ONE WEEK LOAN

RESPECT AND EQUALITY

transsexual and transgender rights

Cavendish
Publishing
Limited

London • Sydney • Portland, Oregon

RESPECT AND EQUALITY
transsexual and transgender rights

Stephen Whittle

Cavendish
Publishing
Limited

London • Sydney • Portland, Oregon

First published in Great Britain 2002 by
Cavendish Publishing Limited, The Glass House,
Wharton Street, London WC1X 9PX, United Kingdom
Telephone: + 44 (0)20 7278 8000   Facsimile: + 44 (0)20 7278 8080
Email: info@cavendishpublishing.com
Website: www.cavendishpublishing.com

Published in the United States by Cavendish Publishing
c/o International Specialized Book Services,
5804 NE Hassalo Street, Portland,
Oregon 97213-3644, USA

Published in Australia by Cavendish Publishing (Australia) Pty Ltd
3/303 Barrenjoey Road, Newport, NSW 2106, Australia

© Whittle, Stephen   2002

British Library Cataloguing in Publication Data
Data available

Library of Congress Cataloguing in Publication Data
Data available

ISBN 1-85941-743-4

1 3 5 7 9 10 8 6 4 2

Printed and bound in Great Britain

ACKNOWLEDGMENTS

I wish to thank all those people who have read and commented on different parts of this book at different times. Catherine Little (Manchester Metropolitan University), who co-wrote the chapter on police employment and who over the years has read many parts of this book, was critical but always constructive, improving my writing skills immensely. Catherine Downs, who co-wrote the chapter on the treatment of adolescents with gender dysphoria. Paula Stephens, who co-wrote the chapters on police employment and imprisonment. Also Siobhan Leonard, who helped considerably with the chapter on Europe. Shannon Minter, Paisley Currah and Jennifer Levi, that indomitable trio of trans lawyers, are deserving of a good thrashing for their cheek and very late calls for advice on briefs – they really have made me realise what good fun it is, despite the hard work. I must not forget Phyllis Frye, who first ensured that I was not alone in seeking justice for people like us.

There are all those who have fought alongside me at the barricades: my fellow vice-presidents in Press For Change, Christine Burns, Claire McNab, Susan Marshall, Sarah Rutherford, Mark Rees and Alex Whinnom, without whom none of this would have been remotely possible. Also the many ground troops, trans people who have marched, lobbied, been the volunteers for the many cases we have pursued, and of course those who did not volunteer, but who because of what happened to them found themselves, reluctantly at first, but enthusiastically in the end, pursuing justice through the legal system. It is a great pleasure to see so many of them continuing this work in their own locales, having gained real expertise and abilities through the work we have done together. There are also a few academics who have shown faith; I say a few because indeed only a minority recognised that this was not just of importance to a few 'misguided poor souls' but challenged the very core of that legal construct: gender. They have provided support in many different ways, and include Steve Redhead, Katherine O'Donovan, Robert Wintemute, Leslie Moran and Julie Greenberg.

Finally, Sarah – you have provided everything whilst I did this. You recognised who I was and you have given me a life, a family, a career and your enduring love. Thank you. This is not a conventional love token, but it is given with my love to you, Eleanor, Gabriel, Lizzie and Pippa.

Stephen Whittle
August 2002

CONTENTS

TABLE OF CASES

TABLE OF UK LEGISLATION

TABLE OF EUROPEAN LEGISLATION

Directives

Treaties and Conventions

TABLE OF INTERNATIONAL LEGISLATION

USA

INTRODUCTION

I have been writing this book for almost 10 years. They have very busy years for me, which have included the commencement of an academic career, and a rise through the ranks at work. They have included the founding of Press For Change, the first trans group to seek not just acceptance and support but also civil rights and equality for its members. I also completed my PhD, and I saw the birth of four children into our family. Those are very good reasons for this book taking so long to come to completion. Nonetheless, the real reason for the delay has been that the last 10 years have seen huge advances in the legal campaign for change to the lives of trans people. As this change has marched forward, every one of the chapters has been altered and revised to try to keep abreast of what is happening out there in the real world.

As this book was going to press, further revisions had to be made as the decisions of the European Court of Human Rights (ECHR) in the cases of *Christine Goodwin and I v United Kingdom Government*[1] were announced. The ECHR held that the government's failure to alter the birth certificates of transsexual people or to allow them to marry in their new gender role was a breach of the European Convention on Human Rights. Given that the Human Rights Act 1998 embedded the European Convention on Human Rights into British law, one might think that this book is now past its sell by date, and that trans people have nothing left to worry about. As it happens, whilst I write, the UK government is refusing to adopt that stance, although I would argue that there is good reason to think that English courts, if asked to address any question of legal status, recognition or marriage, will interpret English law to follow the ECHR's decision.

I had debated pre-empting the decisions in *Goodwin and I*, but could not bring myself to do so, because as a campaigner for trans people's rights, optimism has invariably led to disappointment over the years. The decisions of the ECHR are more than we could have ever hoped for, but the lack of government response is exactly what we might have expected. Despite the fact that transsexual and transgender people have become a feature of our everyday life in Britain, not all is yet rosy. Through my work with Press For Change, I still have an ongoing caseload of individuals who have been subjected to the most appalling treatment in the course of their day-to-day lives and jobs. I suppose I have built a reputation on the misery of others. I do not feel too bad about that, as I too suffered from that prejudice for most of my adult life. I was dismissed from jobs, have been hounded out of my home, received hate mail and even on one occasion a death threat. In fact, it was all that which drove me to take up the law. I was determined to find out why this was happening to my friends and to me, and I wanted to fight back. I cannot claim to be either a great theorist or a great advocate, but I have tried to become a sound lawyer able to recognise injustice and to seek solutions.

---

1   *Christine Goodwin v UK Government*, Application No 28957/95 (1995) ECHR; *I v UK Government*, Application No 25608/94 (1994) ECHR.

This book looks to the law to explain itself. It is not so much a 'call for rights' as a call for people to be given respect and an equal footing before the law. It is intended to give transgender and transsexual people their voice and for their call to law to be heard. When we get into court, our voices are always mediated and translated by others – lawyers, judges and juries who have no idea of what it is to be trans. How can they possibly understand what it is like to be prosecuted or reported as a man when your neighbours have always known you as the 'woman next door'? Can they imagine how, as a father to my children on a day-to-day basis, it feels for my partner and me to be told that I am a stranger to our family? It may be that they cannot possibly empathise, but they could instead respect our need for privacy, our entitlement to rights and our claim to equal treatment.

I start by describing what it is like not to be recognised for who I am. Then, by exploring both the medico-legal construction of transsexualism as a syndrome and the socio-legal construction of the transsexual as a person, I clarify the inadequacy of current legal thinking and law in practice to recognise the 'humanness' of transsexual people. It can be seen that the crimino-legal construction around certain sexual behaviour and the early 20th century medical construction of the homosexual are entwined in such a way that the separate medical and legal category of the person suffering from transsexuality was able to be distinguished. Consequently, the socio-legal construction of the transsexual individual results in a deficient 'common sense' discourse surrounding 'sex changing' and 'cross-dressing'. This enables the transsexual person to be separated out from the rest of humanity and afforded special discriminatory treatment by the law, through their being 'non-human'.

I then give trans people a space to regain that humanness in a discussion of their own construction of self, and this is shown to be quite different from the version of self afforded transsexual people by the non-transsexual. I look to how the 'gender as fluid' approach to their lives, both in theory and practice, has developed into new forms of activism, which are sophisticated, complex, clever and thought provoking in their use of the law to challenge the law.

The remainder of the book concerns the law and the current position as regards transsexual people, particularly in the United Kingdom. The chapters cannot be comprehensive as far as addressing the issues that have come before the courts and the justice system, as every week new issues arise. But they are inclusive of many wide-ranging issues that have rarely been written about before. I consider employment (including a chapter on the employment of trans people as police officers), marriage, parenting, treatment access, the position in European law and imprisonment. These are all 'live' issues in that they make up the bread and butter of my daily legal diet. The chapters include theoretical perspectives, but are actually grounded in the lives of the real transsexual people I know and respect. As such, the book should provide a good guide to tackling the problems of the law. I include at the end of the book some examples of affidavits that have been used in practice to illustrate 'how trans people do law', and to show that we know what we are talking about.

This book provides new insights into the social and medical constructions of the legal categories of transsexuality and the trans person, and it provides a new analysis of current case law in the area, along with solutions to the problems that arise.

As for the campaign for respect and equality for all trans people, I am ever hopeful. That is the art of being a successful lobbyist; if lobbyists gave up every time they fell at a hurdle, pressure groups would be meaningless and governments would face few checks from the public. The decisions in *Goodwin and I* mark the end of a very long battle to reverse Ormrod LJ's 1970 decision in *Corbett v Corbett*.[2] (Female to male) transsexual man Mark Rees made the first application to the ECHR in 1979. Mark's case was to be the first of a series of five brought by transsexual people over the last 23 years. At the time he said, 'There are others waiting in the wings ... They will carry on the fight', as indeed they have done. The ECHR cases have been accompanied by a series of legal applications made here in Britain and in the European Court of Justice. Although far more cases have been lost by transsexual people than won, the wins have been significant, ensuring job protection[3] and access to gender reassignment treatment on the National Health Service.[4]

The ECHR decisions will make a significant difference to the daily lives of transsexual people. Transsexual people can now rely on the principle that they are afforded privacy rights under the Convention, and if those rights are compromised, for example if they apply for a job or a student loan – where their birth certificate has to be shown, they can bring a claim under the Human Rights Act and claim damages. Similarly, they could now get married and argue that they have not committed perjury by declaring themselves to be of their new gender. The marriages may still be open to question as to their validity, but if a couple does separate and seek a divorce or if a pension company refuses to pass on benefits on death on the basis that the marriage is void, then the transsexual person and partner can rely on the *Goodwin* decision.

Older transsexual women facing retirement should now be able to claim their state pension. In fact, the Inland Revenue have recently used their discretionary powers to award pension rights at 60 to a transsexual woman who was born in New Zealand, as she had been able to change her birth

---

2   *Corbett v Corbett* [1970] 2 All ER 33.
3   *P v S and Cornwall County Council*, Case C-13/94 [1996] IRLR 347, ECJ.
4   *R v North West Lancashire HA ex p A, D and G* (1999) Electronic Telegraph, 22 December, issue 1306, QBD.

certificate to reflect her new gender.[5] Several transsexual women who were forced to give up work at the age of 60 or face disclosure of their past, yet who only received social security benefits rather than a pension, could also now make a claim for the lost income and hurt they suffered. In families like my own, where a transsexual man has been refused permission to register as the father of their partner's children by donor insemination, the couple should now marry and jointly adopt the children. Those starting families in the future should be able to register as the parent of the child.

Nonetheless, the ECHR decisions are not the culmination of the campaign, though they could be said to be the beginning of the end. The bureaucratic mess will continue until the law is clarified to ensure that transsexual people in the UK can have their birth certificates amended to reflect a change of sex, and that the change is valid for all legal purposes. Without that, the courts may not regard a new birth certificate as final, leaving the sex of transsexual people open to further challenge. This has already happened in the USA, where some transsexual people have found that new birth certificates were not recognised in court (see Chapter 7). This should not be too difficult, though. Press For Change has drawn up detailed proposals for legislation, which would draw on the best aspects of legislation from other countries. The ECHR's decision means that it is now time for the government to make a clear commitment to legislate for change. The government's Interdepartmental Working Group on Transsexual People, which was recently reconvened in June 2002, would do well to make sure that they use the transsexual community's expertise, ensuring that the sort of half-cocked legal mess that exists in the USA is not created here.

Transsexual people in the UK have proven themselves capable of great staying power, personal bravery, and organisation in this fight. In the last 10 years, they have created a climate in which legal change in these areas was bound to come. In the meantime, as a transsexual man in an unmarried, yet very successful, relationship of 24 years with my partner, I have to debate whether to risk it all by getting married to her. Perhaps marriage would lead to an early divorce. Yet, it would provide pension benefits for my partner, and it would provide security for our children. Maybe we should just sneak off to the registry office with a couple of strangers from the street, in order not to tempt fate. But I think our three daughters would kill us; they are desperate to be bridesmaids.

A note on terms

In the context of this book, I mean, as trans, those people who do not perceive or present their gender identity as the same as that expected of the group of

---

5   Correspondence with KO, May 2002.

people who were given the equivalent sex designation at birth. Cross-dressers (transvestites) are included in this broader grouping, although they do not seek to live as members of the opposite gender. The use of trans delineates a very broad community grouping which includes those people who are transsexual, transgender, cross-dressers and those who identify their gender in some way in opposition or outside of the gender role which they are meant to fulfil as a result of their sex designation at birth.

I use transgender to indicate all those people who live, or desire to live, a large part of their adult life in the role and dress of that gender group which would be considered to be in opposition to their sex as designated at birth. In this context, gender reassignment treatment or the desire for it is not used as the determining factor as to whether a person is trans or not; the desire for gender reassignment surgery delineates the transsexual person who belongs to a sub-group of trans community.

I use the terms trans, transgender, transsexual, cross-dresser as exact terms. If I use the term transsexual, I mean transsexual, that is, someone who is intending to undergo, is undergoing or has undergone gender reassignment treatment. Similarly, when I use the term transvestite or cross-dresser, I mean those people who wear clothing, conventionally of the opposite natal sex grouping, and who do not intend to seek gender reassignment.

CHAPTER 1

DISEMBODIED LAW: TRANS PEOPLE'S LEGAL (OUTER)SPACE[1]

The problem of who I legally am in the world in which I live has been vexatious throughout my adult life. Like other transsexual people, worldwide, I face an inadequate legal framework in which to exist. Some of us live within states and nations that recognise the difficulties and attempt to provide a route way through the morass of problems that arise, others barely, if at all, even acknowledge our being. We are simply 'not' within a world that only permits two sexes, only allows two forms of gender role, identity or expression. Always falling outside of the 'norm', our lives become less, our humanity is questioned, and our oppression is legitimised.

I have spent 27 of my (to date) 46 years of life being known as Stephen. Prior to my adoption of the name Stephen, regardless of the name used for me by others, in my head, my daydreams and my plans for the future, I referred to myself as Peter, a name I did not retain only because other people felt it was old fashioned. I have a beard, I wear a suit and tie to work –not to do so would be considered inappropriate. My partner and I have four children whom we chose to have together and the children all refer to me as daddy. My driving licence, passport, library card and video-club membership have only ever referred to me in the male gender. Yet my National Insurance pension scheme has only ever referred to me in the female gender, if I break the law, I will go to a women's prison and to cap it all, I will depart this life as Stephen Whittle, female.

I frequently face a dilemma as to how I am to refer to myself in various settings. I am all too aware that I am not like most other men. For a start, if I refer to myself as a man, am I claiming some privileged position in the patriarchy? I actually do not want to claim that position; I often do not feel very privileged, having been dismissed from jobs in the past because of my otherness. I have received hate mail and been excluded from social events, both public and private. I find the fact that I cannot ensure my compulsory employment pension contributions are passed onto my partner of 25 years standing, at best, demeaning of our relationship, at worst, an almost criminal extortion of money from me. Where is my privilege?

Furthermore, I have a set of skills imbued in me as a child and teenager that other men simply do not have. Apart from sewing and household cleaning skills, I listen differently and I contribute to discussions differently. My childhood, like that of many I suppose, was unhappy, but the reasons for

---

1   A version of this essay was published as 'The becoming man: the law's ass speaks', in More and Whittle, 1999.

that unhappiness were considerably different from those of most others. I know my attitude to other people and their lifestyles is one of almost excessive tolerance, as long as it involves no harm to others. I simply do not function in life with the same assumptions that other men are afforded through their upbringing and position of privilege.

In social and medical texts, my sort of man has, over time, been referred to as a female invert, urning and gynandrist (Krafft-Ebing, 1893), female transsexual (Stoller, 1975) and as a 'woman who wants to become a man' (Green, 1974, 1974a). More recently, the common descriptor applied to me is that of 'female to male transsexual'. This is on the basis that I was born with genitalia that are regarded as female yet have undergone a bilateral mastectomy, take testosterone on a regular basis and identify myself as male. Yet, am I a man? I prefer to refer to myself as a trans man – my own understanding is that I am a man who was born female bodied and, as I explain to my children, when I was big enough and old enough, I made it clear to other people that I really was a man and I got it sorted out. This leaves me with a personally acknowledged situation that I am a different sort of man; I am a trans man with a transsexual status.

With my status, a trans man, the UK government, because I have undergone some surgical gender reassignment, acquiesces to my request to be regarded as male (and not a man) for some social purposes, but continues to maintain that for legal purposes, I will be regarded as a woman. They choose not to make my life really difficult by making international travel or a driving check embarrassing, but they refuse to allow me many of the privileges that the law affords other men. At worst, they insist that I am a woman.

It is difficult to explain what being a bearded woman means to those who have never experienced that position. If I want to take out life insurance, I am forced to sit in front of an insurance broker who does not know me from Adam (or Eve for that matter) and explain that I am a woman – which always raises the eyebrows. I never ever want to lose my job because the idea of sitting in the dole office waiting for the clerk to shout out 'Miss Stephen Whittle to cubicle 6' makes me feel sick. I find it appalling that one of my children might one day have to register my death and on their return to collect the certificate will find I have been identified as Stephen Whittle, female and that they will simply become 'friend of the deceased'.

The presumption that has been made by most academic writers in the area is that I and people like me are demanding that we be legally recognised in the gender role in which we live. I am not sure if that is the case (though it may be for some) and anyway, surely the role in which I live is that of a trans man. I am willing to be a different sort of man, but I am not willing to be a different sort of woman, because I have never been a woman. I transitioned into living as a man when I was 19 years old; therefore, as I often explain, on that basis, I never reached the exalted state of womanhood. My experience was at most that of being a different girl and certainly not a woman. But even if I was a girl, my experience was significantly different from that of other girls; ask my sisters and they will verify that. My life is different, it is the experience of being a trans man; as such, discrimination has been perpetrated on me throughout my life in an entirely arbitrary manner. I have lost jobs not because I do them badly, but because my life history is that of a trans man. My partner is refused my pension not because my money is not good, but because I have the life history of a trans man.

Yet I am proud to be a trans man, I have surmounted great odds in life, I have had the pleasure of experiencing life in a very unique way, I have learnt a lot about tolerance and I have learnt a lot about bravery, hard work and commitment from the many other trans people I have met. Should it be so hard to be myself, to be a trans man and the operative word in that is 'man'? This essay is in effect a plea to the law. I want to be able to be a visible trans man, to obtain my own identity and to be recognised as myself. But firstly, we must try to understand exactly what is taking place in order to ascertain what we can learn about the nature and construction of the legal culture, and the nature and construction of gender, in itself, by studying the legal problems that transpire because of the emergence of transsexualism in our society.

SEX SIGHTS/SITES

Transsexuals are people whose gender identity, their sense of maleness or femaleness, differs from their anatomical sex. This clash of sex and gender may cause a transsexual much emotional pain, and they must ultimately deal with this issue in some way. (San Francisco Gender Information leaflet, 1992.)

Initially difficulties lie with the semantic understanding of the meaning of the word 'transsexual'. Simplistically, as an adjective derived from the Latin, transsexual is a purely modern term, in that it did not come into existence until the late 1940s. It means crossing (trans) from one sex to the other. But that makes certain *a priori* assumptions: that we know what sex is; and that we know where the 'crossing from' is 'made to'.

The term 'sex' is used to denote sites of physical difference between males and female (as in 'the male sex' and 'the female sex). In that sense, it relates not just to the human state wherein the particular reference points of those sites include complex cultural and social roles (man and woman), but also to many alternative sites that we acknowledge in other species – such as cock and hen, bull and cow. The roles that are tied to these sites are apparently clear; in any species, the sites of sex are based around reproductive roles,[2] but this is by no means the whole story.

2　Reproductive roles do not necessarily indicate reproductive capabilities in the individual within a species, as there are always significant numbers within any species who cannot reproduce for the reasons of age and fertility.

In people, the differentiation process of becoming a man or woman is a multi-step process, involving physiological, social and cultural influences. For each step, there is a window in time that is a critical phase. If the window is missed, then there is no backtracking. Demonstrable brain sex differences only become manifest by three or four years post-natally in the human, and the complex makeup of gender identity is a cognitive process that presupposes language development. The orientation and type of sexual activity does not necessarily belong to one gender group or another. In animal sexology, parallels to gender cannot be found, as sex acts and reproductive roles do not in themselves reveal gender roles (Gooren, 1993, p 4). However, the sexual siting of human beings within the polarised groups 'men' and 'women' is not just dependent upon certain physiological aspects of the body. The major societal organising structure, having a bearing upon access and power within public and private spheres of life, is instead to do with sighting, *what we see* and the cultural constructs which we place around this. Whether it is clothing, mannerisms, physical attributes or genital structure, what we see is how as human beings we determine who or what each of us is, within a limited framework. That framework is culturally and socially dependent, but predominately throughout the modern world, it is a framework made up of binary (oppositional positions). We see good/bad, black/white, able/disabled, man/woman and male/female. The 'man/woman' category has developed historically for many reasons. In some pre-modern cultures, there were other understandings of the variety of gendered positions that could be taken up. Jacobs and Cromwell (1992) illustrated the great potential for diversity of gender in human beings within different socio-cultural environments. Referring to Bogaras's work on the native Siberian tribe, the Chukchi, they describe seven gender categories in addition to the categories 'woman' and 'man' which the Chukchi use. Though individual Chukchi could choose to 'change sex' from man to woman, there were also other genders which Chukchi could take up which do not involve a change from one sex to another, but rather from one gender to another. Most noticeably, they may not have stayed in their original gender, but they did not necessarily become of the opposite gender as defined by the dualistic epistemology of gender that exists in western culture.

However, that modern-western binary man/woman epistemology of gender came to dominate almost all societies and cultures in the 20th century. This undoubtedly arose from the physical limits that reproduction imposed on females, that is, those who bore children. It can be clearly seen that menstruation and multiple pregnancies imposed great restrictions on the lives of the pre-contraception female. The combination of the state of pregnancy itself, the period of breastfeeding and the ill-health and risk of death that pregnancy incurred throughout female's often short lives was such that access to other social roles was without doubt severely limited. The patriarchal system that ensued continues to ensure that females and males are viewed as diametrically opposite. As different creatures they are clearly separate and distinct; they are men and women. As such, society continues to uphold their difference in terms of needs, abilities and social role. In order to ascertain the position in society an individual person is to occupy, we endeavour right at the very beginning of a child's life to place them in the box they are to occupy for the rest of their years. A quick glance at birth determines whether a child has a penis of appropriate length. If it has, it is designated as a boy/man, if not, it is designated a girl/woman. Here in the UK, that cursory glance and the decision made as a consequence is transcribed onto the record of birth, and will remain with the child for ever more. The sighting at birth will be the 'siting' for the remainder of life.

Throughout the modern world, through the written and spoken words of the law, we see the usage of 'man' and 'woman' as pathways to the future relationship of people with the law. It is used to organise many aspects of criminal and civil life, from whether a person can be charged with infanticide through to which prison they will serve a sentence in, from the type of person one is allowed to marry through to whether one can take part in certain sports. The placing of individuals by the law within one of the sites of sex seems to be comparatively easy for the majority of people; however, there are people who challenge the conventional paradigms: transsexual and intersex people. In this book, I want to concentrate on the sites of gender and in particular, on the meaning of 'man' and the group contained in the legal taxonomy 'men'. The question lies: 'Can a trans person of my transsexual background claim a place in that taxonomy?' If we look to the origins of the word, in Old English, it refers to an adult male. The taxonomy of male is 'that which begets offspring – performs the fecundating function'. To fecundate is to render fruitful and productive. On that basis, there are many human beings, infertile men, who are afforded membership of the legal group of 'men', but who are not 'men'. If they can claim it, does that also mean that I can? Furthermore, we need to consider whether the taxonomy afforded means that all people who do not perform the fecundatory role are therefore women. Does not being a man make me a woman, or does not being a woman make me a man? If you are not situated at one place, are you situated in the other?

TRAVELLING

Incorrigible beliefs show up in research about both human and animal behaviour in various ways. A common example is the assumption underlying almost all work on sex and gender that all subjects must be male or female. This shows up in the routine practice of dividing subjects into these two groups before studying them. The very act of dividing a group of subjects in this fashion prejudices the results of any further investigation, because researchers who make this their first criterion are implicitly stating that they have already determined that there are certain

> sex-typed differences and that they are recognisable to them without the aid of empiricism. (Devor, 1989, p 2.)

Correct though Devor's assertion is, that researchers invariably have an obdurate belief in a duality of biological sex types and also probably in gender roles, that does not mean to say that those views have not been challenged. Some of the most eminent thinkers of the 20th century, such as Foucault, Lacan, Baudrillard and Derrida, have produced research and ideas which look beyond the limitations of the modernistic/enlightenment paradigm that constructs a world of dualities, heaven and hell, evil and wickedness, madness and sanity, health and sickness, heterosexuality and homosexuality. They have challenged those basic 'incorrigible beliefs' and shattered their assumptions.

Here, the duality of man and woman (or male and female) is addressed, and this will inevitably call into question other dualities that co-exist alongside this notion. The ethnocentricity of western culture's two sex/two gender model is revealed through the work of many anthropologists and sociologists;[3] this work is reinforced by the many examples in our own cultures of individuals who counter the truth of the paradigm. But the particular dualities man/woman, male/female exist as a controlling paradigm such that you cannot be situated outside of it, so within it, a transsexual travels from one site to another. You cross a boundary of the imagination, a 'not really in existence border' – as we shall see, significant numbers of people, apart from transsexuals, do not fit within the sites of sex. To complicate matters, physically intersex people (as currently recognised by medicine) make up 0.5% of the population; does that mean they are not in existence because they have no site in which they belong? But the physical is by no means the whole story. To be a man or woman is contained in a person's gender identity. Gender identity is the total perception of an individual about his or her own gender. It includes a basic personal identity as a boy or girl, man or woman, as well as personal judgments about the individual's level of conformity to the societal norms of masculinity and femininity. Gender as others perceive it is called gender role. The two concepts are tied together, since most people show their perceptions of themselves in their dress, manners and activities. Clothing is the major public signifier of gender that allows other people to immediately identify an individual's gender role, but there are other signifiers as well, such as mannerisms or occupational choice. For most people, their gender identity, gender role and all the symbolic manifestations of gender will be congruent. But trans people do not necessarily feel that they fit neatly into either the male or female role as designated at birth or that their behaviour is not totally congruent with the rules and expectations of the society they live in for any of the two gender

---

3   See chapters by Cromwell and Rubin in More and Whittle, 1999.

roles offered. Gender identity is the result of a complex interaction amongst three factors:

(1) a sex derivative grade, associated with genetics and hormones. An example would be the general strength differences between males and females;

(2) sex adjunctive differences, not directly associated with hormones, but with their sex derived effects, for example, the division of labour that arose from the physiological need of women to be homebound in order to breastfeed, etc;

(3) sex arbitrary differences related to issues of power and social position, for example, the use of cosmetics and clothing, or the difference in access to particular activities (Money, 1988, p 77–78).

That complex interaction means that it is no longer possible to argue that either nature or nurture alone is the answer to the trans person's sense of self or, for that matter, any person's sense of self. It is clear that both are involved in producing the complex person we call a man or a woman. The physical distinction between men and women is not absolute, since individuals are now scientifically regarded as living on a continuum, with female characteristics at one extreme and male ones at the other. This may result from physical, psychological or social mismatches. The word 'transsexual' is increasingly considered a misnomer, particularly by transsexuals themselves. Being transsexual is not related to any aspect of sexual activity or sexual orientation for the individuals who identify as such, as the physicians who treat such people recognise; nor is it anything to do with 'crossing over'. Transsexual people and their doctors increasingly express the view that the transsexual was always of the gender they now wish to confirm. As early as 1967, in his foreword to Christine Jorgensen's biography, Harry Benjamin, who pioneered research into transsexualism, was casting doubt on the idea that transsexuals underwent sex reassignment treatment. Rather, he forecast a view that would be upheld today by many transsexuals: that they sought out gender confirmation treatment. He says of Christine (who commenced living as a woman in 1952, at the age of 26):

> But was this female gender role really new? The vivid description of her early life supplies a negative answer. This was a little girl, not a boy (in spite of the anatomy) who grew up in this remarkably sound and normal family. (Jorgensen, 1967, p vii.)

The classification of men and women, in everyday life, follows from the biological and social classification. But the legal classification (except in rare exceptions, which I will refer to along the way) arises solely from a biological classificatory process undertaken in a determinatory manner, generally by the courts. The determination can concern any aspect of life; your 'sex' for marriage, imprisonment, a pension, etc. Inevitably, a judge makes the determination.

A LEGAL POSITION(ING)

In English law, the problem came to a head in the 1971 case of *Corbett v Corbett*,[4] wherein the question of sex for the purposes of marriage was decided. In a sense, it embodies the problems of sights and sites. *Corbett v Corbett* concerned the marriage of April Ashley, a transsexual woman (male to female transsexual). On the breakdown of the marriage, her husband petitioned for nullity on the grounds that:

- the respondent remained a male and hence the marriage was void; and

- the marriage was never consummated due to the incapacity of the respondent.

The judge, Lord Ormrod, decided the case on these two issues. For the sex of April Ashley, Ormrod devised a test based upon three factors. Sex was to be considered through chromosomal, gonadal and genital features at the time of birth. These were established as being 'male' at the time of Miss Ashley's birth. However, rather than deciding whether she was then a man, Ormrod referred back to the decision in *Hyde v Hyde*[5] and held:

> Since marriage is essentially a relationship between man and woman, the validity of the marriage in this case depends, in my judgment, on whether the respondent is or is not a woman. I think with respect this is a more precise way of formulating the question than that adopted in para 2 of the petition, in which it is alleged that the respondent is male. (*Corbett v Corbett*, para 48.)

One of the problems with any analysis of Ormrod's judgment is that he constantly mixed the notions of 'male and female' with those of 'man and woman'. For example, he stated in conclusion to this question:

> ... the respondent is not a woman for the purposes of marriage but is a biological male and has been so since birth. (*Corbett v Corbett*, para 49.)

However, he did not attempt to categorise Miss Ashley as a man. He argued that marriage is a relationship based on sex rather than gender so he needed to consider her a 'male'. Yet in fact, the decision in *Hyde v Hyde* is quite clear: marriages are to be between men and women; no mention is made of male or female. His decision to interpret man and woman to mean male and female was almost certainly because he intended to end the marriage by annulment, yet the person he saw in front of him was a socially and culturally acceptable beautiful woman. It might be argued that Ormrod fundamentally misunderstood the sites of sex – of male and female. He did not seem to be aware that 'man' and 'woman' are anthropomorphic signifiers, and that they relate to what we see rather than where we are situated. But perhaps he did, his reinterpretation was there to side-step the dilemma Ormrod faced because he felt unable to define

---

4   *Corbett v Corbett* [1970] 2 All ER 33.

5   *Hyde v Hyde* (1866) LR 1 P & D 130.

the person in front of him as a man yet he felt unable, in law and because of the test he had devised, to call her a woman.

Ormrod, because of his inability to find Miss Ashley to be a woman, declared the marriage void, as it was not a marriage between a man and a woman. Once he had established the marriage was void, there was no reason for him to consider the second ground: whether the marriage could have been consummated. Nonetheless, he did so, and was of the opinion that 'normal' intercourse was not possible between a post-operative male to female transsexual and a man, the difference between that and anal intercourse was a fact 'to be measured in centimetres'. Ormrod distinguished this from the earlier judgement in *SY v SY*,[6] in which a decree of nullity, due to failure to consummate, had been refused on the grounds that a vestigial vagina could have been corrected by forming an artificial passage. Medically, there is little difference between an extended vagina as in *SY v SY* and a wholly artificial one as in *Corbett*, just as there is little difference in any resultant act of intercourse. There is an irony in the distinction made between the two cases, in that it would seem to have been made on the basis that SY was an imperfect woman. Nowadays, it is very likely that she would have been diagnosed as a case of testicular feminisation and accordingly been discovered to be a chromosomal male – in other words, she would not have been a woman for the purposes of marriage on the same basis that April Ashley was not a woman. It could therefore be argued that Ormrod misdirected himself with regard to the distinguishing facts in *Corbett*, as opposed to those in *SY v SY*. Furthermore, the construction of an artificial vagina is not restricted to transsexuals, for some women also have reconstructive surgery in acute cases of vaginal atresia (absence or closure of a normal body orifice) before they are able to have sexual intercourse. Are these people 'not women'?

The case held that a combination of hormone treatment and surgery did not, for the purposes of matrimonial law, result in a change of sex assigned to a person at birth. The sex of a person is, in law, dependent entirely upon their gonadal, genital and chromosomal sex at birth. The decision in *Corbett* has been incredibly influential, despite being from the High Court. It has been followed as precedent in other matrimonial cases such as *Peterson v Peterson*,[7] *Franklin v Franklin*[8] and in the criminal law in *R v Tan*, and the UK government has supported this definition of sex in all of the 'transsexual' cases going to the European Courts. More recently, against all expectations, the Texas 4 Court of Appeals has followed this approach in the case of *Littleton v Prange*.[9] The site you sight is not what it seems – at least not in the law.

---

6   *SY v SY* [1962] 3 All ER 55, CA.

7   *Peterson v Peterson* (1985) *The Times*, 12 July.

8   *Franklin v Franklin* (1990) *The Scotsman*, 9 November.

9   *Littleton v Prange* 9 SW 3d 223 (1999) Texas Court of Appeals, 4 District, www.4coa. courts.state.tx.us/opinions/9900010.htm.

THE ESSENTIALIST/CLUSTER APPROACHES

In 1985, Katherine O'Donovan (1985, pp 64–69) argued that the judicial task of sex determination has been developed along two lines: the essentialist approach and the cluster approach. In the essentialist approach, the court looks to one essential feature and assigns all individuals biologically to either the female sex or the male sex (this was the case in *Corbett*, and the Australian case of an intersex person *C and D*[10]). Following *Corbett*, the current test in the UK of a persôn's legal sex is one which considers three factors only: genital, gonadal and chromosomal sex at birth. Psychological or behavioural sex is not considered relevant.

This apparently inclusive test is fundamentally flawed. For the majority of babies, it is purely genital sex that is used as the determining factor of sex siting. As already mentioned, the Australian case of *SY v SY* referred to the status of an individual born without a vagina, yet who was to be considered a woman. What of those apparent women of whom it is discovered in later life that they have an XY chromosome base and yet androgen insensitivity has prevented the development of descended testes and a penis? The essentialist approach is plainly inadequate and leads to a range of inaccurate sex designations, as we do not at the time of birth test the chromosomal makeup of children, nor do we do more than a cursory examination of genitals, and we have no idea whether a child has ovaries. Currently, medicine recognises an ever-growing number of intersex syndromes and one in every 200 children will be born with some sort of intersex matrix. For some, this will never be discovered, for others, it will only be discovered when they attend a fertility treatment clinic in later life as they struggle to have their own children. Furthermore, the work at the Netherlands Brain Bank on brain sex determination has indicated that transsexual people should possibly be included in the range of physical intersex syndromes. The work supports the hypothesis that there is a brain sex difference between men and women, and transsexual people have the brain sex of that gender group to which they maintain they belong (Zhou, Hoffman, Gooren and Swaab, 1995). The essentialist approach is unable to take on board complex science such as this, which would involve being able to determine a person's sex grouping only after they were dead and their brain was available for dissection.

In the cluster approach, the courts looks to a group of similar features that then suggest the individual falls into one sex site or another. We have seen this approach in the European Court of Human Rights cases of *Van Oosterwijk v Belgium*[11] and *B v France*, also in the High Court in New Jersey in the family

---

10   *C and D (Aus)* [1979] FLC 90-636.
11   *Van Oosterwijk v Belgium* (1980) ECHR Series A, No 40.

law case of *MT v JT*,[12] as well as several other US states. This approach allows concepts of behavioural sex or psychological sex such as masculinity or maleness to appear within the legal matrix. This approach may allow sex classification according to psychological features as well as physiological features; it may also allow personal choice to dictate rather than ascription. However, for a long time, it was an approach rejected as far as marriage was concerned. In two Canadian cases, *C(L) v C(C)*[13] and *B v A*,[14] female to male (ftm) transsexual men were held not to be spouses/husbands for the purposes of marriage and family law if the only surgery they had undergone was a bilateral mastectomy and a hysterectomy. The courts, both in Ontario, followed the doctrine in *Corbett*. In *B v A*, the parties had lived together for 20 years and on that basis had applied for a motion of financial support. Though the (ftm) transsexual man had had birth records changed from female to male, the courts held that the requirements for surgery of the Registrar General were not the same as those required to decide if a relationship was one of husband and wife. The failure to undergo genital surgery on the part of a (ftm) transsexual man would mean that he continued to be female and hence could not marry another female. *C(L) v C(C)* followed this line of thinking, and it was held that the marriage the two parties had undergone was a nullity, and was void *ab initio*. The cluster approach has only recently been accepted for sex determination in relation to marriage, most notably in the Australian case from New South Wales of *Re Kevin (Validity of Marriage of Transsexual)*.[15]

The approach has also been taken in other areas where sex has been found to be an essential element, but then often only in very limited circumstances. We can see how various jurisdictions have tried to limit its use. In Germany and Ontario in particular, the requirement in the legislation that some genital surgery is undergone in relation to gender reassignment before an individual is afforded status in their new sex role has led to questions in the courts concerning to what extent surgical reassignment has taken place, particularly in the case of female to male transsexuals. Michael Wills (1993) mentions the case of *OLG Zweibruken*,[16] concerning a female to male transsexual man, which asks whether in order to achieve what the law calls a 'clear approximation' to the opposite sex, will a bilateral mastectomy be sufficient, or is genital surgery which includes vaginal occlusion and phalloplasty required? The case had been decided in two lower courts in favour of the female to male transsexual applicant, but the state representative appealed (it

---

12   *MT v JT* 150 NJ Super 77 (1977); 355 A 2d 204.

13   *C(L) v C(C)* [1992] Lexis 1518, Ont CJ.

14   *B v A* RFL (3d) 258 (1990).

15   *Re Kevin (Validity of Marriage of Transsexual)* [2001] Fam 1074, CA, www.familycourt. gov.au/judge/2001/html/rekevin_text.html.

16   *OLG Zweibruken* (1992).

has proven impossible to find the outcome of this case). An application was made before the Quebec courts in 1999 for a judicial review of an administrative decision to refuse identity documentation changes for a transsexual man because he refused to undergo vaginal occlusion.[17] In fact, the state settled in that case and allowed the documentation to be changed when evidence was given of the dangerous nature of the proposed surgical procedures. As can be seen even in this approach, there is a presumption that the law distinguishes between the private sphere of gender and the public sphere of sex definition.

In both the essentialist and cluster approaches, though, the law operates on the assumption that the two sexes are separate entities with distinct sites. Concern may be expressed because errors may be made using the essentialist approach or simply that it is inhumane, similarly that the cluster approach simply does not follow its own logic, but the premise that certain areas of the law should be organised around sexual differentiation is not queried. There are still two distinct categories: man and woman.

TACKLING SEX SITE/SIGHT DISCRIMINATION

Because there are these two categories and obvious social inequities have resulted, the law has responded by taking either of two routes. The first has been the taking of an egalitarian approach wherein it is attempted to remove all gendered/sex values from the law, what one might term the 'all men are equal' syndrome of the American Bill of Rights. In this approach, we attempt to write the law as if it is unsexed or as if any sex designation holds some sort of equal value. One example of this approach exists in an obscure section of the Road Traffic Offenders Act 1988, s 25 (which deals with offences requiring disqualification from driving), which states:

(1) If on convicting a person of an offence involving obligatory or discretionary disqualification or of such other offence as may be prescribed by regulations under section 105 of the Road Traffic Act 1988 the court ...

(2) ... does not know the person's sex, the court must order the person to give that information to the court in writing.

(3) A person who knowingly fails to comply with an order under [the above] subsection is guilty of an offence.

One may ask of what relevance it is to the court as to what a person's sex is in these cases. Driving disqualification has nothing to do with sex and vice versa. But, as this is an egalitarian approach, regardless of the sex you have not disclosed, you will have committed an offence of non-disclosure and face a fine on conviction.

---

17 See Chapter 14.

The second route is that of the interventionist approach, wherein we admit that 'all men are not equal' but the law will ensure instead that there is equal opportunity and equal treatment for members of different groups. The law is used in an attempt to control undesirable results of the socio-economic and political values that we give to gender and sex. However, such approaches rarely attempt to provide total equality; instead, they limit their concern to areas which are deemed appropriate for the law's involvement. This is the approach of anti-discrimination legislation such as the Sex Discrimination Act 1975, wherein we provide a legal stick and judicial remedies to try and smooth out inequalities, but its involvement in social life is limited to the areas of employment, vocational training, housing and the provision of goods and services. So, it is legal to have a men's stag night but not to exclude women from a motor mechanics course.

Throughout the law in many jurisdictions in fact, we see no single clearly consistent approach taken; the two approaches frequently work in conjunction alongside each other. This lack of consistency in legal approach arises initially because ostensibly, egalitarian gestures are compromised from the start, as in the statement 'all men are equal'. The supposed neutral subject of law does not yet exist within egalitarian approaches to the law: he is both sexed and gendered male. Women are conceptualised on the basis of masculine parameters; in practice, they are simply 'not men' and as such do not exist within an egalitarian approach to the law, hence the need for an interventionist approach in which their existence is at least acknowledged, though objectified as different.

LIVING IN OUTER SPACE

For the feminist French analyst and linguist Irigary (1977), to have an identity which is not one's own – to be a sex which is not one – is to be excluded from the fullness of being: it is to be left precisely in a condition of dereliction. One is excluded, therefore, from the social contract within which men participate. A Rousseausian design of the social contract inevitably fails because the abstract individual of liberal democratic theory is, as Pateman (1989) has shown, in fact a man. Irigary is referring to women as women, women who never have their own identity – a woman's identity is defined through the social and cultural persona; they are in society but not of society. And this could be seen as an echo of the women in law. A woman is objectified through interventionist law; she never is the law. As such, the egalitarian project of law is doomed through its own history, and the interventionist project in law is doomed through its further objectification. Both deal in a mythical equivalency.

The question then lies on whether there is any other form of project which can address the issue of the inadequacies of sexed/gendered law. I would argue that the site of the trans man informs and addresses us in relation to this project. John Locke asserted in relation to the law that:

... the use of words is to be the sensible mark of ideas; and the ideas they stand for are their proper and immediate signification. (Douzinas, Warrington and McVeigh, 1991, p 228.)

To what extent is the egalitarian project of the words of the Road Traffic Offenders Act 1988 (RTOA) a 'sensible mark of ideas'? In the RTOA, it becomes a separate offence not to acknowledge a sex classification for yourself. Does this then require giving a legally correct classification or is the choice of sex yours, as long as you give one? Do you have to give the one that the court would recognise, and anyhow, do you know what system the court would use to recognise it?

If we consider the situation of the androgen insensitive woman, I (and medicine) refer to her as a woman, yet do we know for the purposes of the law whether she is a woman, or whether she is a man? Is the classification the one afforded on her birth certificate that is based on a cursory glance by a midwife to see whether there is a penis or not – in other words, a process that simply asserts whether someone is a 'man' or a 'not man'? Or should the law follow Ormrod's three-point test devised in *Corbett*? On that basis, her chromosomes would be XY, her gonads would be un-descended testes and her genitalia would include a vagina. In the civil law, therefore, if the court uses the balance of probabilities test, used for ascertaining evidential proof, I suspect she would be found to be a man on a 2:1 rule. However, in the criminal court, if we were to have to prove her sex, say for an offence involving soliciting, would the evidential burden of 'beyond all reasonable doubt' mean that the court would be left with no sex site that they could place this woman in?

As UK law currently stands, the transsexual man, if born in Britain, would be legally classified as a woman for the purposes of marriage,[18] the criminal law,[19] Social Security and National Insurance benefits,[20] immigration[21] and parenting.[22] For the purposes of employment, he would be afforded the special status of 'woman who is transsexual',[23] which simply means a woman with special protection for having an identity peccadillo. If the trans man were born outside of Britain, then his identity in each of these areas of the law would be dependent upon the nation state in which he was born.[24] Yet, the trans man would be classified on his driving licence (through the codification

---

18   *Corbett v Corbett* [1970] 2 All ER 33.

19   *R v Tan and Others* [1983] 2 All ER 12.

20   *Sheffield v UK Government*, Application No 22985/93 (1993) ECHR.

21   *Horsham v UK Government*, Application No 23390/94 (1994) ECHR.

22   *X, Y and Z v UK* (1997) 24 EHRR 143, ECHR, www.echr.coe.int.

23   *M v Chief Constable of West Midlands Police*, Case No 08964/96 (1996) IT.

24   For example, if born in Ontario in Canada, he would be a man for the purposes of immigration into Britain, yet he would be a woman for the purposes of marriage (see the comments earlier in this chapter on the cases of *C(L) v C(C)* [1992] Lexis 1518, Ont CJ and *B v A* 2 RFL (3d) 258 (1990)). If born in Holland, he would be a man for all purposes except (probably) the criminal law.

system) as a man. If the trans man is required to give his 'sex' to the court as he is facing a driving disqualification, presumably the purpose of that disclosure is to ensure that the driving licence records of the correct person are marked up. Should he say he is a man or male, or should he say he is a woman or female? What is the requirement of the law? It is no defence to a criminal act to argue that you had no knowledge of the law, or that you did not understand it. Where lies Locke's 'sensible mark of ideas'; the logic of the law is truly at times an ass.[25]

We must accept there are many problem areas in the law, yet striving to improve it is one of the fundamental demands of justice. There is a need to re-theorise law away from its current notional equivalency projects such as are embodied in the egalitarian definition of rape in s 142 of the Criminal Justice and Public Order Act 1994, wherein the courts had to ask whether a trans woman's vagina was a body orifice or not, or the interventionist approach of the Sex Discrimination Act 1975, in which if you fall outside the man/woman categories, you are not protected. These projects simply highlight the lack that is embodied in the law.

THE BECOMING MAN

The becoming man of this paper is a parody of Irigary's notion of the becoming woman. Women, in order to constitute themselves as truly social beings, need to be able to represent themselves as themselves; they have to overcome the deficit of women un-symbolised as woman, they have to become woman. Similarly, the project currently being undertaken by trans men is to overcome the deficit of the trans man un-symbolised as the trans man.

Though the Rousseausian social contract has produced the identity of collectivity by raising the 'I' (individual) to the power of the homogeneous 'we', the multi-community experience derived through the identity politics of contemporary societies challenges this by effectively proposing an 'identity' that is not just logically based, but is empirically and experientially based. Post-modernism and psychoanalysis seek the subject who inhabits their

---

25 In 1981, I had my driving licence stolen. I reported it to the police and applied for a replacement. The civil service department which issued licences then went on strike. A few weeks later, I was stopped for having a broken rear light on my car, and was charged with failing to produce my driving licence. During this period, I had confirmed by the Driving Licence Authority that I was licensed to drive whilst awaiting my replacement licence. But it is an offence to not produce your licence when asked by a police officer, so I was convicted and fined. Some time later, my licence was discovered by the police to have been in the police station during the said period, having been brought in amongst a large haul of stolen goods. I appealed on the basis of my licence having already been in police possession. My appeal was turned down because I had not produced the licence.

subjectivity, and constructs upon it. The transgender/transsexual community is undertaking a post post-modern reconstruction of the self not only through their lived experience of bodily change, but also through the development of theory, activism and the resultant interrelationship with the law.

Of many possible examples, I would like to consider two legal challenges presented by the transsexual community to the European Courts. The first is the case of *P v S and Cornwall County Council*,[26] which was decided at the European Court of Justice (ECJ) in April 1996. *P v S* concerned discrimination against a transsexual employee. The ECJ was asked whether discrimination against an employee because they were transsexual was contrary to the provisions contained in the 1975 Equal Treatment Directive of the European Economic Council. The court held that it was illegal to discriminate against an individual because they were undergoing gender reassignment. The result is that it is irrelevant whether P is a man or a woman; if her status is that of a transsexual, then that is one 'ground of sex' which affords her protection. This does not mean that she is outside of either the egalitarian or the interventionist approaches, but is contained within both. She is afforded equality because of her humanity and protection because of her difference.

The second concerns the case of *X, Y and Z v UK Government*,[27] which was decided in the European Court of Human Rights (ECHR) in April 1997. The case addressed the issue of 'fatherhood'. Fatherhood lies very close to that initial taxonomy of 'man', the person who performs the fecundatory function – yet fatherhood is increasingly becoming merely a social construction rather than a biological relationship in many circumstances. Addressing the provisions in the Human Fertilisation and Embryology Act 1990 (HFEA), the case concerned a transsexual man whose female partner gave birth to a child conceived using donor insemination at a clinic licensed under the Human Fertilisation and Embryology Authority. Under the HFEA, in providing fertility treatment to any woman, the paramount concern of the clinic, in the provision of treatment, must be the welfare of the child. However, the clinic is obliged, where a woman has a male partner, to obtain the signature of that partner to a statement that they will for all legal purposes be the father of the child. This is to ensure that in the case of couples later separating, the child will have a father to financially maintain it under the provisions of the Child Support Act 1991. In this case, Y, the partner of a transsexual man, X, had received donor insemination and conceived a child, Z.

X (rather than maintaining the common secretive approach taken by many transsexual men in such circumstances) formally applied to the Registrar General for Births and Deaths for permission to be recorded on the child's birth certificate as its father. Permission was refused on the basis that X was

---

26 *P v S and Cornwall County Council*, Case C-13/94 [1996] IRLR 347, ECJ.
27 *X, Y and Z v UK* (1997) 24 EHRR 143, ECHR, www.echr.coe.int.

legally a woman, and a woman could not be recorded as a father. Thus, we see the inherent failure of either the egalitarian or interventionist approaches. Women are not equal with men, nor are they allowed the protection of the law to enable them to have the things that men are given.

Unlike other 'transsexual' approaches to the ECHR, X was not asking to be a man in law, but rather to be afforded the title 'father' as a transsexual man. He sought to become symbolised as the transsexual man, to be as other men, yet different, using the egalitarian approach. Alternatively, he sought to be symbolised as father despite being woman using the interventionist approach. The question is one of being ascribed by the law, then being transcribed by the law, of once being written and then always being wrote, for the trans man. The ECHR found against the applicants on two grounds: firstly, that there is no common consensus throughout the countries who are signatories to the European Convention on Human Rights as to whether a non-biological man can be registered as the father of a donor inseminated child – therefore, the Court maintained that there must still be a wide margin of appreciation for states to act in as they think fit. The second ground, however, is far more problematic. Currently, the transsexual man in UK law is a 'not man' – therefore, he is a woman, and the Court decided that if they gave the transsexual man the status of father, they would be creating a massive contradiction within the law. Can a father be a 'not man' or would a father then become 'man'? Interestingly, the Court found that there was a *de facto* family relationship between the applicants, yet they failed to define the family relationships between the transsexual man and his partner or the child, leaving a highly unsatisfactory result – a family which is beyond our definition, un-symbolised and therefore not in existence.

This mirrors the failure of the law's project. Justice cannot be achieved if, for example, it becomes impossible to inscribe one's self in the letter to the court in which one has to disclose one's sex under the RTOA. That is because in law, the self does not belong to the self; we are inscribed onto the homogenous 'man' without any precursors, such as masculinity or maleness; all that is required is the penis as seen by the midwife. The rest of us who lack merely become derivations.

I am not trying to valorise an incommunicable mental state, or an essential transsexual man. But the process of becoming the transsexual man in law rather than the man in law is a direct counter-discourse to the objectification of man by his own mechanisms. The place created undermines the essentialist approach of the judiciary, and although it bows to the cluster approach, it moves beyond either by demanding a new site, a place in outer space but within the law.

In his preface to *The Order of Things*, Foucault says:

Strangely enough, man – the study of whom is supposed by the naive to be the oldest investigation since Socrates – is probably no more than a kind of rift in the order of things, or in any case, a configuration whose outlines are determined by the new position he has so recently taken up in the field of knowledge … It is comforting, however, and a source of profound relief to think that man is only a recent invention, a figure not yet two centuries old, a new wrinkle in our knowledge, and that he will disappear again as soon as knowledge has discovered a new form. (Foucault, 1994, p xxiii.)

What is a 'becoming man'? A man who is befitting, that is: proper and right, who graces, adorns and embellishes, gratifies and delights our lives. I think I do that quite successfully.

CHAPTER 2

LEGAL MADNESS: TRANSSEXUALISM

THE DIAGNOSIS!

Why is it that we hand over to a group of psychiatrists and psychologists (a group of grey suited men who might have been cloned from the same Sussex stockbroker) the right to define OUR condition and pontificate on the complexities of OUR feelings about gender? (Hennessey, 1990–91.)

Since the publication in 1980 of the American Psychiatric Association's *Diagnostic and Statistical Manual of Mental Disorders* (third edition, revised) (DSM IIIR), transsexualism has been generally assumed by psychiatrists to be a mental disorder that requires their professional intervention. The condition and its treatment had undergone much public and academic discussion since the publicity that surrounded Christine Jorgensen's return to the USA after her reassignment surgery in Denmark in 1953. This discussion took place primarily amongst professionals who worked in areas that were concerned with mental disease: that is, psychiatrists, psychologists and psychotherapists. Such professionals become by their position the authoritative definers of mental disease. There is little evidence until the late 1980s and early 1990s that the people who were defined as *having* transsexualism participated in the discussion about the condition and its treatment. The recent contributions of transsexuals are very much at odds with the clinician's view that they are suffering from a mental disorder. But they remain within a system in which they are viewed as anomalies within the gendered 'norms' of western societies.

Currently, there is little accord by clinicians over its treatment, and even less agreement over its aetiology (Money, 1988, p 89). Transsexualism *per se* has never appeared in any general medical or surgical textbooks despite the fact that the predominate form of relief nowadays provided for somebody who has the 'disorder' is surgical and endocrinological intervention. That is because the history of the diagnosis lies within, not alongside, the medical categorisation of homosexuality, and that has always existed within the field of psychiatry. According to Foucault (1978, p 43):

… the psychological, psychiatric, medical category of homosexuality was constituted [by] … Westphal's famous article of 1870 on 'contrary sexual sensations'.

Yet, it took another 110 years for transsexualism to be included in the DSM IIIR. That was 110 years of research, case studies and discussion before a consensus could be reached on what constituted 'the disease' of transsexualism.

DSM IV

The most recent edition of the *Diagnostic and Statistical Manual*, DSM IV, 1994, removed the classification 'Transsexual' and replaced it with the criteria for 'Gender Identity Disorder'. It could be argued that the differences between the two definitions are insignificant, yet it is important to understand what the American Psychiatric Association (APA) means by the term mental disorder:

> ... a clinically significant behavioural or psychological syndrome or pattern that occurs in an individual and that is associated with present distress or a significantly increased risk of suffering, death, pain, disability, or an important loss of freedom. (DSM IV, 1994, p xi.)

The criteria for gender identity disorder now include the requirement for there to be mental disturbance which must cause 'significant distress or impairment in social, occupational or other areas of functioning'. It might be assumed therefore that the APA recognises that some cross-dressers and transsexuals, who are not significantly distressed to the point where they cannot function in their everyday lives, do not have a mental disorder.

This supposedly more positive attitude towards transgender individuals can, however, present a practical problem. If the transsexual does not appear to suffer from significant distress, they should not be diagnosed as having a gender identity disorder, and hence they should not qualify to receive hormone therapy and reassignment surgery. It is, as one transsexual put it, Catch 22: if you are distressed enough to qualify for surgery, your mental reasoning has been impaired to the point where you probably cannot give informed consent. But if you are not that distressed, you will not be offered the surgery to which you are able to consent.

THE RECENT HISTORY OF TRANSSEXUALISM

The arrival at a consensus of diagnosis of transsexualism has had a much longer history than many think. It is generally considered a recent phenomenon, surgical treatment being developed from the 1930s. The first case of surgical intervention is often cited as being the case of Lili Elbe, who underwent reassignment in Germany in 1931 (Hoyer, 1937), though there are a number of known cases before this. Hirschfeld describes the case of a male to female, Rudolph/Dorchen, who had genital surgery, and a female to male who also had breast tissue removed, both in the 1920s (Hirschfeld, 1948). Harry Benjamin (1969) described how he tried to induce breast growth in a man by means of hormones in the early 1920s. However, the idea of 'sex change surgery' only entered the public and professional consciousness with the publicity surrounding Christine Jorgensen's surgery in Denmark in 1951/52, and Roberta Cowell's surgery at a similar time in England (Cowell, 1954).

The medical words that we currently use for individuals who require 'sex change' treatment were not derived until 1949, when David Cauldwell invented the term *Psychopathia Transexualis* (Cauldwell, 1949, p 274), and the associated word *transexual* (*sic*). Cauldwell was a medical writer of popular articles, and his books were designed to educate the public in sexual matters. In 1953, the endocrinologist Harry Benjamin wrote the first scientific paper to use the word *transsexual*. Between Westphal and Benjamin, psychosexual professionals attempted to categorise individuals who would now be recognised by the public as being transsexual into 'homosexual types', as this was the only framework they could think of where such people might belong.

Historically, the path of the definition of transsexualism can be traced from the search for the aetiology and cure of homosexuality to the present diagnosis specifications recommended in the DSM IV. Ironically, the removal of homosexuality from DSM III's psychosexual disorder category in 1975 coincided with the inclusion in the revised edition of transsexualism under a subcategory of 'Gender Identity Disorders'. In order to understand this paradox, the context of involvement of transsexual people with the psychiatric establishment needs to be understood. For that, it is necessary to look at the general involvement, in a temporal and cultural frame, of transsexual people with all authorities: church, state and medical. Combined with the history of the state and church authorities' response to what would now be termed homosexuality and its associated sexual acts, it is possible to see that the 'transsexual' category arose out of the subdividing of homosexuals into various categories by the 19th and 20th century sexologists. That in turn arose out of the historical treatment of individuals who wore the clothing of the opposite natal sex and their association with homosexuality. The pre-modern responses of the church and state to homosexual acts resulting in the modern retort of medicine was ultimately to lead to the classification of transsexualism as a mental disorder.

A TRANS HISTORY

Since transsexuality was not named until 50 years ago, those people who would today present as transsexual could not be recognised as such. Neither could they have conceived of the possibility of surgical intervention, as it simply did not exist. Since transsexuality as presently defined requires a stated desire for alteration of the body, and was in itself unnamed, it must be acknowledged that such individuals could not have self-identified as transsexual. For the purposes of this discussion, it is therefore necessary to clarify the definition of transsexual people that I will use. For the reasons just outlined, transsexual people will be considered as all those people who have lived, or desired to live, a large part of their adult life in the role and dress of that gender group which would be considered to be in opposition to their sex as designated at birth. They will during that time have been recognised by society as belonging to their 'chosen' gender. These people generally continued in their role to the point of death unless otherwise prevented, for example, by discovery and punishment, or by illness. Included therefore as belonging to that section of the populace who in western culture today would have identified as transsexual would be people such as Frenchy 'Katherine' Vosbaugh (Sullivan, 1990, p 9), Jack 'Bee' Garland (Sullivan, 1990, p 22) and Billy Tipton (Graham, 1989; Wood Middlebrook, 1998) as female to male transsexual people. I will use the umbrella term transgender for these people, as transsexualism is currently dependent upon medical diagnosis and intervention. Others, of whom there is evidence of temporary cross-living or cross-dressing or transvestism, will be referred to as cross-dressers.

In western culture, there is a extensive history of individuals who we would now know as transgender. There are mythological references such as in the Ancient Greek legends of Hermaphrodite and Ganymede, and the Roman story of Venus Castina, the goddess who responded with sympathy and understanding to the yearnings of feminine souls locked in male bodies. Ancient Greek and Roman writers commented on young men who desired to live their lives as women:

> Expending every possible care on their outward adornment, they are not ashamed even to employ every device to change artificially their nature as men into women – some of them craving a complete transformation into women, they have amputated their generative members. (Green, 1974a, p 5.)

Christianity appears to have first called for transgender people to be punished for their behaviour, arising from an apparent prohibition of the wearing of male attire by women, or of female dress by men in Deuteronomy 22: v 5. Consequently, punishment rather than 'treatment' was to be the dominant mode of dealing with the issue until the work of the psychologists of the 19th century.

Cross-dressing was rarely codified against in the secular laws of medieval Europe, but was included consistently in the list of offences against God, or of heresies. When Gratian completed his textbook of canon law: 'A Harmony of Conflicting Canons' (*Concordia discordantium canonum*)[1] in 1140 and included in it an earlier Conciliar condemnation of cross-dressing, it became possible to say that cross-dressing as such was unlawful under the codified church laws. Gratian is recognised as the first church Jurist, and the teaching of his *Decretum* in Bologna led to it being adopted throughout the new universities of the time in Germany, France, England and Italy. Four main decretist schools developed: Bolognese, Parisian, Anglo-Norman and Rhenish. The students of these schools, known as Decretists, annotated and expounded Gratian's work. Few of them attended to the issue of cross-dressing or transgender behaviour.

---

1   Commonly known as the *Decretum*.

But an exception was Stephen of Tournai, of the Parisian school who, in his *Summa* of 1160, distinguished between respectable women who dressed as men in order to protect their chastity and women who lived as men in order to sin more freely (Brundage, 1987).

There is much documented evidence of the medieval and Renaissance cross-dresser, particularly as street prostitute and actor. Evidence of the authorities' role and attitude to the transgender is more difficult to discover. Church and secular law both dealt with the act of sodomy, rather than the relationship that might lead to it. Without the opportunity for surgical intervention, the only options for those transgender people who wished to have a sex life were those acts considered homosexual. In Venice in 1354, Rolandinus Ronchaiai, who had acted and looked like a woman, was burned for sodomy (Goodich, 1979, p 13).

There are many medieval accounts of female saints who were transgender. One such is Pelagia, a dancing girl, who upon conversion to Christianity left Antioch as a man and travelled to the Holy Land where 'he' was admired for his asceticism and holiness. 'His' genital sex was not discovered until death. A saint with a similar name is Saint Margarita Pelagius. Pelagius was so horrified at the idea of marriage that 'he' took refuge in a monastery, lived and worked as a man and was even accused of having made pregnant the portress of a convent. Pelagius lived as a hermit after this accusation rather than face discovery. It was only at his death, when his genital sex was discovered, was Pelagius proclaimed innocent of the crime. There are many similar stories of other saints: St Apollinaris, St Eugenia and St Anastasia are just a few (Bullough, 1974).

There is also the apocryphal story of Pope Joan, known as Pope John VIII, which first appeared in a book by Stephen de Bourbon (1261), then in the *Medieval History of Polonius* (1279) (Addis and Arnolds, 1951, p 35). Joan is reputed to have been uncovered as 'he' gave birth to a child in front of a large crowd of spectators whilst in the midst of a Papal procession. She apparently died shortly after the birth. The story was relegated to legend by the end of the 16 century, but until then, it was held to be true, and Pope Julius III approved the publication of a report of Joan's death (Bullough, 1974).

On the other hand, there is comparatively little evidence of a history or mythology of cross-dressing behaviour amongst men for the medieval period in western society.[2] According to Bullough (1974), this discrepancy may be because transgender behaviour in women was seen as being part of their search for chastity and holiness, and was admired and therefore recorded, whereas it was assumed that transgender behaviour in men was for the purpose of getting close to women, for example, in convents, in order to have sex with nuns. Such persons would have been afforded a low status, and their behaviour was not noteworthy.

---

2   However, there are a great many legends from this period of male to female transgender behaviour amongst the Bedarche of North America and Siberia, and the Mahu of Polynesia (Baynes, 1991; Williams, 1988).

On the other hand, sodomy in medieval Europe was both a secular and an ecclesiastical crime, but as Goodich (1979) and Bray (1982) both argue, it was generally an act privately participated in, in private households. Despite the codification of the canon and secular laws that took place in the 13th and 14th centuries, and the penances and punishments derived for the act of sodomy, there was generally little recourse to using these unless the peace and stability of a community was threatened. The state and church were much more concerned with unacceptable heterosexual behaviour: the production of illegitimate children and adultery. Whilst during this period there were laws against particular sexual acts (sodomy and tribadism), there seem to have been no secular laws against individuals dressing and living in the role opposite to that of their natally assigned sex.

Apparent exceptions are mentioned by Saslow (in Duberman *et al*, 1989) who tells of

> A woman burned at Fontaines, France, about 1535, when authorities discovered that she had been passing as a man in order to marry another woman and 'counterfeit the office of husband' (Saslow, in Duberman *et al*, 1989, p 96),

and two nuns were burnt for penetrative sex using a dildo, in 15th century Spain, but it is likely that the punishments in these two cases were for the sexual acts, rather than for the claims that the people concerned had laid to male prerogatives.

Another possible exception appeared in the laws against witchcraft. First derived in the 10th century against women who followed the goddess Diana, these were codified at the beginning of the 14th century (Addis and Arnolds, 1951, p 840). Green (1974a) states that throughout medieval Europe, there was a belief that witches possessed potions that could change the sex of humans or animals. There was also a belief that demons could change others and themselves into women, and for this reason bishops were requested to look out for throngs of demons transformed into women (Bullough, 1974). The *Malleus Maleficarum* (Sprenger and Institor 1489)[3] contains an eyewitness account of a sex change of a girl into a boy, caused by demons. Green (1974a) points out that this was the book served for almost 300 years as the source of treatment by physicians of the insane.

To illustrate the point that transgender behaviour could be associated with witchcraft and heresy, and was viewed as part of the Devil's works, one need look no further than the famous trial of St Joan. Joan of Arc was burnt at the stake. The charges against her were that she could not prove that her political quest, her voices, or her clothing served God's purpose rather than Satan's. She was only 19 when she was executed in 1431. A peasant girl who heard voices, she had led the French army to several victories against the English until her capture in 1430. She was charged with various heretical acts and

---

3   Known as *The Witches Hammer*.

beliefs, and that her voices were those of demons and not of God, two of the 12 charges against her dealt with the wearing of male costume. After almost a year's inquisition, she repented and promised to wear female clothing. She was sentenced to life imprisonment but in prison, she resumed wearing men's dress. This act led to her execution with the full complicity of the French and the English. She argued that she had not intended to promise never to wear male clothing again and that she would continue to do so because 'it was more lawful and convenient for her to wear it, since she was among men, than to wear woman's dress' (Bullough, 1974). Joan's trial was a rarity, in that few records remain of other individuals condemned on such grounds.

The historian Alan Bray (1982) points out that whilst medieval English society associated 'sex changes' and other unnatural acts such as sodomy with the supernatural and the workings of the Devil, people would be unlikely to recognise the behaviour of their own family or neighbours as demonic. Sodomy and heresy, 'sex changes' and demons, were conceptually linked yet although there was technically abhorrence of such behaviour on theological and religious grounds, the behaviour of individuals was usually tolerated. As Saslow puts it: 'An unsolved problem in this (period) is the wide variation of open violations of official taboo' (Saslow, in Duberman et al, 1989, p 95). In medieval Europe and England in particular, as there was no specific punishment prescribed for cross-dressing, the courts had to deal with incidents infrequently; consequently, no fixed policy was established. Temporary cross-dressing during festivities was an old folk custom. Unless such events got out of hand, or there were political overtones, they rarely came to the attention of the courts. Long term cross-dressing may well have induced a court to pass a heavier sentence upon an individual who had used their 'disguise' to commit crime or fraud (Dekker and van de Pol, 1989), but although there were sometimes laws proscribing transgender behaviour, and on occasion trials of individuals who cross-dressed or cross-lived, local communities as a rule did not condemn such individuals. Only those who were thought to have practised witchcraft on others, or to have been possessed by demons that caused such behaviour elicited punitive sentences. Communities were reluctant to allege witchcraft or demonic possession because of the trials and torments that would accompany official investigation, which inevitably would not be confined only to the initial suspects but would spread fear far and wide. Instead, communities appear to have preferred to deal with such issues locally. Much the same can be said about the enforcement of laws against sodomy and cross-dressing in medieval Europe. Thus, it is easy to understand the small number of prosecutions and lenient punishments for such crimes. For example, Bray (1982) mentions the conviction of Meredith Davy for sodomising his apprentice. Yet, he was not jailed, he was merely required not to do it anymore and he was still allowed to sleep with the boy.

Edward IV had introduced the first sumptuary laws into England in 1463. His successors were to follow his lead passing laws relating to clothing regulations relating to social status. The statues were meant to uphold and continue distinctions in rank by preserving the ancient differences in dress. Thus, the colour, style and fabric of a person's clothing signalled a person's rank in society. Skidmore (1999) says of these:

> It is inherently problematic to know how far such laws contributed to discourses surrounding gender performance, given that notions of sex and gender at this time had not been constructed out of the later-to-be-privileged scientific and sexological discourses ... It is extremely difficult for the late 20th century observer to draw any conclusions without imposing present understandings of sex and gender. And yet we must pose some questions as the legislative texts at times differentiated between 'men' and 'women' and were premised upon gender mappings between clothes and gender identity.

Skidmore debates whether sumptuary laws were ever concerned with regulating same-sex sexual activity. Citing Dollimore (1991), he refers to the report that James I sent instructions to the clergy to ensure the suppression of cross-dressing by women. Was this to ensure that 'lesbianism' was controlled, or was it that some women were usurping male roles in much more general terms, or might it have been that a few were actually 'becoming as if men'. During the period of the Restoration, transgender behaviour started to be clearly documented. Dekker and van de Pol (1989) discovered documentary evidence of 119 'women living as men' in the Netherlands between 1550 and 1839. Nearly all of these though were from the 17th and 18th centuries. Finally, from this latter period, evidence of men who lived as women was beginning to come forward. The Abbé de Choisy (1644–1724) left a firsthand account of a lifelong wish to live and be treated as a woman (Choisy, 1994), and the Chevalier D'Eon de Beaumont's (1728–1810) life as a woman has been written about many times (Cox, 1966).[4]

THE RESTORATION – THE RISE OF THE EFFEMINATE MAN

In England, the church's influence on the state had declined with the collapse of Cromwell's Protectorate in 1660. Though the Witchcraft Act was not repealed until 1736, its influence had mostly died out by the latter half of the 17th century. Popular opinion had began to turn, and increasingly theologians, most notably the Jesuit, Father Frederic Spee, condemned the practice of trial and execution for witchcraft. Thus, the use of laws against witchcraft also declined. Before 1885, there was no comprehensive law

---

4   The Chevalier D'Eon de Beaumont's (1728–1810) name was to be used to coin the term 'Eonism', a sexual activity category describing cross-dressers, by Havelock Ellis in the early 20th century.

relating to male homosexuality in England; the only relevant law was that concerning buggery (the act of sodomy), dating from 1533.[5] It notionally carried the maximum sentence of death. This law was part of the assimilation of established ecclesiastical sanctions into secular law, and marked the surrender to the state of many of the powers of the medieval church, at the time of the dissolution of the Roman Catholic church in England. As such, same-sex sexual behaviour could be said to have been tolerated in many walks of life, despite Christian law since the 12th century holding that sex acts were only to take place within marriage.

Men who did not confine their sexual acts to marriage usually had sex with both adolescent boys and female prostitutes. Prosecution for such acts, as has been seen, was inconsistent. With the Restoration came a social space in which new ideas were to be explored. For the male aristocracy, religious scepticism and republican politics were to become discussion points along with libertinism. Libertinism was originally used to mean 'habitual licentiousness' (1611) but by 1641 also meant 'free thinking in religious matters'. It has been suggested that it appeared in Europe in the 17th century simply because the continent had been exhausted by religious wars; in England, it had the added impetus of a country escaping the strict codes of Cromwell's Protectorate. Whatever its origins, it would mean that those who moved away from the rigours of the medieval church would also consider moving away from its rigid sexual requirements. Trumbach states:

> The behaviour of the relatively small circle of aristocratic libertines in the 1660s and 1670s ... in (whose) world the love of boys certainly did not exclude the love of women; but the love of boys was seen as the most extreme act of sexual libertinism. (Trumbach, in Duberman *et al*, 1989, p 130.)

This was a minority of men, often those with wealth, who played with women what was called the 'love game', involving selection, seduction, subjection and separation. The female victims of this game were often subjected to anal intercourse and sadistic practices. Romantic love was reserved for 'boys' and 'catamites', who were invariably of the servant class. The relationships formed across social classes would also cross the boundaries of clothing as dictated by the sumptuary laws that still existed. We see same-sex activity being made possible through clear social roles determined by clothing. One party would wear finery, the other would be 'rough'.[6] The aristocratic men who played the 'game' came to be known as Rakes, and Trumbach portrays the changing view taken of the Rake on the Restoration stage – from a heterosexual to a bisexual

---

5   25 Henry 8, Chapter 6, which begins 'Forasmuch as there is not yet sufficient and condign punishment appointed and limited by the due course of the Laws of this Realm, for the detestable and abominable Vice of Buggery committed with mankind or beast', and goes on to define it as a felony punishable by hanging until dead.

6   Sex with a 'bit of rough' is to this day seen as desirable role play within the gay men's community.

libertine. Trumbach demonstrates that between 1660 and 1700 in London, there was a temporal change in the social classification of people who participated in sodomy. First: as the man who had a wife, a whore and a boy; later as (bisexual) libertine-rake; and finally as effeminate homosexual. Before this period, male and female cross-dressing had little to do with sexual proclivities. But the changes that occurred over this 40 year period were to have a profound effect on the development of the 19th century psychosexual category of 'homosexual'.

This was the historical period when the concept of the 'self' came into being. The *Shorter Oxford English Dictionary* cites the usage of 'self' in its modern form as first occurring in 1674, defining it as:

> That which in a person is intrinsically *he* (in contradistinction to what is adventitious); the ego (often identified with the soul or mind as opposed to the body); a permanent subject of successive and varying states of consciousness. (*Shorter Oxford English Dictionary*, 1970.)

A sense of personal identity arose, a consciousness of individuality which in turn affected the personal concept of sexuality:

> Sexual activity was increasingly coming to define a particular type of person. In return people were beginning to define themselves as different and their difference was constituted around their sexuality. (Weeks, 1989, p 34.)

The Rakes who were free thinkers viewed their love of boys as being a love of the 'same sex', of other men with like minds and concepts of self. Now it was possible to identify oneself as being a particular 'type' of person and so Rakes began to meet together in order to find lovers of similar type. Sexual activities, rather than being contained within the home, work place and local community, began to centre on special places in urban areas where individuals could be guaranteed to meet others who would wish to participate in similar sexual activities. At the same time, others, like the Abbé de Choisy, and Edward Hyde, Viscount Cornbury (afterwards Earl of Clarendon), were expressing their dissatisfaction with the social expectations of their gender.

It was said of Edward Hyde, Governor of New York and New Jersey (1701–1708) and often regarded as the first known English transvestite, that he:

> ... was a clever man whose great insanity was showing himself in women's clothes. When New Yorkers complained that he had opened their legislative assembly dressed as a woman, he retorted, 'You are very stupid not to see the propriety of it. In this place and particularly on this occasion I represent a woman (Queen Anne) and ought in all respects to represent her as faithfully as I can'. (Davenport-Hines, 1990, p 74.)

However there is no proof that Hyde, the Abbé de Choisy or of the Chevalier D'Eon de Beaumont were sodomites, or practised other homosexual activities. According to Trumbach, there arose at the time the concept of the Fop, an effeminate man. Different from the Rake, the Fop was heterosexual and was not a misogynist – he preferred the company of women to men. Hyde and Choisy could be constructed as extreme Fops.

This was to change in the latter part of the century. The Fop, that is, the effeminate (and upper class or aristocratic) man, began to be associated with the effeminate man who was a passive partner in homosexual activities. Trumbach (1977) puts this down to the fact that it was during this time, with the development of the concept of the self, that women also began to have a 'self'. Whereas in the past they had been housekeepers, child bearers and satisfiers of men's sexual desires, they now had a role as friend and companion to many married men. The companionship that had previously been found between men and boys was now assumed to exist only within the marital relationship. Wives no longer tolerated extra-marital sexual relationships between their husbands and other men. There arose awareness that men should/could only desire women. This assumption led in time to the division of homosexual men into two distinct subgroups: those who appeared 'masculine' (the 'rough') and those who appeared 'as women' (the upper class Fop). The clubs and meeting places for men, which had originated with the Libertines, now became places where men met with other men who were both induced and assumed by society's values to behave 'as women'.

Trumbach argues that:

> ... whenever homosexual behaviour surfaced at the Royal Courts from the 12th to the early 17th century, it was accompanied by what contemporaries viewed as markedly effeminate behaviour ... it is unlikely that the London homosexual sub-culture emerged only in the late 17th century when one considers, if nothing else, the theatrical milieu, with its transvestite boys, in which Marlowe wrote Edward II and Shakespeare his sonnets. (Trumbach, 1977, p 11.)

Despite this, it was not until the early 18th century that trials were seen of effeminate sodomites and evidence emerged of the meeting places of such people. In view of Dekker's and van de Pol's (1989) work on female cross-dressers in the Netherlands, it seems that even if Trumbach's view is correct, the roles of effeminate man or masculine woman were not available to the general populace prior to the 18th century. They were contained in very specific communities – the theatre and the court – in which they were tolerated. However, by the latter half of the 17th century, we see evidence of the Libertine influence permeating down through the class structure. This may have been due to the predilection of the Libertines for relationships with their servants. Whereas in the past, homosexual behaviour had been between individuals of the same class (that is, artisan with labourer or apprentice, or kings with courtiers), it was now taking place between classes. Thus, the effeminate fashions of the court could be passed down through the class structure of society.

Some taverns and houses became men's clubs of mixed social classes where homosexuals could meet. These places became known as Molly houses[7] of which there were estimated to be perhaps 20 in London by the 1720s (Davenport-Hines, 1990, p 72). They were generally in a private house or a tavern and in them:

> ... a new and stricter code of private words, physical gestures, clothing, vocal mimicry and other rituals developed and came to characterise a new sodomite subculture ... There congregants revelled in feminine mimicry and in acting out (with a mixture of mockery and envy) scenes from heterosexual life ... The back room in Molly houses to which men retired for sex was known as the chapel; sexual acts performed there were known as marrying; the first sexual conjunction between two men was known as a wedding night. Some mollies not only assumed female nicknames, or adopted feminine language, but created pregnancy rituals, culminating in mock lying-ins where a 'pregnant' man gave birth to a doll ... In short the mollies were ... playing out the other domestic roles of men and women. (Davenport-Hines, 1990, pp 72–73.)

This did not go unnoticed and the backlash was swift. The Society for the Reformation of Manners was founded by Puritanical Christians in response to the new-found freedoms and functioned between 1690 and 1730. It operated by employing spies, and doggedly prosecuted prostitutes, pornographers, sabbath breakers, swearers and sodomites. Many of its members were to go on to become constables and justices. It pursued several successful prosecutions of the members of Molly houses in 1699, 1707 and in 1726. In 1726, there were purges of homosexuals in both France and Holland. In France, the leader of a 'school and bordello for sodomy' was executed and 200 others were given prison sentences. In Holland, 200 sodomites were executed by drowning, hanging or burning. There were over 2,000 British newspaper reports of the Dutch trials over a two year period (Davenport-Hines, 1990, p 72). In London, in a well organised campaign by the Society for the Reformation of Manners, over 20 Molly houses were raided. The group trials were a national scandal. By 1727, the Society and its various offshoots had persecuted over 94,000 people by their own count, and according to Norton (2000), people simply got sick of them and they declined rapidly. However, Norton says:

> To a great extent the Society for the Reformation of Manners was itself responsible for stimulating the growth of the gay subculture. The gay subculture coalesced under the pressures of this reforming environment. The publicity given to homosexuality by the Societies – in sermons and tracts as well as the publicity attendant upon the raids and trials – must have made gay men aware that a fair number of them were about town, and that they could pick one another up at the cruising grounds helpfully identified by worthy

---

7   'Molly' was originally a term for a female prostitute and, like the word 'queen', later became a term for the effeminate passive male homosexual.

clergymen. The attempt to suppress vice actually may have facilitated the expression of the sexuality of many gay men who otherwise may have thought they were alone in their tastes and who otherwise lacked the courage to seek partners or had no knowledge of where they could be found. And the pressure of persecution may have persuaded gay men that it would be in their interest to form associations to meet in less public places. Self-preservation is a powerful impetus to the consolidation of a subculture. (Norton, 2000.)

This consolidation was to lead to cross-dressing changing in character in the popular perception of the public. From being a form of disguise or theatre with occasional overtones of sodomy, it became the identifier of a form of sodomite. Though not to persist as a pervading image of the homosexual, except in the style of the 'queen', the image of the molly gave rise to the concept of a distinctive homosexual culture and identity, and the development of a protective sub-culture for those involved. Throughout the 18th century, there were prosecutions of sodomites, but it was to be a fragmented response to the issue after the decline of the Society for the Reformation of Manners. Nonetheless, the sodomite and the 'feminine man' had become inextricably linked in the minds of the public and the state. That linking provided a framework for the medicalisation of the feminine man and the masculine female during the 19th and 20th centuries.

THE NINETEENTH CENTURY – THE RISE OF TREATMENT

Before the 18th century, there was practically no social framework for dealing with the insane and no theory of insanity. The deranged beggar was a familiar part of the medieval landscape; other people were supported primarily by families. The only specialised support was that provided by Bethlam Hospital, which had been founded in 1247. At the time of the Enlightenment, as the concept of the self was being engendered, there was the rise of the asylum movement in Europe. Private madhouses were in common use from 1700, but were by their nature limited to the more affluent sections of society. After 1750, demographic changes due to industrialisation and the growth of the cities were the compelling influences in the creation of special institutions for the insane.

Originally places of care and control, in the asylums, there was little concept of treatment or cure of the illnesses from which their inmates suffered. However, from the theories of the Enlightenment evolved the ideas of rationality and irrationality, and the concept of humane treatment. The first acknowledged equation of the insane with other sick persons was by the rational, enlightened Joseph II of Austria. In 1783, he commanded that any religious order whose insane members had been locked up in underground cells 'should treat its own members afflicted with madness with the selfsame care as those suffering from any other ailment' (Doerner, 1981, p 171).

From that first acknowledgment there was, throughout the 18th and 19th centuries, the development of the disciplines of psychology and psychiatry as worthwhile and valued careers for physicians. In 1860, in Zurich, Griesinger converted the existing asylum into a clinic. According to Doerner (1981), Griesinger created the model for university psychiatry that was to last for the next 100 years. Westphal was a pupil of Griesinger's. Like Griesinger, Westphal was a liberal, natural science orientated psychiatrist. Westphal and Griesinger, along with L Meyer, founded the *Archiv fur Psychiaterie und Nervenkrankheiten*, which attacked the asylums and their doctors as inhumane. It demanded free treatment for all, and the abolition of the restraints that had been used in the asylum system. It was this school of psychiatry which was to medicalise those people who practised homosexual acts, or had other 'associated behaviour'.

Meanwhile, in the early 19th century, in Britain and Germany, homosexual behaviour and homosexual prostitution had once again become a major social problem (Weeks, 1990, in Duberman *et al*, 1989). A member of the Home Office wrote in 1822, after the arrest of the Bishop of Clogher for sodomy:

> No event ... is to be more lamented both on public and private grounds. It will sap the very foundations of society, it will raise up the lower orders against the higher, and in the present temper of the public mind against the Church it will do more to injure the Establishment than all the united efforts of its enemies could have effected in a century. (Davenport-Hines, 1990, p 103.)

There was a general feeling amongst those in power that if the public were kept ignorant of the act of sodomy, the 'weak minded' would not be tempted. Unfortunately, for those in power, the trials of sodomites proved excellent fodder for the scandal sheets and were extensively reported. This provoked public and police interest in an offence of which they had previously been scarcely aware. Until 1885, when Labouchere's proposed addition to the Criminal Law Amendment Act[8] was approved, there was still only the 1533 Act[9] under which to prosecute individuals. This had criminalised the act of sodomy or buggery; other homosexual acts such as touching or masturbation were not criminalised. This caused problems for those wishing to control homosexuals, since the proof of sodomy that was required was often difficult to obtain. The only other ground for prosecution of homosexuals, if other aspects of homosexual behaviour could be shown to have taken place, was 'conspiracy to commit a felony'. Furthermore, the punishment was death and though the hangings of sodomites were popular fodder in the 18th and early 19th century (Norton, 1999), as the century progressed, the number of capital crimes was gradually reduced due to social campaigning and public abhorrence. Juries became less and less willing to accept the evidence against those charged with sodomy or convict them.

---

8   48 & 49 Victoria, Chapter 69: 'An Act to make further provision for the Protection of Women and Girls, the suppression of brothels, and other purposes.'

9   *Op cit*, fn 5.

Though there existed the idea of the effeminate man as a sodomite, as shown in the trial of Boulton and Park in 1871, there was little knowledge of the subject. Ernest (Stella) Boulton and Fred (Fanny) Park were arrested in 1870 for indecent behaviour. Two cross-dressers, they were immediately examined for evidence of sodomy, and charged with conspiracy to commit such acts. They had frequented the haunts of female prostitutes for over two years, and the police were of the opinion that they were working as male prostitutes. The authorities lacked knowledge on the subject and based the prosecution on their transvestism and their soliciting of men *as women* rather than sodomy. No conviction could be obtained on these grounds and they were ultimately acquitted of the charge of 'conspiracy to commit a felony by cross-dressing' (Davenport-Hines, 1990, p 118).

By the mid to late 19th century, the authorities' main concern as regards 'sex laws' was with using the law to suppress sexually transmitted disease through the control of female prostitutes. All of these gave the authorities the power to pick young women up of the street and to force them to undergo medical treatment if they were discovered to be diseased. Contemporaneously, there was through the early feminist movement a massive rise in the idea of the Christian family; a great concern about the immorality of the inner city populace; and a concern with the corruption of young people and the weak minded. They viewed all men as being at risk of temptation by vice. However, homosexuals were considered a particular threat in all three areas. They seemed to have no regard for the family and its sacred place in society, they were considered part of the immoral inner city populace both as users and service providers, and they were imagined to be the corruptors of young people.

In 1885, the Criminal Law Amendment Act[10] was enacted. Jennifer Payne (1998) gives a detailed account of how the Act came to the statute books. Its focus to start with was not on homosexual behaviour at all. It was concerned with controlling child prostitution and raising the age of sexual consent for young women. Labouchere proposed a clause for s 11 of the bill that was accepted and passed with little or no comment from either the politicians or the press. Labouchere wished to demonstrate various inadequacies in the proposed legislation, not least the difficulty of enforcing a law that surmised a person's reason for being on the street. His amendment, which criminalised 'any male person who, in public or private commits, or is a party to the commission of, or procures or attempts to procure the commission by any male person of any act of gross indecency with another male person' was not intended to be passed, but rather to provide a point for discussion. However, it was extremely late at night when it made it to the floor of the House, and it went to the vote with hardly a word being said about it. This section of the Act received much publicity during the 1890s as the authorities used the law to

---

10 *Op cit*, fn 8.

crack down on male homosexuality. Probably the most notorious trial that resulted from this amendment was that of Oscar Wilde.

The amendment enabled anyone suspected of being homosexual to be charged without there being any need to prove that they had participated in the act of sodomy. If found guilty, the punishment was imprisonment for up to two years with or without hard labour. This criminalising of private sexual practices, referred to as a 'blackmailer's charter', was sure to drive individuals to visit the doctor. Into this milieu, the clinical system of Griesinger and his contemporaries had:

> ... ushered in an almost 'imperialist' penetration by psychiatry of the (non-psychiatric) somatic brain and nervous diseases, and also – even more portentous – of society as a whole, that is those countless individuals whose 'irrationality' could not previously become visible because they had never been in institutions, who had concealed their problems with society from that society, keeping them locked up within themselves. (Doerner, 1981, p 274.)

The most important innovation in the ushering in of this world was the outpatients' clinic. At these, a new class of patients presented who did not warrant incarceration in asylums but who:

> ... now, as their 'weakness' was becoming 'conspicuous' to the pitiless diagnostic control agent of economic liberalism – efficiency – this army of the 'irritable and weak', the 'abnormal', the 'sexual perverts', the psychopaths, compulsive neurotics – the area in which the borderline between the 'abnormal' and 'normal' is indistinct – began to unburden themselves to the privately practising neurologists or the clinical psychiatrist. (Doerner, 1981, p 274.)

Individuals who were unhappy with what society expected of them now had doctors to go to who could be expected to diagnose them and even 'cure' them. Homosexuals or individuals associated with the homosexual subculture, who lived in fear of the law, could turn to doctors who would hopefully help them to put aside their dangerous desires and aid them towards re-establishing their place in 'normal' society. As homosexuals turned to the medical profession for cure, the doctors were able to collect together case histories of such individuals. From these, they discovered that rather than all homosexuals being the same, there was great diversity, both in individual history and also in practice and desire. This diversity was to allow the separation of transgender people from other 'homosexual' patients.

FIND THE TRANSSEXUAL – THE GAME OF THE CENTURY

In the first half of the 19th century, the authorities had been reticent about discussing homosexuality, for fear that doing so might influence others to 'take up this heinous crime'. Discussion in general was severely limited because of the use of euphemisms and delicacies. Many people were also wary of discussion lest they themselves were thought to be sodomites and would hence risk severe punishment for their surmised crime. But, as Foucault has suggested, the refusal to discuss sex marked sex as *the secret*, and thus it became the centre of discourse. There was an explosion of debate around sexuality at the end of the 19th century. This, combined with the 'visits to the doctor' by people who were 'homosexual' (as well as people with other sexual matters they considered to be problems), allowed the development of the case history form of diagnosis.

Much of the debate around sexuality concerned its relationship to the law. Three of the first 'sexologists as writers', Ulrichs (homosexual), Hirschfeld (homosexual and suspected transvestite) and Ellis (as a result of his wife's lesbian sexual orientation and experiences) could be said to have had 'vested interests'. They wished to decriminalise homosexual behaviour by medicalising it through science.

Foucault claims that Westphal was the first writer to deal with homosexuality as a state of being. However, Casper in 1852 pointed out that homosexual behaviour was some kind of 'moral hermaphroditism' and that attraction to the same sex is inborn. Ulrichs, from 1864, devised the words 'uranian' and 'urning'; he regarded uranism as a 'congenital abnormality by which a female soul had become united with a male body' (Ulrichs, in Ellis, 1948b, p 66). But Westphal was the first medical writer to deal with the subject, and to define a medical category into which 'homosexual' people fell. Foucault says of the category Westphal created that it was:

> ... characterised ... less by a type of sexual relations than by a certain quality of sexual sensibility, a certain way of inverting the masculine and feminine in oneself. Homosexuality appeared as one of the forms of sexuality when it was transposed from the practice of sodomy onto a kind of interior androgyny, a hermaphrodism of the soul ... the homosexual was now a species. (Foucault, 1978, p 43.)

The first sexologist who took a special interest in the sexual impulses of individuals was probably Krafft-Ebbing (1840–1902), Professor of Psychiatry at Vienna. His *Psychopathia Sexualis* was published in constantly revised forms from 1877 until after his death. Krafft-Ebbing in this revision process constantly endeavoured to give clearer and clearer classifications to the manifested behaviours and individual histories of his patients. This resulted in a series of major categories and subcategories, with ever-increasing complexity.

This separation of types enabled Krafft-Ebbing to differentiate from other categories of homosexual those individuals whom we would now recognise as being transsexual. Krafft-Ebbing divided homosexuality into two major categories: Acquired Homosexuality and Congenital Homosexuality. Under both headings, he described transgenderism, under the first as 'Eviration and Defemination' and/or 'Metamorphosis Sexualis Paranoica', and under the second as 'Effemination and Viraginity' and/or 'Androgyny and Gynandry'.

It is sometimes extremely difficult to understand how he distinguished between case histories that today would appear similar; perhaps this is because we no longer have a conception of acquired or congenital homosexuality. The cases Krafft-Ebbing presents are interesting, in that we see the subjects using the same ways of describing themselves as we see in case histories of transsexuals from the 1950s to 1980s. For example, in Case 99, we see the first recorded usage of the term 'I feel like a woman in a man's form' (Krafft-Ebbing, 1893, p 209), which was to become the classic phrase of self-description used by transsexual people in the future.

Magnus Hirschfeld was the next most influential voice. Hirschfeld was not just a doctor, but also a medico-legal expert in Germany's courts. He used his position to advance the science of sex to achieve social justice. He was also gay, Jewish and probably a cross-dresser. He was to be hounded when the Nazis came to power, his Institute[11] was closed and, on 10 May 1934, the Institute's 20,000 volume collection of books was burnt or pulped. Hirschfeld coined the word 'transvestite' from the title of his *book Die Transvestiten*, published in 1910. Hirschfeld divided his 'transvestites' into five subcategories: (1) the heterosexual; (2) the bisexual; (3) the homosexual; (4) the narcissist; and (5) the asexual (Ellis, 1928, p 13). Hirschfeld was the first to suggest that:

> ... homosexuality (was) primarily a biological phenomenon of universal extension and secondarily a ... social phenomenon of serious importance. (Ellis, 1948b, p 74.)

Albert Moll amended Hirschfeld's categories in 1921, and arrived at a classification that included a subgroup of homosexual cases in which cross-dressing constitutes part of the contrary sexual psychic state. However, Ellis (1928), in his commentary on Moll, draws attention to the fact that Moll failed to grasp Hirschfeld's idea of intermediate sexuality for 'pronounced' cases of cross-dressing. Havelock Ellis, who wrote an encyclopaedic seven volume work cataloguing and categorising all types of sexual activity, carefully divided transvestites from transgender people. He called transvestites, as we now know them, Eonists. Transgender people were kept in the group of 'sexual inverts' – that is, homosexuals.

Seven years before creating the Berlin Institute in 1912, Hirschfeld had also been responsible for introducing the first patient to a surgeon to have successful reassignment surgery, albeit partial. That patient was a female to male transsexual who underwent surgery to remove his breasts. More famous though is Rudolph/Dorchen, a male to female transsexual who worked for many years as a housemaid at the institute and who had a penectomy to remove the penis and castration of the testes at the clinic in 1922. In Berlin in

---

11 The Institute for Sexual Science in Berlin, and probably the first clinic in the world devoted to sexology.

1926, at the First International Conference on Sex Research that Hirschfeld had organised, he was to be introduced to a young German doctor who was doing pioneering work in developing field of endocrinology (the understanding of hormones). Harry Benjamin, who was to later make the first medical use of the term 'transsexual', had left his native Germany in 1906 and travelled to the USA, where he had developed an interest in the rejuvenating properties of hormone therapy for the elderly. His meeting with Hirschfeld was to prove one of the most significant in the history of sex changing. Benjamin was to provide Hirschfeld with the expert advice he needed at the Berlin Institute to start developing cross-sex hormone therapy for the clinic patients. The meeting was also to prove to be a catharsis for Harry Benjamin's ultimate career route.

Hirschfeld and Benjamin had little opportunity to work together, but they were greatly influenced by each other. Hirschfeld, with Benjamin's advice, started experimenting with ways of altering the hormones of his patients. The successful results were to lead to Dr Gohrbandt, Director of the Surgical Clinic of the Urban Hospital in Berlin, performing the first complete male to female gender reassignment surgery in 1931. Also in 1931, Dr Felix Abraham who worked at the Institute for Sexology in Berlin published the first medical article on gender reassignment surgery, 'Genital reassignment of two male transvestites', describing Dr Gohrbandt's techniques. The first biography of a transsexual woman who underwent surgery in 1931 at the Berlin clinic was that of Danish painter Lili Elbe (formerly Einar Wegener). Although Lili was to die of complications from the surgical procedures to form a new vagina within the year, her biography, *Man into Woman*, edited by Nils Hoyer, was published in 1933.

Harry Benjamin developed a lifelong fascination in the treatment of cross-gendered individuals. He founded the World League for Sex Research in 1928, and in the early 1930s, he is reputed to have given the 'first scientific talk' on cross-gender behaviour to the Association for the Advancement of Psychotherapy in New York City. He also invited Hirschfeld to his New York apartment in 1930 to give several lectures. When Hirschfeld died in 1935, Benjamin continued, albeit quietly, in the field providing a clinical service to transsexual people throughout the 1940s and 1950s.

It was Hirschfeld who finally separated transgender behaviour from homosexuality (King, in Plummer, 1981), a separation which allowed the medical profession to take a specialised professional interest in the 'treatment' of the former. From the 1950s, Cauldwell's use of the term transexual (*sic*) to describe someone who was 'physically of one sex and apparently psychologically of the opposite sex' (King, in Plummer, 1981, p 166) was being used to justify surgical intervention on behalf of such individuals. But even today, there are still those who argue that transvestism or transsexualism is merely a mask for latent homosexuality.

Through the work of the early sexologists, transsexuality became a recognised phenomenon available for study, discussion and treatment. By the 1930s, an active role was being played by psychologists, psychiatrists, endocrinologists and surgeons in the 'treatment' of transgender people. This continues to this day. There are many arguments about the involvement of so many professions, but that discussion requires a separate space from this one. However, it can be seen as to why the provision of treatment for transsexuals has always been led by the psychiatric profession. Yet we must not ignore the inconsistency in the approach of psychiatric professionals as exemplified by the DSM III, which removed homosexuality from the list of Psychosexual Disorders, whilst at the same time adding transsexuality. For many centuries, the two were inextricably linked; why were they suddenly separated?

The development of the categorisation and diagnosis of cross-dressing or cross-living activity as a mental disorder has been primarily the result of the activities of the 19th and 20th century sexologists. Their interest in transgender behaviour arose for several reasons.

The first of these was the formation of a homosexual identity that arose from the development of a sense of personal self and sexuality. The second came with the 'accidental results' of legislation to control the sexual abuse of young women in the late 19th century, which was to criminalise this homosexual identity. The third factor was the development of the asylum movement and from that, in particular, the outpatients clinic. It was in these clinics that the homosexual sought help to cure an identity that had now been made illegal. Sexologists then divided the homosexual identity into categories in an attempt to show that it was a result of a mental disease, and hence not appropriate for legal control.

From this division, the categories of transvestite and transsexual were developed in the 1930s and 1940s. The involvement of sexologists in this construction of a syndrome enabled the treatment of transsexuals to be in the professional domain, primarily of psychiatrists, rather than surgeons or endocrinologists. The psychiatric world has, by taking this responsibility, failed the transgender by failing to consider the extent to which the labelling of the syndrome as a mental disorder has held back the civil rights of these people. This problem lies alongside the apparent paradox of homosexuality becoming no longer considered as a mental disorder (in fact, it was 'removed' from the DSM III because of those stigmatising effects) at the same time as transsexuality was marked as such.

The church, state, and medicine have taken turns in regulating, through their ideological apparatus, those who have cross-dressed or cross-lived. Social control mechanisms have been passed like a baton in a relay race in much the same way as it has been for other individuals who fall into socially stigmatised categories, for example, black people, disabled people and those defined as insane. Transsexual people, however, are unique, in that as we enter the 21st century, they are still being self-righteously ostracised, even by other oppressed communities who would consider it politically incorrect to oppress any other minority group. As Szaz said in *The Myth of Mental Illness* (1970):

> We call people physically ill when their bodily functions violate certain norms; similarly, we call people mentally ill when their personal conduct violates certain ethical, political, and social norms. (Szaz, 1970, p 14.)

This, a structuralist would suggest, is the result of transsexual people being 'non-human'. 'Man' and 'woman' are used as words to represent the whole of humanity, and since transsexuals fit neither keyword, they cannot be part of humanity. Whatever the reason, the oppression is real – transsexuals have a perplexing legal and medical status, and continue to lose their jobs, their homes and their families merely for being what they are.

One might argue that we must decided whether the transsexual person is 'sick', as was defined in DSM IIIR, and therefore worthy of good treatment, if not cure (which has proved notably difficult to unearth). This would mean that to oppress such individuals is untenably immoral. Alternatively, they just 'are', as homosexuals now just are, and as such must be entitled to the civil rights that other citizens obtain in democratic states. For some time, a difference in civil rights and responsibilities due to being either 'male' or 'female' has been regarded as being inequitable. Is being 'transsexual' so very different from either of these categories?

CHAPTER 3

TRANSSEXUAL DENIAL: SOCIALLY CONSTRUCTING THE LEGAL BODY

As seen in Chapter 1, the transsexual faces the problem of interpretation, As such, they prove a problem to law, in its role as the omniscient protector of truth. If a post-structuralist framework is accepted, legal knowledge is constructed through text; it is secured in language that continually re-examines it, alters it and then recreates it – like a game of Chinese whispers. All legal constructs exist within a series of preconceptions that have been acquired by lawyers through their accumulated knowledge of written texts. To apply the law means to place interpretations on the texts of others, to expound what is within texts and to overlay it onto a new context. According to Goodrich:

> ... it is language which bears tradition and it is through language, through the dense prose of the text, or through the phonic rhythm of the oral history that we remember not simply the appearance of the past but also its discourse ... In discourse, we read language to recollect not simply what was said but the context of what was said. (Goodrich, 1990, p 3.)

As a result, though legal practitioners attempt to be impartial and to seek justice, what in fact occurs is the evolution of a traditional authority over ever-changing circumstances. To legal texts, we must bring the question of meaning, which is in itself a question for the law:

> ... a question of legitimacy of reference, of faith in the linguistic encasing of reality, faith in the capacity of words to act as the notation of things. (Goodrich, 1990, p 7.)

In order to understand the texts of the law, we need to search for and recognise the legitimacy they have in the discourses that construct and are constructed through them.

Texts reproduce discourses; or rather, they reproduce pieces of discourse (Parker, 1992) around subjects. According to Parker, a discourse is 'a system of statements which construct an object'. Realised by their nature of being self-reflecting historically located motifs containing subjects and concerning objects, they have a coherent system of meanings and they refer to other discourses. Parker further defines discourse to be texts (and there are many forms of text, not just the written) that support institutions, reproduce power relations and have ideological effects.

Legal texts, whether case reports, academic commentary or the passing of judgment, can easily be seen to fulfil these requirements; they come from a history and become part of a history, not just of the text, its subjects and its objects, but of the history of law making itself within which they are located.

The texts reflect upon themselves and their legal role, they contain subjects – the villains of the piece (defendants, plaintiffs, etc), and concern objects – the law itself and how it has or has not been broken. Legal texts are seen to be coherent in their meaning, without mistake at the time of their construction; any error appears through time and societal change: it is not 'in' the text, but comes from outside of the text. It can also be seen that legal texts support the state institutions of parliament and the civil and criminal justice systems, within which they reproduce the relationships of power; they support these ideologically through legal decision making processes.

To discuss discourse is to set out on a voyage of discovery, as 'there is no analytic method'. 'Doing' discourse analysis and justifying it as scientific method all too often presents the researcher with the dawning realisation that 'each step rests on a bedrock of "intuition" and "presentation"'(Potter and Wetherall, in Parker, 1992, p 5) and it becomes important to recognise the limitations of what it is possible to accomplish. However, as a type of research, what it does enable us to do is to address a text as one type of truth, rather than as *the* truth. It allows us to see the subject of the text not as a 'real' subject, but as a constructed subject. Post-modern jurisprudes accept, with little difficulty, Hart's view that:

> In most cases, legal terms have a central paradigm meaning that makes their interpretation non-controversial. Occasionally, however, debatable cases arise that exhibit a linguistic or 'motivated' indeterminacy. In these instances, the interpreter must exercise discretion. (Douzinas, Warrington and McVeigh, 1991, p 23.)

Discourse Analysis is a tool that enables the researcher to address the difficulties that arise in maintaining a distinction between Hart's 'core of settled meaning' and the 'penumbra of doubt'. Using Discourse Analysis, it is possible for texts to have both certainty and uncertainty at one and the same time. Certainty appertains to the object of the text to whom the text belongs and for whom it has coherence. Uncertainty concerns the subject who (or which) is constructed through the text, who does not own the text, and who only contributes to the text through being observed. The subject has no certainty, only perceived axioms that are accorded truth by the subject.

Burman and Parker (1993) have listed 32 potential problems with using Discourse Analysis, but go on to say that there may be many more as yet unrealised. Yet, according to Burman and Parker, this does not remove its value as an activity that makes it possible to make 'worthwhile political interventions' by:

- elaborating the contrasting consequences of discursive frameworks;

- promoting existing (possible subordinate) discourses;

- clarifying the consequences of particular discursive frameworks with those who use them;

- commenting upon the consequences of particular discursive clashes and frameworks.

Burman and Parker are working in the discipline of psychology, but the law is also a series of discourses and therefore Discourse Analysis has a place, particularly when we are concerned with those areas which fall into Hart's 'penumbra of doubt'. It could be argued that all legal constructions fall into this penumbra and so there should be little opposition to placing in this shadow the legal discourses that concern transsexual people. Foucault (1971) described how the discourse concerning 'madness' as a medical category was developed, and then considered through his study on Pierre Riviere (Foucault, 1975) how this became interrelated with the power bases of the French criminal justice system. Similarly, we can look at how the transsexual, as a legal category of person, has come into being (or has not, as might be said to be the case in English law), and their meaning to law as a whole.

Discourse Analysis using Parker's methods (1992, Chapter 1) is employed here on two texts to look at the development of social and legal discourses concerning transsexual people through language and meaning. By looking at texts and the discourse that they appear in, it is possible to attempt a retention of objectivity when looking at law. This may appear to initially trap the researcher into looking at the minutiae of text, but in reality, it enables us to develop a theoretical approach to language in the law. The object of study is moved away from that unknown and fluid concept – the transsexual – to the texts themselves, which are fixed and which can be readdressed whenever required.

The two texts, Janice Raymond's *The Transsexual Empire* (1979) and Jonathan Demme's film *The Silence of the Lambs,* appear very different, and hardly legal texts at all. Janice Raymond approaches the issues of the transsexual from her stance as a sex role theorist and feminist who teaches women's studies and medical ethics. Jonathan Demme, as a Hollywood producer, created a thriller/horror movie, with no apparent theoretical approach to transsexuality at all. Consequently, the discourses they participate in appear very different. Yet, both become structuring agencies of the discourses that surround and construct our notion of the transsexual person despite that apparent difference, as it does not hide their 'sameness'.

THE TRANSSEXUAL EMPIRE

In 1979, the Women's Press published Janice Raymond's seminal thesis *The Transsexual Empire*. At the time of its publication, transsexual people in the UK were suffering the legal consequences of the *Corbett v Corbett*[1] decision, which had ended the mechanisms whereby their birth certificates could be altered and their marriages declared void; the decision in *White v British Sugar*[2] had

---

1   *Corbett v Corbett* [1970] 2 All ER 33.
2   *White v British Sugar Corporation* [1977] IRLR 121.

effectively removed any employment rights they might have had. The book became 'the' radical separatist lesbian commentary on transsexualism and has remained so to this day, arguing that transsexual people were engaging in 'the religious and political shaping and controlling of "masculine" and "feminine" behaviour' (Szaz, in Raymond, 1979, 'About the book'). Twelve years earlier, in 1967, an American physician, John Money, had announced that he had solved the dilemma of whether nature or nurture determines gender (Money, 1975). He had encouraged the parents of one of a pair of twin boy babies who had accidentally been penectomised during circumcision to bring the child up as a girl. The boy underwent reassignment surgery to create female genitals. He was never told of his reassignment, and his parents had brought him up as a girl. Money, a self-styled 'missionary of sex' (Calpinto, 1997, p 59) announced that, after long term follow up, the 'girl' had successfully adjusted to her new role and that it was, therefore, nurture and not nature that decided the gender of people. On the basis of one single case, that view was to be dominant until the basis for it was refuted in 1998.[3] It was clear by analogy that transsexualism was not congenital, and that trans people should respond to nurture if it was persistent enough and firm enough.

The nurture overrides nature contention was to be the mainstay of much feminist debate in the 1970s (see Chapter 4), and provided the basis for arguing that women should be treated equally to men, and could consequently achieve as much. Regardless of the benefits that this has afforded all of us in creating social and legal change over the last 30 years, the view that nurture could override all was disastrous to transsexual people. By the end of the 1970s, the film *A Clockwork Orange* (1971) and the work of radical psychiatrists such as Thomas Szaz had thankfully almost put an end to the 'brainwashing' and aversion therapies that psychiatry had forced upon many transsexuals in the past in an attempt to cure them. Yet many medical professionals were, in reality, to continue to place obstacles in the way of gender reassignment treatment. Despite the reality in which people were placed for years on endless waiting lists,[4] during which they were expected to live in their new role, and jump through many social and medical hoops, Raymond used the transsexual as a 'case study' to illustrate the radical feminist call for nurture to be the overriding social force. It might be argued

---

3   In 1998, Professor Milton Diamond discovered the real outcome of John Money's case. The child who had been reassigned as a girl had never been happy in the female gender role; he had always experienced his gender as male, despite his female rearing and female hormone treatment, and as soon as he was able, he had reassigned to his male identity (Kipnis and Diamond, 1998). John Money's findings for his research were revealed as being grossly inaccurate at best, but not before a generation of tertiary specialists had been at least misdirected by someone who, for many of them, had been their mentor and pre-eminent amongst them. From the point of view of trans people, of course, a generation of patients had been inadequately and inhumanely treated.

4   I was told in 1977 that I would be placed on the waiting list for mastectomy surgery, but that the wait would be 11 years.

that *The Transsexual Empire* has little to do with transsexual people; it is nothing more than a rant against male medical/social power. Nonetheless, it did little to challenge the patriarchy, but it did a great deal to further condemn transsexual people to always being of their natal sex.

Raymond's core argument is that transsexual women are medical interventions (by male doctors) which produce pastiches of women, in order to make 'real' women obsolete. In disguise, these (wo)men then seek to invade women's space, to promote reactionary stereotypes of what women should be like, in order to ensure men's control over women's lives and their bodies. Consequently, nurture techniques should be used to force these men to recognise that: (a) they are men; and (b) the real challenge to social role stereotypes would be for them to be feminine as men. As such, the solution to transsexuality was consciousness raising groups and a clear refusal by women to accept transsexual (wo)men as women. The effects of Raymond's thesis are still with us, with Rape Crisis Centres throughout Britain refusing to provide counselling to transsexual rape victims, and statements such as those by Sheila Jeffreys, a radical feminist academic, who recently stated:

> Transsexualism was analysed as a form of social control, ie, to fit malcontents neatly back into one of the categories of the two-sexed, two-gendered system of male dominance, and as being about the profits of a medical empire, but not as constituting the destruction of lesbians (see Janice G Raymond's wonderful *The Transsexual Empire*). (Jeffreys, 2002.)

Jeffreys seeks to explain (ftm) transsexual men as lesbians who have become 'ashamed' of their lesbianism and seek reassignment in order to join the patriarchy, to take part in the 'cult of masculinity'. She says:

> The vast majority of the women who 'transition' have identified as lesbians, or at least lived within the lesbian community and conducted relationships with lesbians. The attribution of masculinity to lesbians historically has formed a major tool of control. ... As lesbians were consigned to lobotomies as a form of social control in the 50s, so transsexualism is the social control of today. (Jeffreys, 2002.)

Jeffreys argues that transsexual men are in effect one of the worst examples of women who 'cut' themselves, only in their cases, they persuade doctors to co-operate in this barbaric self-mutilation. It is a powerful argument, but just like Raymond, Jeffreys presumes that transsexual people have no agency and no control over their personal destiny.

THE SILENCE OF THE LAMBS

The Silence of the Lambs is a complex, multi-layered tale in which a young female FBI agent enlists the aid of a criminally insane ex-psychiatrist to help track down a vicious serial killer, Buffalo Bill (aka Jame Gumb). Buffalo Bill perhaps sees fit to kill people as a way of escaping his own socially abused identity, an idea that is supported by his assumed 'transsexual' identity. The only way he can truly escape his own self-loathing is by transforming his physical appearance; in order to do this, he is making a new 'female body' for himself from the skins of his victims. Buffalo Bill is not, according to the book or the screenplay, a transsexual, as an expert explains:

> ... there's no correlation in the literature between transsexualism and violence. Transsexuals are very passive. ... Billy's not a real transsexual, but he thinks he is. He tries to be. He's tried to be a lot of things ... He wouldn't test like a real transsexual ... Billy hates his own identity, he always has – and he thinks that makes him a transsexual. But his pathology is a thousand times more savage. (Tally, 1989.)

Nevertheless, as we will see through an analysis of the text, what is said about transsexual people through both the book and the film (and which has been reiterated in many previous fictional accounts) is that they 'use up' and destroy the essence of all that is female, making women and, in particular, their bodies outmoded and easily superseded by the technology of men.

As we participate in a discursive approach to both Raymond's work and the film *The Silence of the Lambs*, we will see how the removal of agency from transsexual people leaves them as victims in a war between feminism and the patriarchy, has created myths of perversity and monstrosity, and has left them unable to voice their response. Whenever they attempt to do so, they become nothing more than self-interested, narcissistic, deranged and deluded individuals who by their madness speak only madness. Their place and function in the world is simply as tools of the patriarchy, destroying any place or power of women.

A DISCURSIVE ANALYSIS OF THE TRANSSEXUAL EMPIRE

The first layer of reality that a discourse refers to is the 'apparent object', the layer of reality that is a constructed representation of the world. Raymond is discussing 'the transsexual empire' and her discourse is about man as object, and empire builder. The transsexual is a representative man and the doctors who have created the empire are men. She distinguishes men from masculinity and women from femininity. For her, men and women are 'governed by certain chromosomes' (Raymond, 1979, p 4); masculinity and femininity are 'superficial stereotyping'; transsexuals are examples of that process in action. The discourse of patriarchal hegemony becomes the first layer of reality.

The second level of reality, of objectification, that a discourse can refer to is the discourse itself. Both the transsexual and the doctor as objects are male and, as such, are victims and perpetrators of the patriarchal hegemony of society. The dialogue concerns patriarchy, and this is reflected in the text. Transsexuals (and doctors), as objects, are tools to illustrate a further discourse about patriarchy, which in itself illustrates Raymond's own perspective – that of a feminist discourse.

She presents the transsexual person as an artificially constructed female, naming transsexuality as:

... artifactual femaleness – the 'she-male' is made – ie, constructed, fashioned and fabricated. (Raymond, 1979, p xvi.)

The transsexual (Raymond predominantly features male to female transsexual women) never becomes a member of the sex to which they aspire; they are always men to Raymond. Any femaleness they have is given to them by the empire builders, 'the truly dominating medical/psychiatric fathers who create artificial women' (p 69). The transsexual is never what they profess to be; the male to female transsexual is not a woman, but a man making use of:

... one of the few outlets for men in a rigidly gender-defined society to opt out of their culturally prescribed roles [p 26].

Conversely, the female to male transsexual is never what they proclaim themselves to be, that is, a man. They are:

... the token that saves face for the male 'transsexual empire'. She is a buffer zone who can be used to promote the universalist argument that transsexualism is a supposed 'human' problem ... women are assimilated into the transsexual world, as women are assimilated into other male defined worlds, institutions and roles, that is, on men's terms, and thus as tokens [p 27].

This point is emphasised by her insistence upon referring to transsexual people, at whatever stage of their transition, by pronouns that indicate their natal sex designation, for example:

Paula, formerly Paul, Grossman has sketched a similar portrait of himself. Previously married and the father of three children, Grossman recently lost a test case in the New Jersey courts to postoperatively retain his former public-school teaching status [p 78].

When Raymond feels obliged to refer to the transsexual in their new status, she places the pronouns in quotation marks; for example, in the footnote on p 79, the male to female transsexual woman is referred to as 'her' and 'she':

This is to indicate that, while transsexuals are in every way masculine or feminine, they are not fundamentally male or female [p 4].

Raymond does not try to hide her colours; she speaks as a feminist who is concerned about sex-role oppression and the:

... patriarchal society that has imposed images and definitions of female existence [p 176].

As such, she is not discussing women, she is discussing men, and in this way she has enabled women to become the subjects of the discourse. As a woman, she writes the text that the discourse inhabits, and she writes for a female reader.[5] Women in the text have an important role: they are never the objects of the text, but the discourse concerning transsexuality is objectified through their view. That view though is from the perspective of the woman as victim. She is the victim of patriarchal hegemony; in turn, the transsexual steps from being a victim of the empire builders to being a male perpetrator of hegemonic control over women's roles. For Raymond, theories concerning transsexualism:

> ... neglect the wider and more primary influence of sex-role stereotyping in a patriarchal society, and ... conclude by blaming the mother [p 42].

The theories that blame mothers have enabled the 'father figures' of medicine to redeem the biological mothers' failure. This failure can take one or both of two forms. Raymond uses the work of psychiatrists John Money and Richard Green to illustrate the theory that transsexuality results from pre-natal influences of *in utero* hormones. The psychiatrist's view is that an excess of androgen *in utero* will masculinise a chromosomally female brain, or a shortage will feminise a chromosomally male brain. Thus, women fail to provide appropriate foetal welfare and cause their children to become transsexual.

As her second example, Raymond uses the work of the psychoanalyst Robert Stoller to illustrate a theory in which

> ... mothers of transsexual boys[6] clasped their infants to them too much [p 73],

or the mothers of female to male transsexuals

> ... have been tired, long-suffering, sad or angry women, left too much alone by their husbands. In these families ... the little girl moved into the vacuum created by her mother's sadness and unfulfilled by the husband ... the first fortuitous acts of the little girl may then be so positively rewarded that she will increase such behaviour, and since, to be a proper protector, she will have to take on masculine attributes ... The daughter's own depression, the result of a mother who cannot mother, is then 'cured' only when she does something to which mother will respond warmly: when the girl acts like a protecting husband. (Stoller, 1975, p 243.)

Whichever theory is adopted, either way, women have failed their children. Women are the cause of transsexualism, according to the empire builders: the doctors. Raymond wants to address this accusation on the behalf of all women. She could do this through a defence of women, but that would be to admit that there was a charge to answer. The best alternative is to resort to counter-accusation.

---

5   In the UK, Raymond's book *The Transsexual Empire* was published by The Women's Press, whose aim was to publish texts for and about women.

6   By which she is referring to male children who grow up to become transsexual women.

It is through this counter-accusation that we see a coherent system of meanings in the discourses used in the text. Raymond uses what can be seen as the discourse of 'blame', but directs it at men rather than women. In this way, whilst apparently objectively analysing transsexuality, she adopts the adversarial style of a courtroom battle. Women are the subjects, the prosecutors, who now 'blame' the objects – men – and doctors and transsexuals are token examples of men. The text is a separatist feminist discourse on the hegemony of the patriarchy. The transsexual person is put in the unenviable position of taking up the defence.

Raymond's arguments for the prosecution are undoubtedly powerful, firstly:

> Transsexuals are living out two patriarchal myths: single parenthood by the father (male mothering) and the making of woman according to man's image. (Raymond, 1979, p xx.)

The process of 'medical rebirth' is a process of mythic deception, which was one response, by a male power base, to the second wave of feminism in America in the 1960s. Secondly, transsexual people are one result of a 'socio-political programme', controlled and implemented by the medico-legal hierarchies of, and on behalf of, a patriarchal hegemony which has used them:

> ... to colonise feminist identification, culture, politics and sexuality. (Raymond, 1979, p xx.)

Not only does the patriarchy construct women out of men, but just as the androgynous man assumes the trappings of femininity when he identifies as, and is reconstructed as, a transsexual, so:

> ... the transsexually constructed lesbian-feminist assumes for himself the role and behaviour of the feminist [p 100].

Hence, the transsexual is created as an alternative to biological women who are becoming obsolete. In this way, the Empire does not just attack women; it goes much further. Their sense of self is being penetrated in every way. Women's identities, spirits and sexuality are all invaded. The physical loss of a penis does not mean the loss of an ability to penetrate. In this context, Raymond makes her most damning statement:

> All transsexuals rape women's bodies by reducing the real female form to an artifact, appropriating this body for themselves ... Transsexuals merely cut off the most obvious means of invading women, so that they seem non-invasive [p 104].

This feminist separatist discourse refers to other discourses constantly to substantiate itself. The notion of rape is a legal notion: unlawful sexual intercourse with a woman who does not consent to it. This is what Raymond accuses the transsexual of: penetration without consent. A specific legal discourse is now taking place. Presumably, she wants, like all prosecutors, the sentence afforded by law, and will plead for the maximum: life imprisonment. She does not flinch from the job in hand; she asks for:

The restricting (of) the number of hospitals and centers where transsexual surgery could be performed [p 180].

And for the transsexual to undergo non-sexist consciousness-raising counselling, and to be given peer encouragement to transcend cultural sex role definitions without undergoing surgery – to undertake their lives as men.

The discourse of rape is then followed by a much more subtle one: that of possession, in particular of the flesh of women. When a man penetrates a woman, he is often referred to as 'possessing' that woman. Raymond's constructed transsexual who identifies as a lesbian feminist exhibits:

> ... the attempt to possess women in a bodily sense while acting out the images into which men have moulded women [p 99].

If you want to take possession of the flesh, what better way than to devour it both literally and metaphysically? The transsexual is participating in the beginning of a world where men not only have total power, but become women by 'acquiring the hormones and body of a woman', as Raymond points out in citing Jan Morris's inadvertently (and supposedly) revealing statement:

> I wear the body of a woman. (Morris, in Raymond, 1979, p 126.)

Raymond's final accusation is the most condemnatory of all: the empire builders, the therapeutic fathers, are little different in their ethics from the Nazi physicians whose experiments included the following:

> High altitude tests were done on prisoners to observe the point at which they stopped breathing. Inmates ... were subjected to freezing experiments to observe the changes that take place in a person during this kind of slow death. Experiments in bone grafting and injections with lethal viruses were commonplace ... sterilization experiments were carried out on a massive scale ... for the purpose of seeing how many sterilizations could be performed in the least amount of time and most economically (thus anaesthesia was not used) [p 149].

Despite her disclaimer that she does not intend directly to compare the two sets of doctors, she has made her point in true 'Perry Mason' fashion. She has concentrated the minds of herself and other women, as the subjects, upon the role of the transsexual person as collaborator with these experimental techniques. Those transsexual people who identify as lesbian feminists have become the Kapos of the bunkhouses. She gives details of at least one piece of 'transsexual' surgery having been performed at Auschwitz, and presents a completely unsupported statement that 'some transsexual surgery may' have been developed in the Nazi death camps. Women thus become, of course, justified in thinking of transsexuals not as innocent victims of the patriarchy (which would have been one alternative reading), but as co-conspirators in an attempt by men to possess them and to remake them in a mould that suits them.

The defence does not have a voice in this text. The historical location of the text places it in the history of sex-role, early feminist theory and from it emerges a damning construction of the transsexual. No longer merely a medico-legal construction, transsexual people become part of the (his)story of patriarchal oppression. The institution of feminist theory is reinforced by this discourse; the institution of a medical field of study and praxis is subverted. It reproduces the power relations inherent in radical feminist separatist theory; it provides a place in which 'jobs for the girls' are supported. It begs a response, but the defence has yet to be heard, and there is little space for it.

Finally, the discourse has ideological effects: it promotes separatism as a radical alternative to the patriarchal hegemony; it supports the notion of separatism in that it sanctions an 'invisible' oppression of transsexuals by women. It allows women to become dominant in telling their narrative about their past in order to justify and promote the use of sex-role theory and, in assuming a homogeneity in women's voices, it subsumes any other discourse about gender and sex. In this way, the transsexual story of gender oppression and a search for identity is silenced.

The discourse presented by Raymond is not unique; it exists in other forms, and has been repeated in current cultural artefacts that act as agencies in structuring women's knowledge of the transsexual. Film representations of the transsexual/transgender person also participate in a discourse in which the transsexual 'devours the female flesh' or 'wears the body of a woman'. Although not a part of a feminist separatist discourse, such films invariably promote a discourse in which the subject is the patriarchy and men. Now the transsexual becomes a representation of the worst form of femaleness, once again, a representative of the object, but this time of the object as women.

DO TRANSSEXUALS EAT WOMEN? A POPULAR FICTION

As Sandy Stone, a lesbian feminist transsexual woman vilified by Janice Raymond in *The Transsexual Empire*, puts it:

> ... theorists of gender have seen transsexuals as possessing something less than agency ... transsexuals are infantilized, considered too illogical or irresponsible to achieve true subjectivity, or clinically erased by diagnostic criteria; or else, as constructed by some radical feminist theorists, as robots of an insidious and menacing patriarchy, an alien army designed and constructed to infiltrate, pervert and destroy 'true' women. (Stone, in Epstein and Straub, 1991, p 294.)

The transsexual/transgender[7] (trans) community offers an 'insider's' exploration of the ways they view gender issues and the use of transsexual and transvestite iconography in particular. It is not, however, clear-cut. Their

---

7   'Trans' will be used to refer to the combined cross-dressing/cross-gendered/ transgender/transsexual community and members of it.

theory has amongst its predecessors the work of neo-Marxists and feminist theorists. These theories have their own difficulties in reconciling transgender behaviour with their political stances. However, there is a place for looking at how transsexuality and other aspects of cross-dressing behaviour are portrayed, and to attempt critical ethnographic analyses from the standpoint of the trans participant. Trans people as writers and speakers used to have to be: firstly, apologists; secondly, explainers; thirdly, educators. However, the time has come when we are seeing a new form of trans performativity and text giving: now they have become theorisers about the idea/word/signifier 'gender'. In looking at trans issues from a trans viewpoint, Kate Bornstein in her book *Gender Outlaw* (1994) talks about the way the defenders of gender (by which she means those people who support a binary notion of gender) use humiliation – people laugh at the trans people. But do they also use fear as Raymond did when she laid out the case for the prosecution as we have seen? The film *The Silence of the Lambs* concludes the facts of her case.

The recent iconography of transvestite/transsexual people (in particular) as questioners of gender was clearly rendered in the fortunes of the extremely successful 1993 film *The Crying Game*. Apparently a positive portrayal of the male cross-dresser, it could be contended that it is a direct successor to the story that has been interpreted in Hitchcock's *Psycho*, De Palma's *Dressed to Kill* and Demme's *The Silence of the Lambs*. What exactly is that story and is it little more than an extension of a well known children's fairytale?

In 1960, Alfred Hitchcock released the original slasher movie, *Psycho*, which started a cinema genre that has continued to this day. *Psycho* also happened to give to the world an expressive image of the 'transvestite' at home and at work. That image was of a complex multi-influenced serial killer, who was defined authoritatively to the viewers as a transvestite by a 'psychiatrist' at the film's end. Virginia Prince and the members of the Full Personality Expression Group, which was founded in 1960 as a respectable self-help social group for transvestites (equivalent to the UK's Beaumont Society) were no doubt outraged by this portrayal of their harmless cross-dressing activities, just as transsexuals were later to be outraged by a similar portrayal of themselves in Brian De Palma's film *Dressed To Kill* in 1980.

Other films before and since *Psycho* have addressed transgender behaviour as a lifestyle. Female cross-dressing has been a popular source of film stories since the inception of the film industry. It appears to have less threatening connotations, perhaps owing to the long and well documented history of women who cross-dressed in order to go to war or to sea (Hargreaves, 1930; Dekker and van de Pol, 1989). Many such stories present the woman's cross-dressing as a disguise adopted in order to search for a husband or lover (Hargreaves, 1930), so they do not threaten the social norms. On film, the woman who cross-dresses invariably does it only as a temporary step in order to achieve her acceptance in the world as an adult rather than a child, reverting to their female role when that transition is achieved and they are accepted by 'the real adults' (that is, the men). In films such as *Yentl* (1983),[8] we see women who use male disguise in order to find a place in a man's world. Once there, they learn to understand the world of men but once accepted, they revert to living as women, though it is understood that they have some special knowledge and are as a result 'better' women to the men they know. Much less frequent are films about female cross-dressers in which the women cross-dress as a way of life,[9] such as *Queen Christina* (1933). These portray women who are recognised as such, but wear men's clothes because they prefer to; the activity even then is not associated with any form of sexual activity.

Cross-dressing as male activity has also been used a cinematic artifice throughout the industry's history, most often as a form of disguise and evasion or (often concurrently) as a comic ruse.[10] It is difficult though to accept the view that:

> Indeed, the cinema reflects transvestism in most of its contemporary aspects. (Ackroyd, 1979, p 130.)

However, Ackroyd also cites it as being used as a portrayal of: 'incest and psychosis' *Psycho*; an 'intense and sinister force' *Performance* (1967); and a 'narcissistic and quasi-homosexual activity' *The Damned* (1969). It is difficult to find a film which portrays male transvestism as a serious activity, that is, which shows a man who prefers to wear women's clothes, as opposed to using them for disguise or comedy, which does not end in the ruin or undoing in some form of the male transvestite. The one exception to this is the translation to screen of Monica Jay's semi-autobiographical story *Geraldine* (1993), which was released with the title *Just Like a Woman*.

Unlike films about female cross-dressers, male cross-dressing in films, particularly of the slasher genre, has sexual overtones, and is often used as a portrayal of a Freudian Oedipal complex suffered by the cross-dresser which influences both his lifestyle and his life story. In contrast to the films in which the female cross-dresser enters the adult world via a disguise that enables a rite of passage to be taken, in films about the male cross-dresser, the rights of adulthood that they could have obtained are obliterated. They have been soiled by their transvestism, or their transvestism is a symptom of that rite of passage being spoiled by some external force.

This second type of spoiling of the move from childhood to adulthood of the male is used by *Psycho* as the *modus operandi* of Norman Bates, the killer in the film. Norman has such tremendous desire for his mother that he recreates

---

8   Other films are *Two Girls Wanted* (1927), *The Hoodlum* (1919), *She Loves Me Not* (1934), *Beggars of Life* (1926) and *The Magician* (1959).

9   Others include *Sylvia Scarlett* (1936) and *A Song to Remember* (1945).

10   The classic example is *Some Like It Hot*, more recent examples include *To Wong Foo* and *Nuns on the Run*.

her for himself by his cross-dressing. It is this damaged development of the adult male, the enactment of Norman's Oedipal complex, that the 'psychiatrist' in the film explains to the audience at the time of Norman's undoing.

Dressed To Kill and most recently *The Silence of the Lambs* both have a great deal in common with *Psycho*, but they are not the only films which use cross-dressing/gender confusion as the derivation of the 'slasher' story. Others have been *A Reflection of Fear* (1971), *Deadly Blessing* (1981) and *Sleepaway Camp* (and sequels) (1983), all of which focus on the male cross-dresser. There is one film that uses a female cross-dresser (a girl who had been brought up as a boy) as the killer: *Homicidal* (1961), but that is a rarity. And though the killer in *Friday the 13th* (1980) is throughout the film implied to be male, she turns out to be a woman, a mother avenging her son's death, a situation which can be seen to have parallels with the enactment of Oedipal desire in *Psycho*.

Psycho, *Dressed to Kill* and *The Silence of the Lambs* have all been major blockbusters, bringing in large takings for the studios who made them, and that means they have been seen by more of the general populace than most films and hence are more likely to have influenced the viewer's understanding of the cross-dresser. The killers in these three films are all cross-dressers of different intent and extent, but the common factor, and the main contention within the films' narratives, is that women cause their own deaths and/or the deaths of other women using the hands of the cross-dresser. The cross-dresser in none of these films 'causes' the deaths of women; they are merely tools of women. Women might as well wield the knife upon themselves. The films also have a textual underlay about the power of 'Law': both the formal bearers of justice, the police, and the informal bearers of justice in all three are women. In many slasher films, the 'final girl' who escapes the killer and/or avenges the deaths of other victims is portrayed as 'boyish'. She is seen as resourceful, intelligent and a virgin, and is even named as such having a name such as Stevie, Laurie, Marti or Terry. In *The Crying Game*, the final girl, who avenges the killings perpetrated by Jude, actually turns out to be a boy: Dil.

The films that follow the *Psycho* narrative do not appear to fall into this pattern. Their final girls are not apparently boys or pseudo boys and on that level, the films seem distinguishable from the others. But Liz in *Dressed to Kill*, Lila in *Psycho*, and Clarice in *The Silence of the Lambs* are all made avengers of death by becoming representatives of the law; they become 'law men'. Once again, we cannot leave the meaning the films give us. In order to understand what these films tell the viewer, aspects of *The Silence of the Lambs* narrative are used. However, in the words of Tania Modleski, one has to bear in mind that throughout this:

> I have never really not been discussing *Psycho* – to my mind the quintessential horror film. (Modleski, 1988, p 102.)

PSYCHO – THE TRUE STORY

Psycho is a screenplay taken from the novel of the same name, written by Robert Bloch and published in 1959, less than two years after the events which had inspired its author. Plainsfield, with its population of third and fourth generation French and German dairy farming families, was small, around 700 people. It was nowhere, and nothing ever happened there. But in November 1957 Bernice Worden, a local storekeeper, disappeared. It was remembered that a 51 year old odd-jobs-and-errands man Ed Gein had been asking after her, so the local police visited the 160 acre derelict farm on which he lived. They found the remains of Bernice in the smoking shed next to the house. Throughout the house, they found parts of other human bodies. These were not just collected *per se*, but the skins and bones were made into items of furniture, bowls, etc, and a drum. The skins of female faces were 'made up' and used as wall decorations (reminiscent of the Nazis who made lamps and other decorative items from the skins of their victims). The freezer was well stocked with carefully wrapped human organs. Overall, Gein had tortured and murdered at least 10 women since 1955. Also, since 1945, when his last relative, his mother, had died, he and a friend had exhumed the graves of over 40 female bodies.

Besides the cannibalism, the grave robbing, the torture and the murder, he also made himself partial suits from the skins and hair of his victims, or the cadavers he exhumed. He strapped these female torso skins, masks and 'wigs' to his body whilst he wandered around his farm. Though most of the farm and house had been allowed to run to ruin, his mother's bedroom and parlour had been maintained in pristine order (Woods, 1992). Bloch was to use these details for his novel rather than the more gruesome aspects of the crimes (which have themselves been immortalised in the films *The Texas Chainsaw Massacre* and *The Texas Chainsaw Massacre II*). 'Psycho', the screenplay, was taken directly from Bloch's novel. The person who created the cross-dressing killer of the story, Norman Bates, was Bloch. Bloch actually created many of the visual and linguistic puns that were later to be credited by commentators to Hitchcock. The names of his main characters are intentionally meaningful. Norman is the nor(mal)man and Mary Crane (the name was changed in the film to Marion) can be constructed as the virginal bird (Rebello, 1990, p 11).

A DISCURSIVE ANALYSIS OF *THE SILENCE OF THE LAMBS*

Demme's film is perhaps the most interesting of the films in this genre, in that it accommodates many more details of Ed Gein's story in the Bloch scenario than the others. The following is a hypothetical wandering through the maze of symbolism contained in the film, an attempt to discover a discourse.

The victim in all of these films is a 'bad' woman: she commits a crime against our sense of good womanhood. In *The Silence of The Lambs*, Catherine's main crime is eating too much. She becomes a victim because of being a 'big girl'; she is also shown to have actively taken part in sex games with a boyfriend and photos are found of these activities. It is her size, though, which attracts the killer, Buffalo Bill/Jame Gumb, to her. He is going to kill her because he desires her flesh. Catherine Baker Martin's name has its origins in that of the virgin martyr: Katherine. Like all wicked girls, she has a 'bun in her oven'; she may not be exactly pregnant (it's only that she has over-eaten), but stories do not have to be literal and the point is that she has done her 'baking'. A martin is a type of bird – she is a virginal bird who has erred, and who needs punishment.

The cross-dresser in the film, Jame Gumb, is an ex-psychiatric inmate who preys on large women to satisfy his need to make a female suit out of their skins. Having seen a moth appear from a pupa, he becomes obsessed with the process of change. He abducts young women, whom he kills by hanging or shooting in order to flay them and use their skins. He is making himself a skin in which he thinks he will resemble/change into his mother, whom he apparently adores through two small pieces of film he has of her. Just as Norman in *Psycho* recreates his mother, Jame is trying to recreate his mother through himself. This is the only one of the films that uses the original crime of 'suit making' of Ed Gein.

Clarice Starling, another bird, represents the law in this film. A trainee FBI agent, she sees through the sight and senses of a convicted cannibal, Hannibal Lecter. Hannibal Lecter, nicknamed Hannibal the Cannibal, like the real person Ed Gein, actually consumes parts of his victims, and has even been known to serve up their flesh to his guests. Lecter goes further than Jame with his victims; he desires their flesh so completely, he eats them.

There is much play on Lecter's use of his senses apart from sight. Hannibal constantly penetrates Starling's thoughts, and he sees for Clarice through the enhanced senses he has acquired. How has he acquired these? Is it through the eating of other people, the devouring of other people's powers and sense of being? Clarice very rarely sees for herself but when she does, when she realises that the killer is sewing himself a body suit, it is when she has finally been willing to risk her FBI career, to give up her token position of power in the patriarchy as an official 'law man'. She resumes her role as an FBI agent when she confronts Jame Gumb, and once again, she cannot see. He has infra red glasses through which he can see as he pursues her through the cellar of his house. She is blinded by the darkness but, like Lecter, she eventually sees by using her other senses – in this case, she hears the cocking of the gun. Clarice Starling represents both the formal law, which is blind, and the law of the patriarchy that demands justice for women. It is her insistence on pursuing the case, and risking her career prospects in the FBI, that ensures that Jame Gumb is caught.

The film *The Silence of the Lambs* does not go into the detail that the original novel does. The novel gives more emphasis to Jame's desire for a 'sex' change. He is fixated by moths, and places a pupa in the throat of each of his victims. The term for a moth or butterfly when it emerges from the pupa is 'imago'. An imago is also 'an image of the parent buried in the unconscious from infancy and bound with infantile effect', the Oedipus story once again. Jame looks at two short film sequences regularly: one is of his mother when in a bathing beauty contest; the other is of a woman he imagines is his mother in a swimming pool. He wishes to change into his mother, unlike Norman in *Psycho*, who has already become his mother. The suit of skins that he is making is a suit to make him become his mother, just as Norman did. Thus, his mother, by having rejected him, turns him into a killer, and the ultimate cross-dresser.

Clarice Starling is like Lila, the final girl in *Psycho*, in that she is the college girl. She doesn't have a boyfriend, and we can assume she doesn't have sex; it is only as the case draws to a close that she can show an interest in a man, the biologist who names the pupae that are found in the throats of the victims. Unlike Liz, who as a prostitute in *Dressed to Kill* becomes the final girl by a process of cleansing, she is clean already.

Jame Gumb's victims in the story are large girls. Their crime, like Marion's in *Psycho*, is eating too much, only whereas Marion is a man eater, they are also food eaters. Jame's name is Gumb, a play on the mouth and the process of consuming. Jame is attempting to satisfy his appetite to become his mother, by consuming – that is, using up – female flesh, by killing women and then literally using their flesh to satisfy his desires. He wants to emulate Jan Morris and 'to wear a woman's body'.

WHO SEES WHAT?

Films are made to be seen by spectators, and feminist film theory typically places women in one of two viewing places in relation to these films: either in the place of the female masochist identifying with a passive female character, or as a cross-dressing woman identifying with the active male hero (Modleski, 1988, p 25). That categorisation does not, however, cater for the roles that women take in the films discussed, and hence the female spectator must surely identify differently with the films. The films all place women as victims, but not as masochists. As victims, they are strong women who actually decide for themselves what they want, and it is this strength that makes them the choice as victims. But they are not victims of men; they become victims of all the women who have persuaded them not to support the power structures of the patriarchy. By overstepping the social role of a good woman, they have made themselves victims. Women are also the practitioners of justice in the films: they see, whereas the law is blind, but in this, they are pseudo law men.

The films purport to be about serial killers who are cross-dressers, but when viewed at depth, they are about women. Women are operators at all levels of the text, and hence become the subjects. The cross-dresser is merely a blind to the story; they provide the link between different generations and types of women and, of course, they are the slashers of the stories. This is because to place that slashing in its context, that is, as belonging to a woman, would show up the true inadequacies of the texts to the viewer. The texts are inadequate because women do not as a general rule commit violent crimes, and rarely participate in crimes that involve slashing. The crime of penetration is one perpetrated by men, but the cross-dresser, the apparent trans person, places the act of penetration in the hands of women. The trans person becomes a representative object of those women who ruin their sons, and who deny their sons' sexuality and its rightful place in the patriarchal power mechanism. The final girls, as 'law men', learn the ways of men and to be 'good girls', submissive tools of the patriarchy. Thus the cross-dressed slasher was created, but as the subtext of both *Psycho* and *The Silence of the Lambs* point out, he/she is not a true character at all. Ed Gein was a real person, but not a transvestite or transsexual. Unfortunately, the characters of transvestite or transsexual are used as scapegoats, to illustrate the imaginary female violator.

Neil Jordan, the director of *The Crying Game*, went on to do the same thing. The film initially appears to be a complete reversal of the plot of the other films. The victim is a man, Jody, a black British soldier in Northern Ireland. His crime is to be seduced, and the killer is a straight woman, Jude, the single white female whose career is the IRA, and whose vocation is apparently as a seeker of justice (for the Irish people). The woman as law turns out to be in fact a man, the cross-dresser Dil.

Alter one's point of view though: where does the killing lie in the film? It is the death of Jude at the hands of the cross-dresser Dil that recreates the story of *Psycho*. Mark Simpson in *A Crying Shame* (1994) points to a different interpretation: the film is about 'fear of woman' and Jude represents the vagina dentate, the castrating bitch, the evil and criminal woman who wrecks men's lives. Dil is both the woman killer and the woman with a penis (in that she penetrates and slashes Jude with numerous bullets, and she literally has a penis). She acts for the state in bringing justice against women who commit crimes, yet she also is criminal because of her femaleness. Dil plays the parts of both Norman and Lila in *Psycho*, of Dr Elliot and Liz in *Dressed to Kill*, of Jame Gumb and Clarice Starling in *The Silence of the Lambs*. She is the man who plays the woman, and the woman who plays the man. Once again, real femininity as portrayed by Jude is exterminated, and transvestism is used to do away with the feminine altogether. The patriarchy always wins.

Janice Raymond said that 'all transsexuals rape women'. These films go further and state that all trans people consume women, both metaphysically and through the flesh. This is a misogynist extension of the Red Riding Hood fairytale with the wolf in granny's clothing; the man in his mother's frock who eats up little girls. Killing women is a form of consumption of the flesh of the female. Implicitly to accuse the cross-dresser of participating in the same activity creates an unknown, and unfounded, fear amongst both women and men.

THE CONVICTION OF THE LAW

These two separate discourses both have a subdiscourse, creating a fear of the trans person in both men and women. Raymond uses the discourse of feminist separatism; Demme uses the discourse of the patriarchy. Both use the transgender/transsexual person as the representative object. First, Raymond uses them as the representative man who seeks to consume femaleness, to take it as their own, in order to uphold the power structures inherent in the patriarchy; all women should be frightened of them. Demme uses them as representative woman, to show the fear that the patriarchy and men should have of all women, especially mothers. All men should fear women. He further expands the idea that women must fight their sense of an independent female self, and accept that any power they have will only come through that given by the patriarchy.

Both are legal discourses, in that they expound issues of power and crime, and they place criminal actions in the hands of the trans person. Both charge them with serious and horrific crimes that are on a par with those of Nazi war crimes. And both leave no place for the defence. What defence could there be? There is no defence for war crimes; they are ultimately indefensible, inexcusable and unforgivable. Wars are dreadful events, in which atrocities are often tolerated, both legally and morally. A war crime is an atrocity that can never be atoned, in that it surpasses the morally acceptable at even the most immoral of times.

This may seem an unacceptable and implausible reading of these texts. Yet, Becker says:

> ... a major element in every aspect of the drama of deviance is the imposition of definitions – of situations, acts and people – by those powerful enough or sufficiently legitimated to be able to do so. A full understanding requires the thorough study of these definitions and the processes by which they develop and attain legitimacy and taken for grantedness. (Becker, in King, 1993, p 4.)

Both Raymond and Demme have used their legitimated power to create a scapegoat in the war between feminism and patriarchy. For the transsexual person, it is not a case of 'whose side are you on?', but of 'how on earth can you extricate yourself from always being the defendant at the war crime trials?'. How do you stop being the foot soldier in the Trojan horse that is offered to each citadel? How can you obtain citizenship anywhere?

In Oregon, in 1994, Lon Mabon actively sought to morally mandate transsexuals out of existence with his Initiative 610, which read:

> Any physical alterations to the human body do not effect the natural gender, known at birth or before, of any resident in the State of Washington (O'Hartigan, 1994, p 25),

along with Initiative 608, which sought to circumvent special rights being afforded to transsexuals. How similar that sounds to Raymond's opinion, expressed in the introduction to the 1994 edition of *The Transsexual Empire*, that:

> ... 'male to constructed female transsexuals' are entitled to the same humanity, the same respect and dignity, as is every other member of the human race – but as male human beings or as individuals who have undergone transsexual procedures, not as women.

CHAPTER 4

STILL GENDER FUCKING OR
STILL FUCKING GENDER?[1]

Queer means to fuck with gender. There are straight queers, bi queers, tranny queers, lez queers, fag queers, SM queers, fisting queers in every single street in this apathetic country of ours. (Street leaflet, quoted in McIntosh, 1993, p 31.)

AN INTRODUCTORY NOTE

Stuart Hall says:

> ... movements provoke theoretical moments. And historical conjectures insist on theories: they are real moments in the evolution of theory. (Hall, 1992, p 283.)

To study any culture is undoubtedly a contradictory project. In the process, which is not only one of observation but of textualising[2] a version of the observations, one becomes a 'cultural contribution'. Cultural studies was defined and originated as a political project; 'it holds theoretical and political questions in an ever irresolvable but permanent tension' (Hall, 1992, p 284). To study is in effect to participate. To textualise is to become a historical conjecture. It is an active engagement in a pedagogy with the textual producer about whom one is textualising.

So I become a part of the object of my study by studying it. I politicise, theorise the culture of gender, and in that way, I irreversibly change it. In the politics of gender, sex and the body, the existence of the body is, for us all, a statement of gender from the moment of birth. No matter how hard you try to talk about somebody else, you are always going to be talking about yourself. This book is, in the words of Stuart Hall, a 'moment of self-clarification'. As well as a chronicle of cultural change, it is an intervention in it and we would do well to remember that it has both overt and implicit political aims. I am gendered, not just by myself but by everybody who knows me, by all those who write of me and 'my sort', by all those who work with trans people, and nearly always by trans people themselves. Like everyone else, I cannot escape the hegemony of gendering. Sometimes I do not want to escape. Let's face it, I would not have had the 'sex change' unless I had wanted my gender to be something I could express and celebrate. But at most times, my main concerns are that my needs and those of my loved ones are met. Instead, those needs

---

1   A version of this paper was first published in Ekins and King, 1996. This version has been updated to take on board recent events.

2   Textualising is the production of any output, whether by speaking, writing, image or other form.

are always subsumed under the unpleasant mess which comes of having an appearance that contradicts what was written on my birth certificate.

Evaluating the possibility that 'sex' could be divorced from 'gender' and that the law could move from a 'sexed' framework to one which is either based on 'gender' (O'Donovan's cluster approach) or is divorced from either sex or gender (O'Donovan's egalitarian approach) requires a look at whether anyone has managed to see life beyond these dichotomies.

THEORISING THE SEXUAL

In order to appreciate current theories and cultures of gender blending, it is essential to understand the history of theory surrounding sex, sexuality and gender. The most recent manifestation of that history is Queer Theory, which has its basis in the history of pathologies and dualism that surround these areas. Queer Theory does not stand in isolation; its origins lie in the medico-legal discussions of sexual pathologies, which have been covered in an earlier section of this book. However, it would be naive to interpret Queer Theory without reference to them.

Homosexual pathology was the source of transsexual and transvestite medicalisation, and as such created the medical categories that we know today (see Chapter 2). It could be argued that Queer Theory's first major contribution to academic theory arose from the work done in the late 1960s by homosexuals, and by homosexual psychiatrists and psychologists in particular, to gain that removal from DSM III of homosexuality as a psychiatric disorder. Yet at the time, this work would have been recognised not as the start of a major theoretical movement, but rather as part of the process of political activism. Theory and activism are inextricable bedfellows, especially when it comes to the development of policy and law.

This political process and corresponding theoretical development is now being mirrored today in the contributions that transgender individuals are making to current Queer Theory. In particular, they have contributed to the work that removed from DSM IV (1994) the category of transsexualism. However what has replaced this category is, arguably, an indistinguishable category of 'gender dysphoria'. There is little or no change to the symptomatic requirements, and hence gender dysphoria is really a modern name for an old fashioned view of transsexuality.

Recognising the framework within which transgender behaviour, lifestyle, politics and culture are being employed it is possible to see the powerful contributions trans people are making to theory and hence to public policy and legal development. Queer Theory seemed one of the obvious starting points, along with the specific disciplines of law and psychology, for transgender people. These disciplines, unlike sociology, history and cultural studies, are only just beginning to feel the impact of Queer Theory as a school of thought, and that has probably been indirectly through the work of post-modern theorists. However, Queer Theory is becoming an increasingly powerful force in many other academic disciplines, and its effect is now being seen through many walks of life such as the media and entertainment.

THEORY'S QUEER HER/HIS/STORY

Queer Theory has a very recent history but it is based upon the late 20th century struggles for homosexual equality. The law, through case law and legislation, changed and removed some of the restrictions on individual sexual practice in the 1960s. Some impact was also made through the involvement of lesbians or 'women identified women' in the development of women's study courses in universities in the 1970s. As a result, lesbians and gay men were able to find some respectability and acceptance for their private lives within academic lifestyles.

Throughout the late 1970s and the 1980s, these 'queer' academics explored methods of bringing their own life experiences into the research they undertook. This process was not without problems. Firstly, it took a tremendous effort and will to ensure that lesbians and gay men were not just objects of study, but that they could also be objective 'studiers'. Secondly, though there had been legal change, and some academic acceptance, the activist campaigns that lesbians and gay men had been involved with had not disappeared. Apparent acceptance was tainted by a number of factors: the still unequal footing in law for gay male sexual practice, the lack of employment security and the liberal assumption that with the footholds that had been gained, lesbians and gay men would no longer face fear and prejudices. This was not the reality: young lesbians and gay men still faced justified fears of ostracism if they came out, queer bashing had not been eradicated from the streets, and individual prejudices, often embodied in the forces of the state, were still made manifest. The lesbian and gay community had certainly not gained equality of freedom from fear. Jeffrey Weeks summed up the mid-1970s sense of homosexual self:

> Guilt, evasions, a sense of inadequacy and isolation persisted amongst many homosexuals: inevitably for they had all grown up into families which, by their very nature, seemed to invalidate their experience ... There was a highly uneven integration of homosexuals into society. On the one hand, there were the achievements: the new relative openness, the expanded and more lavish sub-culture; on the other, there was deeply ingrained prejudice, fear of sexual freedom, religious and social norms antipathetic to homosexuality. (Weeks, 1990, p 230.)

The academic community was no refuge from these forces. It provided apparent inside safety, which was then lost outside. Even the inside of the academy was not without its dangers, as individuals fought hard to get their work on their own community accepted as valid and objective. Many, who came out often years later, such as Laud Humphreys, the sociologist and author of the widely acclaimed *Tearoom Trade*, kept their own homosexuality secret in order to achieve academic acceptance.

Activism was still an essential part of the homosexual community's *raison d'être*. Members of the academy recognised that they were potentially powerful voices of their own community, and many of them adopted an activist stance within their own disciplinary fields, as witnessed by those in the field of psychiatry who fought to remove homosexuality as a psychiatric disorder. A typical example of this is the work of Jeffrey Weeks, who in books such as *Coming Out* and *Sex, Politics and Society* brought homosexual activism into the discipline of history.

The gay liberation movement had advanced the idea that as an oppressed minority, homosexuals could be gradually absorbed into mainstream society without too much disruption. By the late 1970s and early 1980s, it became obvious that this was not to prove the case. The public face of lesbian and gay lives became much more prominent, but full legal acceptance proved notoriously difficult to achieve. The opposition movements to this acceptance, such as the religious right in the United States and conservative family values in the United Kingdom, were to gain strong ammunition in the battle with the recognition of the AIDS crisis in the 1980s.

The spread of AIDS in the 1980s posed a great threat to homosexual activism within the academy, just as it did to homosexual activism within the community. There was a grave danger that so many people would die or face death, that activism would become single issue targeted: that is, address the issues of mourning and surviving. However, the lesbian and gay communities did not concentrate their energies in these areas, because AIDS itself also provided the next arrow in their quiver. The emergence of this major health crisis did indeed destroy many lives, but it provided, as Weeks said, 'a major politicization of sex' (Weeks, 1990, p 237). This afforded an impetus to members of the academy, amongst others, to fight a rearguard battle against the new right (republican) attempts to impose retrograde and repressive steps on sexual freedoms.

The gay community fought many causes during the 1980s and the early 1990s. Because of separatist and internal politics within the gay liberation movement (which will be referred to later), they were often only single issue campaigns such as the 'Stop Clause 28' campaign in England, or the 'ACT UP' campaign for free and comprehensive AIDS health care and treatment in the United States. These campaigns though, of necessity, looked to members within the academy to provide the theory and evidence for their arguments. The relationship between gay activism and the academy has remained strong, as seen by the planning and organisation of the 5th and 6th North American Lesbian and Gay Studies conferences that took place in 1991 and 1994. Both conferences, attended by hundreds of people, included activists as well as academics on their organising committees; the appeal of the conferences was to both academics and activists and by 1994, because of campaigning by bisexual activists, the conference held at Iowa State University included 'bisexual studies'[3] in the conference title.

Queer Theory rose from this utilitarian mix of activism and academia. As an interdisciplinary approach, with its potential proponents (queer people) in all walks of academic life, it could be said to provide one of the greatest disruptions to the conceptual thinking of modernist thought there has ever been. Queer Theorists are attempting to undermine the very foundations of modernist thought, the binary codification of our apparent existence, the divergent sex and gender categories of a one-dimensional creed: sexual duality and its resultant heterosexist centrism.

Queer Theory initially arose from the need to conceptualise same-sex desire as if it was not a part of medical pathology nor of legal concern, in order that homosexual behaviours and lifestyles could become part of the mainstream and that homophobic behaviours could be challenged as if they were outside of the law. This has been partially achieved through a dual approach. Gay and lesbian lifestyles and culture, the very sense of community, have been determinedly celebrated and paraded openly. One might say that there has developed a 'balloon culture's celebration of difference'. This has brought homosexual iconography to the forefront of popular culture. Representation is astonishing in its variety, with lipstick lesbianism alongside the butch/femme narrative, homoerotic bonding includes the macho and the femme/paedophile gay body image, and vanilla alongside s-m/bondage as sex practice. Queer Theory and activism has resulted in no one in western culture being able to avoid the real possibilities of same-sex desire.

Alongside this there has been an adoption of the 'respectable'. This has come about to counter the contradictory self-image that many lesbians and gay men faced because of, firstly, legal defects and social reproach and, secondly, the crisis of AIDS which projected the very image of the gay body, whether personal or of the community, as being unwholesome. Respectability and being respectable has become an essential aspect of lesbian and gay lifestyles. Through the adoption of 'family/couple imagery' alongside a move from the casual sex lifestyle of many gay men practised in the 1970s to the practice of safer (serial monogamy) sex in the 1980s, the gay movement and, in particular, the activist and academic interests have moved, as Martin Duberman (1991) puts it, from 'radicalism to reformism'. Respectability,

3   The conference title did not include 'Transgender', which was to become a major issue in the 1994 conference, as lesbian women raised their voices in support of the few transgender academics and activists who attended, but whose issues had been clearly sidelined. At the final plenary, a Dean from the University of Iowa came to the podium and explained that the transgender had been omitted because they felt that the university would not have provided financial support for the conference if it had been included.

Duberman would argue, is typical of the change in priorities that would mark most protest movements. As he says:

> Originating in fierce anger and initially marked by broad-gauged demands for social change, they rapidly evolve into well-behaved self-protective associations, and in the process abandon demands for challenging the vast inequities in our social system, substituting (at best) token liberalism ... pressing for narrow assimilationist goals through traditional political challenges. (Dubermann, 1991, p 392.)

This has led to numerous problems for the queer theorist, who is faced with attempting to reconcile the many diverse representations of gay lifestyles and community thrown up by the balloon culture that celebrates same-sex desire, with the needs of the middle-class liberal view of respectability. As such, today, Queer Theory is faced with several contradictory needs and issues, of which not the least is the trans community and the problems it apparently poses.

Many trans people have made their home in the space inhabited by the homosexual community. There are many reasons for this. Often initial experimentation or experience leads trans people to debate either whether they are gay, or whether it would be easier to try to lead a gay lifestyle with or without sexual involvement, rather than try to achieve the apparently impossible: gender reassignment. Lesbians and gay men have often provided a safe and welcoming space for trans people, no matter what level of commitment they have had to either cross-dressing or cross-living. It may be that many trans people felt like the local gay bar's lucky mascot as they provided the drag revue, but better that than being beaten up down a dark alley as they hustled their bodies for survival. Transgender people can obtain work in the gay community whilst they are androgynous and otherwise unemployable, others work the rent scene as 'she-males' to find the money for hormone therapy and surgery, and find this to be safer in the established 'gay scenes'. Whatever the reason, many find friends and sometimes, after successful transition, choose to stay. However, as transgender activist Leslie Feinberg has put it, though the two communities overlap and interact, they are not the same.

But despite this, even more trans people, especially those who have gone along the transsexual road of transition and assimilation into straight society, do not consider themselves to have any involvement in the gay community. Yet, many have found a home at least on the edge of the gay community's space. After some initial involvement, one might expect them to move on. But during the 1990s, many, including those who have apparently successfully transitioned and would not consider themselves to be lesbian or gay in their new gender role, are staking a claim as actually belonging to and being a part, and an essential part at that, of the gay community.

THEORETICAL DIFFERENCE(S)

Queer Theory is a theoretical attempt to deconstruct the gendered and sexed praxis of academia. Through Queer Theory, the hegemonic-centrism of heterosexism as practised and taught throughout most academic life, thought and writing is being challenged to justify itself or to 'get out of the kitchen'. Queer Theory is about the deconstruction and refusal of labels of personal sexual activity and it is also concerned with the removal of pathologies of sexuality and gendered behaviour. It concerns 'gender fuck', which is a full frontal theoretical and practical attack on the dimorphism of gender and sex roles. Yet, can Queer Theory formulate sex-desire, as opposed to same-sex or heterosexual desire? Queer Theory attempts to be non-gender-specific, but is this possible when the very fact that it foregrounds same-sex desire (according to Sue Ellen Case, 'Tracking the vampire', in McIntosh, 1993, p 30) is gender specific? It could be argued that because of the gay, lesbian and bisexual history of Queer Theory in itself, it can currently do nothing more than expound and further delineate these boundaries. The crossing of them still belongs to the world of 'vogue-ing' and the destruction of them must belong to those for whom they have always been unreal because of their inherent personal incongruity within a gender specific world.

For example, since 1972, when most women left the Gay Liberation front in order to take up the banner of radical feminist lesbianism, one could question whether they were ever involved in 'gender fuck'. Did they rather uphold the idea of women as a separate/different gender, and in doing so, were they reinforcing these binary divisions? They had been complaining that gay men were doing that through their domination of Gay Liberation Front meetings and through their drag parodies such as the Sisters of Perpetual Indulgence. Yet, as radical feminist separatists in the academy, they found it very difficult to do more than introduce an oppositional standpoint to patriarchal values and a reluctant acceptance of some value in ethnographic work, through the sex-role and sex-difference research they became involved in. They were locked into a process of explanation, then deconstruction, of gender differences rather than a reconstruction of a theoretically gender-free world.

That is not to say that this is the current state of feminist theory. But in the young theoretical movement that feminism was in the 1970s, sex-role theory was an essential tool in the fight to clarify and challenge the sexist stereotypes that still pervade western social institutions. But:

> Sex-role theory fail(ed) to situate sex soles within a structural explanation of their origin ... where social structure is missing, biological role is present. Indeed, the terms 'female role' and 'male role', hitching a biological term to a dramaturgical one, suggest what is going on. The underlying image is an invariant biological base and a malleable superstructure. (Messerschmidt, 1993, p 28.)

Bob Connell said that the state of the field of feminist theory and research by the mid-1980s was a paradox. The previous 20 years had produced a mass of factual research and a lively theoretical debate around work that was highly original and very penetrating. But he did not see current work on theories of gender as converging:

> ... the differences between the lines of thought have become more distinct, the conceptual and political differences greater. (Connell, 1987, p 38.)

Feminist theory is now faced with the need to address the dichotomy of biological imperativism and social structure, the differences of sex and gender, which are no longer recognised as synonymous.

Sexual difference was easily quantifiable in the modernist enlightenment view: the sex to which an individual was assigned depended upon the whether the person possessed, at birth, a penis or a vagina. The knowledge of the genital was to predestine a person's life story such that even if their genitals were to be reconstructed in another form, they would not become a member of the other sex grouping. Gender was irrevocably connected to this biological construction of sex differences. An individual's gender was not mutable. Fixed through the knowledge of the genital, any assertion by someone that they had been assigned to the wrong gender grouping was a form of madness. For feminist sex-role theorists, transsexual people and other members of the transcommunity were to become, at best, a surgical construction according to Janice Raymond (1979); at worst, according to Catherine Millot, they are 'the victims of error'. To both, transsexuals did not become members of the opposite sex, but were always part of their original gender grouping; Raymond's researchee's were 'male to constructed female transsexuals' or 'female to constructed male transsexuals' and according to Millot, sexual differences belong to:

> ... the register of the real. It constitutes an insuperable barrier, an irreducible wall against which one can bang one's head indefinitely. (Millot, 1990, p 15.)

As such, she referred to them as male and female transsexuals, the gender designating that to which they were assigned at birth.

The trans community, and its individual members, have a large amount of personal experience of hitting the brick walls of the main foundations of this binary paradigm, the dualities of sex and gender. For many, this led to a process of self-apologia and attempted explanation, which caused self-identified transsexuals to adopt the stance of being a 'woman trapped inside a man's body' (or vice versa). Cross-dressers and transvestites upheld a view that there was a feminine side to their masculinity and maleness, rather than challenging the actual construction of their gender role. It was as if, without genital reconstruction, personal gender roles could not be changed, and even with it, that reconstruction provided the point of change. A transformation took place, and the idea that gender was signified through the genital was repeatedly upheld.

In this way, surgical gender reassignment treatment and the self-organisation of transsexual and transvestite groups in the 1970s and 1980s, according to Anne Bolin, endorsed:

> ... a formula for gender constitution in which social woman is equated with genital woman. (Bolin, in Herdt, 1994, p 460.)

However, the 1990s has seen a change for many in the trans community of their own personal praxis concerning sex and gender, and it is this change and its cultural expression which challenges and offers to expand Queer Theory's 'gender fuck'. Through the real-life post-modernist practice of hearing (and listening to) many voices and the acknowledgment of their individual truisms, gender, sex and sexuality are facing not just deconstruction but also reconstruction in the practices of many individuals and in the community's view of who can claim membership.

The 1990s' contributions to assorted academic disciplines, particularly in the humanities, concerning transgender behaviour, have offered an oppositional standpoint to the assumed 'naturalism' of sexual dimorphism. Marjorie Garbor refers to the 'category crises' of class, race and gender; that is the failure of definitional distinctions that we faced as we entered the 21st century. To her, transvestism:

> ... is a space of possibility structuring and confounding culture: the disruptive element that intervenes, not just a category crisis of male and female, but a crisis of category itself. (Garbor, 1992, p 17.)

In other words, transgender behaviour not only challenges sexual dimorphism in that boundaries are crossed, but it provides a challenge to the boundaries ever being there. These are the boundaries that Queer Theory attempts to deconstruct. The trans community is now facing up to this 'category crisis' in a way which has not yet been addressed in issues of race and class. There are several reasons for this happening at this point in time, and to understand why, it is important to understand something of the recent history and creation of the trans community.

RECENT TRANS HER/HIS/STORY

The trans community is a concept of the 1990s. Prior to the late 20th century:

> Only a few organised groups of cross-dressers appeared in historical accounts, including the Hijiras of India, the Kabuki actors in Japan, and the Mollies of 18th century England. Despite these occasional homosexual cross-dressing groups, there is no evidence in Western culture of what might be called a transvestite consciousness. (Bullough and Bullough, 1993, p 280.)

Early organisation of the community started through the work of Virginia Prince, a cross-dresser and biological male who now defines herself as transgender. She not only organised the Phi Pi Epsilon (FPE)[4] sorority group for transvestites, but extensively published transvestite ephemera under the 'Chevalier Publications' publishing house, and in the 1960s she became involved in a broad-reaching enterprise to educate the public about cross-dressing (Bullough and Bullough, 1993). From these beginnings, a huge network of self-help transvestite groups has come into existence throughout the world, such as the Seahorse Society of Australia, the Elizabeth Club in Japan, the Beaumont Society in the UK and the Phoenix Group in South Africa. They have not, however, always had the same points of view concerning transvestism and other aspects of cross-dressing and the 1980s saw a burgeoning of other publications, many of them coming from different factions within the network of self-help groups that now existed. Initially, generally aimed at the heterosexual cross-dressing male, these groups were often approached by self-identified transsexuals for membership and, similarly, after some time, some members would declare themselves to be transsexual and commence hormone treatment and seek surgical reassignment.

A close network of individuals was very involved in the organisation and motivation of these groups. Ironically, certainly in the UK, they were often the self-identified transsexuals. For example, the Beaumont Society saw itself as a solely heterosexual cross-dressing male organisation, but faced great pressure from the fact that many members of its organising committee and its main activists were transsexual and identified as heterosexual or lesbian women, rather than as cross-dressing men.

Because of the problems of diversity and incompatibility between cross-dressers and transsexual women, the first organisation for transsexual people, as such, in UK, the Self-Help Association for Transsexuals (Shaft), was founded in 1979. Of those involved, certain people stand out. Alice was one of these. A lesbian-identified transsexual woman, she is still involved with the Beaumont Trust and now organises the Gendys, which specifically caters for transsexuals. However, whilst being involved in the running of both organisations, she campaigned actively to remain in the Beaumont Society, to allow other transsexual people to be admitted including female to male transsexual men and, in the late 1980s, to remove the bar on homosexual transvestites from the organisation. Such campaigning was to greatly affect how the transvestite community viewed itself, and to allow a huge level of diversity of gender acknowledgment and of issues to be brought to the fore for discussion.

Worldwide, many associations now exist for transgender people, from local cross-dressers' clubs to international groups such as the two Female to Male (FTM) Networks that now exist and boast over 1,500 members between

---

4   Also known as the Full Personality Expression group.

them. Though primarily North American and European, these FTM Networks have members from as far afield as Alaska, New Zealand, Russia and China.

Important to the understanding of the transgender community's current ideas and thoughts on theories of gender are the transitions that their 'organising centres' have gone through. From the self-help organising of a few transvestite networks in the 1960s and 1970s, there is now a plethora of groups catering for a significant level of diversity in cross-gendered behaviour. However, many of the people participating in the running of these groups have been involved for over a quarter of a century. They have an immense level of personal respect within their own community because of their strong commitment to, and knowledge of, the community and its history. Notwithstanding, many of them have also gone through great changes, personally and socially, both in their own self-identification and in their public lives. This has not just been to do with aspects of their cross-dressing or transgender behaviour, though that could be seen as being pivotal, but with their ongoing fight to get public respect and academic recognition for the work they have done in this area. Their personal roads to understanding gender and what it means have informed the current theories they hold and expound.

It has only been very recently that trans people have felt able to participate in the theoretical discussions. The fight to be included has faced several serious problems. Firstly, any discussion of gender by the trans community has been hampered by the medical discourse surrounding transgender behaviour which makes them both self-interested and decidedly barmy. Secondly, they have been hampered by social and legal restrictions which have made it very difficult to publicly come out as transgender or transsexual and which further adds another aspect of self-interest in any work they might do on gender issues. Thirdly, Janice Raymond's thesis in *The Transsexual Empire* (1979) discredited for a long time any academic voice they might have, in particular, with feminist theorists. As a result of her work, feminists saw transsexual people as misguided and mistaken men seeking surgery to fulfil some imaginary notion of femininity, and furthermore, upholding the gendered sex-role structure inherent in the patriarchal hegemony which sought to discredit feminist work. Fourthly, trans people have not been allowed either objectivity or sexuality. Objectivity was lost because of the combination of the other three factors; also, if they questioned gender and sex-roles, they were put in the invidious position of having to justify any sex-role change they might undertake to accommodate their gender incongruity. Sexuality was lost, as it was constructed for them in the form of repressed homosexuality being appeased through reassignment surgery, or heterosexuality (in their new sex-role) was imposed on them by the medical profession in order to justify what was seen as a 'medical collusion with an unattainable fantasy' (*The Lancet*, 1991, in Raymond, 1994, p xiii).

The transgender community has not avoided these difficulties, but has rather tackled them head on. Firstly, the post-modernist acknowledgment of multiplicity of voices has been adapted to their theoretical stance and there is an ongoing discussion as to whether the medical profession should take a diagnostic or merely enabling role for those people who actively seek hormonal and surgical reassignment treatment. Secondly, the transgender community has consistently fought through the courts and the legislature for legal recognition of any new gender-role adopted, also for anti-discrimination clauses to include not only sexuality but gender identity. Thirdly, trans people have tackled radical feminist separatism by continuously asking for answers to awkward questions. For example, along with male to female transsexuals, Leslie Feinberg, a 'female' transgender person and author of *Stone Butch Blues*, along with James Green, a (ftm) transsexual man, challenged the 'Womyn born Womyn' policy of the 1994 Michigan Womyn's Music Festival (Walworth, 1994, p 27) by asking for their right to enter the festival. Trans people have also been active in addressing hetero-sexism and patriarchy both within and without their own community, demanding not just their right to marry in their new gender roles, but also the right of gay and lesbian couples to marry.

Fourthly, trans people have questioned the whole notion of objectivity; they do not try to claim it and instead they have built upon the tradition that the community has of autobiographical writing to give a voice to their self-acknowledged subjectivity. As to sexuality, they have begun to reclaim it. Through the work begun by Lou Sullivan (a gay (ftm) transsexual man who died of AIDS in 1991) and other gay, lesbian or bi activists, they have come out. The argument is simple: if you can acknowledge in yourself that what makes a person is what takes place between the ears and not between the legs, then you are in a privileged position to know that sexuality is a movable and mutable force within us all.

Unfortunately, the reclamation project by lesbian and gay historians, which could have provided support for the challenge of this sex dimorphism, has placed stereotyped sexual orientations or natally sexed lifestyles on individuals of whom we know little of their sexual activity, choice of sexual partners or platonic lovers. Julie Wheelwright (1989) revealed the 'hidden history of women who choose to live, work and love as men', but it does not occur to her that these 'women' might have in fact been non-gender specific, or even, for that matter, actually men. Jason Cromwell refers to this as a process of 'default assumptions' (Cromwell, 1994, p 4). Default assumptions are (as they always have been) one of the biggest problems facing the trans community's contribution to any academic work or, for that matter, any acceptance at all. There is first the assumption that females do not become men or males become women, they become pastiches, surgical constructions of imaginary masculinities or femininities. As Jason Cromwell says, there are other related default assumptions that arise from this initial one. These take various forms depending upon the social setting, but he cites the director of the film *The Ballad of Little Jo*, Maggie Greenwald, in which she says:

> I stumbled upon some information about the real Little Jo Monihan (*sic*), about whom almost nothing is known except that she lived as a man and nobody had discovered the truth about her until she died. (Cromwell, 1994, p 4.)

Cromwell says:

> The default assumption here is that the truth is that Monaghan was female and thus really a woman. Greenwald vividly reveals her default assumptions when she concludes in the interview 'Women discover themselves – and this is so much part of feminism – that they don't have to be fake men; to be strong; to be powerful ... Jo becomes a woman not a man. She passes through a phase to survive, ultimately to be a woman'. Now let me get this right: Monaghan lived as a man, no one knew otherwise until death, but 'ultimately' was a woman. (Cromwell, 1994, p 4.)

The default assumption that underlies any notion of a transgender existence is that gender (sex) is immutable and fixed through biological constraints, and social construction merely affects any representation that the biological may take. Gender bending thus becomes a social play, a performance of the realms of the imaginary.

Performativity is a notion well known in Queer Theory but it has yet to tackle whether gender is just performance or whether it just 'is'. Lynne Segal has said:

> Studying how we live our sexual and gender identities as highly regulated performances does tell us something which is useful about the instabilities of both categories beginning with the impossibility of insisting, without a brutalising blindness, on their definitive connection. But we are not free to choose our performances or masquerades at will – like a type of 'improvisational theatre'... Mostly we can only enact those behaviours which have long since become familiar and meaningful to us in expressing ourselves. This remains so however much we realise that our self-fashioning was formed through the policing norms and personal relations of a sexist heterosexual culture; indeed however fulfilling or frustrating our routine performances may prove. Challenge to our gendered 'identities' may be more than we can handle. (Segal, 1994, p 208.)

Queer Theory sets up a stall that is apparently deconstructive of categories and subjectives – it is about getting away from binary thinking – but, according to Kobena Mercer:

> ... binary thinking ends up with a static concept of identity rather than the more volatile concept of identification (McIntosh, 1993, p 31.)

Trans activists and academics are attempting to deal with the volatile concept of identification, but it is against all odds; the rigidity of a set of default assumptions concerning sex-roles that pervades all discussion of gender; the two have an incorruptible sameness that makes them all-pervasive.

Yet, gender and sex are fundamentally different to the trans community. They face the everyday reality of that difference in their lives, and attempts to reconcile it have led to it being challenged in unanticipated ways. Many have had to move on from seeking the biological basis for their state of being, as any search for aetiology has been pretty unsuccessful. Any aetiology that has been proposed, whether social or biological, has been torn down by the mass of exceptions. It has been accepted that seeking aetiology is a fruitless occupation as the multiplicity of possible factors increases, and even if found and if there were possible points of interception, would the 'cure' be wanted?

Expressing the move to a theory in which gender and sex roles are clearly separated (at least for a large number of people) and what that means to the modernist view of gender theory is a challenge that the transgender community is not ignoring, nor is it prepared to come up with trite, self-serving answers. Challenging their own sense of self, looking inwards to find who they are, using the process of autobiography that they know so well is producing some very interesting answers. These challenge not only the structured world that Queer Theory inhabits, but the very binary structure of the complacent world in which gender was invented, and by which it has become obsessed. The transgenderist did not after all invent gender. Gender, like God, is a concept of the imagination that belongs within and supports the foundations of a patriarchal heterosexist hegemony. Illustrating this move towards teaching us the limits of one aspect of the imaginary, I wish to look at two 'texts' and what they represent.

GENDER OUTLAWS ON THE RUN!

Kate Bornstein's *Gender Outlaw* (1994) takes us through a life story of sex roles and gender confusion. It uses the politics of respectability, which she has acquired through her position as a respected performance artist, to argue for a fluidity of gender politics. She uses her experience of gender boundaries and the crossing of them to question the basic assumptions that there are only two genders, which are invariant and bound by the genital; that everyone must belong to one gender or another and that this is 'natural' and independent of science or social construction; and that any transfers from one gender to another are either ceremonial or masquerades and any exceptions to the two genders are not to be taken seriously. She argues that there are rules to gender – but rules can be broken; ambiguity does exist – it is how we provide for that ambiguity that matters; but even more than ambiguity, there is fluidity. Fluidity provides for any number of genders:

> ... the ability to freely and knowingly become one or many of a limitless number of genders for any length of time, at any rate of change. Gender fluidity recognises no borders or rules of gender. (Bornstein, 1994, p 52.)

This has meaning in the real world and in the real politics of sex and gender. To be fluid in one's gender challenges the oppressive process of gender and the power processes which use gender to maintain power structures. It makes it hard for them to know who, where or what 'you' are and to set up rules and systems which control. As Bornstein points out, transgender people are at the beginnings of having any sense of community, but gender outlaws exist, though there are still few groups that 'encompass the full rainbow' (Bornstein, 1994, p 68). According to her, however, any community must be based on a principle of constant change to avoid the traps that the rules of gender dictate. But to her:

> A fluid identity, incidentally, is one way to solve problems with boundaries. As a person's identity keeps shifting, so do individual borders and boundaries. It's hard to cross a boundary that keeps moving. (Bornstein, 1994, p 52.)

In her discussion of gender terrorism, she points out that it is not the transgender community who are the terrorists, rather it is gender defenders, those who defend the belief that gender is 'real' and 'natural' and who use it to 'terrorise the rest of us'. She quotes Murray S Davis, who wrote in *Smut: Erotic Reality/Obscene Ideology* (1983):

> Anything that undermines confidence in the scheme of classification on which people base their lives sickens them as though the very ground on which they stood precipitously dropped away ... People will regard any phenomenon that produces this disorientation as 'disgusting' or 'dirty'. To be so regarded, however, the phenomenon must threaten to destroy not only one of their fundamental cognitive categories but their whole cognitive system. (Bornstein, 1994, p 72.)

Bornstein argues that the transgender person as a gender outlaw causes the destruction of the gendered system of reality that most people base major aspects of their lives on. The gender terrorists react with acts of violence which range from the physical; as in the rape and killing of Brandon Teena, a passing female to male trans person in Nebraska, in early January 1994 (Jones, 1994, p 3) to the theoretical; as in the attacks on transsexuals by feminists such as Janice Raymond (in *The Transsexual Empire*) and Catherine Millot (in *Horsexe*).

Bornstein offers a view of real life gender fluidity, a refusal to be categorised by the limited gender roles that are imposed, a refusal to be some cute and humourous representation of the 'third sex' as court jester. Neither is she willing to be invisible; instead, she proposes a play with gender partitioning to ultimately make the partitions meaningless. She is not offering a third sex, but she is creating a third space, a space outside of gender:

> Every transsexual I know went through a gender transformation for different reasons, and there as many truthful experiences of gender as there are people who think they have gender (Bornstein, 1994, p 8.)

WANTED: GENDER OUTLAW

The second piece I wish to look at is Loren Cameron's self-portrait. It could be argued that it is a complete education in the current position of gender blending in the world of Queer Theory. Gender blending is a misnomer to the trans community; gender exists as itself, that is, an idea, an invention, a means of oppression and a means of expression. Many in the community would see themselves as existing outside of gender, of being oppressed by it, but using its icons and signifiers to say whom they are.

© Loren Cameron

Cameron's self-portrait says who he is through a celebration of the body. He resists imposed gender representations and assumptions by his nakedness. He acknowledges that in the struggle for himself, dress as such is not the solution. It cannot direct us to a way out of gendered or sexed roles – it merely directs us further into them. If he was dressed, in the nature of the 'true' disguise that directs us away from questioning, he would lead us further into the traps of gender; as the passing cross-dresser, he would become hidden. The gender outlaw is nearly always hidden in passing and, as a result, the gender defenders are fucked, in that their rules become meaningless because they are constantly broken, and nobody knows when, where or how that is happening.

However, Cameron chooses not to pass. Normally, the nature of 'not passing' means that heads aren't really fucked, because gender rules are not transgressed, they are only highlighted. The transgender person, if they could be a hidden outlaw, has to choose to tell the story themselves, to make the autobiographical statement in order to present the gender fuck. Realistically, many will not, because their outsider-ness, their otherness means they are seeking a form of sanctuary in the gender roles they adopt. Anyhow, once we know – won't we always know, and always have known – so the gender fuck disappears.

However, if the gender outlaw who can pass refuses to pass, then they, once again, present the gender fuck. A world in which gender is transgressed, in which representations are resisted, is a world in which the struggle is presented by subjects rather than objects. Cameron (and Bornstein for that matter) has chosen to show that:

> ... gender is always posthuman, always a sewing job which stitches identity into a body bag. (Halberstam, 1992, p 51.)

The human is first; the gender is an addition. Cameron takes his human form and imposes gender signifiers upon it through the place of the observer. We see a bodybuilder's physique. As Marcia Ian explains in 'How do you wear your body':

> ... bodybuilders plan ... (to) ... display as much tumescent muscle as possible, the skin must be well tanned and oiled, the physique rock-hard, showing striations and bulging veins ... in other words to look as much like a giant erection as possible ... a human fucking penis. (Dorenkamp and Henke, 1994, p 79.)

Cameron becomes the human fucking penis, he is what he does not apparently possess, and which by default we would assume he desires. Yet does he desire the penis? The photograph shows a man who is proud to be without, because his masculinity does not come from a penis but from himself. We see in him the female signifier of 'lack', yet in his case, the meaning of 'lack' is meaningless. He chooses not to wear a phallus because that would not be him, he is without 'lack'. He has gender through himself and because of himself. He shows his fluidity of gender through the fluidity of his tattooed body. The flames signify his flame, he just 'is' and he is proud of his being. Cameron does not 'gender blend'; instead, he escapes gender because the observer can no longer impose it, as the boundaries keep moving.

What has all this to do with Queer Theory and what has all this to do with the law? As said earlier, Queer Theory arose from the mix of academic respectability and street activism. Bornstein and Cameron represent the two sides of that association, but they are, even then, constantly crossing and re-crossing the boundaries. They are both activists and academics in the eyes of their own small community, and they represent the forefront of that community's current political theory around gender and what it is, what it means. However, they choose not to gender blend, they do not claim the position of a third sex (meaning gender); rather, they claim to be unique in their diversity and, most importantly, themselves. This is the lesson that they offer up to the academy:

> The identity politics of Queer Theory permit us, even require us, both to take seriously and experiment with ways of thinking and being which more conventional radical theory is ready to consign to its epistemological closet. (Ian, in Dorenkamp and Henke, 1994, p 77.)

Both are seriously experimenting with ways of 'thinking identity'. Both are bringing to Queer Theory the challenge of diversity not just in terms of race and sex, but also in terms of gender in its most complete and fullest sense. They are challenging the imaginary assumptions through their own imaginations:

> Celebrating and affirming insurgent intellectual cultural practice ... (it is) an invitation to enter a space of changing thought, the open mind that is the heartbeat of cultural revolution. (bell hooks, 1994, p 7.)

This is the challenge to the law: if Bornstein and Cameron can live their gender outside of gender, can the law respect gender without imposing gender? In fact, is there any reason whatsoever to have a gendered basis to law? There may be circumstances of 'sex' which need acknowledgment through law, such as special recognition of the needs of people who may become pregnant, or who are pregnant, but that is not dependent upon how that person identifies or portrays their gender. Acknowledging an individual's gender identity or portrayal by the law, simply through the process of recognition, does not, I believe, induce the law to treat differently. Sex discrimination legislation has come into being in order to protect people who are treated arbitrarily and unfairly. The fact that it has been then used to maintain the misery which arises from prejudice due to a person's gender portrayal or sexual orientation must be anathema to those who drafted these laws. The vision of the law is to provide, as near as possible, a fair and just context in which people can fulfil their lives. The placing of socially responsible citizens outside of its framework continues the law instead as an antiquated, moralistic tool based upon conservative understandings that lack vision. The vision of a non-gendered framework does not just belong to the trans community, but increasingly is also the vision of gay and lesbian people, of women as a social movement and of young people who want to face a level playing field which simply does not curtail their lives because of how they 'look'.

CHAPTER 5

THE TRANS-CYBERIAN MAIL WAY[1]

... the important sociological task is to examine the ways in which this potentially infinite variety of interests is translated into real social structures and processes. (Martin, in Anderson and Sharrock, 1984, p 40.)

When I first started researching transsexual people and the law, the emphasis was centred on the right to change birth certificates and the right to marry. In this chapter, I look at the change in emphasis that has taken place in issues of legal importance. Birth certificate change and marriage are based in areas of personal privacy and personal relationships. But the 1990s saw a significant move in the trans community to concentrate on matters of personal safety and anti-discrimination. This change has taken place throughout the transsexual and cross-dressing communities but, at the same time, the original issues have not been lost. The change has come about as a consequence of the facilities and attributes of cyberspace, and its particular features of disembodiment, community development and spatial reorganisation have been critical in re-organising political activism for this minority group.

In particular, this chapter looks at how the properties of cyberspace have enabled transsexual and cross-dressing people to create and promote a new self-identification category, transgender, which has resulted in a re-drawing of boundaries to create a new community identity: trans. This flexible self-identification category and the resulting diverse community lines have then been utilised to both multiply and concentrate the activism and campaigning base addressing all potential members of the new community. Specifically in the context of academic 'gender politics', it is moving the discussions away from those legal issues which were, in fact, merely of concern to a minority of transsexual people.

TRANS-THEORY – A NEW RAILROAD

Feminist theory has consistently failed to afford transgender people a voice. Feminist and queer analyses continue to find the transgender issue volatile and divisive, and have proved incapable of moving beyond the binary discourses of sex and gender (Stone, in Epstein and Straub, 1991). For example, Judith Butler (1993) re-reads the death of Venus Extravaganza in *Paris is Burning* as a 'tragic misreading of the social map of power'. For Butler,

---

1   This chapter was originally published in (1998) 7(3) Social and Legal Studies 389–408. It has been updated for this book.

Extravaganza dies because she represents a poor Latino woman sex worker rather than because her 'John' killed her when he discovered she was a pre-op transsexual. Extravaganza's death becomes representative rather than identified; transgender people exist but they merely mirror the gender and sex troubles of the rest of the world. In an even more deliberately transphobic vein, Jacquelyn N Zita, when considering transgender subjectivity, dismisses the notion of the male lesbian as oxymoronic (Zita, in Card, 1994, p 129), imputing the condition to her new kitten in her contributor's notes.

By failing to take on board transgender identity as valid and experiential, queer and feminist theory initiates and then justifies the homosexual and women's movement's ignorance of the real oppression trans people face. Whether resulting in Rape Crisis Centres refusing access and help to either transsexual men or transsexual women (Radical Deviance, 1996, p 93) or the Michigan Womyn's Music Festival's refusal to allow transsexual women to participate through its 'womyn born womyn' policy, the failure of theory has great repercussions.

Most post-modern theory has repudiated the mechanisms whereby the social reconstruction projects of macro politics can exist, so – although recognising the oppression of social norms, institutions and practices, and valorising the subjectivity of the individual, which might respect the essential sense of self of the transgender person – it disallows any effective place for group activism because it:

> ... lacks an adequate theory of agency, of an active creative self, mediated by
> social institutions, discourses and other people. (Best and Kellner, 1991, p 283.)

However, despite, or perhaps because of, this lack of theoretical grounding, the new trans community has, after Stone (in Epstein and Straub, 1991), refused to categorise itself as a class or problematic third gender, but sees itself as:

> ... a genre – a set of embodied texts whose potential for productive disruption
> of structured sexualities and spectre of desire has yet to be explored. (Stone, in
> Epstein and Straub, 1991, p 296.)

There has been the development of trans-theory, with a transgender ontology theorising the metaphysics of the self as abstract, a personal science of the essence of their gendered being. Arguably essentialist, trans-theory does not, however, avoid social construction in that it recognises the artefacts of gender and sex that render them specific to any given social situation. In order to understand the changes in trans activism that occurred during the 1990s, it is important to understand the trans community's new understanding of their actual, as opposed to virtual or real, identities. The virtual self, the point of communication in cyberspace, has created a space in which an actual self, the trans person with a trans identity, is to be recognised. Being trans becomes the primary organising centre of activism, which is then translated through the real self into becoming transgender rage:

> ... by mobilizing gendered identities and rendering them provisional, open to strategic development and occupation, this rage enables the establishment of subjects in new modes, regulated by different codes of intelligibility. (Stryker, 1994, p 248.)

The technology of the home PC and the Internet has been a catalyst in enabling this otherwise spatially diverse group of people to create an online cyber-community that was never possible in the real world. That online community is undergoing a post post-modern reconstructive project and is developing an activism based around consequences rather than just through reaction, which has so often been the organising response of most minority groups. This organising is now proving to be exceptionally influential within the spheres of state that affect them, through what I will call the street-Net-street effect.

DIS-EMBODIMENT: A VIRTUAL IDENTITY

> ... a holographic reality, where identity is defined by the consensual hallucination of a being's component parts. (Rushkoff, 1994, p 226.)

Transsexual and transgender people have always spent large parts of their lives managing a 'virtual identity'. By using Goffman's concepts of the 'virtual social identity' as opposed to 'actual social identity' (Goffman, 1990), we can see that the trans person, whether they are pre-transition (ie, in those times before they start living in the gender role to which they wish to be ascribed) or post-transition, spends large amounts of their time involved in social intercourse pretending/pastiching a person whom everyone else assumes or demands 'in effect'. Whether pretending to be a person of their natal gender designation or performing gender as if a non-trans/gendered/sexual person of their new gender role, there are in the real world very few opportunities in which their identity as trans can be fully disclosed (Whittle, 1995). The real world has medically, socially and legally failed to afford a place in which they can authenticate themselves.

Daily, trans people are involved in portraying a holographic version of the self that cultivates the others' consensual hallucination. Thus, the cyberworld of virtual reality, virtual space and virtual beings is not a new and strange world to the trans person; it is a world in which they have in-built expertise and of which they already have a range of experiences, albeit that these were gained outside of cyberspace. Ironically, the cyberworld in which others have to learn how to manage their virtuality is a world in which the trans person's actual identity can thrive. For the trans person, in a new theoretical understanding that is being developed, the actual needs have no relationship to the external real world of the body as:

A figural use of transgender identities is obviously deficient when it comes to accounting for transgender realities. (Namaste, in Beemyn and Eliason, 1996, p 194.)

This 'thriving' of the actual has resulted in the creation of a massive 'virtual' publication bank, a series of online news groups, both on the Internet and through private listings operated via email, and, most importantly, a huge activist base which does not require any of the 'real body' to exist in 'real space' other than those aspects of the body required to participate in cyberspace. As Rushkoff said, in terms unintentionally appropriate to hormone takers:

Cyberia is made up of much more than information networks. It can also be accessed personally, socially, artistically, and perhaps easiest of all, chemically. (Rushkoff, 1994, p 79.)

THIS-EMBODIMENT – A REAL IDENTITY

When I first opened an America Online account, I tried to establish the nom de'net 'stone butch' or 'drag king'. I discovered these names were already taken. As I later prowled through AOL and UNIX bulletin boards, I found a world of infinite sex and gender identities, which cyberspace has given people the freedom to explore with a degree of anonymity. (Leslie Feinberg, author of *Stone Butch Blues* and *Transgender Warriors*, in Leshko, 1996.)

By now, everyone who uses a computer as a means of long distance communication will know the old joke that somewhere a dog sits at a computer surfing the Net, and yet nobody knows it is a dog. Seen by many as one of the greatest advantages of computer technology is the 'potential offered by computers for humans to escape the body' (Lupton, 1995, p 100) in the same way as the dog does.

That 'escape from the body' is not just of interest to those who study the Net. In recent years, it has become a cultural obsession transformed by Judith Butler (1993) and others into the study of gender performativity, and the linking of the materiality of the body with utopian analyses of the gendered world's future. Interestingly, the analyses that exist about both disembodiment and computers have never come from the dog (in as much as he has not admitted his authorship). However, as far as the trans users of the Net are concerned, as allegorical dogs, in recent years, they have found their bark within a series of online discussion and mail groups.

For the trans community, the actual sense of gender that was previously theoretically tied to their bodies, whether through social construction, performativity or biological essentialism, has been successfully re-codified within cyberspace to successfully detach gender from such limiting paradigms. That is not to say that the paradigms do not exist for the trans community, but the paradigms have been successfully deconstructed as irrelevant to transgender lives, other than as external mechanisms of power and oppression. To understand the resultant changes in activism, one needs to understand both the dynamics that have historically existed within the trans community and the way that cyberspace both motivated and facilitated the initial deconstructive project. One must also understand how, as Kate Bornstein has put it, gender defenders 'bang their heads against a gender system which is real and natural and who then use gender to terrorise the rest of us' (Bornstein, 1994, p 72). The 'rest of us' are trans people for whom gender is 'real and natural' (neither merely biologically determined nor mere performativity), a concept at the heart of the issue of the newly developed trans activism. Cyberspace affords the place in which the actual self can be subjectively, but also validly, experienced as real and natural.

If that is the case, it begs the question: what about those people who 'pose' as trans people in cyberspace? Undoubtedly, there are those who do, but our concerns are with the battle lines as redrawn through cyberspace and their impact on street activism. The minority who participate in gender bending on a transient basis could benefit from the experience and hopefully integrate into their real lives their virtual experiences.

However, for the trans community members, the experience of locating a virtual self in alliance with an actual self has enabled them to reconstruct their understanding of the mechanisms of oppression that exist in the real world. Before the development of that understanding, it had been:

> ... difficult to generate a counter-discourse if one is programmed to disappear. (Stone, in Epstein and Straub, 1991, p 95.)

For example, one of the frequently condemned features of a transgender life is that it abounds in stereotypes that reinforce oppressive gender roles. As Raymond puts it in her introduction to the 1994 edition of *The Transsexual Empire: The Making of the She-male*:

> ... transgenderism reduces gender resistance to wardrobes, hormones, surgery and posturing – anything but real sexual equality. A real sexual politics says yes to a view and reality of transgender that transforms, instead of conforming to, gender. (Raymond, in Ekins and King, 1996, p 223.)

If this is indeed the case, then the trans movement would indeed have little to offer, other than as a self-help network in which people are 'taught' how to reinforce the values of a white, heterosexist patriarchy. They would endeavour to 'pass' as the oppressor, leaving the others behind to bear the brunt of the struggle and the worst of the discrimination. Such a view singularly fails, in trans theory, because if the pundits are right and there are far more transsexual women than vice versa, they are in fact struggling to become the oppressed, and to leave behind a position of privilege.

But the reality of an oppressed experience is, in fact, all too true for the majority of the trans community. It is this oppression that the community ultimately wishes to address, but for there to be the change in emphasis in what is considered oppressive, the doors had to be opened to those who were previously unable to have a voice in the politic surrounding transgender (or, as it was then, transsexualism) because of their social position, both within and outside of the community.

Very few members of the community would argue against the fact that there had been in the 'real world' a hierarchy within the community itself[2] that was very much based around issues concerned with 'passing'. 'Passing', some notion of feminine or masculine 'realness', does provide for many a physically safe, although restricted and unauthentic, way of living in the real world. Furthermore:

> ... the principle of passing, denying the destabilising power of being 'read', relationships begin as lies. (Stone, in Epstein and Straub, 1991, p 298.)

But the truth of the matter was that even the most 'passable' transsexual woman could find themselves vulnerable, as witnessed by Caroline Cossey (Tula),[3] when her privacy disappeared after the *News of the World*[4] published an exposé of her transsexual status in September 1982.

The hierarchy that existed based on 'passing' within the community was such that those who were the most 'non-trans' looking were awarded status and privilege, whilst those who were most obviously transsexual or transgender were often the butt of private jokes and exclusionary behaviour (Green and Wilchins, 1996, p 1). By default, they were also to be the 'front line' of any political or social movement that existed. By not 'passing', they daily faced the street issues which often result in emotional, financial and even physical scars. The privileged few would, however, get to dictate the terms as to what were 'important and significant' issues. If you 'pass', then the issues are bound to be based around issues such as: further privacy rights, that is, the right to have birth certificates reissued, and further relationship rights, that is, the right to marry in one's new gender role. Feinberg, who in particular has asserted that the community can no longer afford to use this assimilationist approach to activism, states it as one consequence of early minority rights activism, and in such a small movement, it is far too limiting:

> When a young movement forms, it gets a great deal of pressure to put forward only its best dressed and most articulate – which is usually a code word for white ... These 'representatives' are seduced into thinking the best way to win is to not rock the boat and ask for only minimal demands. A more potent strategy relies upon unified numbers ... We need everyone and cannot afford to

---

2   This hierarchy still exists in parts of the trans community, but is increasingly being broken down as the liens between cross-dressers and transsexual people are seen as problematic. Many cross-dressers go on to seek surgical reassignment, and many transsexual people are rejecting aspects of surgical reassignment, particularly those in which there is a risk of losing the capacity for sexual pleasure.

3   Caroline Cossey was a successful model and even a Bond Girl. She challenged the refusal by the UK government to legally recognise her new gender in the European Court of Human Rights: *Cossey v UK* (1991) 13 EHRR 622, ECHR.

4   A 'tabloid' style Sunday newspaper and scandal sheet.

throw anyone overboard. After all, we could never get rid of enough people to please our enemies and make ourselves 'acceptable'. (Leshko, 1996.)

The plain fact is that the majority of transgender or transsexual women (by whom I mean trans people whose sense of actual gender means that they self-identify as belonging in that place in the gendered framework that most natally designated women automatically belong in) cannot and will never 'pass', and so assimilationist politics are wholly inadequate. For these women, their issues are not necessarily going to be those of the privileged few who could seek integration. For them, such rights are meaningless in the context of their lives. If you cannot pass, beyond the most casual of inspections, then any reissued birth certificate will certainly not prevent your discovery (whether by prospective employers or by observers on the street) as a transsexual woman, and you are very unlikely to find a relationship which is so conventional that marriage matters. Only by opening the forum to these people could a unified group form which could address fully the legal issues that caused real external oppression. But as Stone puts it:

> For a transsexual, as a transsexual, to generate a true, effective and representational counter-discourse is to speak from outside the boundaries of gender, beyond the constructed oppositional nodes which have been predefined as the only positions from which discourse is possible. (Stone, in Epstein and Straub, 1991, p 295.)

Deconstructing the demands of passing, just as enunciated by gays, lesbians, and people of colour in their articulation of arguments for solidarity, suggests that all transsexuals must take charge of the history of all of their community (Stone, in Epstein and Straub, 1991).

Cyberspace initially affords a place in which the body is 'fully malleable, indeed even disposable' (Lajoie, in Sheilds, 1996, p 165). The body is not seen or felt 'in passing'. Cyberspace is a locale in which transsexual women have been able to discuss over whether 'looks' are important without 'looks' getting in the way. However, as argued by Argyle and Sheilds:

> Technology mediates presence ... Bodies cannot be escaped, for we express this part of ourselves as we experience together. Although some attempt to conceal the status of their bodies, it is betrayed unless we resort to presenting another kind of body in our communications. (Argyle and Sheilds, in Sheilds, 1996, p 58.)

This failure to escape without taking on a further presentation is what is essentially advantageous in re-drawing community relationships in the trans community. However, the real presentation of the body can be escaped in cyberspace, the actual is signified through the pure signifier of the self, the name (of the word). Baudrillard states the idea of the virtual as:

> ... the radical effectuation, the unconditional realisation of the world, the transformation of all our acts, of all historical events, of all material substance and energy into pure information. (Baudrillard, 1995, p 101.)

The ongoing presentation of pure information without the body has re-drawn the battle lines for many trans women. The issues of concern have changed, and instead of birth certificates and marriage (which are to do with the further privacy of 'passing'), they are about the right to personal physical safety, about the right to keep a job regardless of a transgender status and resultant lifestyle, about the right to be treated equally before the law and the right to medical (including reassignment) treatment (to all of which, 'passing' should be irrelevant).

For transsexual men, the pre-eminent issues were to be different. For most men, 'passing' was never an issue. Any transsexual man can take testosterone, grow a beard, have his voice break, and pass anywhere, anytime, with great success. The issue was 'does the penis make the man?'. The hierarchy within the male transsexual world was based around surgical status. But phalloplasty is a notoriously difficult surgical procedure, with few successful results. Furthermore, the 'good' results were only obtained at a very high price; several years of frequent hospital visits as an in-patient and an awful lot of money.[5] Yet many men felt driven to complete their 'passing' by undertaking these procedures. If it is extremely difficult to be a women with a penis, imagine how much more difficult it is to be a man with a vagina. Without the penis, no matter how well they 'passed' when clothed, they would always have to disclose in intimate relationships, never participate in men's sports where showers and baths were the norm, or even where it was just customary to go and pee up against a wall or bush. In a male world where 'cunt' and 'pussy' are the ultimate insult, the penis became the object of desire, the definitive and supreme sign of passing.

Green and Wilchins (1996) argue that the potential for 'passing' has cost transsexual men a great deal, not just in terms of their failure to become involved in political activism, but also:

> ... in hospital rooms across the country, trans-identified men continue to happily sacrifice their bellies, forearms, thighs, and whatever tissue and tendons are left, in pursuit of the Magic Phallus, and there are more than a few of them on crutches for life as a result of such operations. Many more bear hideous scars on large sections of their bodies in exchange for a tube of skin that hangs ineffectually, forever dangling, a mocking reminder that they cannot 'get it up'. (Green and Wilchins, 1996, p 1.)

One problem with phalloplasty, and in particular those which had poor results, was that many transsexual men were left severely disabled, unable to work and ashamed to socialise. Wearing incontinence diapers is not conducive to a good self-image. Cyberspace provided a space in which the (invariably

---

5   Phalloplasty has become more successful in recent years, providing an aesthetically pleasing phallus. There are still problems with urethral connection, and the new phallus will rarely be sensate. Even those with some sensation do not have sexual sensation. Costs are extremely high, and can rise to over £50,000.

housebound) victims of such surgical procedures could talk freely about their experiences, without presenting their failed body image, and others who had not yet undergone the procedures could assess whether they wanted to take such great risks in an attempt to 'fully pass'. This opened a discussion around what makes a 'real' man, and the body was able to be dismissed as a socially controlling mechanism that dictated power roles, but which in the transsexual man was shown to be an inadequate mechanism which missed their authenticity. Many transsexual men started to view the body differently and as a faltering 'sight' of 'passing'. In order to pass, the manipulation had to go beyond the real into the hallucinatory. Frequently in online discussions, we see the 'dick' referred to, but it is a virtual dick:

> When I do IT, I feel as if I have a dick – does anyone else feel this 'phantom' dick? (lbear)

> I think we all feel that – it isn't just sex, but often my 'dick' makes its presence felt (max)

The equation has changed from penis = man to dick = man. The penis is a signifier within the real world; the dick (which is an actual rather than a real reference) is the signifier within the actual world of transgender men's experience.

This combination of 'manipulating the body image' and the potential privacy of a public display of the personal, along with the nature of controlled extensive publication, alongside the new spatial dynamics of and within cyberspace has contributed, over the last five years, to the immense change in trans politics. Cyberspace presents a safe area where body image and presentation are not amongst the initial aspects of personal judgement and social hierarchy within the trans community, so extending the range of potential community members and voices. Further, as we shall see, it has allowed the trans community to participate in what was previously, for its members, an un-enterable world of local and national politics where, in this televisual age, 'image' is all.

RE-EMBODIMENT: THE NEW COMMUNITY

The denotational process of the community has been simultaneously re-ordered and this is, to an extent, because of the influence of cyberspace. This means that we no longer see the definitions provided by the medical profession being adopted by the community as its boundary distinguishers. In 1990, the Gender Trust, a UK self-help membership group for transsexuals, defined its members as having:

> ... a profound form of gender dysphoria, and persons thus affected have the conviction of being 'trapped in the wrong body' and feel compelled to express themselves in the gender to which they feel they belong. (Gender Trust Handbook, 1990.)

By 1996, the online TransMale Task Force defined itself as:

> ... a grassroots organisation of transsexual and transgender men who are committed to creating action on major issues affecting our community. Our membership is open to all those who identify as male but were born with female anatomy. Some of us have or are seeking medical treatment to change our bodies – others are not. Many of us live full time as male, while others are either just beginning their process or are still considering it. We are a diverse group, comprised of all ages, races, sexual orientations, professions and lifestyles. (TMTF Mission Statement, 1996.)

The Mission Statement then goes further:

> The usage of the term 'transgender' has undergone a tremendous amount of change over the past decade, and is currently used in a number of different ways. Some political action and educational groups are promoting its use as an umbrella term to include transsexuals, transgenderists, cross-dressers (transvestites) and other groups of 'gender-variant' people, such as drag queens and kings, butch lesbians and 'mannish' or 'passing' women. However, it must be realised that many people belonging to the aforementioned groups do not wish to be included under this umbrella, and prefer to retain their distinct identities ... Some transgender people consider themselves a third sex, neither male or female but combining characteristics of both (also called an epicene or 'third'). Most commonly, transgender people live as, identify as and prefer to be treated as belonging to the 'opposite' sex, but do not wish to change their bodies through surgery. (TMTF Mission Statement, 1996.)

In the six years between these statements, we see a series of changing emphases. Firstly, there is a move from a medical naive paradigm, which excludes most people, to a complex paradigm, which is inclusive rather than exclusive. Secondly, because the defining process is no longer medicalised, the community boundaries are not based on surgical procedures, or even in themselves controlled in any way by physicians. Instead, the boundaries are flexible and encompassing whilst not prescribing. Thus, the definitional limits are experientially informed by the self who chooses inclusion, rather than being medically informed and hence inclusion being forced upon the individual through specific medical intervention.

It is perhaps this aspect of 'choice' that is most interesting because it is a reflection of the process of re-embodying the self which has taken place within cyberspace. Because inclusion in the cyber-trans community is by choice, it removes the need (as felt by many in the past) to aim for the status of being a 'non-trans/gendered/sexual person'. Historically, the authors of 'transsexual' autobiographies have often fought hard to distinguish themselves from the rest of the trans/gendered/sexual community by claiming some sort of intersex disorder such as Klinefelter's syndrome (see Cossey, 1991; Allen, 1954; and Langley Simmons, 1995). Whether a true reflection or not of their situation, there are certainly many reasons, not least the social and legal difficulties associated with transsexualism being a choice rather than a medical imperative, and the hierarchy as it was in the community itself, why such people should wish to portray an identity 'in effect' in the real world.

However, the choice for inclusion within cyberspace is about choosing to represent the actual rather than a performance of an 'in effect' gender. Thus, we see a virtual space of (un)dress rehearsal in which passing, an automatic process of such space, enables the practice of non-passing. Large sections of the new voices of the community who fail the stereotyped gender tests as dictated by the gender defenders of the real world learn to redress that failure and to turn it to a successful sense of self, develop a sense of home within the cyber community and no longer need to deny their trans self. Thus, the community both within and without cyberspace has formed a new identification based upon failing rather than succeeding at 'passing'. The actual rather than the real becomes authentic.

The change of community identification has enabled the creation of a new political activism, it has rekindled Rheingold's 'sense of family – a family of invisible friends' (Robins, 1995, p 148) amongst a group of otherwise disparate people who were felt to have little mutual interest. Success is no longer dictated through the striving for invisibility as trans that had been dictated through the medical models of transsexuality. The invisibility afforded to the body that is the 'real' in cyberspace has enabled a level of personal 'actual' visibility that was not previously possible. As a result, in the trans community, the visibility of the non-passing gender outlaw has a new value in itself and the invisible outlaw (those who do pass and can perform the other genders) have become the shock troops who can infiltrate the outside community and then drop the odd bomb(shell), so destroying the gendered bases of so many gender defenders.

RE-EVALUATION OF THE LEGAL ISSUES OF EMBODIMENT

The resulting recreation of the community, both in terms of its hierarchical structure and the prioritisation of issues, which are a circular process, has resulted in a re-evaluation of the legal issues that are important. The reality was that for most women, the issues were not of individual privacy, but of personal safety regardless of trans-visibility and, for most men, they were to do with expressing the actual masculinity of the self through a failed body site which would never in itself afford legal status as men. The virtuality of the body in cyberspace has re-entangled actual gender with the sense of self, and the community now participates in the 'consensual hallucination of the being's component parts'. You speak (or rather type) yourself through your words, and the text becomes the entire signifier of the body.

SPATIAL RE-ORGANISATION OF THE BODY POLITIC

> Electronically mediated communications have proliferated in recent years, introducing a fragility and tenuousness to traditional systems of signification, expanding social worlds, and generating new forms of community, social bonds, networks and intimate relationships. (Wiley, 1995, p 145.)

The overall use of the Internet is extremely large – figures for the first week in January 2002 estimated that 175 million Americans have Internet access, of which 77 million regularly use it.[6] A result of this supposed ease of access is that it has become all too easy to focus on the downside of the Internet. The horrors of supposedly freely accessible child pornography, bomb making instructions, suicide kits and marijuana gardening tips have put the rapid assimilation into the real world of what was, until recently, an extremely useful academic tool into the legal domain. Service providers face the difficulty of complying with the laws of the many countries in which they operate. The laws in different countries are often in conflict, and this creates new challenges unique to the emerging online industry. In February 1996, the US government passed the Communications Decency Act, authored by Senator James Exon, a bill that would give the Federal Communications Commission the power to regulate 'indecency' on the Internet, but this has turned out to be a 'toothless' law. However, the issue of control has not gone away:

> Xerox Corporation fired 40 people in October 1999 for excessive non-work-related use of the Internet and visiting inappropriate sites, such as pornography and gambling sites – in violation of corporate policy. 1970s glam rock star Gary Glitter was convicted of possessing pornographic pictures of children that he downloaded from the Internet (November 1999). On 9 December 1999, UK police arrested 11 men in connection with Internet porn, as part of a countrywide raid aimed at catching those in possession of or distributing indecent images of children. (Quoted in GFI, 2000.)

Yet this concentration on control of the uncontrollable seems to have missed the point for many Internet users; that is, the amazing ability it gives people to publish to others: to publish as often or as little as desired, at very low capital cost, with even less ongoing cost. A message can travel huge distances, crossing political borders on the way, the only restriction for potential readers being the choice of language and their own ability to gain access to the hardware necessary to read it. A message will stay in the 'reading area' for as long as the author wants; nobody can 'throw it in the bin'.

It can be further disseminated by the direct readers reprinting it in another medium and distributing it further to secondary readers who do not have the necessary initial access. Furthermore, of particular relevance to discussions of

---

6 Nielsen//NetRatings Audience Measurement Service, week end 6 January 2002, http://209.249.142.27/nnpm/owa/NRpublicreports.usageweekly.

the trans community's use of the Net, readers can be targeted by simply focusing the first lines of text, so that the numerous search engines available on the Net will pick it up when specific key words are searched. In this way, a specific 'interested' audience can be reached, and further directed using hypertext, to other readings contained in documents that the author thinks are important. This publishing ability has created the two apparently incompatible and oppositional standpoints in relation to the Net and its use.

There is the first view that this ease of publication, and hence ease of access, to so many to so much has created an environment in which the perverse and evil adults of the world can approach and corrupt others, most particularly the young. This is constantly proposed and re-iterated as one of the main uses of the Net, with journalists repeatedly citing the Carnegie Mellon study in which Martin Rimm found 450,620 pornographic images, animations, and text files which had been downloaded by consumers 6,432,297 times. What they fail to say is that these were actually found on 68 commercial 'adult' websites which require consumers to register their credit card details and pay large fees every time they access – and that they are completely separate services from the Net, and though some small number can be accessed that way, they still cost a lot more than ordinary Net access (Riley, 1995).

The alternative view is of a super information highway that allows an ease of cyberspace travel between cultural groupings and communities, creating a global village, a sort of cyber Disneyworld in which everyone comes together to celebrate diversity within a democratic means (Robins, 1995). It is a version of this utopian process of spatial re-organisation that has enabled the transgender community to build within their fresh boundaries a new form of political activism. The problems, in the future, likely to be faced by the trans community's use of cyberspace will be concerned with the incomparability of this freedom and the continued clamour for control and censorship in order to control the flow.

TRANSGENDERING CYBERIA

Like a prison escape in which the inmates crawl through the ventilation ducts towards freedom, rebels in cyberia use the established pathways and networks of our postmodern society in unconventional ways and often towards subversive goals. (Rushkoff, 1994.)

Community: A word rich in symbolic power, lacking negative emotions. (Cohen, 1985, p 116.)

According to a Durkheimian perspective, a society exists in the minds of its members – it cannot exist without, firstly, an extensive agreement on morality amongst its members; and secondly, some awareness on the part of its members of the fact of agreement amongst them. If a society is a moral community, then it must have a sense of internal unity and external difference. It cannot exist without setting itself apart from outsiders. Community has in this sense a loosening of geographical ties. There are areas of 'imagined' community based on notions of comradeship, social interactions, identity definitions in which the members may never meet, yet of which there is a communion (Rothenberg, in Bell and Valentine, 1995). The communion of the transgender community has been realised within the space outside of space. As Stuart Hall says:

> Identity is formed at the unstable point where the 'unspeakable' stories of subjectivity meet the narratives of history, of a culture. (Hall, 1987, p 14.)

Cyberspace has allowed networking on an unprecedented scale through the creation of that meeting point for transgender people. The mechanics of the new identity formation that has taken place in the community could not have existed outside of cyberspace. Despite the re-drawing of the margins of community identification, there are still only very few transgender people in any one geographical locale at best. Though it is reasonably easy to form a chapter of 'The Transsexual Menace' in New York, the three transsexual people I know who live on the fragmented islands of the Shetlands would face a great deal of practical difficulties. Cyberspace provides a neighbourhood in which many people, otherwise separated by great distances, can interact at a local level. Furthermore, users have in both their personal and local geographical areas been able to reach out over long distances to the expertise contained within their community; without having to travel, incur great expense or to even meet with others, they are able to read and ultimately participate with a huge network of individuals. Such networking was, in fact, not possible prior to the development of cyberspace.

For the trans person who logs into any of the Usenet groups that exist specifically around the issues, cyberspace is often originally used for 'initiation', that is, to find out how to deal with personal matters such as family problems, accessing medical intervention. But they will find themselves surrounded by a hive of active threads concerning political and activism issues. The trans Net crawler will find themselves confronted with a vast library of materials that call for their response or personal action. There are numerous sources of materials – most of these concentrate on three issues: starting out in a transgender life; activism materials and 'calls for action'; and community news. However, because of the close nature of the community, these three areas are often linked and invariably connect. The connections enable the experienced activist to easily contact the rest of the community.

The 'public' areas of the Net are, however, not the only areas which new users will reach. There are several private, yet regularly promoted, areas that take the form of private mail lists. Lists such as TMTF (TransMale Task Force), AEGIS (American Educational Gender Information Service), TSMENACE (The Transsexual Menace) and TAN (The Transgender Academic Network) operate to create activism cells within cyberspace. Focusing on specific issues (for example, AEGIS is primarily concerned with health care and TSMENACE is primarily concerned with street activism and events), these private listings operate to inform and mobilise small groups of committed activists. They are, however, operated by seasoned activists, who have total control, who can include or exclude list members, and hence who can restrict access. In this way, control and privacy can be afforded to both users and 'sensitive' materials. These activists are in the position of a circumscribed sysop, so the control of the sysops on the commercial systems such as America Online or the USENET itself is avoided. They also all know each other in the real world, are veterans of many campaigns and have long since learnt to compromise their differences in favour of the larger battle tactics. Thus, they all share and disseminate information when appropriate.

These veteran activists have an immense level of respect within the community, because of their strong commitment to and knowledge of the community and its history. As a result, their voices are considered to be not only powerful, but also rational. Most of them have undergone great changes, personally and socially, during the last 25 years and now hold new paradigms of gender, which inform their praxis (Whittle, in Ekins and King, 1996). Many of these veterans were to be at the forefront of Net use. They were amongst the first 'home computer users', as they initially looked to the computer as a means of production of low cost magazines and the associated mailing lists with which to 'keep in touch' with their community. As such, they became computer literate when others were still trying to work out what to buy. It was a small step to becoming peripheral members of the underground cyberian network, and so they were in incalculable ways to create the dynamics of the Net community. They are also at the forefront of 'real world' activism, so the two sets of activities have become intertwined, and it is no longer possible (if it ever was) to distinguish them. What happens on the street-happens on the Net-happens on the street! The actual self has been enabled to exist through effect in the real world, and the Net could be said to have become the street on which the transgender community lives.

TRANSGENDERING SIBERIA

To illustrate the process and changes that have taken place, two examples will be given of this street-Net-street effect. The first concerns the issues of personal safety.

In December 1993, a female to male transgender person, Brandon Teena, was murdered in Lincoln, Nebraska. The murder came about when a local newspaper outed Brandon after he was discovered to be biologically and legally female by local police following his arrest on a misdemeanour charge. One week later, on Christmas Day, Brandon was assaulted and raped by two men whom he identified as Marvin Nissen and John Lotter. However, the local police did not file charges against them, despite Brandon's sister ringing the County Sheriff, Charles Laux, two days later to ask why Nissen and Lotter had not been arrested. Brandon's sister quoted Laux as saying 'you can call it "it" as far as I'm concerned' when describing Brandon. The Sheriff's deputies later testified that they were directed not to arrest Nissen and Lotter (Laux was later to be defeated in his bid for re-election as sheriff). On 31 December, Nissen and Lotter went to the home of Brandon's girlfriend Lisa Lambert and killed her, Brandon and a friend of theirs, Phillip DeVine. Nissen and Lotter have since been tried and convicted of the murders.

Violence to, and even the murder of, transgender people is not in fact unusual. Since Brandon Teena, there have been at least three other murders of transgender people reported on the Net. But that's the point: from being small inside page reports in local press, they have now become international news, albeit only within the transgender community. A Nebraskan transgender Net user picked up the local report on Brandon Teena's murder, and posted it on the Net. Within a day, it had been picked up by Riki Anne Wilchins, founder of Transsexual Menace and member of the TSMENACE list, who then went on to disseminate it throughout private and public news groups. Within a short space of time, it was world news and reported in the magazines of numerous transgender and transsexual groups.

Several vigils of support were mooted over the Net, and many of these took place with the approval of Brandon's family. These were to culminate in a quiet vigil held on 15 May 1995, in Falls City, NB, outside the Richardson County Courthouse, as the trial of John Lotter opened. Over 40 transgender people travelled from all over the United States to participate. They had co-operative support from the local authorities and extensive television coverage.

Before the development of cyberspace and a trans community, such an event would not have happened, and Brandon Teena's death would have disappeared into a void. Moreover, since then, local trans groups have taken up the issues surrounding personal safety and many are involved in local campaigns for appropriate policing policies (Press For Change, 1997). The successes and failures of these in turn are published on the Net, and a whole area of expertise is being built on in matters like these.

One other response to Brandon's death, and this is perhaps partly due to the 'Net effect' itself, is that at least two film production companies have proposed a movie. One of these, Diane Keaton's, was to star Drew Barrymore and be based on the book titled *All She Wanted* (Jones, 1996). Immediately, the trans 'Net' community responded to this suggestion. Arguing that Brandon died for the right to be man, members of the Trans-male Task Force, an online email group, commenced a letter writing and email campaign to get Keaton to take on board the issues around transgender men and to recognise that Brandon was not be sanitised into a 'girl who liked dressing up'. The Net was also used to repost these concerns on to the Gay and Lesbian parts of the Net, and now groups like the Lesbian Avengers have taken up the issue of transphobia (*in Your FACE*, Issue 2, Fall 1995).[7]

The second example concerns the issue of employment protection. The Employment Non-Discrimination Act proposes to give federal employment protection to gay, lesbian and bisexual people, but it will not include transgender or transsexual people, gender or sexual identity, etc. The Human Rights Campaign Fund (HRCF) who drafted the bill had originally included gender identity, as well as sexuality, as a category requiring protection, but this was withdrawn as the bill got closer to a hearing in July 1995.

When this happened, the Net was used as the main form of information dissemination and activism organisation. Net users were asked to email HRCF directors, to get others to write and to organise demonstrations at local HRCF meetings and fundraisers. The number of responses was tremendous, and the HRCF national office found its email system collapsing under the weight of the postings. On a local level, throughout the United States, HRCF groups found themselves facing peaceful demonstrations at fundraising events and being asked to explain national policy. In turn, many of these groups took up the cause of the trans people they met at these demonstrations.

In September 1995, the HRCF Executive Director, Elizabeth Birch, agreed to a meeting with leading transgender activists, and on the 18th, after a four-hour encounter, the HRCF issued the following statement:

> HRCF has made a commitment to work with representatives of a spectrum of the transgender community with a specific focus on hate crimes. HRCF has also committed to assist transgender representatives with an amendment strategy in the context of ENDA (*in Your FACE*, Issue 2, Fall 1995).

Inclusion of the trans community was now back on this particular agenda.

Both examples used are US-based examples, but as use of the home PC continues to rapidly increase throughout the rest of the western world, the street-Net-street process is beginning to take place elsewhere. Users of the TSMENACE list include transgender activists from all over the world, including the United Kingdom, Japan, Columbia, Australia, New Zealand and Thailand, so literally creating a worldwide web of 'cells'. These cells bring their own issues into the forum where they are commented and advised on, but they also take on board the values and issues of the forum as it already is. Thus, on one level, we see a 'North Americanisation' of the problems, but already that version is constantly undergoing a subtle change.

In this way, the trans community itself is constantly being redefined, and the issues of importance are shifting. The personal recognition of the actual

---

7   The final film, *Boys Don't Cry*, starring Hilary Swank in the role of Brandon Teena was very well received by the trans community.

self, internally defined, as opposed to the real self, which had been externally dictated, has meant that a huge shift has already occurred in transgender politics; from personal privacy and personal relationships to personal safety and anti-discrimination issues, particularly in employment. The body or its performativity is no longer the dictator of gender. Gender has become who or what you experience as actual – what you type at a keyboard, nothing more. Cyberspace, as shall be seen, has further accelerated the decline of the legitimacy of the politics of 'passing' for the trans community, and it has provided both the catalyst and the mechanism for that decline.

Originally a US-based effort, in the last five years, the trans cyber-community has relocated its nodes of communication both within cyberspace and outside of it and is now becoming an increasingly international movement. Internationalisation, along with the increasing diversity of community participants' lifestyles and experiences, has further reshaped the political nature of the legal activism that the community is involved in. Thus, the 1990s saw the domain of operation move from a local system that was disparate, and which often could simply not exist because of geographical constraints, and a social hierarchy which emphasised difference in interests, to a nationwide and international response mechanism that encompasses the parts. The Net has been the agent of this change.

The gendered orders of law and of medicine in the real world have been severely undermined for a significant group of people. Yet this has not undermined the nature of gender itself; the paradigms that exist in the real world have been shown to be inadequate to addressing the trans community's issues, but the community is not so naive as to think that reconstruction is a completed task. The future is by no means certain in this area. There is already the beginnings of an online discussion on the tactics needed to take hold and redefine the medical processes and its practitioners: from gate keepers to prescribers, its users; from sufferers of a mental disorder to owners of a physiological syndrome, and its mechanisms; from state gift to personal right. In turn, this will create new legal battles for activists to undertake.

CHAPTER 6

INSTITUTIONALISED EMPLOYMENT DISCRIMINATION AND TRANSSEXUAL PEOPLE[1]

The applicant claims that in 1990–92 some colleagues, including management, attempted holding [her] to see what was under [her] skirt, feeling [her] breasts. She attempted unsuccessfully to take a case of sexual harassment to the Employment Tribunal on Sex Discrimination, but was allegedly told that she has no case as she is legally considered a man. The applicant was dismissed from her job on grounds of ill-health, the real reason allegedly having been that she is a transsexual.[2]

After my explanation, he said that he employed me for my talents and abilities and that he saw no problem in continuing doing that. Are you sure, I asked, since if not, we could part and I could get another job? Yes, he was sure; yes, he still offered a new, much improved contract. The rest is legal history: the office emptied in my absence, the ban on speaking to my staff, followed by the ban on speaking to clients and the setting of impossible targets. We talked; my union negotiated; and I was dismissed. The post another organisation offered me was withdrawn when my ex-boss told them that I had been an unsatisfactory manager. (P, 1997.)

My experience of being involved for over 25 years with the self-help groups that exist for trans people in the United Kingdom, alongside my personal work experience,[3] has led me to believe that discrimination in the field of employment is probably the issue of greatest concern to trans people. A job, or lack of one, is of primary concern to most of us. Without a job, our place and status in the community in which we live is tenuous. We are known by and through our job; the first thing we ask on meeting a new person is '... and what do you do?'. We gain access to social contacts through the workplace; the financial rewards of a job allow us to enjoy those social contacts to the full along with giving us participatory and consumer access to the goods and

---

1 A shorter version of this chapter was published as 'New-ism's transsexual people and institutionalised discrimination in Employment Law' (1999) 4(1) Contemporary Issues in Law. This chapter has been extensively revised to include more background and to bring it up to date.

2 *Christine Goodwin v UK*, Application No 28957/95 (1995) ECHR.

3 I transitioned whilst in post as a laboratory technician, but in less than two years, I left because of the attitudes of fellow employees, who made it very difficult for me to perform my job tasks. Later, in 1982, I was dismissed from my post as a project manager for an Urban Development Project sponsored by the Church of England's Manchester Diocese, for failing to disclose my transsexuality at the time of my interview. In a later position where financial irregularities became of concern to me in my post as Head of Finance, I was threatened with being 'outed' to the tabloid press by members of the management team if I persisted in my investigations. I left the job rather than risk the possible consequences of becoming a party to possible fraud charges if I maintained my silence.

services which, in their own turn, provide more jobs for others. By having paid work, we are fully able to participate in our society.

A job becomes even more essential for the transsexual person. If seeking surgical reassignment, a job or full time college place is one of the requirements of the real-life experience as promoted through the Standards of Care for Gender Identity Disorders (HBIGDA, 2001). It also provides the material resources that allow access to medical treatments that are becoming increasingly rarely funded by state-run or private health insurance schemes.[4] Finally, the workplace provides a place in which transsexual people retain social contacts; social stigma is such that many transsexual people are cut off from friends, family and neighbours during the early part of transition. The social contacts made in work may at first be problematic, but Christmas comes and the 'ladies luncheon' arrives on its annual visit. It is one thing to not to be happy working alongside a transsexual women; it would be a cruelty beyond the bounds of most office politics not to invite her to the lunch. Such small events can smash huge walls and, before long, she is accepted as 'one of the girls'. However, for many transsexual people, a job is often still an illusory prospect.

In 1992, an extensive survey was carried out amongst transsexuals who were both pre and post-'transition', pre and post-surgical reassignment (Whittle, 1995).[5] Responses were elicited on a range of issues that were shown to be of concern through in-depth interviews with transsexuals.[6] The survey was repeated in 2002 with a further range of questions to determine whether there had been any improvement with the social and legal changes of recent years. The 1992 responses provided empirical support to what had previously been speculative ideas concerning legal issues that were of importance to the transsexual community. It also enabled there to be a ranking of those issues in terms of their importance to the community's members. The 2000 survey showed some slight improvement, but supported the hypothesis that being

---

4   In the US, Medicare funding for gender reassignment surgical procedures is extremely difficult to obtain, and in the UK, applications for reassignment treatment are increasingly being turned down by District Health Authorities, using funding priority arguments.

5   Surgical contributions to gender reassignment will often require several procedures, generally a penectomy and vaginoplasty for the male to female transsexual, a bilateral mastectomy and hysterectomy for the female to male transsexual. It is rare in the UK for female to male transsexuals to undergo phalloplasty to create a phallus because of the poor results available from current procedures. The survey undertaken required self-definition, and as such respondents were enabled to classify themselves as pre or post-operative transsexuals, with no specific surgical requirements being made.

6   In-depth interviews were undertaken with 15 transsexuals, both male to female and female to male. Also, many informal interviews and conversations were undertaken with members of the transsexual community in the UK.

transsexual was not conducive to retaining work or enjoying the workplace environment.

Legal work on transsexual people has tended to concentrate on 'quality of life' issues, such as the transsexual's right to birth certificate change, their right to marry and the medico-legal issues of treatment and surgery, but it has rarely concerned itself with employment rights or employment protection for this minority group.[7] Yet, employment law is also concerned with 'quality of life' questions. Plainly, it seems senseless to require that the transsexual person obtain and keep work prior to surgical procedures, and for physicians to then follow through such procedures on the basis that life quality is being improved, unless they concurrently recognise that this outcome cannot solely be provided by the slice of a surgeon's knife, nor a piece of paper acknowledging a name and status change. All such efforts become pointless if the transsexual person can then be excluded from most jobs on the essentially arbitrary grounds that they are undergoing or have undergone gender reassignment treatment. There is no doubt that those working with transsexuals are working hard to develop a 'care package' mentality in which access to employment is as important as access to hormone therapy, surgery, counselling and legal status change.

1992 SURVEY RESULTS

However, of the 122 (of 157 potential) respondents to the question on job status, 53 (35%) now living in their new gender role were unemployed. This was an astonishing figure, even in view of then high rates of unemployment, and supports the view that even though transsexuals may be happy in their new role,[8] they are likely to face severe financial hardships.[9]

Of the 157 respondents, 87 (56.9%) had been living in their new role for three years or less, of whom 48 (30.5%) had been doing so for a year or less. Only 17 (11%) had been living in their new gender role for 15 years or more. The length of time that a person has been living in a new gender role must have some bearing upon the issues being discussed. The longer an individual has been living 'in role', the more confident they will often feel, their appearance is often less ambiguous and their employment record (if they have

---

7 An exception is Pannick, D, 'Homosexuals, transsexuals and the Sex Discrimination Act' [1983] Public Law 279.

8 Of the 157 potential respondents, 146 provided valid responses to the questions concerning their personal sense of well being. Of these 146, 143 strongly agreed or agreed with the statement 'I am happy with my decision to seek a sex change'. Only one respondent did not agree that they were happier since changing roles, but they did say they were happier now than before.

9 44.5% of the respondents felt that they had suffered financially since changing over, but 54.8% felt that they had neither suffered nor gained financially.

managed to remain in work) will often be more fitting to their new gender role. In the early stages of transition, individuals can often present a rather androgynous appearance, which may make employment difficult to obtain. Many of them will be dealing with (at what is an already difficult time) family issues such as divorce or rejection. Clinical requirements are such that they may find themselves unable to take up some jobs, or maintain an old job because of time needed for hospital visits, electrolysis, etc, and many transsexuals will in fact choose to leave a job rather than face the possible humiliation or risk that goes with trying to transition in a place of employment.[10]

Asking respondents to classify their job, both before and after transition, assessed change in employment status and earning capacity due to gender role change. A large number of the 122 respondents who completed this question had been in professional jobs before undergoing reassignment: 63 (51.6%) were in professional and managerial roles, whereas only 7 (5.7%) were in unskilled work. Of the 53 who were unemployed at the time, 40 were male to female transsexual women, of whom 28 (70%) were pre-operative; 13 were female to male transsexual men, of which 9 (69%) were pre-operative. Looking at the numbers who became unemployed, it can be seen that all groups have suffered from a similar level of job loss, even those in very high earning posts whom one might expect would have the ability to safeguard their positions. Overall, there was a 'downward' trend, in that many transsexual people who had been in high profile jobs took jobs below their abilities in order to stay in work, and undoubtedly received less money.

Legislation and case law at the time of the survey afforded little protection in work from the vagaries of employers and employees alike. Worldwide, many transsexual people still suffer, both financially and socially, because of the inadequate protection the law affords them. The survey supported the notion that though it may be psychologically beneficial for the transsexual to undertake gender reassignment, it could be disastrous in terms of personal finances and career prospects. This must partly be because the law on employment as it relates to transsexuals was at that time, and in many parts of the world still is, a somewhat nebulous area, which provides very uncertain protection to them in their jobs at the times when crises may be reached.

---

10 However, it must be said that even if a transsexual person chooses after some time not to remain in a job in which they have transitioned, those who do succeed in getting support to remain in post whilst undergoing transition will often find that their employment life will be much easier in the long run, compared to those who have chosen to leave or who have been forced out at such a difficult time.

2002 SURVEY RESULTS

Compared to the 1992 survey, unemployment rates were greatly reduced. In 1992, 35% were unemployed. By 2000, this figure had reduced to 9% (of 207 respondents). However, if including those who were economically inactive due to claiming sickness or disability benefits, the total comes to 17%. I refer to sickness/disability as for many transsexual people, the social stigma they face leads to their general practitioners' collaboration in supporting this route rather than risk their mental health by insisting upon them working in very stressful situations, or the regular 'signing on' that is required of the unemployed. The reduction in unemployment may be partly due to the overall reduction in unemployment rates but, at the same time, there has been a large increase of the overall numbers in the general population claiming long term sickness benefits. However, in February 2002, national unemployment rates were 5.1%,[11] which is considerably less than that experienced by transsexual people.

It was then looked to see how many respondents were now working for the same employer they had at the time of transition. 79 responses (51% of 152 valid responses) elicited indicated a change in employer. As can be seen from Table 1, 49 of the 79 (62%) in other words, 2 in 3, had changed jobs because their employer forced them to leave or the conditions were such that they had had to leave.

Table 1: Why are you no longer working for the same employer?		
	Number	%
Left voluntarily	23	29.1
Employer forced leave after transition	26	34.1
Left because of conditions due to transition	23	29.1
Left – personal circumstances	7	8.9

The figure of only 1 in 3 people changing their job with the real freedom of choice as to whether to go or stay is a terrible indictment of the problems faced by transsexual people in the workplace. However, considering whether there had been the expected significant improvements since the decision in *P v S and Cornwall County Council*[12] at the ECJ, the results are equally damming, with analysis showing that:

11   ONS, 2002b, p 3.
12   *P v S and Cornwall County Council* [1996] IRLR 347, ECJ.

- *post-P v S/pre-1999 Regulations*: 7 out of 21 respondents (33%) claimed they were forced to leave their employment due to their employer or the conditions they faced;

- *post-1999 Regulations*: 5 out of 32 respondents (16%) claimed they were forced to leave their employment due to their employer or the conditions they faced.

The drop from 62% to 16% is significant, but it is still the case that more than 1 *in 6* transsexual people have no real choice in whether they stay or leave their jobs, despite there being legislation supposedly affording them full protection from discrimination. The figures showed that the experience of (mtf) transsexual women and (ftm) transsexual men was equally bad, and so any question of whether people are more prejudiced against 'men in dresses' rather than vice versa is not relevant. Most (ftm) transsexual men will profess to having 'bent' any dress code throughout their working life, choosing to wear jeans and baggy shirts whenever possible, or the smart equivalent. It appears simply to be that as soon as a person states that they are undergoing gender reassignment, their transsexual status is the sole source of prejudice. As transsexualism is recognised as a medical condition,[13] one must ask whether co-workers and employers would behave in a similar way to any other worker with a medically diagnosed illness.

Further analysis by job type indicates that an 'employment' move has taken place amongst respondents. At the time of transition, just 45 (28%) of those employed worked in the public sector, which includes the civil service, local authority, education, health and social services work. This rose to 67 (42%) for current employment. The reason for this is unknown, but we might speculate that it may be due to the difference in private and public sector equal opportunity policies and practices. There is a long history of the public sector being at the forefront of improving equal opportunity policies in a variety of areas, including issues of ethnicity and race, disability and women's work. The involvement of a strong trade union movement in the public sector has meant the introduction, even before relevant legislation, of improved working practices. As such, it may well be that the public sector provides a far better and more welcoming working environment to transsexual people, with far less emphasis being placed on 'looks' or prior medical history. Furthermore, the public sector is increasingly a struggling sector when seeking to recruit skilled and highly motivated workers, and so transsexual people are more likely to find a job there, as their skills will supersede other factors, such as their gender reassignment history.

Statutory law alone cannot change attitudes, as was seen with the Race Relations Act 1974, the Sex Discrimination Act 1975 and as will certainly be

---

13 *R v North West Lancashire HA ex p A, D and G* (1999) *Electronic Telegraph*, 22 December, Issue 1306, QBD.

seen with the Disability Discrimination Act 2000. However, they do provide an educational impetus, with public sector employers in particular leading the way in setting in practice change and developing new workplace practices. These in turn lead to an increased visibility for the 'discriminated' group, and consequently they 'become acceptable' within society at large. Private sector employers, particularly larger ones, are able to adopt new policies and practices. They do this for two reasons: firstly, because they wish to be seen as leading fair employers for the purposes of merit-based recruitment and retention; and secondly, in order to increase or extend their customer/client base, so improving profitability.

The remainder of this chapter will consider the history of discrimination in employment against transsexual people, whether there is institutionalised discrimination within all levels and types of employment and whether this is condoned by government.

THE AMERICAN EXPERIENCE

The failure of the Sex Discrimination Act 1975 (SDA) has little in fact to do with the issue of birth certificate change or any other form of legal recognition, as can be seen by examining the American situation. In the US, to date, no court has found Title VII of the 1965 Civil Rights Act applicable to discrimination cases brought by transsexuals. The statute provides:

It shall be unlawful employment practice for an employer:

(i) to fail or refuse to hire or to discharge any individual, or otherwise to discriminate against any individual ... because of such individual's ... sex.

In the few years from the first reported case in 1975 of *Voyles v RK Davies Medical*,[14] in which an employer was granted permission to dismiss a male to female transsexual who asked to be called by her new name, to the 1979 decision in *Kirkpatrick v Seligman & Latz Inc*,[15] in which a beauty salon employee was dismissed, the American courts made discrimination claims by transsexuals impossible to pursue. According to the 1993 Employment Law Project of the International Conference on Transgender Law and Employment Policy, the courts have:

... gone out of their way to find that existing federal non-discrimination laws do not apply to transgendered individuals. (ICTLEP, 1993, p A6-2.)

---

14 *Voyles v RK Davies Medical* 403 F Supp 456 (1975) (ND Cal), comment in Wein, SA and Remmers, CL, 'Employment protection and gender dysphoria: legal definitions of unequal treatment on the basis of sex and disability' (1979) 30 Hastings LJ 1075–1129.

15 *Kirkpatrick v Seligman & Latz Inc* MD Fl 636 F 2d 1047 (1979).

The courts have repeatedly held that the word 'sex' in Title VII is to be given its plain meaning and is not to encompass transsexuals, the major thrust of the legislation being to provide equal opportunities for women. Protection under state employment practices, acts and non-discrimination laws has also proved elusive, as in the case of *Sommers v Iowa Civil Rights Commission*,[16] where the Iowa Supreme Court held that an Iowa statute prohibiting dismissal on the grounds of sex or disability did not prevent discrimination against transsexuals. Similarly, laws protecting disabilities in particular have proved of little help.[17] Even in those cities or states that ostensibly provide protection at the local level, it has proven elusive.

Attempts have even been made by the religious right in some states of the US to promote bills that would allow discrimination against gays or lesbians. None has yet included transsexual or transgender people. The only one to be passed to date is in Colorado, but this was refused permission to take effect by the Colorado Supreme Court, which held that it was unconstitutional to put any class of person's civil rights to a vote of the people (ICTLEP, 1993).

The trans community in the US cannot see a way out of the legal mess, which allows most of them to legally 'change sex' yet affords them no protection from discrimination in or dismissal from their jobs. The lesson that must be learnt is that legal recognition of a 'sex change' will not automatically provide protection in the workplace (or other parts of life, for that matter).

AN ALTERNATIVE APPROACH

In 1992, a pre-transition female to male transsexual, who worked as a games teacher at a large comprehensive secondary school, decided to undergo gender reassignment treatment. He informed the headmaster and the personnel officer of the Local Education Committee (LEA). Their response was unsupportive, the headmaster recommending that the individual 'move to Brighton, where people like you are accepted'. The transsexual man felt that there was no real reason why he should not continue in his job. Originally employed as a teacher of 'games' to girls, as the school was mixed, he had throughout his time there also taught games to boys and supervised them in other sessions. Furthermore, he also taught history, and felt that even if he could no longer teach games, there was sufficient space in the curriculum for him to teach solely in that area. He was asked to provide a sick note in the initial stages of 'transition' and not to attend school. This he did for four months, but he became aware that if he stayed off sick for six months, he could be forced to take early retirement. Being in his early 30s, he was not

---

16 *Sommers v Iowa Civil Rights Commission* 337 NW 2d 470 (1983).
17 *Jane Doe v Boeing Co* 823 P 2d 1159 (1992) (Wn Ct App).

willing to lose the benefit of 13 years of pension contributions and the career he had worked so hard at. After consulting with his doctor, who was supportive and who did not, in any case, consider him to be sick, he decided to return to work. At that point, when he informed the school of his intentions, he was suspended on full pay.

He then received a request to resign. He took a simple line: he was fit to work and wished to do so. As to his gender reassignment, in English law, he had not changed his sex, he was still a woman, and hence he could still fulfil his contractual duty to teach games to girls. As to the beard he was growing, many women had facial hair – and they were allowed to work, and the hormone therapy he was receiving was an approved and prescribed medical treatment provided by the National Health Service. His name change was irrelevant; under English law, one could use any name and if he had wished to be known as Mickey Mouse, that was his own private concern. If the LEA and school chose to dismiss him, he would fight the case on these grounds. In the end, the LEA provided a personal pension to the transsexual, after a suspension on full pay for over a year. This class of pension means that he was still able to take up a teaching post elsewhere. He is now teaching in a primary school where the head and the LEA have full knowledge of his circumstances (and it is not in Brighton!). One of the ironies of this case is that throughout the period of his reassignment, many of the children he taught and their parents met him and nobody was hostile – if anything, he was given wholehearted support. This is one possible form of attack that transsexual people, overall, have failed to take up. Yet, if they cannot legally have 'changed sex', then they could use the law to emphasis that point.

TRANSSEXUAL PEOPLE AND INSTITUTIONALISED DISCRIMINATION IN EMPLOYMENT LAW

A society in which everyone is treated equally is beyond price (MacPherson, 1999). In the Report of the Stephen Lawrence Inquiry, Sir William MacPherson refers to the 'Report into the Brixton Disorders', in which Lord Scarman said:

> If, by [institutionally racist] it is meant that it [Britain] is a society which knowingly, as a matter of policy, discriminates against black people, I reject the allegation. If, however, the suggestion being made is that practices may be adopted by public bodies as well as private individuals which are unwittingly discriminatory against black people, then this is an allegation which deserves serious consideration, and, where proved, swift remedy. (MacPherson, 1999, para 6.7.)

MacPherson considered whether this allegation carried any weight today and concluded that:

... institutional racism, within the terms of its description set out in paragraph 6.34 above, exists both in the Metropolitan Police Service and in other Police Services and other institutions countrywide. (MacPherson, 1999, para 6.39.)

After the report of the Lawrence Inquiry, the focus on discriminatory practices within public institutions was once again brought to the fore. It has almost solely been referred to as an issue of race or ethnicity, but MacPherson provided a clear definition:

The collective failure of an organisation to provide an appropriate and professional service to people because of their colour, culture, or ethnic origin. It can be seen or detected in processes, attitudes and behaviour which amount to discrimination through unwitting prejudice, ignorance, thoughtlessness and racist stereotyping which disadvantage minority ethnic people. (Macpherson, 1999, para 6.34.)

The above can be broadly adapted and interpreted as relating to many groups within our society, not least of all transsexual people. In 1999, unwitting prejudice, thoughtlessness and stereotyping at the most senior levels of government and the executive led to the passing (by negative resolution, so avoiding any parliamentary debate) of the Sex Discrimination (Gender Reassignment) Regulations.

The Regulations are intended to prevent discrimination against transsexual people because of their gender reassignment, both in pay and treatment in employment and vocational training. However, in some circumstances, the Regulations make provisions whereby it may not be unlawful to discriminate on grounds of gender reassignment, for example, where the job may involve conducting intimate searches pursuant to statutory powers (for example, the Police and Criminal Evidence Act 1984). The Regulations also provide temporary exceptions when it may not be unlawful to discriminate. These relate to the period when a person is undergoing gender reassignment treatment and include circumstances, for example, where individuals have to share accommodation in the workplace, or where a post involves providing 'vulnerable' people with personal services.

Supposed to end discrimination in the workplace, in effect, the Regulations formalise discrimination in a way that directly contradicts the clear instruction of ECJ. They have resulted in a loss of many of the rights which had been won by transsexual people through the decision of the ECJ in *P v S and Cornwall County Council*[18] (*P v S*), and which had been affirmed by the Employment Appeal Tribunal in *Chessington World of Adventures v Reed*.[19] After the decision of the ECJ in *P v S*, leaders of the trans community in the UK really thought that a major step forward had been taken in achieving their

18 *P v S and Cornwall County Council* [1996] IRLR 347, ECJ.

19 *Chessington World of Adventures Ltd v Reed* [1997] IRLR 556, EAT.

aims of respect and equality for their community members. In that decision, the Court clearly stated that:

> In view of the objective pursued by Council Directive 76/207/EEC of 9 February 1976 on the implementation of the principle of equal treatment for men and women as regards access to employment, vocational training and promotion, and working conditions, Article 5(1) of the Directive precludes dismissal of a transsexual for a reason related to a gender reassignment.[20]

P v S concerned a male to female transsexual woman, P, who worked as a senior manager in a Cornwall education establishment. On informing her employers that she was undergoing gender reassignment and wished to come to work as a woman, she was given notice of the termination of her contract. She was not allowed to return to work during the period of her 'transition', that was, when she was living full time as a woman but before she had undergone surgical genital reassignment, and her period of employment ultimately terminated without her returning to work. P brought an action before an employment tribunal, claiming that she had suffered discrimination on the grounds of sex. Both S and Cornwall County Council claimed that, on the contrary, she had been dismissed due to redundancy.

The employment tribunal found that whilst there was a case for redundancy, the true reason for dismissal was the objection to P's intention to undergo gender reassignment. At this stage, the employment tribunal found that English law provides no protection to transsexual people, it long being understood that under the SDA 1975, all that an employer needed to show was that they would have treated a transsexual person of either (natally recorded) sex in the same manner.[21] However, the ECJ approached the question differently. It was asked not whether P would have been dismissed if she had in fact been a female to male transsexual, but rather whether she would have been dismissed if she had remained a man. Holding that she would not have been, the ECJ could see no reason for not upholding that there had been discrimination by reason of sex.

The ECJ's Advocate General Tesauro pointed out, in his opinion to the ECJ, that for the purposes of the Equal Treatment Directive, sex is important as a social convention. Discrimination is frequently to do with the social roles of women rather than their physical characteristics. Similarly, discrimination suffered by transsexual people is linked to moral judgments which have nothing to do with their abilities in the sphere of employment.[22] As the Court has a duty to ensure that the general principles of Community law are upheld and as these include a respect for certain fundamental rights, one of which is

---

20 [1996] IRLR 347, ECJ.

21 *White v British Sugar Corporation* [1977] IRLR 121.

22 Advocate General's Opinion in *P v S and Cornwall County Council*, Case C-13/94 [1996] IRLR 347, ECJ, para 20.

the elimination of discrimination based on sex as expressed in the Directive, then the Directive must be held to cover changes from one sex to another as much as it covers whether a person is discriminated against because they are a man or a woman.[23]

The decision was a historic one for transsexual people. It meant that throughout Europe, it would be unlawful, as regards any aspect of employment or vocational training with the state or any emanation of the state, to discriminate against a transsexual person on the grounds that they are going to undergo, are undergoing or have undergone gender reassignment. It was the first piece of case law to come into existence anywhere in the world which prevents discrimination because a person is a transsexual (Whittle, 1995). Further, the scope of the decision was very broad. Not only did it affect all employers who were emanations of the state, through the principle of direct effect,[24] but also, potentially, all other employers through the principle that national courts are required to interpret national law and, in particular, the provisions of a national law specifically introduced to implement the Directive[25] to achieve the results referred to in the European Directives. So it has been successfully argued that the SDA 1975 must be construed so as to apply to transsexual people. In *Chessington World of Adventures v Reed*,[26] it was also found that there is no requirement for a male/female comparator[27] and:

> ... therefore the Sex Discrimination Act can be interpreted consistently with the purpose of the Directive as interpreted in *P v S*.

As such, it is potentially the case that transsexual people are not only protected from discrimination in the sphere of employment and vocational training, but also in those other areas not covered by the Equal Treatment Directive but covered by the SDA. That would extend protection to the provision of goods, services, housing and of areas of education, effectively making illegal virtually all discrimination based upon a person's transsexuality.[28]

---

23 *Ibid*, para 14.

24 *Marshall v Southampton and SW Hants AHA*, Case 152/84 [1986] IRLR 140.

25 *Marleasing SA v La Commercial Internacional de Alimentacion SA*, Case C-106/89 [1990] ECR I-4135, ECJ, para 7.

26 [1997] IRLR 556, EAT.

27 *Webb v EMO Air Cargo (UK) Ltd (No 2)* [1995] IRLR 645.

28 The Equal Opportunities Commission have taken several such cases, for example: 'AM' had been an amateur musician who played at Irish music sessions in the pubs of Manchester. In her mid-50s, she commenced gender reassignment treatment. However, upon starting to live and dress in her new gender role, the managers of two pubs where she had played music for almost 25 years barred her from using the pubs. All of the cases to date have been settled out of court.

Finally, if it is the case that if the SDA can be interpreted by the national courts in line with the Directive and the decision in *P v S*, then it affords protection as the enabling legislation of the Equal Treatment Directive. As such, the protection effectively came into existence from the date of the Equal Treatment Directive. Potentially, therefore, transsexual people who were discriminated against prior to the decision in *P v S* could make a claim, within the appropriate time limit, from the date of the ECJ decision rather than the date of the discrimination. Such a claim has been allowed in the case of *Marshall v DPP*.[29]

A CONSULTATION PROCESS?

In 1996, I wrote:

> Case law and legislation cannot possible stop all discrimination on otherwise essentially arbitrary grounds, but they do provide an educational thrust which forces those in positions of power to reconsider their practices, especially when not to do so might cost them far more than a little adaptation over the use of the staff toilets. (Whittle, 1996.)

Such was my genuine belief in the educational thrust of these decisions that I was frankly shocked when, in February 1998, I received and read the contents of a consultation document from the Department for Education and Employment (DfEE, 1998) which proposed amending legislation to the SDA 1975. The vice presidents of Press For Change[30] wrote in the introduction to their response to the consultation document:

> The document is absolutely horrifying. It basically proposes *taking away* many of the rights which we won in the European Court of Justice. It sets out to create an interminable list of exceptions when it will be acceptable after all to discriminate. It also shows a startling ignorance of the medical and social factors relating to transsexualism and of the process of so called gender reassignment. (Whinnom, 1998.)

One example from the consultation paper typifies the contents of the proposed Regulations:

> It will be lawful for the employer to specify that the transsexual individual must use particular facilities for that period [during gender reassignment] (for example, the male or female lavatories or those for disabled people). The individual will have the right to request a change at the point of believing that he or she would, when observed by a reasonable person, appear to be of the new sexual identity. (DfEE, 1998, para 14.)

---

29 *Marshall v Dame Barbara Mills and the Crown Prosecution Service* (1998) IT.
30 Press For Change is a campaigning and lobbying group seeking 'respect and equality for all transsexual and transgender people'.

It was not surprising, then, to see, shortly afterwards, a cartoon showing doors to the ladies and gents toilets with a bucket situated inbetween them and a sign over it saying 'transsexuals' (Press For Change, 1998). The DfEE consultation document showed a clear misunderstanding of the issues and problems faced by transsexual people in employment and, albeit not relevant to this paper, the manner in which the department gained its information is an interesting footnote on the mechanism of government.[31] It was argued by many in the community that the problem areas envisaged in the DfEE's consultation paper could be immediately resolved if current scientific knowledge and best European practice (Liberty, 1997) was followed and transsexual people were able to be legally recognised in their new gender role for all purposes. For example, The Gender Trust said:

> Transsexual people do not want specific provisions in domestic law for their protection! Surely, if they were legally recognised in their true gender, then there would be no need for this legislation. In other countries where legislation has been enacted on behalf of transsexual people, it has been to enable full recognition of their new status in law. Thus, women are women and men are men and inappropriate legislation such as this is therefore unnecessary. Would it not be more fruitful for the government to come into line with the rest of the world in this regard? (Gender Trust, 1998.)

This echoes Advocate General Tesauro's position in his recommendation to the ECJ:

> First, transsexuals certainly do not constitute a third sex, so it should be considered as a matter of principle that they are covered by the directive, having regard also to the above-mentioned recognition of their right to a sexual identity.[32]

But, as we shall see later, the idea of a 'third sex', that is, the sex of 'being a transsexual' is a recurrent theme throughout the approach that the UK has taken to the ECJ's decision in *P v S*.

---

31 In 1997, a Native American spirit (ie, trans) woman who was a psychotherapist and a psychiatric nurse who worked in a Gender Identity Clinic in a northern city formed a training company by which it was intended to train employers and others in trans issues. It has since been confirmed by Alan Lakin of the EOC and one of the partners in the company that they held a training session for civil servants from the DfEE and the Prison Service in late 1997. After the morning training session concluded, apparently the civil servants from the two departments went for a private meeting with Dr S, who was the consultant psychiatrist in charge of the clinic where the nurse worked. Dr S was well known in both the trans community and the medical world for being out of date and conservative, in both his medical practice and personal opinion of transsexual and transgender people. He retired from medical practice shortly after this meeting. However, the civil servants at the meeting were not to know that Dr S was no longer considered within the medical world to be an appropriate physician in this field, and so took his opinions as being a truthful and valid view to hold.

32 Advocate General's Opinion in *P v S and Cornwall County Council*, Case C-13/94 [1996] IRLR 347, ECJ, para 22.

As said, many aspects of the consultation paper were ill-informed about the transsexual condition, its treatment and the processes undergone, and what can be achieved in individual cases. Nor did the paper take into account the many diverse ways in which individuals are affected by the condition and the lifestyle choices they are obliged to make because of the current social stigma attached to it. In particular, it singularly failed to be aware of the treatment processes of gender reassignment and its limitations. The consultation paper presumed that there was a moment at which a person becomes a transsexual and a moment at which they are no longer a transsexual:

> The first stage involves the individual reaching the conclusion that he or she is transsexual, ie, is in the wrong body and deciding to consult the medical profession. ... The fourth stage is post-operative, when the individual will have a re-assigned gender, including name, and will aim to return to a normal routine within their new identity either in the old job or in a new job. (DfEE, 1998, Annex B.)

In fact, it is difficult to define a distinguishing moment when a person might be considered transsexual. They might be said to be so from birth to death, and so should warrant appropriate protection from inappropriate discrimination throughout their lives, just as the law provides protection for women and people from ethnic minority groups. It is unrealistic to mark the start of protection as being at the point of time when individuals seek medical intervention. Many transsexual people have no choice, because of family or social difficulties, to try other than to accommodate their trans lifestyle without seeking treatment. Further current NHS funding policies mean that many transsexuals find it impossible to obtain medical treatment. Area Health Authorities are refusing even an initial consultation for assessment on the basis that if that assessment means that the individual is diagnosed as transsexual, this would commit them to the funding obligations required to provide treatment.[33] This means, for example, that many transsexuals attend work in an androgynous mode of dress prior to any treatment – surely they should also be afforded full protection in the workplace from harassment and dismissal, so long as they work within the broad range of workplace dress codes? Practice guidelines, to ensure that such rules are not excessively onerous in terms of gender conformity except where necessary, would be easy to promote, as they have been in San Francisco where all city employees are afforded protection regardless of their gender presentation (Green, 1994).

Because of NHS funding policies, many transsexual people now resort to seeking private treatment on an *ad hoc* basis. Further, there are doctors who refuse to acknowledge that an individual is transsexual. These people

---

33 This has been challenged successfully through judicial review. The decision was appealed, but was upheld by the Court of Appeal. See *R v North West Lancashire HA ex p A, D and G* (1999) *Electronic Telegraph*, 22 December, Issue 1306, QBD.

ultimately obtain surgery privately, having had to save for many years, yet they successfully participate in society and the workplace. There are also many transsexual people who underwent gender reassignment many years ago; should they now be forced to seek medical confirmation of what has become, for them, a fact? All of these people might well find it socially or practically impossible to meet the requirements of regulations which were intended only:

> ... to protect from discrimination someone who has formally recorded with a relevant medical practitioner or qualified psychiatrist that he or she has a settled intention to achieve a new sexual identity; is in the process of doing so; or has achieved a permanent new sexual identity. (DfEE, 1998, para 11.)

The reality is that for many transsexual people, it is not possible to identify what is the period of gender reassignment. Many transsexual people will not have a defining point of commencement and, for many, there will not be a defining point of completion.[34] For even more, there will be a very long period wherein they may well be defined, in purely medical terms, to be undergoing reassignment, yet they will have successfully transitioned into their new gender role and their work colleagues will be none the wiser as to their history. And for some transsexual people, no amount of medical intervention will ever enable them to reach a point whereby others are not able to tell that they are a transsexual person. Therefore, any proposals to exclude people from workplace protection based upon notions such as completion of treatment or the ludicrous concept that they would, when observed by a reasonable person, appear to be of the new sexual identity (DfEE, 1998, para 14) would effectively exclude most transsexual people from that protection, if not forever, then at least for a considerable period of their working life. Effectively, all talk of defining periods of exception (or protection) creates that third sex category that Tesauro rejected, and is contrary to the decision of the ECJ itself that precludes dismissal of a transsexual for a reason related to a gender reassignment.[35]

However, it is not just a case of acknowledging that for some transsexual people, obtaining and completing gender reassignment treatment will not be straightforward or timely. For some, it might also produce long periods when they are unable to work due to health-related reasons because of treatment and its potential complications. It would seem fitting, for the purposes of employment protection, to regard difficulties faced because of gender reassignment *treatment* itself to be comparable to the difficulties faced as a result of pregnancy. As such, following the logic of the ECJ in *Dekker*, as only a transsexual person undergoes gender reassignment just as only women undergo pregnancy, discrimination because of gender reassignment treatment

---

34   For most transsexual men, genital surgery is not an available (or even desirable) option within the NHS.

35   *P v S and Cornwall County Council* [1996] IRLR 347, ECJ.

must be direct discrimination on the grounds of sex.[36] Similarly, any medical complications or long term illness associated with gender reassignment treatment should be held comparable to another individual undergoing lengthy medical treatment, just as the ECJ responded to the problem of pregnancy-related illness during employment.[37]

INSTITUTIONAL TRANSPHOBIA?

The specific Genuine Occupational Qualifications proposed in the consultation paper are very informative as to the unfounded and institutionalised fears that surround transsexual people. The government proposed that during the process of gender re-assignment:

- It will be lawful for the employer to specify that the transsexual individual must use particular facilities for that period (for example, the male or female lavatories or those for disabled people). The individual will have the right to request a change at the point of believing that he or she would, when observed by a reasonable person, appear to be of the new sexual identity.

- During the period and for one year afterwards, it will be lawful to exclude the individual from jobs which involve intimate physical contact with members of the public or customers (for example, body searches by the police, Prison Service, Customs and Excise and airport security, or beauty therapy/massage); or close personal interaction with vulnerable people whom the employer reasonably believes would be disturbed, such as those seeking counselling for rape, or people with mental disabilities.

- During the period and for six months afterwards, it will be lawful to exclude the individual from jobs involving contact with members of the public or customers who are changing, for example staff in health clubs, clothes shop assistants, home helps, swimming attendants, etc. (DfEE, 1998, para 14.)

There is apparently a national neurosis about toilets, despite the fact that we all share toilets in our own homes. The FTM Network[38] sensibly responded:

Toilets have doors which are designed to give individuals privacy. FTMs always have to use a cubicle rather than a urinal. Hormone treatment very quickly allows the FTM's voice to break and beard growth to develop, for them to use the lady's loo would, we are sure, be extremely threatening to the women who used them. It is FTMs who are likely to feel fearful in public toilet

---

36 *Dekker v Stichting Vormingscentrum voor Jong Volwassen Plus* [1991] IRLR 27.

37 *Handels-og Kontorfunktionaerernes Forbund i Danmark (acting for Hertz) v Dansk Arbejdsgiverforening (acting for Aldi marked K/S)* [1991] IRLR 31.

38 A self-help group for female to male transsexual men.

areas; many find the fear of discovery very debilitating. To be forced to use an inappropriate toilet or a disabled toilet would be cruel, and would lead to a fundamental failure of the requirements of the real life test imposed by the medical profession, which is required before any surgical treatment will be provided. (Whittle and Wong, 1998.)

The notion of the proposed 'reasonable person' test assumes that all people in society fit in neat little boxes. Many people would fail such a test; should employers be able to insist that a woman with facial hair or a man with Klinefelter's syndrome and visible breast growth use the disabled toilet? Objective tests based upon the 'reasonable person' have proven notoriously difficult in other areas of law[39] and it is doubtful whether they have any substantial basis.

If transsexual people are to be excluded, at any time in their employment, from close personal contact with others, it would exclude (and, in the past, has excluded) many from their jobs. Trainee doctors, masseurs, chiropodists, physiotherapists, occupational therapists, nurses, security guards, etc, could all be excluded from protection. Surely in these circumstances, the public is only seeking the treatment provided by these people; patients with flu really do not care whether a male or female doctor sees them; similarly, both male and female chiropractors treat both men and women. In effect, once again, we see the idea that transsexual people are a third sex. Therefore, perhaps transsexual men and women should complain if they were to be treated by non-transsexual men and women. After all, if it is about being attended to by a person of the same sex, this is the logical response. The Gender Trust responded:

> This exception would prevent a doctor from working in the same surgery, a nurse working in the same hospital. The bottom line is that it means that people are having to give up EVERYTHING in their lives in order to make the transition. They have to give up enough already without legislation adding to their burdens. (Gender Trust, 1998.)

As previously stated, the notion of a period of reassignment in which treatment is started and then concluded is fundamentally flawed. To specify such points in time for transsexual people would bar many people from the jobs they are already undertaking successfully. The consultation document, however, went on to compound matters by providing proposed 'genuine occupational qualifications' for those who had completed gender reassignment:

- where the employment has to comply with the doctrines of an organised religion;

- where the transsexual seeks to return to the same employer and activity, and to work with the same people (for example, patients) who were of an

---

39 For example, in criminal law, the *Caldwell* test with regard to risk assessment, and the test for discerning the response of battered women in the case law on provocation.

unusually vulnerable nature. This exception seeks to recognise that in such exceptional cases, some vulnerable people could be disturbed by the fact of gender reassignment in someone they know. (DfEE, 1998, para 16.)

As regards religious exceptions, this seems to do nothing more than enable organised and systemic prejudice against transsexual people. As regards the exception for those working with vulnerable people, the response from the FTM Network was:

> As regards vulnerable people: many network members are 'out' about their gender status and we know of no instance where 'vulnerable' people have felt threatened in any way by the transsexuality of their carer. In fact, it has been stated by several public and private sector employers that their FTM employees bring a great understanding of their clients' difficulties to these posts, and several of our members work with patients with mental health difficulties both in hospitals and in the community. (Whittle and Wong, 1998.)

The consultation paper then considered the position of the transsexual person who had been in a 'single sex' occupation prior to transition:

> In very rare cases a person who has been through the process of gender reassignment may find themselves in a job lawfully restricted to the other sex (for example, in a single-sex hospital). The Sex Discrimination Act's genuine occupational qualification exceptions expressly cover acts in the course of recruitment, training, transfer and promotion, but not dismissal. The Regulations would make it lawful to dismiss a transsexual from a post restricted to someone of the 'original' sex. (DfEE, 1998, para 17.)

An apparently logical conclusion, but it makes an assumption that is crucial to the discussion about transsexual people – can they now change their legal sex? Despite all the government assurances to the contrary, both in the national courts[40] and in the European Court of Human Rights,[41] this was perhaps the first indication that such a thing was possible. The notion that recognition of changed legal status could be obtained, albeit only to lose your job, was inherently tempting to transsexual people, but there were no guarantees. Such a move could only be acceptable if full legal recognition were to follow gender reassignment; if not, in this case, the UK government was asking to have its cake and eat it. It could otherwise result in a situation whereby employers would be able to dismiss, or refuse to employ, a transsexual man for a male post because they were legally a 'woman' and they could refuse to employ the same man in a female post because they looked like a man.

Then the consultation paper added insult to injury by asking for advice on:

> (i) ... whether there should be a specific exception for jobs which involve working with children. If so, should all children be regarded as vulnerable

---

40 *R v Registrar General for England and Wales ex p P & G* (1996) unreported, HC.
41 The most recent example has been the case of *Sheffield and Horsham v UK* (1998) 27 EHRR 163, ECHR, www.echr.coe.int.

up until 18, as in the Children Act 1989, or is this unnecessarily restrictive? Information would be helpful about the merits of a comprehensive approach permitting discrimination against transsexuals for all jobs in schools, and for any work involving substantial contact with children under age 18, during the gender reassignment process plus one year, as at 14(b); or

(ii) a narrower approach which allowed employers to exclude transsexuals from work bringing them in contact with children regarding changing facilities (for example, swimming trips) and sleeping accommodation (for example, boarding schools) during the gender reassignment process plus six months as at 14(c). (DfEE, 1998, para 18.)

Many transsexual people work with children both professionally and as volunteers. Whether scout masters or teachers, such posts are not barred to either men or women. To bar transsexual people would be to exclude them from posts to which they are already bringing expertise, enthusiasm and skills. The notion that transsexual people are a danger or a threat to children in any way is confusing sexuality (and in particular, dangerous sexualities such as paedophilia) with gender. Transsexual people are perhaps even less of a threat because, to my knowledge,[42] there has never been a serious charge or a conviction of a transsexual person for molesting children. As to whether children find their own gender identity threatened or damaged by knowing a transsexual person, in reality most children would never know. Of those who do, such children have shown a greater understanding than most adults. Further, many transsexual people are parents, whether biological or not, and bring up children very successfully (Green, 1974b).

Finally the consultation paper proposed that the EOC should not have the power to help an individual take a complaint to other courts under the SDA's provisions for goods, facilities, services and education (DfEE, 1998, para 19).

This sums up the prejudices and thoughtlessness of those in government. There can be no reason why a transsexual person should not be afforded the support of the EOC, just as other people have it, to claim the protection they have under the SDA, and not just in the workplace. To remove this potential support would be in itself contrary to the SDA and the spirit of it, discriminatory and a legalisation of bigotry. It would drive far more transsexual people into the dreadful spiral of secrecy that has ruined enough lives already.

---

42 I have spent almost 25 years giving advice, specifically legal advice, to community members and such a situation has never arisen. However, I have been dismissed from a job where the rumour that was spread around by my ex-employers as the reason for my dismissal was that it was 'something to do with children'. On two other occasions, I have been asked to advise people whose jobs have been threatened when accusations of paedophilia have led to the threat of dismissal. On each occasion, the threat was shown to be entirely unfounded and based entirely on a malicious response to the discovery of the individual's transsexual status.

The proposals contained in the consultation paper were fundamentally ill-informed as regards the issues faced, the medical treatment undergone and the relationships between gender, sex and sexuality in trans people's lives. They were short sighted as regards the legal implications of attempting to remove the protection already afforded to transsexual people by the courts both here and in Europe, and they legitimised discrimination on the grounds of gender behaviour, which is seen as 'different'. The emphasis on the completion of treatment contradicted the very essence of the decision of the ECJ in *P v S*, wherein the Court outlawed discrimination on a(ny) reason related to a gender reassignment.

WAS THERE ANY NEED FOR THE LEGISLATION?

A primary issue must be as to whether any proposal for legislation in this area is necessary at all. The decisions of the ECJ in *P v S*[43] and the Employment Appeal Tribunal (EAT) in *Chessington World of Adventures v Reed*[44] appeared to hold that any discrimination in employment due to an individual's transsexualism, no matter what stage of treatment they are at, was illegal. As such, transsexual people appeared to have successfully achieved the law's protection in the workplace without any need for supplementary regulations. Surely, all that was needed was a set of guidelines for employers to ensure that both they and their employees were aware of the implications of the rulings, and that their equal opportunity policies were up to date. Therefore, the need for new legislation to embody the decision in *P v S* at national level must be questioned. There are, though, three possibilities which may have contributed to the driving force behind the government's desire to create supplementary regulations.

Firstly, the possibility of a *Francovich*[45] action from a transsexual person may well have been foremost in the minds of the civil servants in the DfEE. Such an action would enable a claimant who is employed by an emanation of the state, such as 'M' in *M v West Midlands Police*,[46] to have made a claim against the state for failing to implement the Equal Treatment Directive. Such a claimant would have to show that the Directive conferred rights on them, which it is now possible to claim after the decision in *P v S*, and that they have suffered a loss which was caused by the state's failure to implement the Directive. Alternatively, there is the chance that an individual could ask the Social Affairs Directorate of the European Commission to investigate whether

---

43   *P v S and Cornwall County Council* [1996] IRLR 347, ECJ.
44   *Chessington World of Adventures v Reed* [1997] IRLR 556, EAT.
45   *Francovich v Italian State* (C-6/90 and 9/90) [1992] IRLR 84.
46   *M v Chief Constable of West Midlands Police*, Case No 08964/96 (1996) IT.

the UK government had met its obligations under the Treaty, and then to bring infringement proceedings under Art 169. Such cases of alleged violations are often instigated by individuals and it is now possible, albeit unlikely, if such a case is proven, for a state to be fined under the provisions of the Maastricht Treaty and Art 171. Finally, what can be clearly argued when looking at the Regulations[47] that were to result after the consultation paper is that the UK government has a desire to ensure that 'undesirables' are kept in their place, which is not in certain workplaces.

THE SEX DISCRIMINATION (GENDER REASSIGNMENT) REGULATIONS 1999: SOME FUNDAMENTAL PROBLEMS

Firstly, it is worth saying that after the initial consultation paper in February 1998, which provided a very short period for response[48] and which caused an outcry amongst the transsexual community,[49] there was no further formal consultation. Representatives of the Parliamentary Forum on Transsexualism were promised on 26 March 1998 by the then minister, Alan Howarth MP, that there would be a further consultation following the preparation of draft guidelines for employers (Doerfal *et al*, 1998) to be produced by the Forum. A few members of the Forum, after a great deal of pressure was placed upon the DfEE by several sympathetic Members of Parliament, were finally given confidential (that is, no further disclosure was allowed to anyone else of the contents) access to the draft Regulations.[50] But no consideration was given to the fact that the people best qualified to comment, that is, Press For Change legal experts and the other members of the Parliamentary Forum, were volunteers with jobs and families and six or seven days was simply not sufficient time for a reasoned and comprehensive response.

To begin with, it is of great concern that, by default, it appears that the sections of the SDA concerned with discrimination in the areas of the provision of housing, goods and services are excluded from the legal effect of having the SDA interpreted as the enabling legislation of the Equal Treatment Directive 1975. Currently, the EOC regularly supports cases involving such discrimination. It is entirely possible that any court would be able to justify

---

47 Sex Discrimination (Gender Reassignment) Regulations 1999.

48 The total period was six weeks, but relied upon a series of voluntary and unfunded organisations to consult with their members at their own expense.

49 Over 350 responses were sent to the DfEE in the short space of six weeks.

50 Four people were given access, of whom only two were legally qualified, and any response had to be provided within a week. As it happens, the Regulations were published before the week was up, though the respondents had managed to make their submissions prior to publication. However, no changes were made as a result of the submissions and in fact, none could have been made in the overnight period that was available, as it turned out.

excluding transsexual people from protection on the basis that 'if Parliament had intended, Parliament would have made clear their intention'. There is no statement of intention to include this protection and therefore it would be only right that there must be a clear statement that there is no intention to exclude this protection. It would therefore be appropriate to include in the guidelines that accompany the Regulations a statement to the effect that:

These Regulations are not intended to do anything other than address the obligations of government as regards the Equal Treatment Directive 1975. Judicial interpretation of the provisions within the SDA to provide protection against discrimination for transsexual people in the areas of the provision of housing, goods and services, is still possible and these Regulations are not intended to affect that possible provision.

Secondly, the final version of the Regulations contained, in ss 4 and 5, several new insertions in s 7 of the SDA (ss 7B(2)(a), (b), (c) and (d)) and s 19 of the SDA, which introduced new 'Genuine Occupation Qualifications' (GOQs) relating to transsexual people. Despite Advocate General Tesauro's clear and express dismissal of the treatment of transsexual people as belonging to a 'third sex', these new GOQs, without a doubt, intimate that transsexual people are neither male nor female for a period of time or permanently in those circumstances where they have to perform intimate physical searches, or seek employment in a private home. The decision of the ECJ made it quite clear that transsexual people are not to be regarded as belonging to a third sex. The exclusion of transsexual people from all 'sex-specific' tasks is fundamentally in breach of EC non-discrimination legislation as it is, *ipso facto*, incompatible with the overall purpose of the Equal Treatment Directive and the comparative approach adopted by the ECJ.

In particular as regards the inserted s 7B(2)(a), this section clearly pre-empted the decisions in the two '*Police*' cases forthcoming at that time. To implement regulations before then was an attempt to pre-determine the outcome of those cases. In fact, the case of *A v West Yorkshire Police*[51] was decided just days before the publication of the Regulations and the tribunal held that the failure to appoint a transsexual woman by a police service was contrary to the SDA. How this decision now tallies with the Regulations has yet to be decided and is currently being appealed to the UK's Court of Appeal. It would undoubtedly, however, be a nonsensical situation if 'A' was able to be compensated for a failure to appoint her prior to the introduction of the Regulations, but that any possible remedy of appointment was now unavailable as the police service in question could now plead the protection of the Regulations.

Finally, there is a third major problem with the GOQs created in the inserted s 7B(2)(c) and (d). Section 7B(3) states that these sections will not only

---

51 *A v Chief Constable of West Yorkshire Police*, Case No 1802020/98 (1999).

apply to people who are undergoing gender reassignment, but also those who intend to undergo gender reassignment. Almost certainly, the intention was to ensure that those transsexual people who had completed gender reassignment were not caught within the ambit of these GOQs. In other words, if treatment was completed, then a person would be regarded as of their new sex in the designated circumstances. What has in effect happened, though, is that any transsexual person who intends to start gender reassignment in the future has been excluded from the protection of the SDA in jobs which involve sharing accommodation or working with vulnerable people. So, a transsexual person who has not started living in their new role, or even yet visited their doctor, and who works in one of these areas would have to ensure that they did not discuss their proposed life changes with anyone before visiting the doctor, just in case word got back to their employer, which could result in them losing their job. This is very reminiscent of the situation that gay and lesbian people still face in employment as a result of the decision in *Saunders v Scottish National Camps*.[52] In this, merely to be gay is sufficient reason to be dismissed, if any other reasonable employer may have used the same reason for dismissal. This was thought for a long time to be the situation in employment law as regards transsexual people, but the whole purpose of the decision in *P v S* was to ensure that this was not the case.

THE SPECIFICS OF INSTITUTIONALISED DISCRIMINATION

(a) Section 7B(2)(a)

The Sex Discrimination (Gender Reassignment) Regulations, by the inserted s 7B(2)(a), creates a GOQ where:

(a) the job involves the holder of the job being liable to be called upon to perform intimate physical searches pursuant to statutory powers.

Presumably, this is intended to allow police services not to employ or continue the employment of transsexual people. The ambit of this and s 7B(2)(b) is very broad, allowing employers to exclude transsexual people whether before, during or after completion of gender reassignment treatment. Further, s 7B(2)(b) would allow discrimination, by an emanation of the state, which was specifically barred by the decision in *P v S*. There are two issues to be addressed here.

This section is clearly contrary to EC law as it stands. It seeks to bar transsexual employees from carrying out physical searches on *either* sex, hence treating such employees as belonging to a third sex. No justification of such sex discrimination on grounds of transsexuality could be invoked pursuant to Art 2(2) of the Equal Treatment Directive, as neither being a man nor being a

---

52 *Saunders v Scottish National Camps* [1981] IRLR 277.

woman constitutes a GOQ for employment in a profession carrying out intimate searches. For example, in the police services, *both men and women become police officers*. In excluding transsexual people from any employment requiring the carrying out of such searches, the Regulations seek to justify the initial discrimination against transsexual employees by relying on the fact of the discrimination itself. In order to justify sex discrimination under Art 2(2) of the Equal Treatment Directive, however, an objective factor independent from the discrimination has to be relied upon (other than the non-recognition of a transsexual person's change of legal status). Even presupposing that a justification could be adduced for barring transsexual people from performing intimate physical searches (which, as I have argued elsewhere, it clearly cannot), this would *not* justify the exclusion of transsexual employees from a sector of employment ('job') altogether (rather than solely from tasks of a sex specific nature).

The mandatory nature of the principle of equal treatment requires strict adherence to the principle of proportionality to ensure that derogations remain within the limits of what is appropriate for achieving the aim in view. As *Johnston v Chief Constable of the RUC*[53] established, such reconciliation may require, *inter alia*, the re-allocation of tasks and would not allow the taking into account of financial or organisational concerns as material factors. In the interpretation of *Johnston*, the court had held that derogations from the Directive must be interpreted narrowly. Crucially to the inserted s 7B(2)(a) of the SDA, the Art 2(2) exception could be invoked in relation to particular duties, *not* general activities. Section 7B(2)(a), by seeking to exclude transsexual people from any *job* involving intimate physical searches, clearly breaches EC law and, as such, must be omitted. It is perhaps worth noting here that only s 55 Police and Criminal Evidence Act 1984 searches are defined as intimate, and are so few that they can easily be accommodated within an operational framework. The EAT decision in a first appeal to the decision in *A v West Yorkshire Police* supported this view, holding that the operational circumstances currently existing in policing (in which there are so few intimate searches) were such that a transsexual officer could easily be accommodated simply by asking another officer to perform the duty (for a further discussion of this, see Chapter 11).

The only solution would be to remove this section completely. However, in the meantime, until decided upon by the ECJ, for the protection of transsexual people who do serve in police services or similar professions, there could be included in any supplementary guide to the Regulations a statement such as:

> Where a transsexual person might incur a civil or criminal liability for assault, if they perform a search of an intimate nature, which statutory powers require to be performed by a person of the same sex as that of the person being

---

53 *Johnston v Chief Constable of the RUC*, Case 222/84 [1987] ECR 1651, ECJ, para 38.

searched, then it is the transsexual person's responsibility to bring the possible legal anomaly of their status to their employer. If they do not do so, then the employer will incur no vicarious liability as regards any intimate search that the employee carries out.

(b) Section 7B(2)(b)

This inserted section creates a GOQ where:

(b) the job is likely to involve the holder of the job doing his work, or living, in a private home and needs to be held otherwise than by a person who is undergoing or has undergone gender reassignment, because objection might reasonably be taken to allowing such a person–

   (i) the degree of physical or social contact with a person living in the home, or

   (ii) the knowledge of intimate details of such a person's life, which is likely,

because of the nature or circumstances of the job or of the home, to be allowed to, or available to, the holder of the job.

This is entirely irrelevant and unnecessary, as provision is already made in the SDA for the exclusion of inappropriately sexed people from employment in a private home.

This regulation again indicates a third sex position, in which the transsexual person is of neither sex for a period of time or, in this case (see above), throughout their working life. The problem lies with the inadequacy of a transsexual person's current legal status. And as already pointed out, it is perfectly possible for a transsexual person in the UK to simply claim that they have not changed sex.

The nature of the GOQ in s 7B(2)(b) does not allow the transsexual person to have any civil sex status at all. They become neither a man nor a woman for employment within a private home, yet surely they could insist that they must be one or the other and, therefore, they must be able to work as one or the other. If they do not change sex, then they are always of their original sex – therefore, they surely must be able to work in that capacity. If we recognise that there may be a difficulty in employing someone who appears to be man in a job normally reserved for women, then there is an obvious solution. Simply allow the transsexual person to change their status for the purposes of employment. This already happens in many other spheres of the law. For example, driving licences are altered and apparently, as such, the transsexual person changes sex for the purposes of driving a vehicle. When looking at the next GOQ in the Regulations, it is possible to see how a similar position might be achieved in the sphere of employment.

(c) Section 7B(2)(c)

This creates a GOQ where:

(c) the nature or location of the establishment makes it impracticable for the holder of the job to live elsewhere than in premises provided by the employer, and–

(i) the only such premises which are available for persons holding that kind of job are such that reasonable objection could be taken, for the purpose of preserving decency and privacy, to the holder of the job sharing accommodation and facilities with either sex whilst undergoing gender reassignment, and

(ii) it is not reasonable to expect the employer either to equip those premises with suitable accommodation or to make alternative arrangements.

Presumably, this section is intended to prevent the employment in the armed services, and other bodies which might have single sex dormitory accommodation, of transsexual people who have not undergone genital reconstruction. The phrase 'whilst undergoing gender reassignment' is vague and fails to indicate what constitutes gender reassignment and needs clarification, and further presumes that there is a period when a person is of neither sex. Further, if it is interpreted as that period of time before genital reconstruction is undergone, this potentially creates a situation of indirect discrimination against female to male transsexual people in particular. It would either effectively bar them from such jobs or drive them to seeking dangerous surgical procedures (because of the limited nature of phalloplasty surgery currently available here in the UK) in order to maintain their employment. This would certainly be open to challenge. Similarly, s 7A (the requirements of single sex employers) and s 7B(2)(b) of the Regulations (see above) would also disproportionately affect female to male transsexual people.

It seems that the Regulations should instead provide a clear definition of a point when a person changes sex for the purposes of employment such as:

For the purposes of employment a transsexual person will be considered to be of their new sex, when they:

- present documentation from their medical supervisor stating that they are undergoing or intend to undergo gender reassignment in order to permanently change their gender and that henceforth they wish to be considered to be of that new gender for the purposes of employment; and

- they present a statutory declaration stating they are changing their gender permanently from male (female) to female (male) for all purposes; and

- they present a statutory declaration with details of any name change; and

- they state their declared intention to henceforth attend the workplace in their new gender role.

These requirements are very similar to those that already exist for transsexual people when they wish to change the sex designator on documentation such as passports, driving licences, medical cards, etc. They have worked satisfactorily in those areas of civil status for many years; is there any reason to suppose that they would not do so in this area?

(d) Section 7B(2)(d)

This creates a GOQ where:

> (d) the holder of the job provides vulnerable individuals with personal services promoting their welfare, or similar personal services, and in the reasonable view of the employer, those services cannot be effectively provided by a person whilst that person is undergoing gender reassignment.

This is an extremely problematic proposal, regardless of the statement in the accompanying guidelines (DfEE, 1999, Part 2) that it is envisaged that this will be used in very rare circumstances. There is a huge problem with the meaning of the word 'vulnerable'. This is a broad term, with a vast scope for judicial interpretation. After some pressure,[54] the guidelines accompanying the Regulations state:

> It is envisaged that this exception will apply only in very rare circumstances and is not a general defence for discrimination on gender reassignment grounds against individuals who provide such personal services. It should not be assumed that vulnerable people automatically include children, patients undergoing medical treatment, elderly people, mentally ill people or any other group. The onus is on the employer not only to show that a particular individual or individuals are vulnerable, but also to show that he or she acted reasonably in concluding that the personal welfare services in question could not be effectively carried out by a person undergoing gender reassignment. (DfEE, 1999, Part 2.)

There is, however, no real guidance as to whether 'the reasonable view of the employer' is to be determined objectively or subjectively. An appropriate test might be similar to that used for the defining of dishonesty under the Theft Acts, such as:

> Would such a view be held by reasonable people who were in the employer's position? If no, then this subsection would not provide a defence for discriminatory treatment of a person who was in the initial stages of undergoing gender reassignment. If yes, then did the particular employer themselves genuinely believe that the services provided could not be adequately provided by the particular employee in their initial stages of gender reassignment?

---

54 See fn 50, above.

There should also, at the very least, be added a time limit such as 'three months from the point of social change' to the definition as to being the period of 'the initial stages undergoing gender reassignment' and a legal requirement that the employer carry the burden of proof that the services could not be adequately provided. The employer should also have to show that neither re-allocation of duties within the workplace was possible, nor could the workplace accommodate a temporary period of paid or unpaid leave. As such, they would be obliged to show that neither could they, for example, accommodate the needs of a pregnant worker, which as we have already seen is a very difficult test.[55]

As this section stands, regardless of the guidelines to the Regulations, the Regulations apparently introduce many areas of work wherein people may be dismissed or refused employment. For example, the question will certainly arise as to whether children should be classed as vulnerable. Much legislation[56] and case law makes the presumption that children are vulnerable. As such, a transsexual school teacher, working in a reception class and therefore involved with children's toileting, could be dismissed from their job when they indicated they are going to undergo gender reassignment, whereas almost certainly, a short sabbatical or period of unpaid leave would resolve almost all of the possible problems in this area.

(e) Section 5

This states:

In section 19 of the 1975 Act (ministers of religion, etc) after subsection (2) there shall be inserted the following subsections–

(3) In relation to discrimination falling within section 2A, this Part does not apply to employment for purposes of an organised religion where the employment is limited to persons who are not undergoing and have not undergone gender reassignment, if the limitation is imposed to comply with the doctrines of the religion or avoid offending the religious susceptibilities of a significant number of its followers.

(4) In relation to discrimination falling within section 2A, section 13 does not apply to an authorisation or qualification (as defined in that section) for purposes of an organised religion where the authorisation or qualification is limited to persons who are not undergoing and have not undergone gender reassignment, if the limitation is imposed to comply with the doctrines of the religion or avoid offending the religious susceptibilities of a significant number of its followers.

The exceptions as regards ministers of religion, etc, are incredibly badly worded pieces of legislation. The notions of 'religious susceptibilities' (do they

---

55 *Dekker v Stichting Vormingscentrum voor Jong Volwassen Plus* [1991] IRLR 27.

56 Eg, the Children Act 1989.

in fact mean sensibilities?) and 'significant number of its followers' are extraordinarily vague. Is a significant number five or 500? How could a court ascertain what comprised a significant number of people of the Roman Catholic faith? An alternative wording could sensibly be:

(3) In relation to discrimination within section 2(a), this Part does not apply to employment for the pastoral purposes of an organised religion where the published doctrines of that religion exclude employment to persons who are undergoing or have undergone gender reassignment, if the limitation is to comply with those published doctrines.

5(4)(a)   the definition of pastoral purposes in section 5(3) applies only to those positions, which are stipendiary or ministerial, in that the person involved would administer the sacred rites of an organised religion.

Such a section might also be helpful to transsexual and other members of a religion, as organised religions would be obliged to publish their stance on gender reassignment, and transsexual people and others would know exactly the nature of such a religious organisation.

There are many problems with the Sex Discrimination (Gender Reassignment) Regulations 1999. Yet, despite the possibility of a *Francovich* action or an Art 169 referral by the European Commission, there is, I would argue, clearly no need to regulate in this area. The decision in *P v S and Cornwall County Council* was quite patent, plain and unambiguous. Employment tribunals and the Employment Appeal Tribunal have had no great difficulty in interpreting the SDA 1975 as providing protection in line with the spirit and intention of that decision. In fact, it is much more likely the case that the Regulations as they stand will lead to *Francovich* actions or an Art 169 referral by the Commission.

If that is the situation, then why did this happen and what should have happened instead? The 'why' is answered quite easily. Despite the wonderful portrayal of the transsexual woman 'Hayley' on Britain's biggest soap, *Coronation Street*,[57] it is clearly the case that transsexual people are still misunderstood. Yet few in positions that affect transsexual people are prepared to admit how little they understand us, perhaps because they are not even aware of that fact. The 'Interdepartmental Working Group on Transsexuals'[58] did learn from this disastrous exercise. It prioritised listening

---

57   The UK's 'best loved soap', which appears four times weekly on UK prime time television.

58   Announced by the Right Hon Jack Straw MP on 14 April 1999 in a written answer to Dr Lynne Jones MP who tabled the question: 'to ask the Secretary of State for the Home Department what plans the government has to review the legal status of transsexual people? [81107] Mr Straw: My officials will chair an inter-departmental Working Group on transsexuals. This will have the following terms of reference: "To consider, with particular reference to birth certificates, the need for appropriate legal measures to address the problems experienced by transsexuals, having due regard to scientific and societal developments, and measures undertaken in other countries to deal with this issue".' (*Hansard*, 14 April 1999, col 257.)

and learning from those who really do know what it is like. However, it is crucial whilst we wait for further legal developments in this area to provide full protection in the workplace for transsexual people. Work is the primary social contact and source of welfare provision for all people. The triple 'added value' for transsexual people that

> They must work in order to meet the requirements of the medical 'Real Life Test', without meeting those requirements, they are effectively barred from medical and surgical treatment.

> Access to work provides, for many, access to such treatment through the private sector, as treatment is increasingly 'rationed' within the NHS.

> The workplace provides a re-integration into civil society at a time when many face social ostracism from their family, church, and sometimes friends,

is even more important as we try to develop a socially and culturally diverse society for the new century. The Regulations could have been quite simple:

> The Sex Discrimination Act is to be interpreted as to afford full protection from discrimination in the spheres of employment and vocational training (and there could be included in here, by a government truly willing to end all arbitrary and unfounded discrimination, the provision of goods, services, housing and education) due to any ground related to gender reassignment.

It really is not too much to ask – but the reality was that the government department involved was not willing to truly consult or listen to the results of the meagre consultation process they instigated; they were prejudiced and they thought they knew the answers. They then spent 18 months creating a legal nightmare and finally they were too haughty to back down.

In the meantime, much could be done. Few employers have policies in this area, and even fewer unions. Clearly, there is every need for employers to adopt equal opportunities policies that recognise gender identity as a protected category. Unions have often found this a difficult area to deal with, many union 'men' being of the old school. Unions, though, are changing, as the nature of work changes. As most workforces will now contain more women and as they become increasingly involved in union politics, it is hoped that unions will find it easier to respond positively in this area. Whilst the law provides uncertain protection for the transsexual, policy and legal issues aside, it is clearly no wonder that many transsexuals remain unemployed or have to do jobs which put them socially at a disadvantage.

The understanding of the self that transsexuals offer us means that gender, as a problem, should not lie solely in their domain. It is an issue which needs regular critical appraisal by society and by state institutions, particularly the courts. Biology, we all know, does not have to be destiny, and as in the late 20th century, equal opportunities are being sought by many minority groups.

Transsexual people, even though belonging to one of the smallest minorities, should not be forgotten as rights are recognised and embodied through the law. It also needs to be remembered by all of those involved in helping transsexual people fulfil their potential that medical treatment is only one small part of the task in hand, and support needs to be given to ensure that a job, along with all its ensuing benefits, does not become the unobtainable dream that surgery was in the past.

CHAPTER 7

SEX AND MARRIAGE:
GO TOGETHER LIKE A ...?[1]

Many transsexual people seek marriage in their new gender role. Like others, transsexual people want the opportunity publicly to declare their commitment to and love for their partners. But marriage is not just a religious or spiritual ceremony; it is also a civil contract under which the parties acquire various responsibilities, rights and social benefits. Transsexual people also want to be able to provide economic and emotional protection for their families. Yet, at the moment, they are uniquely placed in British law in being unable to contract a legally secure marriage with a partner of either sex. In a recent submission to the government's 'Interdepartmental Working Group on Transsexual People',[2] the leading campaigning groups in this area said:

> In many cases, transsexual people have already been economically disadvantaged due to lengthy periods of time in which career aspirations had to be put on hold, as medical treatment was sought and undergone. For many of us, social pressures will have meant our education has suffered. Job insecurity, or failure to get a job due to prejudice, will mean that we will have spent time being unemployed. Finally, as we achieve some sort of social acceptance, we then discover that without the right to contract a marriage [we are denied] many of the financial benefits that accrue on marriage [such as survivors' pensions] ... [B]ecause only spouses and legally related children can benefit ... [w]e find ourselves having to buy extra financial security for our families, and yet we are invariably already financially worse off than our peers for all of the other reasons, such as entering a career late, or having missed out on formal education. (Change *et al*, 2000a.)

---

1   This chapter was previously published in Wintemute, R and Andeaes, M, *Legal Recognition of Same Sex Partnerships*, 2001, London: Hart. It has been revised and updated for this book.

2   Home Office, *Report of the Interdepartmental Working Group on Transsexual People*, April 2000, www.homeoffice.gov.uk/ccpd/wgtrans.pdf. The group was asked 'to consider, with particular reference to birth certificates, the need for appropriate legal measures to address the problems experienced by transsexual people, having due regard to scientific and societal developments, and measures undertaken in other countries to deal with this issue'. The group identified three options to put out to public consultation: 'to leave the current situation unchanged; to issue birth certificates showing the new name and, possibly, gender; and to grant full legal recognition of the new gender subject to certain criteria and procedures' (para 5.5). With regard to marriage, the Working Group noted: 'Legal recognition of a change of sex would have implications for pre-existing marriages. If a subsisting marriage continued after one of the partners had changed sex, this would conflict with the current legal position that a person can be married only to someone of the opposite (legal) sex' (para 4.17).

CIRCUMSCRIBING MARRIAGE I

Marriage confers an enhanced form of citizenship; in US federal law, there are an estimated 1,049 legal rights and responsibilities associated with civil marriage.[3] Marriage is not, as is often thought, simply a recognition of one contractual relationship, that between the respective contractors. It is also a mechanism whereby a far more complex set of relationships is put in place. These relationships are not just between the marriage partners themselves, but also between the marriage partners and the children brought into or resulting from the marriage, between the state and the marriage partners, and between the state and the children of the marriage.

Marriage delineates the extent of the dependency claims between the partners, and in relation to the state. For example, in effect, marriage partners agree to forgo the enhanced levels of state welfare benefits afforded to single people when they are, for whatever reason, unable to work or to provide for themselves. In return, the state in effect pledges to ensure that the marriage partners will be able to transfer their pension rights to each other in the event of the death of one partner. Whilst marriage still affords these sorts of benefits – which exist within our modern welfare state primarily to ensure that children and spouses are not left seeking welfare benefits – it is a strange aberration that people who want to provide for their families, by entering the institution that confers these automatic rights, are excluded from doing so. It is even more of an anomaly at a time when state welfare benefits continue to be eroded in the name of 'protection of the public purse'.

CIRCUMSCRIBING MARRIAGE II

In the UK, the definition of a valid and legal marriage is contained in the *ratio decidendi* of the 19th century case of *Hyde v Hyde*:[4]

> ... marriage is a voluntary union for life of one man and one woman to the exclusion of all others.

It is easy to criticise this historical definition as no longer being 'good law'. Of the four components contained within the decision (a voluntary union, for life, the exclusion of all others, a 'man and woman'), three are no longer needed for a legal and valid marriage.

Consider the voluntary nature of the union. In *Kaur v Singh*,[5] a Sikh was forced by his parents to marry a woman in India. His petition for nullity was

---

3 See Rep No GAO1, OGC-97-16 (31 January 1997),
   www.gao.gov/AIndexFY97/abstracts/og97016.htm.

4 *Hyde v Hyde* (1866) LR 1 P & D 130.

5 *Kaur v Singh* [1981] Fam Law 152, CA.

rejected; respect for the cultural traditions which practise arranged marriage seemed to be a major policy factor in the decision (Bainham, 1995, p 242). Under s 12(c) of the Matrimonial Causes Act 1973, an involuntary union will render a marriage voidable rather than void, so it will not be void until the court exercises its discretion and declares it so. Therefore, an involuntary union could, given the right circumstances, be a valid marriage, apparently contrary to the definition in *Hyde*.

As regards the requirement that a marriage is for life, the availability of divorce would indicate that this requirement is no longer taken literally. In England and Wales, there are approximately 150,000 divorces per year, two for every three marriages that take place. Peter Pace, citing the case of *Nachimson v Nachimson*,[6] claims that this requirement is satisfied if the couple, at the time of celebration, intend their marriage to last for life (Pace, 1992 p 16). This intention often falls short of an actual lifelong union. A divorce does not mean that the marriage is void, it simply ends the marriage, and the marriage was valid whilst it lasted.

Similarly, the requirement that a marriage is to the exclusion of all others is no longer an essential aspect of the contract as far as the courts and marriage are concerned. Although adultery accounts for almost 30% of all divorces (Bainham, 1995, p 237), it does not make a marriage void, and the parties are not required to seek a divorce when they discover that their partner has committed adultery. Many married people no longer see monogamy as an essential requirement for marriage. Furthermore, polygamous marriages are recognised in UK law for some purposes, although they cannot be contracted here. *Radwan v Radwan (No 2)*[7] concerned a polygamous marriage that was not contracted in the UK. It was held to be valid for the purpose of temporary residence rights in the UK, as the parties intended to reside permanently in Egypt where polygamy was permitted. This, along with the adultery statistics, shows that, often, a marriage is not to the exclusion of all others.

When considering the obstacles to marriage for transsexual people, the fact that three of these components are no longer, or not always, requirements for the validity of a contemporary marriage is indicative of the changing nature of marriage. It could be said to have become a civil contract of aspirations reflecting contemporary social mores. It is a mechanism whereby family life can be regulated and contained, in which responsibilities and rights within the nation state are delineated and in which citizenship is improved, but it is not a static concept and has historically undergone frequent changes.

---

6 *Nachimson v Nachimson* [1930] AC 217.
7 *Radwan v Radwan (No 2)* [1972] All ER 967.

However, a marriage between two people who are not respectively male and female is void, *ab initio*, under s 11(c) of the Matrimonial Causes Act 1973. Such marriages were also void before the Act. An example was *Talbot v Talbot*,[8] concerning the voiding of a marriage between two women. The most infamous case was *Corbett v Corbett*.[9] The husband of a (mtf) transsexual woman sought a decree of nullity, alleging that the respondent was biologically male and that the marriage had not been consummated. It was not in dispute that marriage is a heterosexual union between a man and a woman. What was in dispute was whether one of the parties was in fact a woman for the purposes of marriage.

I have argued, earlier, that a major criticism of Ormrod J's decision in *Corbett* must be that he:

> ... constantly mixed the notions of 'male and female' with those of 'man and woman' ... He argues that marriage is a relationship based on sex rather than gender, so he really needed to consider her to be a 'man' ... [A]lmost certainly Ormrod was faced with a dilemma that arose from his being unable to define the person in front of him as a man yet he felt unable, in law and because of the test he had devised, to call her a woman. (Whittle, 1996, p 366.)

I would consider this to summarise many of the problematic issues surrounding the determination of the sex of the transsexual person for the purposes of marriage. How do we decide who is a man or a woman, and should such a decision be based solely on biological factors?

In 1977, a mere seven years after the decision in *Corbett*, the evolving medical evidence surrounding the complexities of determining sex was recognised in the case of Renee Richards. In *Richards v US Tennis Association*,[10] a transsexual woman was determined to be exactly that, a woman, for the purpose of playing sport. Yet, as regards marriage, the courts have continued in many cases to refuse to take on board the new scientific and medical knowledge in these areas. Is that because marriage is considered predominately a matter of biology?

There has been a retreat over the years, in many courts and jurisdictions, from Ormrod's decision in *Corbett*. But we can see in the recent case of *Littleton v Prange* in the Texas Court of Appeals[11] the social stigma surrounding transsexual people to this day, and the inability of some courts to recognise what marriage actually is: a social and contractual arrangement which has little to do with sex, sexuality, sexual orientation or sexual activity. Rather, as

---

8   *Talbot v Talbot* (1967) 111 SJ 213 (Ormrod J).
9   *Corbett v Corbett* [1970] 2 All ER 33.
10 *Richards v US Tennis Association* 400 NYS 2d 267 (1977) (SC, New York County).
11 *Littleton v Prange* 9 SW 3d 223 (1999) Texas Court of Appeals, 4 District, www.4coa.courts.state.tx.us/opinions/9900010.htm.

long ago as 1965, marriage was defined by the US Supreme Court in *Griswold v Connecticut*[12] as:

> ... a coming together for better or for worse, hopefully enduring, and intimate to the degree of being sacred. It is an association that promotes a way of life, not causes; a harmony in living, not political faiths; a bilateral loyalty, not commercial or social projects ... It is an association for as noble a purpose as any.[13]

Despite *Griswold*, courts determining the validity of marriages continue to be trapped in discussions of biology and hence sexual activity, even though this is not the primary aim or motivation of many marriages.

CIRCUMSCRIBING SEX I

Ormrod J set out in *Corbett* how sex is to be determined for the purposes of marriage. He considered sex to be decided through three factors: chromosomal, genital and gonadal characteristics at birth. His reasoning can be criticised. According to Yatoni I Cole-Wilson (1998, p 4), there was general agreement among the expert medical witnesses in *Corbett* that there was a fourth factor (which Ormrod J disregarded), ie, psychological characteristics. This factor had in fact proven to be crucial in an earlier case, *John Forbes-Semphill v The Hon Ewan Forbes-Semphill*,[14] in which a question of title inheritance depended upon the sex of the petitioner (who would almost certainly nowadays be classified as a transsexual man). Lord Hunter held that the predominance of 'masculine attributes, behaviour, and desires' was instrumental in his decision that Ewan Forbes-Semphill was a man. However, in *Corbett*, Ormrod excluded psychological characteristics, justifying his exclusion on the ground that marriage was essentially heterosexual in character, by which he meant that 'physical characteristics' were what counted.

There is now evidence that transsexuality is in fact related to biological factors, which may in themselves be determined by, or determine, the form taken by chromosomes, genitals and gonads (Zhou *et al*, 1995). The scientific evidence to date is inconclusive as to the 'cause' of transsexuality, but it is also becoming increasingly inconclusive as to the biological determinants that will result in chromosomes, genitals and gonads being congruently of the male or female form. For example, the Intersex Society of North America estimates that one in 500 people have a karyotype (sex chromosome pattern) other than XX (female) or

---

12 *Griswold v Connecticut* 381 US 479 (1965).

13 *Ibid*, para 486.

14 *John Forbes-Semphill v The Hon Ewan Forbes-Semphill* (1967) unreported, Scottish Court of Administration.

XY (male).[15] The sex chromosomes determine whether the gonads will be ovaries or testes. When the pattern is not XX or XY, the result is intersexuality (hermaphroditism). An example of one such condition is Androgen Insensitivity Syndrome (AIS), where the body's cells are unable to respond to the 'male' hormone androgen. Testes develop, but due to the lack of response to androgen, the genitals 'differentiate in the female, rather than the male pattern'.[16] So, the gonads are male, but the genitals appear female. According to Ormrod's criteria, would a person with AIS be male or female? This condition causes as many problems for his criteria as April Ashley did in *Corbett*, with the added factor here that the chromosomes, genitals and gonads have never been congruent.

Corbett has not been followed in other jurisdictions, because of the distinction that was made between biological (physical) sex and psychological gender. In *MT v JT*,[17] the New Jersey Superior Court (Appellate Division) agreed with Ormrod J that marriage must be between a man and a woman, but they used a dual test of anatomy and gender identity to determine the sex of a person:

> ... for marital purposes if the anatomical and genital features of a genuine transsexual are made to conform to the person's gender, psyche or psychological sex, then identity by sex must be governed by the congruence of these standards.[18]

In *Attorney General v Family Court at Otahuhu*,[19] Ellis J was:

> ... unable to accept the decision in *Corbett* because the law of New Zealand has changed to recognise a shift away from sexual activity and more emphasis being placed on psychological and social aspects of sex, sometimes referred to as gender issues.[20]

Ellis felt that if society allows a person to undergo surgery to change their sex, then it ought to allow them to 'function as fully as possible in their reassigned sex, and this must include the capacity to marry'.[21] In addition, there was no social advantage to not recognising such a marriage, and no 'socially adverse effects ... or harm to others, particularly children'.[22]

Chisholm J provided what appeared to be a resounding destruction of the *Corbett* decision in the recent Australian federal case of *Re Kevin (Validity of Marriage of Transsexual)*.[23] He said of Ormrod's flawed logic:

---

15 See www.isna.org/index.html (FAQ).

16 See *ibid*.

17 *MT v JT* 150 NJ Super 77 (1977); 355 A 2d 204.

18 *Ibid*.

19 *Attorney General v Family Court at Otahuhu* [1995] NZ Fam LR 57.

20 *Ibid*.

21 *Ibid*.

22 *Ibid*.

23 *Re Kevin (Validity of Marriage of Transsexual)* [2001] Fam CA 1074, www.familycourt.gov.au/judge/2001/html/rekevin_text.html.

The asserted legal proposition, that 'true sex' is the test for the validity of marriage, is true only if 'true sex' is the sole criterion of determining whether a person is a man or a woman. The judgment thus again exploits a subtle shift in terminology which gives the impression that an argument has been made, when in fact the proposition to be established is merely *assumed*.[24]

Chisholm J said that to argue that the decision that a person was a man or a woman for the purposes of marriage was based 'solely on the person's biological sexual constitution' has no support in law whatsoever. In fact, the unsound reasoning of Ormrod in *Corbett* becomes the only authority, and that is how the decision was arrived at. Chisholm J reasoned that contemporary usage and understanding of the terms 'man' and 'woman' included transsexual men and women, that there was no sound reason not to find for the applicants and thus declared Kevin to be a man for the purposes of marriage. Unfortunately, the decision is now being appealed.

However, even in the UK, Ward LJ suggested in *ST v J* that, in the light of 'new insight into the aetiology of transsexualism', it may be appropriate that *Corbett* should be re-examined.[25] And in *Bellinger*,[26] though the majority decision in the Court of Appeal followed *Corbett*, the dissenting judge, Thorpe LJ, said:

> In those societies which do permit it, it seems to me to be difficult to justify a refusal to recognise that successful gender reassignment treatment has had any legal consequences for the patient's sexual identity, although the context in which, and conditions under which, a change of sexual identity should be recognised is a complex question. But for the law to ignore transsexualism, either on the basis that it is an aberration which should be disregarded, or on the basis that sex roles should be regarded as legally irrelevant, is not an option. The law needs to respond to society as it is. Transsexuals exist in our society, and that society is divided on the basis of sex. If a society accepts that transsexualism is a serious and distressing medical problem, and allows those who suffer from it to undergo drastic treatment in order to adopt a new gender and thereby improve their quality of life, then reason and common humanity alike suggest that it should allow such persons to function as fully as possible in their new gender.[27]

However, not all recent developments have been 'anti-*Corbett*'. In *Littleton v Prange*,[28] the Texas Court of Appeals asked:

> Can there be a valid marriage between a man and a person born as a man, but surgically altered to have the physical characteristics of a woman?

---

24 *Ibid*, para 79.

25 *ST v J* [1998] 1 All ER 431, 447.

26 *Bellinger v Bellinger* [2001] EWCA Civ 1140, CA.

27 *Ibid*, para 159.

28 *Littleton v Prange* 9 SW 3d 223 (1999) Texas Court of Appeals, 4 District, www.4coa.courts.state.tx.us/opinions/9900010.htm.

In holding that, for the purposes of marriage, a (mtf) transsexual woman was male and therefore any marriage to a man was invalid, the court relied on a chromosomal test and expressly referred to *Corbett*. In her dissenting judgment, Lopez J hits at the nub of the matter:

> Particularly material to this case, the legislature has not addressed whether a transsexual is to be considered a surviving spouse under the Wrongful Death and Survival Statutes.

Christie Lee Littleton is a transsexual woman who, from a very early age, had felt extreme discomfort at living the life of a boy and a male. At the age of 23, she started treatment to undergo gender reassignment. Upon completion of her treatment, Christie had to petition a court to get her birth certificate amended. After hearing expert opinions, the court granted an amendment because there was now satisfactory evidence to show that the original birth certificate was inaccurate. In 1989, Christie married Jonathon Littleton in the state of Kentucky, and lived with him until his death in 1996. Jonathon was fully aware of her background and the fact that she had undergone gender reassignment surgery. In 1996, whilst undergoing surgery, Jonathon died on the operating table. Christie filed a medical malpractice suit under the Texas Wrongful Death and Survival Statute in her capacity as Jonathon's surviving spouse.

The sued doctor, Dr Prange, filed a motion for summary judgment in the trial court, after having found out that Christie was a transsexual woman when she had to answer the deposition question 'Have you ever been known by another name?'. This motion challenged Christie's status as a proper wrongful death beneficiary, asserting that Christie was a man and could not therefore be the surviving spouse of another man. The trial court agreed and granted summary judgment; Christie appealed to the Texas Court of Appeals. However, their judgment concluded that: at the time of birth, Christie was a male, both anatomically and genetically; the facts contained in the original birth certificate were true and accurate; and the words contained in the amended certificate were not binding. The court went on to state:

> There are some things we cannot will into being. They just are ... [A]s a matter of law, Christie Littleton is a male. As a male, Christie cannot be married to another male. Her marriage to Jonathon was invalid, and she cannot bring a cause of action as his surviving spouse.

The Texas Supreme Court refused to review the case, as did the US Supreme Court.[29]

Dr Greer and Dr Mohl, who had psychiatrically assessed Christie, testified that true (mtf) transsexual women are, in their opinion, psychologically and psychiatrically female, both before and after the sex reassignment surgery, and that Christie was a true transsexual woman. Dr Greer served as a principal

---

29 See http://christielee.net/main2.htm.

member of the surgical team that performed the gender reassignment surgery on Christie. In Dr Greer's opinion, the anatomical and genital features of Christie, following that surgery, were such that she has the capacity to function sexually as a woman. Both Dr Greer and Dr Mohl testified that, in their opinions, following the successful completion of Christie's gender reassignment treatment, Christie was medically a woman.

Christie had suffered years of pain growing up as a boy and as an adolescent, and further years of trauma participating in medical and psychiatric treatment, trying to persuade doctors and medical experts to believe her and correct her anatomy to coincide with her deep psychological conviction that she was a woman. Despite those same medical experts testifying in court that, as far as medical opinion was concerned, Christie was a woman, at law she was still a male, at least for the purposes of marriage. Hence, her seven-year marriage to her husband Jonathon was reversed at a stroke and made void, as was the validity of her gender reassignment surgery and her new identity as a woman. She may still be able to drive or travel abroad as a woman, but that does not compensate if she is called a man in other areas of her life, such as relationship formation, or employment. The undeniable tragedy of this case is that the questions surrounding Jonathon Littleton's death may now go unanswered, with nobody having to take responsibility, and the wife he cared and provided for throughout the years of their marriage being left impoverished, despite all their efforts as a married couple to the contrary.

✵ CIRCUMSCRIBING SEX II ✵

The second issue in *Corbett* was whether the marriage had been consummated – what were the requirements as regards sexual activity in marriage. Ormrod J decided that a post-operative (mtf) transsexual woman and a man would not be able to have 'normal' intercourse. In reaching this conclusion, he distinguished *SY v SY*,[30] where a woman was capable of marriage, despite suffering from a vaginal defect that prevented what Ormrod referred to as 'normal' intercourse. There is, in fact, little difference between a wholly artificial vagina (as in *Corbett*) and an extended one (as in *SY*), both medically and sexually. Indeed, based on modern medical knowledge, it is very likely that *SY* would have been diagnosed as a case of testicular feminisation and accordingly been discovered to be a chromosomal male. If that was the case, Ormrod J misdirected himself in distinguishing *Corbett* from *SY*.

A separate criticism comes from Pace (1992), who argues that by stressing the capacity for heterosexual intercourse as a requirement for marriage, Ormrod J would also render void the marriage of a person without such

---

30 *SY v SY* [1962] 3 All ER 55, CA.

capacity due to age or injury. Yet, incapacity for these reasons is no longer considered a ground for automatically voiding a marriage:

> Marriage has also long moved beyond the point of being little more that consummation, procreation and property transfer. As a society we would not dare to consider refusing the right to marry to a person with a disability that meant they could not consummate the marriage through penetrative sexual intercourse. (Change *et al*, 2000a.)

The Press For Change Submission argues that:

> ... to protect spouses, failure to consummate could lead to the dissolution of a marriage, just as it can in other marriages where there has been *prior deceit as to the ability to consummate*. As the law stands, failure to give material information to a spouse, such as *implying that procreation is possible*, is a material fact that can lead to the dissolution of any marriage. (Change *et al*, 2000a.)

This would mean that a spouse of a transsexual person would have a legal recourse if, for example, a transsexual man implied prior to marriage that he had the ability to participate in ordinary sexual intercourse when he had, in fact, not undergone any genital reconstruction.[31] Moreover, sexual intercourse and procreation are no longer considered the primary purpose of, or perhaps even essential to, the modern concept of marriage. As Lauw has said:

> There has never been any attempt to prohibit unions between a sterile woman and a fertile man, or vice versa. Nor does legislation exist which 'requires' a married couple to have children. If procreation – or the lack thereof – were a real concern of the legislature, it is probable that there would be legislation regulating marriages by sterile and handicapped persons. The fact that the laws do not do this suggests that procreation is not a primary concern. (Lauw, 1994.)

Nevertheless, as the law is currently understood, Ormrod J ruled out marriage for the majority of transsexual people (and hence 'same-sex' couples) on two counts. Firstly, that the partners must have had, at their birth, chromosomal, genital and gonadal congruent male and female features respectively; and secondly, that the couple must be able to consummate the marriage through 'normal' heterosexual intercourse. However, though there have been many criticisms of *Corbett* and many other jurisdictions have chosen not to follow it, none of the criticisms suggest that same-sex couples should be able to legally marry. So, while *Corbett* may have been overruled in some jurisdictions, it has not been done in a way that would allow same-sex couples to marry, including homosexual or lesbian transsexual people and their 'same-gender' partners. There is a certain irony to this, though; in those jurisdictions where transsexual people cannot marry in their new gender role, they can marry in their 'old' gender role. Thus we see a situation in which 'same-sex' marriages are contracted, as gay transsexual men marry their male partners, and lesbian

---

31 Few transsexual men actually undergo genital reconstruction, as such surgical procedures are life-threatening and rarely successful.

transsexual women marry their female partners. Some of these marriages may be voidable under the consummation requirements for 'normal' heterosexual intercourse, but by no means all of them.

It has also been said that:

> As Hyde was a reflection of mid-19th century morality, it may be questioned whether, and if so why, public policy should prevent post-operational transsexuals from contracting a valid marriage. (Pace, 1992, pp 16–17.)

The moral values of the mid-19th century, thankfully, no longer prevail in most walks of life. We would be horrified if there was any suggestion that they should; therefore, we must ask whether those values are still pertinent to modern day marriage.

CIRCUMSCRIBING RIGHTS, CIRCUMSCRIBING BENEFITS

Civil marriage provides legal benefits that thousands of people take for granted. It is important to remember that marriage also brings obligations, such as spousal support on the breakdown of the marriage. A marriage is not only a commitment between the couple, but also a contract with the state. In looking at how the law affects transsexual people and their partners who are unable to marry because they are considered, in effect, to be 'same-sex' couples, there are three areas I wish to examine briefly: firstly, the couple themselves during their relationship; secondly, the couple's conceiving children and their responsibilities as parents; and finally, the couple's separation, either through death or breakdown of the relationship. It is impossible to list all of the legal benefits and obligations of civil marriage because there are too many.[32]

The couple

Firstly, with regard to immigration, a non-European Community national whose partner is a British national whom they are legally unable to marry, cannot claim residency in the UK until they have lived for two years in a relationship 'akin to marriage' with their British partner.[33] In many cases, the couple have no right to live in the foreign partner's country either. For example, in the US, the Immigration and Naturalization Service does not recognise 'same-sex' relationships, no matter how long-standing they are. This causes problems in satisfying the 'akin to marriage' requirement, because the foreign partner is not allowed residency in the UK, and the British partner is often not allowed residency in the foreign country. Even though the UK government's current policy is a huge improvement on the pre-1997 policy, it

---

32 Text accompanying note 3.
33 Immigration Rules, paras 295A-295O, www.ind.homeoffice.gov.uk.

is still much easier for a non-transsexual person to get a visa by marrying a person of the opposite sex, having met them two weeks before, than it is for a transsexual person in a 10-year, long-distance relationship with their opposite-gender partner.

In many countries, transsexual people can solve their immigration problems by marrying. At least 35 of 43 Council of Europe countries,[34] every Canadian province, much of the US, Israel, South Africa, Namibia and New Zealand provide mechanisms whereby transsexual people can be recognised in their new 'sex' as regards civil registration procedures. This does not guarantee that their marriages to their opposite-gender partners are entirely secure, but any marriages they contract are recognised for many purposes, including immigration. The fact that a transsexual person can marry in many US states, but not in the UK, means that the UK immigration service would recognise the immigration rights of a US non-transsexual woman who had contracted a marriage, in the US, to a US transsexual man who had residency rights in the UK. Yet, they would not recognise the immigration rights of a US transsexual man who had married a British non-transsexual woman, wherever their marriage had been contracted.

An example of British non-recognition of a transsexual person's marriage, validly contracted outside the UK, was cited to the European Court of Human Rights in *Sheffield and Horsham v UK*.[35] Rachel Horsham had been registered as a boy at her birth in the UK. She had undergone gender reassignment in the Netherlands, and had become a Dutch citizen through naturalisation. In the Netherlands, she had received a 'Certificate of Reassignment', which had allowed the Dutch authorities to issue her with a new birth certificate showing her sex as female. This allowed her full rights as a woman in Dutch society, including the right to contract a marriage to a non-transsexual man, which would be recognised throughout the world for immigration purposes. However, if she contracted a marriage with a non-EC national, that marriage would not be recognised if they chose to move to the UK, because her original birth certificate would be that used for immigration purposes, and her marriage would be considered void, ie, that it had never existed.

The second detriment to transsexual people and their partners (who are often viewed in law as same-sex couples) is in relation to fringe benefits and employment. In *Grant v South-West Trains*,[36] the ECJ held that Art 119 (now

---

34 Excluding the UK, Ireland, Andorra and Albania. No information is available regarding Armenia, Azerbaijan and Georgia. A bill *(Proposición de Ley sobre el Derecho a la Identidad Sexual)* passed by the Spanish Senate on 7 March 2001 would allow a transsexual person to change their civilly registered 'sex', rather than just their first name. See EuroLetter No 87 (March 2001), www.steff.suite.dk/eurolet/eur_87.pdf, See also www.stonewall-immigration.org.uk.

35 *Sheffield and Horsham v UK* (1998) 27 EHRR 163, ECHR, www.echr.coe.int.

36 *Grant v South-West Trains*, Case C-249/96 [1998] ECR I-621, ECJ.

141) of the EC Treaty, which prohibits sex discrimination in relation to pay, was not violated by a refusal to grant travel concessions to a lesbian employee's female partner. The decision was based on three grounds:

(1) the employer's requirement that the partner be of the opposite sex applied regardless of the sex of the worker, because travel concessions were also refused to gay male employees;

(2) EC law has not yet adopted rules stating that same sex relationships are equivalent to marriages or stable opposite-sex relationships; and

(3) *P v S and Cornwall County Council,*[37] where the ECJ held that dismissal 'for a reason related to a gender reassignment' was sex discrimination contrary to the Equal Treatment Directive,[38] could be distinguished from *Grant.*

This decision is considered bad law by many commentators (Koppelman, Bell and Waaldijk, in Wintemute and Andenaes, 2001), as there is a potential inconsistency between *P* and *Grant.* If it is contrary to EC sex discrimination law to discriminate against a person because they are undergoing or have undergone gender reassignment, then would it still be sex discrimination if a transsexual employee were denied a benefit for their legally 'same-sex' partner? Or would it be the same sort of legal discrimination that Lisa Grant and her female partner suffered, if Lisa Grant had instead been a transsexual man called Liam Grant? The ECJ will have to answer this question in *Bavin v NHS Trust Pensions Agency,*[39] which concerns the denial of a survivor's pension provided to 'spouses' to a transsexual man who is the partner of a non-transsexual female employee, who is legally unable to marry him. The Employment Appeal Tribunal had doubts about the law as it is at present in relation to non-traditional partnerships, saying:

> ... we can and do invite those who are responsible for such matters to consider whether it is sensible in modern times for eligibility to any concession or benefit to depend upon the marital status of the people concerned. It is the experience of the members of this court that many if not most pension schemes give trustees a discretion to make payments where relationships outside marriage are stable. We can think of no good social reason why travel facilities or derived pension benefits should not be available where there is a stable long-term relationship between two unmarried people, whatever the reasons for not being married. Such a change would not have to address the more complicated and difficult question as to whether persons of the same sex should be permitted to marry or transsexuals be permitted formally to change their birth certificates.[40]

---

37 *P v S and Cornwall County Council,* Case C-13/94 [1996] IRLR 347, ECJ. See also the Sex Discrimination (Gender Reassignment) Regulations 1999, SI 1999/1102 (amending the Sex Discrimination Act 1975).

38 Council Directive 76/207/EEC of 9 February 1976, OJ [1976] L 39/40.

39 *Bavin v NHS Trust Pensions Agency* [1999] ICR 1192, EAT referred to the ECJ by the Court of Appeal (England and Wales) on 4 October 2000; registered as Case C-117/01, *KB v National Health Service Pension Agency.*

40 *Ibid,* para 19.

I would argue that, since the interpretation of *P* by the EAT in *Chessington World of Adventures v Reed*,[41] there is no need for a specific comparator in cases concerning gender reassignment under the Sex Discrimination Act 1975 (Great Britain). Instead, the courts, in the light of *P*, should determine what 'feature' caused the discrimination, ie, the court should consider what position the claimant would have been in if she had not had that feature, compared to the position she is in now. For *Bavin*, the feature was that she was a non-transsexual woman with a transsexual man as partner. The discrimination must be based on sex, because if her partner were a non-transsexual man, she would have been able to contract a lawful marriage to him, which would have qualified him for the survivor's pension benefits. Alternatively, if she had been a non-transsexual man with a transsexual man as partner, they could have contracted a valid marriage and the partner would again have qualified. Therefore, the discrimination against *Bavin* was based on sex and, because it relates to pay, violated both Art 141 EC and the Equal Pay Act 1970 (Great Britain). In *Bavin*, the ECJ will have to decide whether to apply *P* or *Grant*. If the ECJ applies *Grant*, then British couples where one partner is transsexual will have to look to any protection for 'same-sex' partners provided by the EC Directive[42] prohibiting sexual orientation discrimination in employment (Bell and Waaldijk, in Wintemute and Andenaes, 2001).

The couple's children

Transsexual men and their (non-transsexual) female partners often form families by bringing children into their domestic unit. Sometimes they are the biological children of the transsexual man, born before his transition to his new gender role, and sometimes the children of the female partner from a prior relationship. On occasion, though, female partners have children within their relationship with the transsexual man. These children are conceived by the female partner either having an 'affair' with a non-transsexual male or by donor insemination. Many partners of transsexual men now seek the help of donor insemination services provided through licensed fertility clinics. Clinics are bound to keep as their paramount concern the welfare of any child who is born by the treatment they provide.

A prospective transsexual father cannot keep his status a secret in this process. Many clinics will not treat unmarried women at all (Douglas, Hebenton and Thomas, 1992, p 488) because of the requirement in s 13(5) of the Human Fertilisation and Embryology Act 1990 that:

> ... a woman shall not be provided with treatment services unless account has been taken of the welfare of any child who may be born as a result of the treatment (including the need of that child for a father).

---

41 *Chessington World of Adventures v Reed* [1997] IRLR 556, EAT, www.pfc.org.uk/legal/chess.htm.

42 Council Directive 2000/78/EC of 27 November 2000, OJ [2000] L 303/16.

Hence, the transsexual man needs to be involved in the application for treatment in order for the first barrier to be crossed. Then the male partner will be investigated as to whether he is the cause of the infertility within the relationship. This requires the giving of sperm samples, etc. It is far easier for the transsexual man to be open about the situation from the beginning. Indeed, if a transsexual man has to consider keeping his status 'secret', it implies that being transsexual would somehow make him less able as a parent. I argue that:

> Just as in the history of negative eugenics it becomes illogical to discuss the 'best interests' of the child, if the child can never be born, if the claim is made that transsexual people are not suitable for parenthood, then they are refused access to parenthood ... this supports the claim because there is no evidence to the contrary. (Change *et al*, 2000b.)

In these cases, the consultant often refers the matter of the treatment of the partner of a transsexual man to his Ethical Committee, which advises doctors on whether certain treatments or experimental work they may do are within ethical boundaries. The role of the Ethical Committee in fertility treatment cases is merely advisory; it is not a decision making body and it is doubtful whether a committee could veto the decision of a doctor to provide fertility treatment. Furthermore, *R v Ethical Committee of St Mary's Hospital ex p H*[43] held that a decision by an Ethical Committee could be reviewed where, for example, there was a policy of refusing treatment to anyone who, for example, was Jewish or Black.

Once treatment is obtained and a child conceived and born, in the UK, the transsexual man is not in a position to be registered as the child's father[44] (see Chapter 10). The mother of the child can choose to give the child her partner's surname, and this will be entered upon the child's birth certificate (the short form has no space for details of the child's parents, so may be preferred by such a family as documentary evidence of the child's birth; however, the full certificate has a space for the completion of the father's details). Undoubtedly, many transsexual men ignore the law and, with their partner's consent, register themselves as the father of the child, just as many other non-biological fathers do. However, unlike other social fathers, the transsexual man is committing an offence under the Registration of Births and Deaths Act 1953. This would be on the grounds that he is not entitled to be treated as the father of the child under s 28 of the Human Fertilisation and Embryology Act 1990, even though he is compelled to agree to be the child's father in order that his partner will receive treatment. Section 28 provides that, if treatment using donated sperm is provided for a woman together with a man, and although the embryo was not created using the sperm of that man, that man will be

---

43 *R v Ethical Committee of St Mary's Hospital ex p H* [1988] 1 FLR 512.

44 *X, Y and Z v UK* (1997) 24 EHRR 143, ECHR, www.echr.coe.int.

treated as the father of the child for all purposes. As the transsexual man is not a 'man' under English law, he cannot become the father of the child, though he will be allowed to share parenting under the provisions of the Children Act 1989.

Various legal anomalies appear. The transsexual man may claim the additional tax allowance that is available to the parent of a child if he can show that he maintains the child. At the same time, for all welfare benefits purposes, the child's mother will remain legally a single parent and the income of the child's transsexual father will be ignored. This means that the mother may claim the additional single parent's allowance and, if she is not working, or working only part time, she will qualify to claim income support for herself and the child, or family credit.[45] The Child Support Agency (CSA) is obliged to ask mothers who are claiming benefits for details of the child's father, in order that maintenance may be claimed from him. But children who are born through donor insemination, provided by a licensed clinic to a transsexual man's female partner, currently have no legal father. In practice, the mother merely needs to inform the CSA of the nature of the child's conception, and any further action is dropped.

There is no reason why a transsexual parent cannot apply to adopt a child, as an unmarried individual. The attitudes of some local social services in London and elsewhere have recently changed their views towards gays and lesbians adopting a child, and the courts have confirmed their eligibility.[46] However, if a transsexual person's partner is of the same natal sex (that is, a transsexual woman lives with a non-transsexual male, or a transsexual man lives with a non-transsexual female), and that partner is the parent of a child, the transsexual person would not be able to adopt that child without the biological parent losing their parental rights. Section 14 of the Adoption Act 1976 states that a joint adoption order may be made only on the application of a married couple. As the transsexual person and their partner cannot get married, it is not possible for them to be joint parents, though it may be possible for them to share parental rights and duties under the Children Act 1989.

After the child has been born, there are legal obstacles for the family, including the child. The partner who is not the legal parent of the child does not, in the eyes of the law, bear parental responsibility as a married partner would. The most that can be done by the co-parent is to apply (jointly with the legal parent) for a residence order in both of their names. In law, the transsexual man and his non-transsexual female partner are currently treated as if they were two cohabiting women, which makes case law on lesbian

---

45 Letter from Virginia Bottomley, Secretary of State for Health, to Gerald Kaufman, MP, 4 July 1992.

46 See, eg, *Re W (A Minor) (Adoption: Homosexual Adopter)* [1997] 3 All ER 620.

couples relevant. In the Manchester High Court on 24 June 1994, a lesbian couple obtained joint legal recognition as parents of a two-year-old baby, through a 'joint residence order'. The judge held that the child's welfare was his first and paramount consideration, and that the evidence in the case overwhelmingly pointed to the making of such an order.[47]

A joint residence order would be available to a transsexual man and his partner, but it has limitations. It allows the transsexual parent to make decisions with the legal parent, for example, to authorise medical treatment. However, it is not the same as a parental responsibility order, which only unmarried biological fathers can obtain. A joint residence order only exists whilst the partners cohabit and disappears immediately on the separation of the couple, or on the death of one of the partners. Potentially, therefore, the birth parent could die and leave the children of the family 'parentless' and hence 'homeless' in law. It is also important that a transsexual man write a will leaving his property appropriately, because his partner and children (if not his own biological children) are not covered by the intestacy rules that provide for family dependants. The Stonewall lobbying and litigation group in London is arguing that same-sex co-parents should be entitled to seek parental responsibility orders, and that a child should be allowed to inherit from a co-parent who has a joint residence order or a parental responsibility order.

These orders (and wills) would not be necessary if transsexual people and their opposite-gender partners were able to marry. The married (or unmarried) transsexual male partner of the mother of children conceived by donor insemination would automatically be their legal father; either partner's children from a prior relationship could be adopted by the other partner; and unrelated children could be adopted jointly. The right to marry would also force an end to the presumption that transsexual people do not form meaningful relationships, and therefore do not provide a suitable environment for children.

The couple's separation

When a transsexual person and their opposite-gender partner separate, they do not have the protection of Part II of the Matrimonial Causes Act 1973. They are treated as though they were strangers by the law and must rely on, for example, property law to determine ownership of land. There is no legal duty to support a partner who is economically dependent during the relationship, as there is when a marriage breaks down. This is also the case for children; there is no obligation to pay child maintenance and no right of access for the non-birth parent of the children.

---

47 News Release, Otten & Skemp Solicitors, 28 June 1994.

Since *Fitzpatrick v Sterling Housing Association*,[48] a long standing same-sex relationship (including that of a transsexual person and their opposite-gender partner) does give the surviving partner a right of succession to a tenancy under the Rent Act 1977, but as a 'family member' and not a 'spouse'. In the Act, protection given to a family member is not as great as that given to spouses.[49] Nor does the Act apply to public sector tenancies. Despite the *Fitzpatrick* decision, transsexual people and their partners generally do not qualify as next of kin, unlike married couples. This means that if their partner is ill or dies, they do not have the rights and responsibilities that a spouse would have in relation to hospital visits and consultation, and funeral arrangements. Some of these rights and responsibilities can, however, be obtained by using Powers of Attorney between the partners.

There are also financial disadvantages to not being a surviving spouse. For example, in relation to inheritance, there are three problems. Firstly, if there is no will, the rules of intestacy mean that the estate will pass to the nearest blood relative, not the unmarried partner. Secondly, if there is a will, and the estate is worth more than £234,000,[50] it is subject to inheritance tax. Married couples are exempt from this. Thirdly, where a pension scheme provides for a survivor's pension, if the scheme member dies before his or her spouse, it generally does not apply to an unmarried partner.

It is true that there are some benefits to transsexual people and their partners in not having their relationships recognised by the state, because the partners' incomes will not be combined in relation to social security and eligibility for legal aid. But these advantages do not outweigh the disadvantages. Additionally, the advantages to these couples of non-recognition of their relationships are disadvantages to the state. Therefore, it is not beneficial, either to these couples or (in a more limited way) to the state, not to recognise their relationships.

CIRCUMSCRIBING HUMAN RIGHTS

Three Articles of the European Convention of Human Rights are relevant to marriage. Firstly, Art 12 states that:

> Men and women of marriageable age have the right to marry and to found a family, according to the national laws governing the exercise of this right.

---

48 *Fitzpatrick v Sterling Housing Association* [1999] 4 All ER 705.
49 A surviving family member of the original tenant is entitled to a life interest (an assured tenancy), but a surviving spouse becomes the statutory tenant and can pass on the tenancy to a family member or subsequent spouse.
50 Limit for the tax year 6 April 2000 to 5 April 2001.

This confers a right to marry on all people of marriageable age. However, the ECHR has held that it does not apply to transsexual men and women. In *Rees v UK*, the Court indicated that the primary purpose of Art 12 is to 'protect marriage as the basis of the family'.[51] Therefore, the inability of *Rees* to procreate entitled the UK to refuse the right to marry, even though many married couples cannot procreate. Nevertheless, the Court concluded that 'the right to marry guaranteed by Article 12 refers to the traditional marriage between persons of opposite biological sex' and that the challenged rule was not such that 'the very essence of the right is impaired'.[52]

In 1991, the Court followed *Rees* in *Cossey v UK*.[53] However, four dissenting judges strongly criticised the Court's view that procreation is the basis of marriage. Katherine O'Donovan (1993, p 50) notes in particular the dissenting opinion of Judge Martens based on 'humanistic principles of dignity, freedom and privacy'. Mirroring the decision of the US Supreme Court in *Griswold*,[54] Judge Martens claimed that marriage is:

> ... far more than a union which legitimates sexual intercourse and aims at procreating ... it is a societal bond ... a species of togetherness in which intellectual, spiritual and emotional bonds are at least as essential as the physical one.[55]

The second relevant Article of the European Convention of Human Rights is Art 14. It provides that:

> [T]he enjoyment of the rights and freedoms set forth in this Convention shall be secured without discrimination on any ground such as sex, race, colour ... or other status.

Although one might presume that gender identity is included in this list as an 'other status',[56] the Court ruled in *Sheffield and Horsham* that:

> ... not every difference in treatment will amount to a violation of [Art 14]. Instead, it must be established that other persons in an analogous or relatively similar situation enjoy preferential treatment, and that there is no reasonable or objective justification for this distinction.[57]

Clearly, opposite-sex couples enjoy preferential treatment because they have access to the benefits of civil marriage. Cohabiting opposite-sex couples also have more of these benefits available to them than cohabiting couples who are considered in law to be of the same sex. According to Simon Foster (1998,

---

51 *Rees v UK* (1986) 9 EHRR 56, www.echr.coe.int: para 49.
52 *Ibid*, paras 49–50.
53 *Cossey v UK* (1990) ECHR, Series A, No 184, www.echr.coe.int.
54 *Griswold v Connecticut* 381 US 479 (1965).
55 Above at fn 53, para 4.5.2.
56 See *Salgueiro v Portugal* (1999) 31 EHRR 47, ECHR, www.echr.coe.int: para 28.
57 *Sheffield and Horsham v UK* (1998) 27 EHRR 163, ECHR, www.echr.coe.int: para 75.

p 328), the 'objective justification' for the difference in treatment is 'administrative or other inconveniences'. These reasons are hardly an adequate justification for restricting civil liberties or refusing human rights.

The third relevant provision of the European Convention of Human Rights is Art 8, which provides a right to respect for private and family life. Article 8(2) allows a state to interfere with this right if the interference is in accordance with the law and necessary in a democratic society. In 1997, in *X, Y and Z v UK*, the Court confirmed that 'family life' in Art 8 could include *de facto* family relationships, other than those joined by marriage. The Court identified a number of factors which evidenced a *de facto* relationship:

> ... whether the couple live together, the length of their relationship and whether they have demonstrated their commitment to each other by having children together or by any other means.[58]

On the facts of *X, Y and Z*, the Court found that there was a *de facto* family relationship.[59] However, the UK's refusal to allow legal recognition of the relationship between X (an ftm transsexual man) and Z (his child conceived through donor insemination) was held not to amount to a breach of Art 8. The Court weighed 'the disadvantages suffered by the applicants' against the 'general interests' of the 'community as a whole' (the community interest in maintaining a coherent system of family law; uncertainty as to whether amendments to the law would be to the advantage of children such as Z; the implications that amendments would have in other areas of family law) and found that the general interests prevailed.[60] As there was no common ground between the member states of the Council of Europe, and as 'X is not prevented in any way from acting as Z's father in the social sense', the UK had to be given a wide margin of appreciation.[61]

In 1998, in *Sheffield and Horsham*, the Court rejected a claim by two (mtf) transsexual women of a violation of Art 8[62] for two main reasons. Firstly:

> ... the applicants have not shown that [since *Cossey*] there have been any findings in the area of medical science which would settle conclusively the doubts concerning the causes of the condition of transsexualism.[63]

In addition:

> ... it continues to be the case that transsexualism raises complex scientific, legal, moral and social issues, in respect of which there is no generally shared approach among the Contracting States.[64]

---

58   *X, Y and Z v UK* (1997) 24 EHRR 143, ECHR, www.echr.coe.int: para 36.
59   *Ibid*, para 37.
60   *Ibid*, paras 47–48.
61   *Ibid*, paras 44, 50.
62   They also claimed violations of Arts 12, 13 and 14.
63   *Sheffield and Horsham v UK* (1998) 27 EHRR 163, ECHR, www.echr.coe.int: para 56.
64   *Ibid*, para 58.

Secondly, the Court was not persuaded that:

> ... the failure of the authorities to recognise their new gender gives rise to detriment of sufficient seriousness as to override the respondent State's margin of appreciation in this area.

However, in a dissenting judgment, Judge van Dijk expressed the view that 'the very existence' of a legal system that:

> ... keeps treating post-operative transsexuals ... as members of the sex which they have disowned psychically and physically as well as socially ... must continuously, directly and distressingly affect their private life.[65]

Will the UK's Human Rights Act 1998, in force since 2 October 2000, be any more helpful with regard to giving transsexual people, their partners and their families the benefits of civil marriage? It seems unlikely because, although UK courts are not bound by decisions of the European Court of Human Rights, they must take these decisions into account. To date, both the High Court and the Court of Appeal in *Bellinger v Bellinger*,[66] where a transsexual woman and her 'husband' have sought to overturn the *Corbett* decision, have followed *Rees, Cossey, X, Y and Z* and *Sheffield and Horsham*. The European Community's Equal Treatment Directive, as interpreted in *P v S and Cornwall County Council*, would more be likely to provide protection (see Chapter 10) through the financial and social mobility benefits that marriage brings. However, all this is to change.

AN INVITATION TO A WEDDING?

In January 2002, headlines in *The Independent* and *Daily Mail* newspapers announced 'Transsexuals to win right to marry'. It was not technically true; the stories 'officially' resulted from a leak, which should not have happened, from a junior member of the Lord Chancellor's Department. The truth was much more mundane but the headlines did give an indication that transsexual people in the United Kingdom may look forward to a brighter future. On the day of the leak, the Office of National Statistics Population Studies (ONS), which includes the Office of the Registrar General who is responsible for all births, deaths and marriage registrations, published the White Paper *Civic Registration: Vital Change* (ONS, 2002a). Covering all aspects of civil registration, for most people the main interest is the fact that marriages will be able to be celebrated at a far wider range of venues in the future.

However, a small section entitled 'A through life record: the creation of a central database of registration records provides the opportunity to make

---

65 Above: para 12.
66 [2001] EWCA Civ 1140 (CA).

improvements in line with developments in other countries' (p 23) potentially promises much for British transsexual people. One small paragraph says:

> There is strong support for some relaxation to the rules that govern corrections to records. Currently, once a record has been created, the only corrections that can be made are where it can be shown that an error was made at the time of registration and that this can be established ... in future, changes (to reflect developments after the original record was made) will be made and formally recorded. Documents issued from the records will contain only the information as amended, though all the information will be retained. The level of evidence, other than that based on legal proceedings, on which changes to the records will be authorized, will continue to be at the discretion of the Registrar General. (ONS, 2002a, p 25.)

The press read this as government putting in place a mechanism whereby the birth certificates of transsexual people could be changed after they underwent some aspect of gender reassignment. After all, as Steve Doughty of the *Daily Mail* said to me: 'Who else, apart from Geri Halliwell (in order to knock ten years off her age), would want their birth records changing?'

The Lord Chancellor's Department maintains the line that these proposals have 'nothing to do with transsexual people', yet the fact is that this year (2002) will see four high profile cases, brought by Press For Change activists, being heard by the senior courts. *Bellinger v Bellinger*,[67] which requests retrospective recognition of the marriage of a transsexual woman and her male partner, will be heard at the House of Lords this year. *A v West Yorkshire Police*[68] has been referred to the Court of Appeal, raising the question 'what sex would a transsexual police officer be for the purposes of searching?'. *Bavin v NHS Pensions Trust*[69] was heard in the European Court of Justice at the end of April, seeking the pension position of a woman who 'fell in love with a man who just happened to be transsexual' but whom she cannot legally marry. These will follow on from the (just announced) decision of the ECHR in the case of *Goodwin and I v UK*,[70] which challenged the refusal to change birth certificates and the question of marriage rights. This 'royal flush' has not come about by accident; rather it is the result of long term planning by Press For Change, the UK's lobby group for trans people. The fact that the four most senior courts will hear cases which all challenge Ormrod LJ's *Corbett* criteria for determining sex for the purpose of marriage has, undoubtedly, brought great pressure to bear on the UK government. That one of these courts, the ECHR, has now made its decision and found a breach of Article 12 of the

---

67 [2001] EWCA Civ 1140 (CA).

68 *A v Chief Constable of West Yorkshire Police*, Case No 1802020/98 (1999) IT.

69 *Bavin v NHS Trust Pensions Agency* [1999] EAT ICR 1192, referred to the ECJ by the Court of Appeal (England and Wales) on 4 October 2000; registered as Case C-117/01, *KB v National Health Service Pension Agency*.

70 *Christine Goodwin v UK*, Application No 28957/95 (1995) ECHR; *I v UK*, Application No 25608/94 (1994) ECHR.

Convention means that the government will have to act. The question, though, is in what way will they act, and will they avoid the travesty of the US system, which still fails to recognise the marriages of many transsexual people?

A *Goodwin* in Europe

The decision of the European Court of Human Rights in *Goodwin and I v UK* was clear and to the point. The two applications were on five specific points:

- the failure of the UK government to award a pension at the age of 60 to Christine Goodwin;

- the refusal of the UK government to issue Christine Goodwin with a new National Insurance number;

- the refusal of the UK government to allow Christine Goodwin to marry her male partner;

- the requirement of the UK government that 'I' produce a birth certificate detailing her 'old' sex in order to undertake a nursing course;

- the requirement of the UK government that 'I' produce a birth certificate detailing her 'old' sex in order to obtain a student loan.

Fortunately, the Court addressed the root causes of these problems rather than confining itself to these matters, holding that the government's failure to alter the birth certificates of transsexual people or to allow them to marry in their new gender role was a breach of the Convention. The decision needs to be considered under the two Articles that were breached.

Article 8: the right to privacy

The Court said:

> The United Kingdom National Health Service, in common with the vast majority of Contracting States, acknowledges the existence of the condition and provides or permits treatment, including irreversible surgery. The medical and surgical acts which in this case rendered the gender reassignment possible were indeed carried out under the supervision of the national health authorities. Nor, given the numerous and painful interventions involved in such surgery and the level of commitment and conviction required to achieve a change in social gender role, can it be suggested that there is anything arbitrary or capricious in the decision taken by a person to undergo gender reassignment. In those circumstances, the ongoing scientific and medical debate as to the exact causes of the condition is of diminished relevance.[71]

---

71 *Christine Goodwin v UK Government*, Application No 28957/95 (1995) ECHR, para 81.

The basis for the Court's argument is that gender reassignment is properly recognised medical treatment; further that gender reassignment is not easy, and so any argument that it is a matter of 'choice' or 'fancy' is no longer viable. The medical debate on aetiology is, in itself, of no great importance when it comes to legal matters; the fact is that trans people exist and cause is irrelevant in matters of human rights.

The Court finally buried the *Corbett* test, saying that biological factors at birth are not sufficient to determine a person's sex in later life. Other factors must be taken into account:

> ... a test of congruent biological factors can no longer be decisive in denying legal recognition to the change of gender of a post-operative transsexual. There are other important factors – the acceptance of the condition of gender identity disorder by the medical professions and health authorities within Contracting States, the provision of treatment including surgery to assimilate the individual as closely as possible to the gender in which they perceive that they properly belong and the assumption by the transsexual of the social role of the assigned gender.[72]

The other factors must include the fact that the state permits gender reassignment treatment and surgery. So, for transsexual people, sex is to be determined through chromosomes, gonads and genitals at birth and gender reassignment treatment.

The Court then said:

> ... the unsatisfactory situation in which post-operative transsexuals live in an intermediate zone as not quite one gender or the other is no longer sustainable.[73]

Put simply, post-operative transsexual people can no longer be left with a 'no-sex', 'intermediate sex' or 'both sex' legal status. Interestingly, in the light of the decision of the Australian Federal Court in *Re Kevin (Validity of Marriage of Transsexual)*,[74] at no point does the ECHR define what is meant by post-operative. This could enable a broad view to be taken. The Court said:

> Where a State has authorised the treatment and surgery alleviating the condition of a transsexual, financed or assisted in financing the operations and indeed permits the artificial insemination of a woman living with a female-to-male transsexual (as demonstrated in the case of *X, Y and Z v United Kingdom*), it appears illogical to refuse to recognise the legal implications of the result to which the treatment leads.[75]

---

72 *Ibid*, para 81.

73 *I v UK Government*, Application No 25608/94 (1994) ECHR, para 70.

74 [2001] Fam 1074, CA, www.familycourt.gov.au/judge/2001/html/rekevin_text.html. See above.

75 *Christine Goodwin v UK Government*, Application No 28957/95 (1995) ECHR, para 79.

So the state would have to ban all gender reassignment treatment to avoid having to afford the recognition of the 'new' sex of a transsexual person.

Interestingly, this paragraph, by commenting on the provision of artificial insemination to the female partner of an ftm transsexual man, has, to all intents and purposes, overturned the Court's previous decision in *X, Y and Z v UK*[76] and enables the partners of trans men to ask again for their partner's name to be put on their children's birth certificates as the father.

In the past, the UK government has argued that the matter is complex and that the interests of others override the interests of transsexual people. The Court addressed this, saying:

> No concrete or substantial hardship or detriment to the public interest has indeed been demonstrated as likely to flow from any change to the status of transsexuals and society may reasonably be expected to tolerate a certain inconvenience to enable individuals to live in dignity and worth in accordance with the sexual identity chosen by them at great personal cost.[77]

Accordingly, transsexual people are entitled to the dignity that would come from recognising their new legal status. There must be a real reason showing a substantial detriment to the public interest before any consequence flowing from that legal change could be withheld. In simple terms, transsexual people must be given full legal status and recognition unless the government can show very good reason for not providing it.

Summing up, the ECHR has determined that whilst gender reassignment treatment is available and permitted in the UK, whether on the NHS or not, the 'new' sex of post-operative transsexuals must be recognised for all legal purposes (though see below for a question mark in the area of marriage), unless the government can show substantial detriment to the public interest. Even if such detriment is shown, the sex may not be recognised in that area only. Post-operative, as it is undefined, we might presume to be judged by current and appropriate medical knowledge, so it would appear to be dependent upon:

- what is available and possible under current medical knowledge;
- what is appropriate to that particular person.

Thus trans people who 'fit' the following requirements:

- are permanently living full time in their new gender role;
- have had gender reassignment surgery which is appropriate to them, bearing in mind current medical knowledge,

---

76 *X, Y and Z v UK* (1997) 24 EHRR 143, ECHR, www.echr.coe.int.
77 *I v UK Government*, Application No 25608/94 (1994) ECHR, para 71.

should be able to have their new sex recognised on all documentation and in relevant service provision in the following areas:

- driving licence;
- passport;
- medical records (provisional upon their medical history remaining intact, for medical purposes only);
- student records;
- Inland Revenue and National Insurance records;
- birth certificate.

The last two of these are of course the ones which have been consistently refused since the *Corbett* decision in 1970. The Court's endorsement of the rights of 'post-operative' transsexual people is the minimum line behind which the UK government cannot retreat. It must provide legal registration for these people. In spite of this, it is perfectly possible for the government, when implementing legislation, to go one step further and to make legal recognition available to those who are post-treatment and thus include legal recognition rights for those trans people who, for health, disability or other reasons, are unable to undergo surgical intervention.

Article 12: the right to marry

The Court said of the Matrimonial Causes Act 1973:

> It is true that the first sentence refers in express terms to the right of a man and woman to marry.[78]

This is used to void a marriage unless between a man and a woman. In many ways, pre-empting the next legal discussion in sexuality law, that of same-sex marriage, but at the same time steering clear of it, the Court states that it:

> ... is not persuaded that at the date of this case it can still be assumed that these terms must refer to a determination of gender by purely biological criteria (as held by Ormrod J in the case of *Corbett v Corbett*).

So for marriage, the terms 'man' and 'woman' do not mean men and women whose sex is determined only by biology, but also includes men and women whose sex is determined through gender reassignment. The government has always argued that transsexual people do have a right to marry, but to a member of their opposite natal sex grouping. The Court went on to say:

---

78 *I v UK Government*, Application No 25608/94 (1994) ECHR, para 80.

... it is artificial to assert that post-operative transsexuals have not been deprived of the right to marry as, according to law, they remain able to marry a person of their former opposite sex ... In the Court's view, [they] may therefore claim that the very essence of [their] right to marry has been infringed.[79]

Thus post-operative transsexual people must have the right to marry a member of the opposite gender, in other words, someone of the same natal birth sex. The Court further retreated from its decision in the very first transsexual case from the UK, that of *Rees v UK*,[80] that marriage was linked with procreation, saying:

Reviewing the situation in 2002, the Court observes that Article 12 secures the fundamental right of a man and woman to marry and to found a family. The second aspect is not, however, a condition of the first and the inability of any couple to conceive or parent a child cannot be regarded as *per se* removing their right to enjoy the first limb of this provision.[81]

However, the Court did still insert potential conditions whereby a union may not be a marriage. It held that:

... it is for the Contracting State to determine *inter alia* the conditions under which a person claiming legal recognition as a transsexual establishes that gender re-assignment has been properly effected or under which past marriages cease to be valid and the formalities applicable to future marriages (including, for example, the information to be furnished to intended spouses).[82]

Thus the state retains a final say, though the ECHR does itself see marriage as probably only being possible when there has first been legal recognition of transsexual people's 'new' sex. This means that transsexual people must first go through any legal recognition process before they can contract a marriage that might be valid. According to the Court, though, the UK government has little say in what conditions are attached to legal recognition of the 'new' sex, but it does have the right to determine conditions under which transsexual people have the right to marry. According to the Court, these might be:

- post-operative status;

- a requirement in which future spouses are told of the transsexual status.

Consequently, the conditions required to obtain a valid marriage to a member of the opposite gender may well be stricter than the requirements required to have birth certificates changed. Finally, if these requirements, or others, are met, then, apparently according to the Court, there could be a situation

---

79 *I v UK Government*, Application No 25608/94 (1994) ECHR, para 81.
80 *Rees v UK* (1986) 9 EHRR 56, www.echr.coe.int.
81 *Christine Goodwin v UK Government*, Application No 28957/95 (1995) ECHR, para 98.
82 *I v UK Government*, Application No 25608/94 (1994) ECHR, para 83.

whereby former marriages could cease to exist. This could prove very problematic for those transsexual people who contracted a marriage in their old gender role, and who after gender reassignment have retained that marriage under the current legal system. The retention could be for many reasons, but the dissolution of the marriage could have disastrous consequences. For instance, a woman married to a person who is now a transsexual woman could face losing property rights, inheritance tax benefits and pension rights upon the death of her spouse if the marriage has been, to all intents and purposes, forcibly dissolved.

This is very problematic. There is currently no situation in English law where parties to a marriage, which was valid at the time it was contracted, can be required to dissolve that marriage or to choose between the continuation of that marriage and the recognition of other legal rights. It is ironic that if such a legal event happened, or was forced before legal recognition of a transsexual person's new sex, then they, their partners, and quite possibly their children would have a claim under the Human Rights Act to assert their rights under Article 8 of the European Convention on Human Rights: 'Everyone has the right to respect for his private and family life ...'

Certainly, dissolution or requiring nullity proceedings in the case of current (apparently same-sex) 'transsexual marriages' would be likely to lead to legal uncertainty and prolonged litigation both for the individuals involved and for the state, as transsexual people and their same gender spouses seek to protect the rights they have built up during the marriage. On the other hand, permitting pre-existing, pre-(new sex) recognition of 'transsexual (same-sex) marriages' to continue would require the addressing of some minor administrative issues relating to other areas of law which distinguish between married and unmarried persons, such as tax and social security provisions. It is worthy of note that in effect such 'same sex marriages' have existed for some time already, without society being in the slightest bit affected. Where such marriages survive gender reassignment of one of the partners, society and government departments have succeeded in accommodating the changed situation. There appears to be no good reason why they should not continue to do so, though some adjustment of administrative procedures might be useful to clarify the situation for all concerned and to preserve privacy. The alternative would be to strip some loyal older women, who have stuck by their partners through one of the most difficult changes a marriage could face, of financial security.

Summing up the decision, the validity of a marriage between a transsexual person and a member of the opposite gender group is no longer to be determined by the *Corbett* criteria alone. The new criteria are:

- post-operative status (which is again undefined);

- any other conditions laid down by government (apart from the almost certain infertility of one of the partners).

At the time these conditions are met, and the right to future marriage claimed (which would be after a new legal status has been claimed), former marriages might cease to be valid (dependent upon the government's conditions). These are obviously potentially tougher requirements than those required for the changes in legal status in other areas, though that, in itself, may cause other legal problems. It is clear that valid marriage will not necessarily flow from birth certificate change, but on the other hand it may. It is for the government to decide.

But in whatever way the right to marry is afforded transsexual people, as the Press For Change submission to the government's Interdepartmental Working Party noted:

> ... the remaining steps to enhance our social inclusion are, we believe, not only necessary, but can be done easily ... They would make a massive difference in the quality of life not just for the many transsexual people who are citizens of these islands, but also for the friends, family and colleagues with whom we share our lives and who also suffer through our lack of recognition.

> ... Any nation which legitimises, even unintentionally, the social exclusion of any of its citizens simply because of a condition, increasingly recognised in scientific medicine as one of the many possible intersex conditions that exist, and which has no bearing at all on their ability to participate fully in society cannot be a nation worthy of the name.

> Whether it is one person, or as in this case, maybe 5,000 people, this social exclusion must not continue. Many other nations have successfully responded to the needs of the transsexual people in their societies ...

> ... As our knowledge of all sorts of ... conditions grows, as medicine increasingly admits to there being a significant number of births in which it is impossible to guarantee that the sex designation given is unquestionable, and as our society increasingly removes the barriers to equality between the sexes, it may be that 'sex' is no longer something that we should record about the individual. (Change *et al*, 2000a.)

The ECHR decision does not detract from the importance of 'sex' to marriage, but it does call into question what we mean by 'sex'. Some commentators, probably correctly so, see sex/gender as becoming no longer relevant to the modern concept of marriage, as we increasingly recognise the true worth and value of marriage to our society. It is a matter of contractual relationships and agreements of dependency 'for richer or poorer, in sickness and in health' based upon mutual respect, an 'association for as noble a purpose as any', in which sex, whether chromosomal or an act, is increasingly nothing more than the icing on some people's cakes.

CHAPTER 8

GEMEINSCHAFTSFREMDEN[1] –
OR HOW TO BE SHAFTED BY YOUR FRIENDS:
STERILISATION REQUIREMENTS AND LEGAL
STATUS RECOGNITION FOR THE TRANSSEXUAL

This chapter explores the problem of 'demanded sterilisation' that arises when seeking to legislate for transsexual 'rights' in the light of the recent movements within the trans community towards self-definition, both legally and medically. By concentrating on the matter of reproduction rights, it highlights how eugenics discourses, that are thought to be historically dormant, still govern the policy processes that take place within the contradictory stances that govern notions of family rights. It illustrates the hegemonic processes of government that continue to set the boundaries within which normalisation and absorption into society is allowed for 'outsiders'. To the extent that the 'trans' person is to be given limited acceptance, those limits exclude what is constructed as their potential invasion of the bodily integrity of others; in this case, children. It has not proved easy for non-trans people to acknowledge both the imperative existence of trans people and their claim to the law's protection, but it has proved even harder for them to accept fully the consequences of the *discourse interruptus* that the community is offering in their new theorising of sex and gender roles, because of that theory's mandatory removal of gender and sex from legal praxis. This persevering failure to comprehend the re-constructive nature of such a stance has instead meant that the 'gender neutral' or 'gender crossing' sites of trans-bodies are still seen as lacking some essential aspect of humanness.

RESISTING THE ISSUE

The 1990s have seen increasing calls from transsexual people, throughout the world,[2] for legal recognition of their gender status in their new role. In the UK, this campaign has led to the formation of a cross-party Parliamentary Forum which is seeking to draft appropriate legislation for this. A question that arose

---

1   *Gemeinschaftsfremden* is the German language title of the 1943 Nazi draft law on the 'handling of social aliens', which provided the framework for the compulsory castration of homosexual men in Nazi concentration camps. This chapter was originally published in Beresford, S, Monk, D and Moran, L (eds), *Legal Queeries*, 1998, London: Blackwell, pp 42–56. It has been revised and updated for inclusion here.

2   Transsexual people have been involved in recent calls for recognition (or further recognition) of their legal status in Italy, France, Australia, Thailand, Japan, Brazil and Argentina.

was whether the transsexual person who is seeking legal recognition, for example, birth certificate amendment, should be certified as being permanently sterile at the time of recognition. The legislation from several jurisdictions, including Germany, Sweden, Holland and some North American states, requires this to be certified as a matter of course before a legal change of 'sex' or 'gender' will be allowed. For example, the German legislation (TSG) requires that the transsexual person is 'continuously non-reproductive' (TSG (1980) Second Section, Subsection 8(1)(iii)). Similarly, Swedish law requires that an applicant for a legal recognition to effect a change of sex must:

> ... have been sterilised or at least incapable of procreating. (*Lag om andring i lagen* (1972, p 119) Section 2.)

At the 1993 XXIIIrd Colloquy on European Law, 'Transsexualism, Medicine and the Law', Professor Michael Wills of the University of Berne took the view that 'sterility [of the transsexual person] must be absolutely certain and permanent' (Wills, in Council Of Europe, 1993, p 88) before a full recognition of gender change is afforded in law. But Wills does not explain his reasoning; it is presented as a natural common sense assumption. It also appears to be a common sense assumption of many of the medical practitioners who provide gender reassignment treatment. At the 1993 Colloquy, no fewer than four rapporteurs mentioned the sterility requirement without 'batting an eye' (see Wills, Hage, Delvaux and Doek, in Council of Europe, 1993).

This assumption of sterility before legal recognition begs certain questions. It seems an almost obsessional demand as, in reality, in almost all cases, after a few years the hormone therapy undertaken by transsexual people will for all practical purposes have rendered them infertile at that time when they might be considered to have sufficient commitment to their new role for any legal recognition of a status change. If they undergo genital reconstructive surgery, they will certainly be permanently unable to procreate.

There are, though, some transsexual people who, for health reasons, cannot take the high hormone levels normally prescribed; nor can they necessarily undergo extensive surgery. Should they then, by virtue of being unable to be rendered permanently sterile, be denied recognition? Furthermore, for female to male transsexuals, even if they are physical able, should they be forced into undergoing a hysterectomy; a major surgical procedure which will involve some high level of risk, for no therapeutic reason other than to qualify for a legal 'sex change'? The German legislation further requires that there is a 'clear approximation to the phenotype of the desired sex' (TSG (1980) Second Section, Subsection 8(1)(iv)). Must the female to male transsexual have to undergo surgery to occlude the vagina, which can lead to loss of sexual sensation, and further surgery to create a penis, a notoriously difficult and often unsatisfactory procedure (Hage, in Council Of Europe, 1995, p 107)? Should individuals be obliged to undergo specific surgical procedures and their associated health risks before they will be recognised by the law as the social man or woman that they are? There are also those people who identify as transsexual but who do not wish to undergo the surgical procedures involved in gender reassignment. The development of the 1990s term 'transgender' (see Chapter 4) in the trans communities specifically caters for the inclusion of these people in the political processes concerned with access to healthcare, anti-discrimination and anti-hate crime policies and practices.

The legislative requirements for sterility and specific surgery clearly illustrate the medico-legal discourse of the transsexual body, which highlights the ways in which particular bodies are constructed and controlled by the state. Further, they throw light on the particular eugenics and mental hygiene discourses that still surround deviant bodies today.

The eugenics movement, built on Galton's[3] principle of enhancing a biological group on the basis of alleged hereditary merit which was very much grounded in Social Darwinism, was a powerful force well into the 20th century. All too often seen, nowadays, as a thing of the past which resulted in either a series of monumental policy mistakes, as in the US Supreme Court decision in *Buck v Bell*,[4] in which it was held that 'three generations of imbeciles are enough', or the practical embodiment of extreme racism as in the Nazi sterilisation and killing programmes of the 1930s and 1940s, the eugenics movement[5] may have apparently disappeared, but in reality its principles live on. David Smith (1994) argues that eugenics continue to influence attitudes and behaviour toward people who are perceived to be non-productive or defective. Worldwide, court decisions concerning the non-consensual sterilisation of the intellectually disabled may talk about the 'basic right to reproduce', but that apparently becomes irrelevant when considering the best interests of such women (Little, 1992).[6] Such best interests are defined and delineated by 'qualified experts' who are, of course, medical experts.

---

3   Francis Galton coined the word 'eugenics' in his 1883 book *Inquiries into Human Faculty and its Development*, reprinted in 1973 by AMS Press: New York.

4   *Buck v Bell* 274 US 200 (1927).

5   The eugenics movement might be best defined as a Euro-centric collection of campaigning groups, individual physicians and policy makers, who throughout the late 19th century and early 20th century held that racial miscegenation and 'poor breeding' were the causes of poverty, mental health problems, learning difficulties and other sorts of 'social disease'. In the later 20th century, many aspects of their theories, although seen to be racist or bigoted at an intellectual level, have entered the social discourses surrounding parenting rights.

6   Little (1992) goes on to emphasise how the vast majority of sterilisations are performed on women rather than men, despite the fact that female sterilisation procedures are far more dangerous than a vasectomy for men.

Medical experts, both scientists and physicians, have in fact had a long and dishonourable history in the field of eugenics, creating a common discourse on degeneracy and the role of both hereditary and environmental factors in the production of 'deficiency' (Garton, 1994, p 181). For much of the 20th century, following the decision in *Buck v Bell*, the eugenics movement promoted mass forced sterilisation and the segregation of the 'feeble minded' members of society. Numerous American states passed legislation and, consequently, over 60,000 individuals diagnosed as mentally retarded were non-consensually sterilised in the USA (Smith, 1993). The movement recreated the legal, social and ethical environment of those who were seen as different or less than human. As Rafter (1992) explains, no longer did science (eugenics) go through a claims making process, which was then endorsed so creating a response; rather the claims are made, the response follows and this provides the endorsement.

Throughout the western world and up until the 1960s, the sexuality of people of racial and social difference was regulated by denial and suppression in order to control their reproduction (Kempton and Kahn, 1991). The 'deficient' body became the origin of deviance and the site of control. As Rafter states, the early eugenics campaigns:

> ... constituted a very early attempt to criminalize not an action, but the body itself. (Rafter, 1992, p 17.)

In this way, the body is, in itself, the social problem and the solution to social problems is to prevent their (re)production by ensuring that the body can no longer produce. The relationship between the state, science and the individual was irrevocably changed through early eugenics. This paradigm shift may have been questioned, in terms of practice, but it has by no means dissipated as we enter the new century.[7]

Indeed, the theoretical discourses of the 'hereditarily deficient' are still extremely powerful to this day. Whether looking at the family planning threads within the 1994 Cairo World Conference on Population and Development or at the social theories of Charles Murray (Murray, 1990), they bear reminders of some of the theoretical underpinning devised and promoted by eugenics movements throughout history.[8] Negative eugenics

---

7   The controversies surrounding theoretical eugenics are still very much with us, as could be seen with the publication of the book, *The Bell Curve* (Hernstein and Murray, 1994), the withdrawal from publication of Edinburgh University's Christopher Brand's book (Ofori, 1996) and the criticisms of the Pioneer Fund funding of American and European Academics (ABC News, 1994; *Irish Times*, 1994).

8   In May 1995, China introduced a law promoting the sterilisation of people suffering from genetic disorders. If either partner is diagnosed as having a 'serious genetic disorder', then marriage will only be allowed if they both agree to long term contraception or surgical sterilisation (Agence France Press, 1995). The law was always intended as 'social engineering', with Prime Minister Li Ben reported as saying: 'All of China's family planning policies – mandating late marriages, restricting families to one child have been aimed at improving China's population both in quantity and quality' (Maier, 1995).

(which are being discussed here as opposed to positive eugenics) are fundamentally concerned with the prevention of reproduction to deplete certain societal groups. In turn, this was adapted by the mental hygiene movement into a movement concerned with controlling who could become a parent (the right to parenthood) and the ways in which parenting was to be practised.

TRANSSEXUAL CONCERNS

Transsexual people may seem to have more to worry about than their right to reproduce. Yet, the problem they face is gradually being resolved in many states and this has allowed the agenda to be widened by members of the community to include other issues that are seen as fundamental human rights. Furthermore, the changes that the community has undergone in recent years, including changes in self-identification, alongside new reproductive technologies, have led to the possibility of procreation no longer being excluded from the post-transition transsexual person. Transsexual parenthood, albeit not genetic, is certainly on the agenda, as witnessed by the ECHR case of *X, Y and Z v UK*.[9] These issues cannot be viewed in isolation; the 'common sense' discourses that have surrounded the drafting of any legislation relating to transsexual people can be seen to have been informed by eugenic principles. These principles are concerned with the idea that some people are less worthy people than others, and because they are lesser people (and by that I mean 'less human'), they have less of a right to reproduce, to become a parent and to practise parenting. Yet, as in other anti-discrimination movements, transsexual people argue that arbitrary and irrelevant factors should not be used to exclude people from the basic forms of social interactivity, such as getting and keeping a job, bringing up children or registering relationships. The new trans community is demanding that the body be extracted from gender praxis (see Chapter 4).

The removal of the body from status means that judgments based upon status but imposed upon the body become problematic. Negative eugenics practice is based substantially within jurisdictions over the body. If the normative organisations, status and identity, fail the jurisdictional site, then the structural value of the 'hereditarily deficient' theses is faulted. Mainstream academic theories of deviance, such as the Durkheimian tradition or Labelling, Foucauldian or feminist theories of deviance, locate identity as a formulation of later life, of cause and effect rather than of ancestry and birth. It may be the case that trans theorists may deny gender as cause and effect (see Chapter 4), but neither do they see it in terms of biological process.

---

9   *X, Y and Z v UK* (1997) 24 EHRR 143, ECHR, www.echr.coe.int.

PARENTHOOD: A NATURAL STATE OF AFFAIRS?

Generally, the law might now be said to prevent interference in the right of the individual to become a parent. From the decision in *Roe v Wade*,[10] where the US Supreme Court held that a woman's reproductive rights were protected under the privacy clause of the Constitution, to Art 12 of the European Convention, which protects the right to found a family, the right to become a parent is as a general rule available to all.

However, we must not make the assumption then that everybody has the right to become a parent – the right to found a family is principally, as Feldman (1993, p 906) says, 'a negative right – a right to be free of state interference'. Yet this freedom from state interference is even then not available to all and, in the UK as elsewhere, judicial paternalism plays a significant role in authorising the sterilisation of women who would be unable to adequately care for any resultant children.[11]

MOTHER OR FATHER?

The notion of what is meant by parentage itself, until very recently, has not been in question, with all legal systems regarding it as a factual progenitory relationship (unless resulting from statutory adoption). However, in England, the Children Act 1989, though privileging the progenitory relationship, has gone some way to conceding and granting that there is a concept of social parenthood which may be worthy of recognition. By emphasising parental responsibility rather than biological relationship, it has gone some way towards recognising that parenting is about the quality of relationship between child and adult rather than a series of rights that adults acquire over the body of another.

But recent advances in reproductive technology have led to a questioning of what exactly is meant by the terms 'mother' and 'father' (McKnorrie, 1994). Again, in English law, the Human Fertilisation and Embryology Act 1990 has removed the genetic imperatives that used to signify parentage. There is no longer any requirement for a legally recognised father to be the person who performed the fecundatory role in the conception of a child, nor does a mother have to have any genetic or birth relationship with a child. However, public and private presumptions still prevail in that a father is required to be a man, and a mother, a woman. There are many problems, however, with this simple view and, in law, the question of what is a man or a woman still requires a tremendous amount of clarification, particularly with regard to transsexual people, as can be seen in the case of *X, Y and Z v UK* (see the discussion of the *Corbett v Corbett* decision in Chapter 7).

---

10 *Roe v Wade* 410 US 113–52 (1973).

11 For an example, see *Re F (Mental Patient: Sterilisation)* [1990] 2 AC 1.

THE NEITHER MAN NOR WOMAN IN LAW

The definitional problems associated with the dichotomous view of gender, and in particular, the right to reproduce, are not just confined to the UK. To illustrate the issues, I want to look at two particular instances: a state that requires sterility in its legislative provision for transsexual people; and one that does not.

The German legislation requests that the transsexual person has:

> ... undergone an operation to alter their other sexual marks, so that a visible closeness to the appearance of the other sex has been achieved. (TSG (1980) Second Section, Subsection 8(1)(iv).)

However, it does not specify that the operation be penectomy and vaginoplasty, or hysterectomy and phalloplasty. Nevertheless, in the case of *OLG Zweibruken*,[12] concerning a transsexual man, the courts have been asked to ascertain what the law requires for a 'clear approximation' to the opposite sex. Would the bilateral mastectomy undergone by the applicant be sufficient (Council of Europe, 1995, p 89)? Interestingly, one of the lower court's reasons for rejecting the state's arguments for compulsory vaginal occlusion was that occlusion of the vagina was unnecessary as hormone therapy would diminish the size of the vagina, so precluding sexual activity as a woman. This makes several false assumptions: first, that the vagina diminishes in size; second, that women always have vaginal intercourse; and third, that transsexual men are never gay. The decision and commentary on it by Wills (Council of Europe, 1993) are indicative of the lack of understanding of transsexualism, its features and the effects of reassignment treatment, and it highlights the continuing problems of ignorance in this area.

An earlier German case concerned a transsexual man who had undergone a bilateral mastectomy but was unable to continue hormone therapy and unwilling to undergo any further surgery. The legislation requires that the transsexual person be completely non-reproductive. In this case, the courts granted a name change with no problem, but would not allow the change of sex designation because regular menstruation showed that the applicant was still fertile. In *obiter*, the court held that a reversible interruption of the fallopian tubes might be sufficient, because a transsexual man would be very unlikely to seek such a reversal.[13] However, Wills argues that this does not preclude the possibility of *in vitro* fertilisation; therefore, such practice, according to him, must not prevail (Council of Europe, 1995, p 88).

It may stretch the imagination to think of a man giving birth, or a woman impregnating and fathering a child, yet where does the law define that a mother must be a person of XX chromosomes with a womb and vagina and a

---

12 *OLG Zweibruken* [1992] 47–53.
13 *OLG Hamm* (15 Feb 1983).

father a person of XY chromosomes with testes and a penis? For that matter, where does it define a man as having XY chromosomes, and a woman XX chromosomes? It is in Ormrod LJ's decidedly problematic decision in *Corbett v Corbett* where we see these criteria being upheld.

The requirement that the transsexual person should not be able to reproduce through the biological mechanisms concordant with their natal sex designation is not the only issue. What if future surgical techniques enable a transsexual woman to carry a child – should this be restricted? Where do we draw the lines? It is not possible to do more than touch upon this issue; however, it is, I think, one that will increasingly be put on the agenda by transgendered people themselves. The truth of the matter is that these difficult questions are all too easily avoided because we do not see the people or their issues as being meritorious enough to command our time and our thoughts. Gender and sex are merely linguistic signposts which should be used to help us to deal with difficult issues, not to dictate them. And in law, we really should not base legislative decisions around 'gut feelings'.[14]

In contrast, it is possible in the various US and Canadian states to obtain legal recognition of a new gender status without having to undergo sterilisation. In British Columbia, under s 21a of the Revised Statutes British Columbia 1974, Chap 66, an unmarried transsexual person may apply to have the Director of Vital Statistics 'change the sex designation on the registration of birth of such a person in such a manner that the sex designation is consistent with the intended results of the transsexual surgery' (s 21a(1) of the RSBC 1974 1), but there is no specific requirement of sterility. However, the problems that have arisen under German law have also arisen under Canadian law. In *C(L) v C(C)*[15] and *B v A [1990]*,[16] the ftm transsexuals were held to have become men but not husbands, as the only surgery they had undergone was a bilateral mastectomy and a hysterectomy. If not a man for the purposes of marriage, could they be men for the purposes of fatherhood?

RESISTING THE ISSUE II

In the initial draft of the Private Members' Bill, which was to be unsuccessfully presented by Alex Carlile QC, MP on 2 February 1996 before the UK Parliament, a similar provision was included, but after prompting by the transsexual members of the Parliamentary Forum, it was removed. They argued that, in reality, most transsexual people will be medically sterile as a

---

14 In 1995, I had lunch with Professor Michael Wills, rapporteur at the XIIIrd European Colloquy and brought up some of these issues. He was genuinely astonished that I should concern myself with them as they were, according to him, 'self-evident truths'.

15 *C(L) v C(C)* [1992] Lexis 1518 (Ont CJ).

16 *B v A* 29 RFL (3d) 258 (1990).

result of their treatment and surgical reassignment, so to talk of a sterile post-operative transsexual person is a tautology. However, on a very rudimentary level, they also asked 'who else *has* to be sterilised before they are allowed to take up their full legal rights and responsibilities?'. The question was to arise again, when the Interdepartmental Working Group on Transsexuals also posed the question:

> The transsexual community's concern about discrimination has, however, to be set against the great concern felt by the general public if someone who was legally a man gave birth to a child or someone who was legally a woman became the father of one. (Home Office, 2000b, p 21.)

Again, the trans community responded, saying:

> Any proposed restriction on fertility will achieve little if anything. Without these restrictions, transsexual people are already generally infertile shortly after commencing reassignment treatment. Yet despite this infertility many of them already participate in the raising of children. Any such restriction will fail, as medically induced infertility already fails, to ensure that children do not have an experience of being raised by a transsexual person, and it is undoubtedly the case anyway that children who are cared for by transsexual people do not suffer from that care. (Home Office, 2000b, p 47.)

They argued that any requirement of compulsory sterility for legal recognition of the new gender status could not be imposed equitably. To do so would coerce transsexual people with poor health to undertake inappropriate and even dangerous surgical procedures. Further, it would be contrary to the principles of human rights:

> The idea of excluding from parenthood a set of people because they have certain characteristics which have no relevance to their ability to be a good parent must be outlawed because it runs counter to the dignity of human beings, who are unique, free and responsible for their actions. (Home Office, 2000b, p 48.)

Finally, the requirement could not be policed in practice, as transsexual people have always found ways of living in their new gender role regardless of any legal recognition, and this has included the raising of children. This is shown simply through the numbers of those who already do so, despite the lack of recognition.

From the late 1990s, we have seen many transsexual people simply ignoring society's conventions as regards the birthing and raising of children. Several transsexual men have chosen to withdraw from hormone therapy for a period of time in order to conceive and give birth to a child (Dylan More, 1998). Many more are raising children conceived by their female partners, as fathers. Some are freezing their eggs for possible implantation in the womb of a female partner or a surrogate mother, and many transsexual women are choosing to freeze their sperm for possible future use.

THE INTERNATIONAL BILL OF GENDER RIGHTS

The International Bill of Gender Rights (IBGR) is one way in which the trans community promotes the issues relating to the community's legal and social status. The most recent version as adopted in Houston, Texas, US, 17 June 1995 is a theoretical proposal that formulates basic human rights from a trans perspective. These rights are not seen as special rights, but rather as universal statements of human rights. None of the customary labels – gay, lesbian, bisexual, transgendered, transsexual, transvestite, bi-gendered, cross-dresser, etc – are used in the IBGR. There is only one label needed to qualify for all of these rights – be a human being.

The tenth right states:

> ... individuals shall not be denied the right to conceive, bear or adopt children, nor to nurture and have custody of children, nor to exercise parental capacity with respect to children, natural or adopted, on the basis of their own, their partner's, or their children's chromosomal sex, genitalia, assigned birth sex, initial gender role, or by virtue of a self-defined gender identity or the expression thereof. (ICTLEP, 1995.)

Thus, it states that the right to be a parent should not be dictated by gender identity, and that living in an oppositional gender role should not prevent the procreation, conception or bearing of children, dependent of course on ability. This means that an individual who lives and is legally recognised as a male, but who for some reason has not taken enough hormones nor undergone enough surgery to render it otherwise, could bear a child. This is not such a far-fetched concept: many transsexual men identify as gay and have penetrative sexual relationships. Similarly, many transsexual women identify as lesbians.

Should those who do not understand what it is to experience a gender identity that is discordant with the body decide whether the transgendered person experiences of life are not worthy enough to pass on? Research that has been done has shown that the children of transsexual parents are just as likely to grow up well-adjusted (and as heterosexual) as any other child (Green, 1974b). However, it becomes illogical to discuss the 'best interests' of the child if the child can never be born. Just as in eugenics, if the claim is made that transsexual people are not suitable for parenthood, then they are refused access to parenthood, and this supports the claim because there is no evidence to the contrary.

Sterilisation procedures are generally irreversible, and in gender reassignment, genital surgery which involves the expunging of the relevant tissues is all the more so. In the English case of *In Re D (A Minor) (Wardship: Sterilisation)*,[17] it was held, on interpretation, that any sterilisation performed

---

17 *In Re D (A Minor) (Wardship: Sterilisation)* [1976] 1 All ER 326.

in the absence of consent and for non-therapeutic reasons involves a deprivation of that right (Lee and Morgan, 1989, p 136). The IBGR argues for recognition of that basic human right in the 'revolutionary' framework of a unified humanity. Lee and Morgan consider that the argument that liberties are dependent upon usages that others consider reasonable or valuable is a very dangerous one, and they cite Bernard Williams:[18]

> ... there is no slippery slope more perilous than that extended by a concept which is falsely supposed not to be slippery. (Lee and Morgan, 1989, p 152, note 25.)

By assuming that the surgically reassigned transsexual person has voluntarily given up a right to reproduce begs the question. There is little, if any, scope for the giving or refusal of consent. The individual is faced with the lesser of two evils, a choice of choosing to live as a whole person or to reproduce and give life to another person at the cost of one's self. There is no real choice if we do not provide in law (or medicine) either a space in which the legal status change sometimes afforded to the gender reassigned does not require procedures demanding sterility or, alternatively, a universal framework in which sex or gender is no longer a delineator in law. The IBGR promotes a new vision of the world in which childbearing and child rearing is by and about the development of people rather than by and about the development of men and women. This vision is symbolic of the re-constructive project of the new trans community; going beyond the deconstructive enterprise of modernity, Feminist and Queer, all of which privilege sex and gender. Instead, it privileges the unity of humanity.

Science and society is changing all too rapidly for us to know now what will lie in the future, but it is not so long in the past that negative eugenics, the forced sterilisation of unfit, asocial groups of people was accepted medical practice in some states. Perhaps it is of interest here that sterility requirements for the transsexual person are features of the juridical systems of these countries rather than of states which might be seen to have a far worse human rights record, such as Turkey and South Africa. Undoubtedly, the discourses which led to the 'hygienic' practices of the past are still just bubbling under the surface. The trans person could be regarded as the ultimate non-being, neither man nor woman, a-gendered and hence asocial, therefore, a danger to all our futures. Yet, just like the rest of us, throughout history, they have been carrying their genes alongside ours:

> The only way to oppose eugenics is to ensure that human rights come first. The idea of scientifically manufacturing a set of people exclusively composed of individuals with certain characteristics must be outlawed because it runs counter to the dignity of human beings, who are unique, free and responsible

---

18 Williams, B, 'Which slopes are slippery?', in Lockwood, M (ed), *Moral Dilemmas in Modern Medicine*, 1985, Oxford: OUP, pp 126–37.

for their actions ... In the words of the American novelist Paul Auster, 'Each man is the entire world, bearing within his genes a memory of all mankind'. (Elnadi, 1994, p 5.)

CHAPTER 9

SEEKING A GENDERED ADOLESCENCE: LIABILITY AND ETHICS SURROUNDING ADOLESCENTS WITH GENDER DYSPHORIA[1]

Doctors face complex clinical questions and legal responsibilities when they are requested to provide puberty suppression drugs by adolescents who are gender dysphoric and who are indicating that in the long term, they will be requesting gender reassignment treatment. These young people often an express a desire to receive medical intervention in the short term: firstly, to prevent the development of secondary sexual characteristics. This request is made so that:

> ... female to male gender dysphoric adolescents will avoid the traumatic experience of menstruation and later avoid the major surgical procedures to remove breasts, which will have developed with puberty.

> ... male to female gender dysphoric adolescents will be able to avoid having their voice break and the long term social problems that will arise from living as an adult woman with a masculine voice, also the avoidance of future electrolysis to remove beard growth that will develop with puberty.

Secondly, to enable them to continue their education in a gender role that is more comfortable to them. This may not be completely in their proposed new gender role, but with the support of their schools and colleges, they may well be able to spend significant parts of their education being socially accepted by their peers as being a young transsexual. Thirdly, to allow them time, without dealing with the unwanted (and often hated) effects of puberty, to decide whether gender reassignment is the appropriate route for the adolescent in the long term.

In 1997, *The Sunday Times* reported that 'Children as young as 14 are receiving sex change treatment on the NHS' (Rogers, 1997). Suitably shocked in its tone, it was reported that there were an estimated 600 girls and boys, some as young as 7, who suffer gender identity disorders in Britain, and that the disclosure that a growing number of children were seeking treatment for gender dysphoria had resulted in an intense debate amongst medical specialists. The report continued:

> While some psychiatrists believe children should be helped to change sex early, others insist that they should only take that decision after reaching maturity.

The article, which highlighted this issue, said that one psychiatrist, Russell Reid:

---

1   Co-author Catherine Downs. This essay was first published in Heinze, E, *Of Innocence and Autonomy: Children, Sex and Human Rights*, 2000, Aldershot: Dartmouth.

... believes that children as young as 13 should be offered preliminary drug treatment to prevent puberty,

whereas Dominic Di Cegli, who runs the Portman Clinic Gender Identity Development Clinic, stated that:

... up to 1 in 4 of the teenagers who at 14 seemed convinced of their desire to change sex would later change their minds.

It is important to read these reports, as all newspaper reports, with suitable cynicism. However, it would be foolish to say that the last five years have not seen a significant increase in the number of adolescent children, with the support and guidance of their parents, seeking medical help of some sort to deal with their perceived gender dysphoria.

There are several reasons for this here in the UK. Recently, there has been an increased awareness, in society, of transsexuality and gender identity disorders. Further, there has developed the knowledge that gender identity disorders can be suffered by anyone from any social group, or at any age. Much of this awareness has been achieved through the news coverage of the 1990s campaigns undertaken by groups such as Press For Change and the Gender Trust. There has also been increased access to resources and information through helplines and websites such as those of the Gender Trust. But in particular, for young people, there have been three significant events.

The first of these is the creation, in 1989, of a clinic, initially at St George's Hospital in London and led by Dr Dominic Di Cegli, which provides a service for young people with gender dysphoria (Di Cegli, 1992, p 1). Secondly, in 1996, Channel 4 screened a two-part film in a series entitled *The Decision*.[2] The film concerned three ftm transsexuals and their trip to Holland to look at the treatment and service provided by the team at the Gender Clinic at the Free University of Amsterdam. The film included a young female to male transsexual, 'Fredd', aged 13, and showed his supportive parents as they sought some way of providing Fredd with support through his difficult adolescence. The film highlighted and contrasted the treatment regime of the London Gender Identity Development Clinic for adolescents, under Dr Di Cegli, with the treatment provided to young people at the Free University Gender Clinic under Dr Peggy Cohen-Kettenis. It showed several young Dutch female to male transsexuals who had started pubertal suppression treatment at the ages of 13 and 14 in order to prevent unwanted changes to their secondary sexual characteristics. When aged 16 or 17, they had gone on to start active hormone therapy to change their secondary sex characteristics to those of their chosen gender role, followed by surgical gender reassignment surgery from the age of 18. It showed them as content and fulfilled, handsome young men. The third event of significance was the setting up of a support group, Mermaids, for children and teenagers who have gender identity

---

2   Windfall Films, *The Decision*, 6 February 1996, 13 February 1996, Channel 4 Television.

disorders. The group also aims to support their families, their friends and the professionals who work with them. Mermaids has enabled the networking of young people and their families and the realisation that their experiences are not unique. It has also enabled young people and their parents to compare treatment regimes and the alternative approaches taken by doctors working in this field.

As a result of these three events, clinicians are now faced with, in young adolescents with gender dysphoria, a well informed patient group who know what they are asking for before attending a clinic. Often, this patient group has the full support of their parents in their request for active medical intervention to support a medical plan, which will ultimately lead to gender reassignment.

THERAPY OR CURE

Generally, clinicians treating young people who display gender dysphoric behaviour see their therapeutic role, through early intervention, as the prevention of later problems. This is achieved by developing a framework in which the family, the young person and other interested parties, for example, the school, can find ways of dealing with and understanding the child's behaviour so that it does not become an excessive burden to the child or the family (Zucker and Bradley, 1995, p 269). The fundamental question the clinician must address is: 'What would be the right treatment to give a child with such a syndrome?' This question is not asked simply because of the clinician's duty of care to the patient. Because there are still so many social stigmas associated with gender dysphoria and gender reassignment, the clinician may find themselves facing a personal crisis as to what is the best treatment for a young person in the light of this social stigma.

There are three possible routes when it comes to treating young people with gender dysphoria. These may be simply categorised as follows (though they may be combined):

- The clinician will attempt to 'cure' the young person of their gender identity problem, so ensuring that they do not grow up into a transsexual adult.

- The clinician will help reconcile the young person and their family with the behaviour and social stigma that results from the gender identity problem, so enabling the young person to have some good experiences of adolescence. This aims to allow suppression of any active intervention until the young person is an adult. Quite often, such an approach will involve friends, the school authorities, etc, so that the alternative gender behaviour of the young person is not treated punitively, albeit that it may not be encouraged.

• The clinician provides active medical intervention, initially by postponing puberty, which would allow the young person to more easily to undergo hormonal or gender reassignment at a later stage if that is their chosen path.

Though, undoubtedly, there are still some clinicians who still attempt to 'cure' patients with gender dysphoria, this is becoming an increasingly outmoded approach. In the case of adults presenting for gender reassignment treatment, it has become increasingly acknowledged that 'it is exclusively and primarily the person himself or herself who will decide for sex reassignment' (Pfafflin, in Bullough and Bullough, 1993, p 342). In other words, although it is possible for clinicians to participate in the diagnosis of gender dysphoria, it is the patient who will ascertain, for themselves, whether it is appropriate to continue to full gender reassignment. Thus, the primary role of therapists and counsellors becomes one of ensuring that the patient is fully informed of both the possibilities and risks of gender reassignment treatment, so that they may make an informed decision. Yet, when considering young people, some clinicians view the role of the therapist as not merely to provide information. Nor is it just to provide liaison psychiatric services to deal with the social stigmatisation processes that are linked with cross-gender behaviour, but that, as expert clinicians, they also have a role in the prevention of transsexualism in adulthood. Zucker and Bradley state this as being:

> ... so obviously clinically valid and consistent with the ethics of our time that they constitute sufficient justification for therapeutic intervention. (Zucker and Bradley, 1995, p 269.)

This is despite also arguing, in the same book, that any aims of treatment designed to prevent adult homosexuality are far more problematic. Though Zucker and Bradley go on to state that there are simply no studies demonstrating that therapeutic intervention in childhood alters the developmental path to either transsexualism or homosexuality, they do not in fact equate the two states as far as the clinician's therapeutic goal. Their apparent inconsistency sums up the problem faced by young people when seeking intervention from clinics. Clinicians are gatekeepers to the hormonal and surgical reassignment that many young people with gender dysphoria seek as a solution to their problems. Whereas the adult transsexual is, at least nowadays, acknowledged as being someone who decides whether or not to undergo reassignment, young people are faced with a clinical situation wherein doctors still feel a cultural imperative to 'cure' them.

Consequently, a significant amount of their clinic experience (and that of the parents who accompany them) is perceived as 'stalling tactics' and 'lies' on the part of doctors. These delays are perceived as existing simply in order to delay the individual's quest for active treatment leading to gender reassignment, whilst the doctors instead seek to cure them.[3] These stalling

---

3   L Howse, Children with GID versus the Medical Profession (12 February 1998), unpublished personal comment.

processes are also perceived as existing even when clinicians are aware of the futility of attempting to cure their patients, and instead are seeking to help with the social problems associated with gender identity problems. As a result, there is often a long delay in which distress and misery is undergone by the adolescent patient and their parents, whilst puberty advances and nothing appears to be happening to prevent the inevitable arrival of adult transsexual treatment and its associated problems.

It is acknowledged that hormonal or other medical interventions are inappropriate in pre-pubertal children,[4] but there may be medical options that clinicians might consider in young people under the age of majority. However, in the second route, because adolescence is viewed as a time when many aspects of identity are still being developed, many professionals fear that by 'interfering' with gender identity formation and gender role performance, they may cause more problems than they resolve (Cohen-Kettenis and van Goozen, 1997, p 263). What we see is a situation wherein the doctor decides that the adolescent is 'simply not old enough' to make up their own mind as to whether pubertal suppression would be appropriate. This is condensed into the view that any young person with gender dysphoria is not able to consent to such treatment until they are at least 18 years old. This is a particularly problematic area as regards any young person's right to access treatment and this will be considered in the second part of this chapter.

The third routeway seeks, in the cases of those children who have shown consistent and extreme patterns of gender dysphoria with a strong cross-gender identification, to provide an alternative that leads to hormonal and gender reassignment in early adulthood. The arguments for taking this path are that by starting some sort of active intervention, it prevents unnecessary feelings of hopelessness whilst the young person waits for adulthood and 'permission' to start reassignment. It also improves greatly the prospects of an enhanced physical appearance in the new gender role they will adopt, and it prevents the onset of permanent secondary sexual characteristics, such as a deep voice in male to female transsexuals, which would be blight their future life in their new gender role. It has been shown in numerous follow-up studies that the earlier gender reassignment is commenced, the greater the chance of a favourable post-operative outcome (Cohen-Kettenis and van Goozen, 1997, p 264). This route in the Amsterdam clinic is only offered to those young people with a very favourable prognosis. The young person must be psychologically stable, they must have a lifelong, extreme and complete cross-gender identification, and they must function well with good family and social support. The initial treatment afforded to an adolescent who meets

---

4   See the studies of Green, R, *The 'Sissy Boy Syndrome' and the Development of Homosexuality*, 1987, New Haven: Yale University Press; also Zuger, B, 'Early effeminate behaviour in boys: outcome and significance for homosexuality' (1984) 172 Journal of Nervous and Mental Disease 90–97.

these clinical requirements involves providing pubertal suppression hormones that block the actions of sex steroids in a reversible manner, followed by full non-reversible hormone treatment at the age of 18. If the patient has in the meantime concluded a favourable 'real-life test' (that is, has lived in their new gender role successfully and happily for at least one year), then consideration will be given to any request for surgical reassignment. This model of treatment has been tried with several adolescents in the Gender Clinic of the Free University Hospital in Amsterdam, with reported success; however, also alongside a call for many more follow-up and prospective studies (Cohen-Kettenis and van Goozen, 1997, p 271).

The real issue is on what basis does a doctor chooses which route to take? What are the ethical questions that doctors should consider when deciding which of these three routes to follow with the young adolescent with a confirmed desire for gender reassignment? And, if the doctor because of his/her clinical judgment chooses to either attempt a 'cure' of the patient or to delay active treatment, what are the possible legal consequences if the patient or their family chooses, at some later stage, to sue the clinician because they deem them to have led to unnecessary suffering? This is perfectly possible in a world where hormonal and surgical gender reassignment is increasingly accepted as being the only solution to the transsexual person's plight and in which, furthermore, the medical profession's own follow-up studies have shown a consistent 97 to 99% success rate in the case of those people reassigned (Pfafflin, in Bockting and Coleman, 1992, pp 69–86).

It could be argued that where young people, with the support of their parents, seek active intervention in these cases, if a doctor chooses either of the first two routes, they may well be leaving themselves open to litigation in the future unless they have clarified the questions regarding clinical judgment leading to refusal. We may well reach situations where, for example, an ftm transsexual man may decide that, because of a refusal to treat them whilst younger, they were forced to undergo unnecessary breast reduction surgery and that they deserve compensation for their pain and suffering. An mtf transsexual woman may well sue for the costs they have incurred in obtaining beard reduction through electrolysis, and what if a parent sues because their child was one of the small percentage of untreated transsexual people who committed suicide? These are situations wherein doctors may be called upon to justify the route they took. In particular, we wish to address the legal issues surrounding that all too often heard phrase: 'well of course young people, aged 14 to 17, are simply not old enough to decide whether they are transsexual.' This is almost certainly insufficient legal justification for the withholding of pubertal suppression treatment. The dilemmas that doctors face in these circumstances are undoubtedly difficult, the patients are desperate, and social pressure is great. This is all the more reason for clinicians to look carefully at the problems involved in either refusing or providing pubertal suppression treatment and ensuring that they have not only safeguarded their patient's best interests, but that they have made clinical judgments of the highest standards.

LEGAL ISSUES OF CONSENT

The first legal issue to be considered is that of consent to treatment. The first thing to say is that, in most of these cases, consent to treatment will *not* be an issue. A healthcare professional cannot treat any patient of full capacity without receiving consent from them to that treatment. If medical treatment is provided without informed consent having been obtained, the professional is liable to be sued in tort,[5] either for trespass or for negligence, and may even be guilty of criminal assault. Children under 18 are *generally* deemed incapable of giving consent to treatment because of their minority. Health professionals have to rely on consent being given by their parents or under the inherent jurisdiction of the court following an application to court. However, in the case of older children who are still under 18, there are two main ways in which they, if they have full mental capacity, can give consent to their own treatment.

For minors in the age group of 16–18, s 8(1) of the Family Law Reform Act 1969 lowers the age at which an individual can give consent to medical treatment from 18 to 16. For the purposes of consent to medical treatment, consent by a minor aged 16 or above 'shall be as effective as it would be if he were of full age'. The minor can only consent to certain kinds of treatment, namely surgical, medical or dental treatment including, according to subsection (2), diagnostic and ancillary procedures. The subsections do not make it clear whether the treatment must only be therapeutic or whether it also includes non-therapeutic treatment, which is arguably the definition of treatment for transsexual people (McMullen and Whittle, 1994, p 85). The only case in which s 8 of the Family Law Reform Act has been discussed is *Re W*.[6] In this case, the suggestion by Nolan LJ was that the phrase 'surgical medical or dental treatment' is used in a narrow sense in the Act because of the need in subsection (2) to elaborate by including for clarification diagnostic and ancillary procedures. If s 8 is limited by this narrow approach to therapeutic treatment only, then there may be restrictions on the treatment to which those aged 16 to 18 can give consent. However, it is not clear whether this restrictive interpretation is correct and these patients may still be able to rely on giving effective consent under s 8 of the Act.

Minors who are under 16 can give effective consent to treatment under the common law following the decision in *Gillick v West Norfolk and Wisbech AHA*.[7]

---

5   *Chatterton v Gerson* [1981] 1 All ER 257.

6   *Re W (A Minor)* [1992] 4 All ER 627.

7   *Gillick v West Norfolk and Wisbech AHA* [1986] AC 112.

This case established that children under 16 can give a valid consent to medical treatment without parental knowledge or consent, provided that the doctor treating them is satisfied that they understand the nature of the proposed treatment. There are no clear-cut grounds as to at what age this independent right comes into existence, but the test put forward by Lord Scarman is that a child must have 'sufficient understanding and intelligence to enable him or her to understand fully what is proposed'.[8] There are problems in putting the *Gillick* test into practice because of its subjectivity and the lack of clarity in the House of Lords' decision as to the actual test to be applied. Lord Scarman indicated at least in relation to contraceptive treatment, although the test must apply to other kinds of treatment, that the minor must understand not only the nature of the medical advice regarding his or her treatment but also be mature and understand the family, moral and social issues involved. Lord Fraser indicated that the patient must be capable of understanding the doctor's advice. These tests are often hard to satisfy and in fact, adults of full capacity do not have to show the same level of understanding that adolescents must show, when they consent to treatment.

Therefore, it is possible that the patients, if they are 16 or older, can give consent to treatment in exercise of their statutory right under the Family Law Reform Act 1969. If they are under 16, then they may be *Gillick* competent and still be able to give effective consent to treatment under the common law. Even if they are under 16 and not assessed as *Gillick* competent, then their parents can give consent to treatment on their behalf. Importantly, lack of parental consent should not affect the validity of the consent given by the minor either under statute or the *Gillick* test. Difficulties with regard to the issue of consent will therefore only arise in cases where the patient's parents do not consent to the treatment *and* the patient is under 16 *and* not assessed as being *Gillick* competent. In reality, in most of the cases involving gender dysphoric adolescents, the parents of these patients support their child's desires for treatment and in many cases are also prepared to pay for the treatment abroad if necessary.

However, even if consent to treatment is not a real problem, the decision whether to treat at all and the kind of treatment to be administered is a difficult issue, as it depends on the exercise of the doctor's professional judgment. In *Re J*,[9] it was held that a doctor can never be forced by the courts to administer a particular kind of treatment contrary to their professional clinical judgment. In this case, after an accident, a baby was acutely handicapped. The medical staff did not want to put the baby on a ventilator but the mother did. The mother was unsuccessful in trying to force the medical staff to give her baby the treatment that she wanted, even though she

---

8   *Ibid, per* Lord Scarman, p 186.

9   *Re J* [1992] 4 All ER 614; [1992] 2 FLR 165.

had a medical expert who supported giving that treatment. Lord Donaldson said that doctors should be free to treat in accordance with their best clinical judgment, and for the court to intervene:

> ... would require the practitioner to act contrary to the fundamental duty which he owed to his patient ... which was to treat the patient in accordance with his own best clinical judgment.[10]

Notwithstanding, the Court of Appeal decided against overruling the decision of a mother concerning medical treatment for her child. In *Re T*,[11] the mother of a small child did not want him to undergo a liver transplant even though medical opinion favoured such treatment. This involved a slightly different issue, in that the mother did not want access to treatment, she wanted to be able to refuse a certain kind of treatment on behalf of her child. However, Butler-Sloss LJ held that the welfare of the child must be the paramount consideration even if, in this particularly acute case, that meant allowing the mother to decide on her child's future treatment rather than automatically making a decision to prolong life. The decision affirms the 'welfare of the child' test and if followed, may indicate greater recognition being taken of parents' wishes. In general, though, it seems that patients are dependent on whether or not a doctor is willing to administer a certain kind of treatment. The courts will not usually intervene to force doctors to administer any particular treatment or to administer one form of treatment in preference to another regardless of the wishes of the patient or their parents.

The problem in the cases of gender dysphoric adolescents is not one of access to treatment *per se*, but access to a specific form of treatment. Specific forms of treatment have to be recommended and administered by the patient's doctor. If one particular doctor refuses to give the treatment that a patient wants, it is usually open to a patient to try and seek a second opinion in order to gain access to that treatment. If there is no doctor available in this country who would be prepared to treat these patients by the third route referred to earlier, this gives the patients no choice about the treatment that they are given. However, we do know that there are doctors in the Netherlands who are prepared to administer this treatment. As this is the case then, it may be possible for patients to question the clinical judgment of doctors in this country who are unwilling to give such treatment when colleagues abroad are giving this kind of treatment and have been doing so for a number of years.

Patients seeking to establish negligence need to establish that their doctor owes them a duty of care. Once they have been accepted as a patient (in the case of the specialist) or have been registered with a general practitioner and sought treatment, then this duty of care is established. The law of negligence

---

10 *Ibid*, p 615H.
11 *Re T* [1997] 1 WLR 242, CA.

requires that healthcare professionals exercise reasonable care in the performance of their duties. The standards expected of a reasonable professional were examined in *Bolam v Friern HMC*.[12] The standard expected is:

... to act in accordance with a practice accepted as proper by a responsible body of medical men skilled in that particular art.

Even if there are different practices which take different views of the appropriate mode of treatment, then a healthcare professional will not be condemned by acting in one way rather than another, provided that they can justify the approach that they have taken.[13] A body of skilled and experienced doctors must correctly accept the practice adopted as proper.[14] Even though the *Bolam* test can be criticised, in that it allows doctors to set the standard of treatment that they are to give and as such is very paternalistic, it still sets a high standard. Doctors needing to show standards of excellence within their field of specialism must now demonstrate an awareness of current practices and this must, in this modern age, obviously include research and work carried on outside the UK. The introduction of evidence based medicine which requires compliance with treatment on the basis of research evidence further makes it difficult to justify failing to follow up-to-date procedures and treatments which are supported by research findings. Doctors may justifiably be cautious in giving new forms of treatment, but if a particular new approach to treatment has the support of research findings, then it may be difficult to justify not following this new approach. This will be relevant in the case of the gender dysphoric adolescent. The clinic in the Netherlands does, in some cases which have been carefully selected on the basis of prognosis and individual circumstances, offer this different and novel kind of treatment and this has been shown to be successful over a number of years (Cohen-Kettenis and van Goozen, 1998).

Any action in negligence would be taken on the basis of the doctor or NHS Trust failing to give the most effective and up-to-date treatment for this syndrome and any subsequent loss arising from this failure to treat effectively. A patient trying to sue for compensation for a doctor's negligence would have to establish causation. They would need evidence that failure to treat, in a way that they allege would have been more effective, has caused or contributed to the progress of their particular medical condition and thereby caused loss. This may be difficult to establish, but doctors need to be aware of the possibility of legal actions for negligence and take steps to ensure that they have considered the most appropriate treatment for each individual patient.

12 *Bolam v Friern Hospital Management Committee* [1957] 2 All ER 118.
13 *Maynard v West Midlands Regional Health Authority* [1985] 1 All ER 635.
14 *Sidaway v Board of Governors of the Bethlem Royal and the Maudsley Hospital* [1985] 2 WLR 480.

Hospital ethics committees may also have a role to play in the decision-making process concerning treatment available for patients. In *R v Ethical Committee of St Mary's Hospital ex p H*,[15] the judge stated that the role of an ethics committee was not to decide on particular cases but to provide a forum for discussion amongst professionals in an informal context. The only situation in which the advice given by the ethics committee would be subject to legal scrutiny would be if it were to advise that a section of the population should be refused treatment based on, for example, race or religion. Any ethics committee, in these cases of treatment for gender dysphoric adolescents, needs to ensure that doctors can explain the clinical rationale behind decision. Doctors should seek the advice of the ethical committee on whether or not to treat a gender dysphoric adolescent and discuss the appropriate form of treatment on an individual case basis. A prudent doctor should be able to justify the clinical approach taken in the light of current practice in their field of specialism. This must include taking into account recent developments, research and treatment in other countries and at other clinics. A failure to act in accordance with successful new techniques may become more difficult to justify as more research evidence becomes available to support these new approaches to treatment. Patients are reliant on their doctors to give them the most appropriate and effective treatment for their condition and their specific personal circumstances. A doctor must be able to demonstrate that they have considered what is the most relevant treatment for each individual patient. The obvious risk in failing to demonstrate that each patient has been considered individually and that there is no blanket ban on treatment is that of being sued for negligence if the patient suffers harm as a result of a policy of non-treatment.

At the beginning of this chapter, three possible methods of treatment for adolescents with gender identity problems were considered. The first route of treatment has been shown not to work and should never be recommended by a doctor or endorsed by a hospital ethics committee. The second should only be used if it can be shown to be therapeutically beneficial for a particular patient. As shown, there is no need to wait until the patient is 18 to obtain an effective consent to treatment, if the third route is requested. As such, the 'holding' approach which delays any active intervention and treatment should only be used as a positive choice if it is appropriate for an individual patient. If the second route is being adopted, then the ethics committee, which clinicians refer to for guidance, may need to consider developing guidelines such as those proposed below, bearing in mind the overall requirement to consider the welfare of the child.

---

15   *R v Ethical Committee of St Mary's Hospital ex p H* [1988] 1 FLR 512; (1988) 137 NLJ 1038.

PROPOSED GUIDELINES FOR THE TREATMENT OF ADOLESCENTS REQUESTING PUBERTAL-SUPPRESSION TREATMENT

When considering treatment for a gender dysphoric young person who has a favourable prognosis for gender reassignment as an adult and who has parental support for such treatment, a doctor should ask the following questions:

- What treatment is the preferred treatment of the patient and their parents? Is there a clinical reason not to follow their choice?

- What is the likely prognosis for this patient? Is there a clear indication that they are unlikely to go on and seek gender reassignment as an adult?

- Can the doctor justify delaying access to pubertal suppression treatment in this particular patient's case, bearing in mind the unhappy nature of their adolescent years and that such treatment is entirely reversible?

- Would the non-provision of such treatment actually prove beneficial for this particular patient?

- Has the clinician ensured that the correct procedures will be used if pubertal suppression treatment is not given?

Any decision must consider the age of child and the likely support they will receive for their cross-gender lifestyle from their parents, school or college, friends, etc.

This leaves us with the third route of treatment, which should be used in all cases unless there are positive reasons for choosing the second route. If this mode of treatment is not being used, then it is necessary to show that the second route of treatment is therapeutically beneficial, as we know that the first route of treatment can never be therapeutically beneficial.

CONCLUSION

Doctors, and the ethics committees advising them, must think very carefully before deciding to refuse pubertal suppression treatment to any gender dysphoric adolescent who has a good prognosis for future gender reassignment treatment. The question of whether an adolescent is old enough to consent is generally a 'red herring'. Often, the patient's parents consent to pubertal suppression treatment and that parental consent then overrides any issue of the child's competence, so the issues of age and consent must be discarded, whether an adolescent is judged to be *Gillick* competent or not.

In deciding what path to take in the treatment of these adolescents, clinicians increasingly need to consider the possibility of future litigation for refusal to treat. It is recommend that the clinician must ask themselves three questions before referring to the ethics committee for advice:

(1) Is there any clinical basis for refusing treatment because this individual can be cured of their gender dysphoria?

The answer to this, at present, is no. Severe gender dysphoria is currently assessed as not being susceptible to any treatment other than hormonal (and surgical) gender reassignment:

(2) Is valid consent to the treatment available from either the adolescent or the adolescent's parents?

If an adolescent's parent consents to such treatment, then regardless of the child's level of competence to consent, pubertal suppression treatment should not be refused unless there are specific contra-indications. If parents refuse their consent, then an adolescent's competence, under the rules in *Gillick*, should be assessed if they are under 16. If over 16, their competence should be assessed according to s 8 of the Family Law Reform Act:

(3) Are there specific contra-indications to pubertal suppression treatment in this patient? These might be that the adolescent does not have extreme cross-gender identification, or they do not function well socially (apart from any anxiety or depression caused by the social stigma resulting from their cross gender identification).

If no, then pubertal suppression treatment should be provided. It is reversible, it relieves anxiety and distress and, perhaps importantly for the clinician involved, it removes the threat of possible future litigation as a result of the consequences of failing to provide such treatment.

The well documented experiences of the Dutch model of treatment have shown that this particular form of treatment is, if clinically indicated, a therapeutic approach to the treatment of young people with gender dysphoria.[16] The alternatives have, to date, not been shown to effect anything other than continuing distress in the individual adolescents, and to allow the development of secondary sex characteristics which will require extensive, painful and expensive medical intervention in later life. Gender reassignment treatment is no longer a medical practice in its infancy, having been initiated at the end of the 19th century and provided regularly since the late 1960s. The prognosis for patients is excellent and it could be said that the younger they are allowed to commence some sort of treatment and cross-gender lifestyle, the better. However, the social stigmas associated with gender reassignment, and the resulting concerns of those clinicians that provide it, are still great.

---

16 See the studies of Cohen-Kettenis and van Goozen, 1997, 1998, also Cohen, L, de Ruiter, LC, Ringleberg, H and Cohen-Kettenis, PT, 'Psychological functioning of adolescent transsexuals: personality and psychopathology' (1997) 53(2) Journal of Clinical Psychology 187–96.

Doctors must step back from their own prejudices and fears. They need to assess the best long term medical interests of an adolescent patient before refusing active intervention. Seeking guidance from their ethics committee would ensure they have shown why they have chosen a particular route, its benefits to the patient and, in the long term, this process of justification could safeguard the clinician and health authorities from potential litigation. It will also safeguard the individual patient and ensure that they receive a treatment plan best suited to their clinical and social needs.

CHAPTER 10

EUROPEAN TRANSGENDER RIGHTS: NEW IDENTITY POLITICS FOR A NEW AGE

It would be very easy to think that over the last 50 years, 'human rights' campaigning and lobbying in Europe would have resolved all the problems and issues faced by disadvantaged groups – whether because of ethnicity, skin colour, religion or sex. In fact, we know this not to be true, and the concepts surrounding human rights are constantly being expanded. In particular, the last 10 years have seen a rapid rise in the campaigning and lobbying of new community groups as more and more people start to claim new political identities such as disabled, queer and transgender. These new identities have led to people who belong to those groups developing:

- a community consciousness;

- an awareness of disadvantage based upon those identities;

- an awareness that those disadvantages affect more parts of life than originally thought. For example, for gay people, it is not just about equalising the age of consent for same-sex relationships, but also about partnership rights such as pension protection. For disabled people it is not just about equal access to public buildings, but about the right to have workplace protection;

- a use of the European institutions to tackle those disadvantages.

In Europe, the two institutions seen as having the judicial ability to rectify these problems at the level of the nation state are the European Court of Justice (ECJ), the court of the European Community (EC) and the European Court of Human Rights (ECHR), the court of the signatories to the European Convention on Human Rights. In recent years, we have seen all sorts of disadvantaged groups deliberately developing cases which could be referred to one or other of these courts.

First, though, we must look at people's understanding of what these two courts do. There is a public consciousness in Europe that the EC is not just about economic freedoms, but is also about social improvement. The general public in Europe looks to the European Courts as providing justice at a level above and beyond the requirements of the nation state; they look to Europe to set standards that are higher than can be achieved at home. At the same time, of course, they perpetually moan about the high standards that are being set in Europe – especially when it comes to the state of a nation's sausages.

Many members of the public confuse the two courts. The ECJ and the ECHR are often seen as being one and the same, and even if different, there is little recognition of their differing roles. Thus, the public often sees a decision from one as having the same meaning and legal result as a decision from the other. This is plainly not the case, as we shall see later, but in terms of changing public awareness of what sorts of discrimination or prejudice are socially acceptable and what aren't, the fact that the two courts are seen as being one and the same means that at ground 'public' level, the effect is the same. A decision from either means that people's attitudes are changed, their social practices adjusted and to those involved in campaigning for identity based 'human rights', the end result is a huge shift in public awareness and a great step forward to achieving the equality and respect they are fighting for.

Initially, it would seem that issues of discrimination, especially at the level of the state, should be considered in the ECHR. Article 14 of the Convention provides that all the other articles of the Convention should be met without any discrimination on grounds of sex, race, colour, language, religion, political or other opinion, national or social origin, property, birth or other status. And in fact, many minority groups did indeed, throughout the 1980s, seek rectification of social disadvantage through the ECHR. One of these groups was the newly formed trans community. However, from the first case presented to the ECHR by *38 Transsexuals v Italy*[1] in 1981 through to the last decision before that in *Goodwin and I v UK*,[2] they have in fact found the Court to be singularly ineffective in providing a resolution to the problems and discriminations they face. In the 1990s, there was an apparent victory by a transsexual woman in the ECHR: the case of *B v France*.[3] It was held that the French government must recognise transsexual people as being of their new sex for social purposes. However, the French government have simply gone on to refuse virtually all gender reassignment treatment in France, so making effective sex change impossible. They have then refused to recognise any transsexual person treated abroad, and they have insisted that transsexual people make individual applications to the French courts every time they want any piece of documentation changed, if they want to get married, if they wish to make under a claim under the rules of succession. This means that their lives become bound up in court procedures reminiscent of Dickens's Chancery in *Bleak House*.

The remainder of cases brought by transsexual people before the ECHR, until the decision in *Goodwin and I v UK*, have gone on to fail. Most of these cases have concerned the 'traditional' transsexual person and what might be considered the traditional issues: the right to change birth certificates to recognise the new sex and the right to marry in the new sex role.

---

1   *38 Transsexuals v Italy*, Application No 9420/81 (1981) ECHR.
2   *Christine Goodwin v UK*, Application No 28957/95 (1995) ECHR; *I v UK*, Application No 25608/94 (1994) ECHR.
3   *B v France* (1992) ECHR, Series A, No 57.

In 1995, I wrote that:

> ... though transsexuals are seeking a unique set of freedoms that are related to the process of undergoing gender reassignment or assertion, they are not seeking a new set of rights. Transsexuals are seeking for the law to acknowledge that they have rights, not as transsexuals, but as men and women who have finally become appropriately recognisable through medical intervention. (Whittle, in Bullough *et al*, 1997, p 443.)

My view that transsexuals are seeking a set of freedoms related to gender assertion has not changed, but I would now argue that the identity politics of transsexual people as a subgroup of the larger trans community has shifted considerably. They are no longer asking the law to recognise them simply as men and women, but rather they are seeking for the law to recognise them as trans men and trans women – a status that goes beyond the dichotomous structures of sex and gender roles recognised within and by the law (see Chapter 1). This will be evident in the following section which aims to explain and analyse the early cases dealt with under the ECHR, to contextualise them and finally to explain how human rights issues in this field have evolved beyond the traditional stereotypes, to encompass basic questions concerning recognition of the civil status of members of the trans community.

CLAIMING A LEGAL STATUS

It would be facile to say that the trans community wishes to be recognised as having a unique position, a third gender or rainbow gendered approach to their legal status. The massive paradigm shift within the trans community of the last few years may have seen a move from claims of rights within gender roles to claims of needs regarding the expression of gender roles, but there is a pragmatic acceptance that gender roles, as defined by those outside of the community, still exist. Most importantly though, within the community itself, as we move into the new millennium, members no longer privilege 'passing', the ability to hide a transsexual identity in a new gender role. Passing had been, for over 50 years, the defining political movement in transsexual identity politics. This could be seen in the demands for birth certificate and identity card amendment along with the right to marry, in the 'transsexual' cases before the ECHR in the 1970s and 1980s.[4]

To date, all of the applications in the transsexual cases have claimed a violation of Art 8 of the Convention and all have in essence sought an identical solution: the legal recognition of their true gender identity (after

---

4   *Van Oosterwijk v Belgium* (1980) ECHR, Series A, No 40; *Rees v UK* (1986) ECHR, Series A, No 106; *Cossey v UK* (1990) ECHR, Series A, No 184; *B v France* (1992) ECHR, Series A, No 57.

gender reassignment) in all civil status documents, whether birth certificate or identity card. Article 8 of the Convention states:

(1) Everyone has the right to respect for his private and family life, his home and his correspondence.

(2) There shall be no interference by a public authority with the exercise of this right except such as is in accordance with the law and is necessary in a democratic society in the interests of national security, public safety or the economic well being of the country, for the prevention of disorder or crime, for the protection of health or morals, or for the protection of the rights and freedoms of others.

Until very recently (in *X, Y and Z v UK*[5] and *Roetzheim v Germany*[6]), the cases have demanded that transsexual men and women are issued with new civil documentation that recognises them as non-transsexual men and women. This relies upon the state accepting a positive obligation to appear to recognise as a fact something that many have argued is a fiction, or if not a fiction, then at the very least an assertion based on scant scientific evidence.

This call for a response to a positive obligation arises out of a possible interpretation of para 1 of Art 8 of the Convention. Paragraph 2 of Art 8 appears to imply that public authorities simply have a duty not to interfere with private and family life, home and correspondence. But para 1, which stipulates the right to 'respect for private and family life', has been interpreted by the Court and the Commission 'as a basis for expanding the duties in Art 8(1)', thus giving rise to a state's possible positive obligations to fulfil its duty under Art 8.[7] The Court itself has stated:

[Article 8] does not merely compel the state to abstain from ... interference: in addition to this primarily negative undertaking, there may be positive obligations inherent in the effective respect for private and family life.[8]

The extent of the state's possible positive obligations under Art 8 in the 'transsexual' cases by the ECHR has proved to be a moot point. In *Van Oosterwijk v Belgium*,[9] the Court upheld, by 13 to 4, the Belgium government's position of 'non-exhaustion of domestic remedies', despite the fact that there was no indication that domestic remedies could in any way resolve the problems faced by the transsexual applicant, as was pointed out by the dissenting judges. In *Rees v UK*,[10] the Court held, by 12 votes to 3, that an amendment of the applicant's birth certificate would impose new duties on the state and the rest of the population, by insisting that they recognise current

5   *X, Y and Z v UK* (1997) 24 EHRR 143, ECHR, www.echr.coe.int.
6   *Roetzheim v Germany*, Application No 31177/96 (1997) ECHR.
7   *Kroon and Others v Netherlands* (1994) ECHR, Series C, No 297.
8   *X and Y v Netherlands* (1985) ECHR, Series A, No 91, para 23.
9   *Van Oosterwijk v Belgium* (1980) ECHR, Series A, No 40.
10 *Rees v UK* (1986) ECHR, Series A, No 106.

civil status rather than historical record, and that the Court could not impose duties of such magnitude.

In *Cossey v UK*, the Court refused to distinguish this case from *Rees*, preferring instead to consider whether there were persuasive reasons for departing from its previous decision. By 10 to 8, the Court re-iterated that the refusal to amend the applicant's birth certificate, or to allow her to marry a member of the opposite gender, did not constitute an interference with her private life. The Court said that the applicant was invoking a positive obligation, and this obligation was subject to the wide margin of appreciation afforded to the differing practices of member states, that is, the striking of a fair balance between the general interests of the community and the interests of the applicant. In this case, it was held that although there had been some social changes, the nation state had not contravened its obligations under the Convention.

All of these cases have concerned the 'traditional' transsexual person and what might be considered the traditional issues: privacy and marriage. However, the next UK case posed the questions differently. *X, Y and Z v UK* presented an alternative way for the Court to look at the civil status of the transsexual. It cited Art 8 and also Art 14, which reads as follows:

> The enjoyment of the rights and freedoms set forth in the Convention shall be secured without discrimination on any ground such as sex, race, colour, language, religion, political or other opinion, national or social origin, association with a national minority, property, birth or other status.

The case concerned a transsexual man, X, his partner, Y and her birth child, Z, who had been conceived using donor insemination. The family had been refused permission to register X as the father of Z on her birth certificate, on the basis that only a biological male could register as the father of a donor inseminated child, albeit not biologically related. The family invoked Art 8, arguing that it had been contravened in relation to family privacy. They did not request that X be recognised as a man, or that he be allowed to marry a woman. But they were hoping that if he could be recognised as the father of Z, then the UK government would be obliged to consider the other two issues.

The Court unanimously decided that Article 8 was applicable in this case as they considered that *de facto*, family ties did exist between the three applicants, despite arguments to the contrary by the UK government. However, did this mean that the state had a positive obligation to recognise the *de facto* family, through civil registration procedures? The Court, most unfortunately, went on to say that there was little common ground amongst the member states of the Council of Europe as to whether any non-biological father should be recorded on donor inseminated children's birth certificates. Accordingly, as there was no common European standard with regard to the granting of parental rights to transsexuals, then the law here was in a transitional stage, thus, states must be allowed a wide margin of appreciation.

On the question as to whether a fair balance had been struck between the interests of the applicants and the interests of the state, the Court then held that because transsexuality raises complex scientific, moral and social issues, Art 8 could not, in this context, be taken to imply an obligation for the state to recognise as the father of a child a person who was not a biological father. That being so, the failure of UK law to recognise the relationship between X and Y did not amount to a failure to respect family life. The court further held that the complaint made under Art 14 was tantamount to a re-statement of the complaint under Art 8 and consequently raised no separate issue. In view of their findings, there was no need to examine the issue again in the context of Art 14.

The case raised many issues and its failure tended to say more about the state of the ECHR than the state of transsexual rights in the UK. In this, as in other recent decisions, the width of the margin of appreciation that the Court accorded to member states in this area could be said to be increasing in many areas of the Court's jurisdiction; this does not bode well for the future of human rights in Europe. However, the case itself made some progress, not least that the Court held that Art 8 was applicable because there was a recognisable *de facto* family relationship in existence. The decision though failed to recognise that in this area, there are, or should be, limits imposed on the respect for fundamental rights guaranteed by the Convention. In the *Cossey*[11] case, Judge Martens held in his dissenting opinion that the refusal of a new identity in law for those who had undergone gender reassignment treatment 'can only be qualified as cruel'.[12]

In *X, Y and Z*, if we look to the dissenting opinions, Judges Casadevall, Russo and Makarczyk argued that the government should accept the consequences of allowing X to have gender reassignment and of allowing Y to have fertility treatment during which X was obligated to acknowledge his role as the future father of any child born by donor insemination. This they considered to positively obligate the government to take all measures needed, without discrimination, to allow the applicants to live a normal life. Judge Thor Vilhjalmsson, also in dissent, argued that as other non-biological fathers are allowed to be registered on the birth certificates of donor inseminated children, to refuse to allow X to do so was discrimination on the grounds of sex under Art 14. This also led him to conclude that the family ties between X, Y and Z were not being respected under Art 8. The fact that the male partner is a transsexual should be irrelevant. Judge Foighal, who also dissented, argued that in *Cossey*, the Court held that, though the law was in a transitional state, legal measures should be kept under review to take account of medical, social and moral developments. He maintained that the majority decision in *X, Y and*

---

11 *Cossey v UK* (1990) ECHR, Series A, No 184, www.echr.coe.int.
12 *Ibid*, dissenting judgment at para 64.

Z did not reflect the changes that have taken place in recent years, although the Court was given ample evidence of those changes. He also stated that it is part of our common European heritage that governments are under a duty to take special care of individuals who are disadvantaged in any way. The government did not advance any convincing arguments with regard to competing interests, nor had they attempted to justify their failure to help X further by ensuring that his change of sex received legal recognition, even though this would help him and harm no one. These reasons led him to conclude that in his opinion, a violation of Art 8 had occurred. Following the dissenting judgment of Thor Vilhjalmsson, he similarly found a contravention of Art 14. Judge Cotchev also argued that a contravention of both Articles had occurred, but from the standpoint of the 'welfare of the child', which should, in his opinion, be the prevailing consideration. He stated that this obligates a state to allow what had been unanimously agreed upon as *de facto* family ties to be legally safeguarded so as to render possible from the moment of birth, or as soon as practicable thereafter, the child's integration into the family. This would include recognising X as Z's father.

In many areas, nation states appear to have been afforded a wider margin of appreciation by the Court than would seem to be required as a result of recent social and legal developments within the membership of the Council of Europe and the rest of the world. Indeed, the margin appears wider than the balancing test supposedly applied by the Court to its decisions would appear to indicate. Doerfal (1998) has argued that the reason for this is that these decisions are a reflection of 'the apprehension and prejudices' of the majority of the Court's judges. Is it that the Court's judges cannot imagine recognising the transsexual person as being of equal worth to others? It is perhaps in response to this, and the theoretical and social changes that transsexuals have achieved over the last decade, that X, Y *and* Z did not ask for X's right to marry or to have his birth certificate changed. Rather, the demand being made was that the transsexual man be recognised for what he is, namely a transsexual man, but that that should not exclude him from recognition as a social and legal father. By considering these social changes and the more recent case of *Roetzheim v Germany*,[13] decided by the Commission, it is possible to see both how many transsexual and transgender people are claiming a new class of civil status and the implications for sex and gender categories as we know them. The dissenting opinions in X, Y *and* Z gave some hope, in that they provided possible ways forward for the future. However, they also acknowledged that identity documentation is not the same as status recognition, nor will it necessarily provide privacy, personal safety, employment or relationship protection. Some members of the trans community are now arguing that it is only status

---

13 *Roetzheim v Germany*, Application No 31177/96 (1997) ECHR.

acknowledgment as transsexual men and women that will afford true protection on these levels.

A NEW AGENDA

Legal activism in this area has tended to concentrate on 'quality of life' issues such as the transsexual's right to birth certificate change, the right to marry and the medico-legal issues of treatment and surgery. In recent years, the issues of concern have changed within the new community, the emphasis on birth certificates and marriage (which are to do with the further privacy of 'passing') giving way to concerns about the right to personal physical safety, to keep a job regardless of a trans status and resultant lifestyle, to be treated equally before the law, particularly in the area of relationship rights, and the right to medical treatment (including reassignment), to all of which 'passing' should be irrelevant (see Chapter 5).

The 1990s cases before the European Courts have clearly illustrated some of these trends, with cases concerning employment rights,[14] parenting,[15] the right not to face arbitrary discrimination in areas such as cross-border immigration, marriage status, employment regulation and the right not to have to disclose medical treatment except where absolutely necessary.[16]

The essence of the problems can be seen in the contradictory nature of legal status recognition provided by European nation states to transsexual people. An ongoing case in Ireland illustrates the issues, as the question of marriage is related to nationality and immigration status.

SPOUSAL AND FAMILY RIGHTS – A HISTORY OF DENIAL

Transsexual people seeking to set up home outside their country of origin have been bedevilled by problems in relation to attainment of legal recognition of their gender reassignment. As early as 1972, it was possible to foresee how problems might arise for the post-operative transsexual person.

In Canada, under the provisions of the pre-1978 Immigration Act, the state was able to bar the entry of persons practising 'homosexualism'. Among those affected by these provisions was a transsexual woman who was legally classified as a man. Her relationship with her male partner was considered a same-sex relationship and she was refused immigrant status as a practising homosexual.[17] Again, in Canada in 1980, the Immigration Board found a transsexual woman acting as the sponsoree for her husband to be of the same

---

14   *P v S and Cornwall County Council*, Case C-13/94 [1996] IRLR 347, ECJ.

15   *X, Y and Z v UK* (1997) 24 EHRR 143, ECHR, www.echr.coe.int.

16   *Sheffield and Horsham v UK* (1998) 27 EHRR 163, ECHR, www.echr.coe.int.

17   *Sherwood Atkinson (Sheri de Cartier)* [1972] Imm App Cas 5, 185.

sex as her husband, and therefore not his spouse within the meaning of immigration regulations.[18] Despite the fact that the woman concerned had undergone gender reassignment surgery, and the two had legally married, for the purposes of immigration, the marriage was held not to be valid.

Within a European context, and specifically within the context of the European Union, the main problems faced by individuals who have undergone gender reassignment have occurred in relation to partnerships where one partner is a national of the EU and the other is not. In accordance with EU law, an EU national is able in theory to travel to and/or reside in any member state of the 15 strong organisation. Traditionally, this freedom of movement has had a strong economic link. Most migrants exercising this right do so within the context of taking up or looking for work opportunities. The provisions also include professionals and self-employed service providers and enable all those exercising freedom of movement rights in this way to bring with them to the host country certain family members. In summary, this would include the 'worker's' spouse, that is, their married partner, their dependant children and certain other ascendant dependent relatives and more remote relatives who, in a given case, can prove a relationship of dependency.

On the face of it, these provisions appear generous, but when scrutinised in any detail, can prove problematic for partnerships where the union has not been sealed by a marriage contract. Unmarried partners and their families cannot avail themselves of these rights to gain entry to another EU state, though the intended move may still be possible if the excluded partner can establish that he or she is entitled to avail him or herself of free movement opportunities in their own right. Where difficulties mostly arise, however, is in relation to partnerships where the 'worker's' partner is not an EU national. Where a traditional partnership between an EU national and non-EU national has been sealed by marriage vows, and the marriage, no matter where it has been celebrated, is recognised as valid, the non-EU national is treated as if he or she was an EU national, under EU law. However, if the partners are not married, the non-EU national will be denied entry, unless he or she has separately accrued a right to work in the EU, subject to a series of fairly stringent conditions.

However, further complications may arise where one of the partners has undergone gender reassignment. If unmarried, unless the non-EU national has accrued the right to live and work within the EU separately, that partner will not be entitled to stay and work in the EU for an extended period of time. The situation is not much better where the partners have been legally married in one country but move to a state where that marriage is not recognised in law. This is the crucial issue for EU nationals and their non-EU partners where the marriage involves at least one post-operative transsexual person. As it

---

18 *Vulpen v Minister of Employment and Immigration*, File No V79-6100, 29 August 1980 (Immigration Appeal Board), reversed A-179-81, 1982 (FCA).

currently stands, the lack of consensus among EU member states as to the recognition of these marriages has led to each state developing its own rules on the matter and applying these in such a way that the rights of third country transsexuals may be diminished by factors such as place of domicile, gender status at birth and/or place of birth.

A case in point, which highlights these issues, is the *Krivenko* case. This is the most recent case where a nation's failure to recognise the validity of a marriage transacted between a transsexual man who has undergone gender reassignment and his female partner will be declared legitimate under both national and EU law. Nicholas Krivenko is a Russian citizen and non-EU national. His wife, Sybille Hintze-Krivenko, is a German citizen and EU national. The country in question is Ireland and a judicial review application has been made to the Irish courts because of the stringent application of Ireland's immigration rules. The rules do not in themselves conflict with current EU law on freedom of movement rights. In October 2000, Nicholas and Sybille were given leave to take judicial review proceedings against the Irish authorities over their failure to extend his residence permit, though as yet, the case has not come to trial.

Nicholas Krivenko was born in the USSR and registered as a female on his birth certificate with the Christian name of Nadia. In 1995, he began hormone therapy to reassign his gender, changing his name to Nicholas. The Russian authorities issued a new birth certificate in December 1998, showing his gender as male and his Christian name as Nicholas. He came to Ireland in November 1996, together with his partner Sybille. In August 1999, the Dominican Republic authorities issued a new passport showing his gender as male. Nicholas and Sybille lived together in Austria and the Dominican Republic before moving to Ireland, where they set up a food-exporting business. On that basis, he was given a temporary residence permit, but it was not renewed. In September 1999, he and his partner married in a Limerick registry office and in February 2000, he applied for a residence permit on the basis of being married to an EU national. He was told to attend his local Garda (police) station to receive his permit and the stamp. There, a Department of Justice official told his solicitor that there was a 'serious problem' with the application, based on Nicholas's gender reassignment.

Interestingly, this case may never have arisen if Sybille had been the person who had had gender reassignment. Under German law, she would have not only been able to have her birth records changed, but all aspects of her gender status for German law. As such, if Sybille had become Simon, Simon would have been in a position to have his gender status as a male citizen of Germany recognised throughout Europe by virtue of his being an EU national. Nadia would then have been able to marry Simon and almost certainly have that marriage recognised as valid throughout Europe. Nadia would have been a non-European national marrying, as a woman, a European national recognised as a man. As things stand, Sybille is a European national marrying, as a woman, a non-European national whom Ireland does not recognise as a man. While Sybille as an EU national could exercise her right to freedom of movement under EU law, her husband is legitimately excluded from enjoying basic economic and attendant social rights to which he would otherwise be entitled if he had contracted a traditional marriage with an EU national. It is likely that the exclusion will be upheld under Irish national law.

EU CITIZENSHIP

So far, we have discussed this case specifically on the basis of EU nationality which is strongly, though not exclusively, associated with the enjoyment of predominantly economic rights and a scattering of social rights, the latter in the main flowing from the former. On the other hand, since 1992, a new concept has appeared on the EU statute books, the notion of EU citizenship, which requires some discussion in the light of these issues. Its introduction represents an overt political attempt to move the EU away from its almost exclusively economic roots by introducing the non-economic based concept of EU citizenship. It has been described as a fundamental and personal right, which may be exercised independently of economic rights and entitlements by everyone with EU nationality. However, as is made clear in the legislation which frames and discusses the scope of the right, while it confers the right to 'move and reside freely [within the EU], ... this is... subject to the limitations and conditions' laid down in EU law. So, in effect, would Sybille's invocation of her EU citizenship have any effect on the outcome of the case in question? It does not appear to do so in the context of our previous discussions. The constitutional court of the European Union has stated as much in a recent case where the principle was invoked: '... citizenship ... is not intended to extend the scope *ratione materiae* of the Treaty to internal situations which have no link to community law.'

The discrimination suffered by Sybille and Nicholas Krivenko at the hands of the Irish authorities would appear to apply whether Sybille was Irish or German and occurs in an area not presently regulated by EU law, therefore taking the case out of the present debate on citizenship. Unfortunately for the Krivenkos, apart from reasserting the existing rights of EU nationals in the area of freedom of movement and residence, and bestowing some basic political rights, the new concept falls short of filling the void in EU law in relation to the position of transsexual people, their partners and children. The concept of EU citizenship is symbolic, but adds little. The newly signed Charter of Fundamental Rights not only presently lacks legal status, but also, unsurprisingly, does not address the specific problem faced by the Krivenkos, despite asserting that the rights protected include the right to family life (Art 7), the right to marry and to found a family (Art 9) and a whole chapter dedicated to 'equality' (Chapter 3). Where do the Krivenkos go from here? The answer must be, as ever, to the European Convention, whose contents are by and large incorporated into the Charter. The ECHR has seen a number of high profile applications in this area, though the protection given to transsexual people and their families in this arena has traditionally fallen short of being complete, as is illustrated by cases such as *X, Y and Z v UK*[19] and *Sheffield and Horsham v UK*,[20] though the decision in *Goodwin and I v UK* is a promise of better to come.

In the case of *Horsham*, the applicant once again encountered legal problems due to her altered gender status, though of a slightly different nature. As a British born citizen, she held a British birth certificate, but she also held a Dutch 'Certificate of Reassignment' by virtue of her treatment and residence in Holland. Consequently, she was afforded the legal status of a woman in Holland and could legally marry a man. However, if she and her spouse then returned to the UK, her marriage would become void – that is, it would automatically disappear in law. If she married a fellow European national, it would not necessarily be a major problem, albeit humiliating and embarrassing. But if she married a non-European national, his rights of free movement, as they would ordinarily derive from her, would in effect disappear upon arrival on British soil.

Unfortunately, in its judgment, the ECHR barely touched on this matter, stating that 'since it relates to the recognition by that state of a post-operative transsexuals' *foreign* marriage rather than the law governing the right to marry of individuals within its jurisdiction', it was not an issue for the Court to address. Does this statement contain a crumb of hope for the Krivenkos, given that their marriage was transacted on Irish soil? What comfort it might have offered was taken from them in the next breath. The judges went on to say that: 'Furthermore, it cannot be said with certainty what the outcome would be were the validity of her marriage to be tested in the English courts.'

The reality is that as the law stands, until the UK government responds to the *Goodwin and I* decision, it is in a position of untenable uncertainty. Rachel Horsham might marry her non-EU national male partner in Holland, and her partner could then obtain derivative rights in EU law exercisable theoretically upon the couple moving to another member state. However, should she move to the UK, her marriage would be declared void and her partner could not claim family rights under EU law. Alternatively, she could attempt to marry her non-EU national partner in the UK. The couple could then move to Holland where he still would not have gained a right to EU citizenship unless he then married Ms Horsham again in the Netherlands. They could then move to Andorra, which would recognise a Dutch marriage, but would not recognise a British marriage in these circumstances, and would not allow them to marry validly in Andorra. However, if they went to Italy, a Dutch

---

19   *X, Y and Z v UK* (1997) 24 EHRR 143, ECHR, www.echr.coe.int.
20   *Sheffield and Horsham v UK* (1998) 27 EHRR 163, ECHR, www.echr.coe.int.

marriage would be recognised, the British marriage would not be recognised, and nobody would be sure at all if an Italian marriage would be recognised. This is also the predicament faced by the Krivenkos. Should 'family rights' be based upon such an arbitrarily obtained contract as marriage, on which it appears there is little agreement across the European states?

The above dissection of the Krivenkos' marriage and the state's failure to recognise it leads to the conclusion that a spousal or family contract made upon marriage demands revisiting conceptually as well as on several levels. We would argue that the modern concept of the family now exceeds the purely traditional definition, which has shaped the development of national, European and global law impacting upon family relationships. People who live in alternative family forms are inadequately protected, as compared with those living within traditional, usually biologically linked, and nuclear relationships. The law leaves them without the rights needed to protect their 'own'. They are unable to live where they wish with family members, nor can they ensure that their wealth, whether property, money or pension rights devolves to their 'families' upon death. They are unable to provide the protections that the traditional family format affords for the people they wish to spend the rest of their lives with, and to ensure that those rights are passed to future generations of the family unit. There are, however, two alternative solutions: either we agree a common European framework for marriage; or we agree a common recognition of a group of trans people with need for added protection. One particular application to the European Commission on Human Rights sums up the essence of the new campaign issues surrounding gender identity rights, and further illustrates this need.

Roetzheim v Germany[21] concerned the application by Dora (formally Theodor) Roetzheim to the Commission, alleging that the German government had failed in its obligations, in that its refusal to recognise her new gender for civil status purposes violated Art 8 of the Convention. German law provides two remedies for transsexuals: firstly a change of forenames, which does not require there to have been any surgical intervention; and secondly, an amendment of public registries following surgical reassignment treatment. Particular features of the application were that Roetzheim, although living as a woman and taking female hormones, had not undergone any gender reassignment surgery and, further, that she had given up a well paid job in order to work as a woman. Accordingly, she argued that her maintenance obligations to the children of a former marriage should be reduced. The local courts had held that without genital surgery, there was no obligation to amend her public status and further stated that because of the lack of surgery, there was no reason why she should not resume her male role

---

21 *Roetzheim v Germany*, Application No 31177/96 (1997) ECHR.

and take up her former profession, hence retaining the value of her maintenance obligations.

Roetzheim had argued that the requirements of s 8 of Germany's 1980 Transsexuals Act (*Transsexuellengesetz*) for a change of civil status that a person must be unmarried, permanently unable to procreate and have undergone gender reassignment surgery with the consequence that the outer appearance resembles closely the phenotype of the opposite sex, was a violation of her right to respect for her private life under Art 8 of the Convention. Fundamental to Roetzheim's argument was that her gender identity should be recognised regardless of her body morphology. The Commission was to find unanimously that Roetzheim's application was ill-founded and declared it inadmissible.

Roetzheim's claims before the Commission closely mirror those made in the International Bill of Gender Rights (ICTLEP, 1995) wherein fundamental human and civil rights are articulated from a gender perspective. The rights claimed are to be regarded as universal rights both claimable and exercisable by any and every human being, regardless of gender or sex. These range from the right to define and have free expression of gender identity for one's self, to the right to conceive, bear or adopt children, to nurture and have custody of them regardless of a self-defined gender identity or the expression of such identity. These rights are both transformative and embedded in notions of personal liberty and free expression. They provide a framework for the claims of the new trans community and as such, are increasingly being seen as the paradigms that inform the legal battles the community is undertaking. They may be seen as being too revolutionary for justice systems yet they are simple truisms with which it is hard to argue. For example, 'the right to train and to pursue an occupation ... nor to be denied ... employment ... or just compensation by virtue of chromosomal sex, genitalia, assigned birth sex, or initial gender role' reflects what we might see as essential interpretations of the Equal Treatment Directive of the European Community, or the Sex Discrimination Act. Yet for trans people, those rights have to be fought for and clearly articulated, as was to happen in *P v S and Cornwall County Council*[22] in the ECJ.

The decision in *P v S* provided a huge boost throughout Europe to the recognition of transsexual people as being ordinary members of society, deserving of the same respect and equality as others. The reality is that employers throughout Europe have now to retain transsexuals in their jobs. Further, the press has given an immense amount of positive coverage to transsexual people who have transitioned in the professional roles as teachers, doctors, lawyers, etc. Overall, as a result, there has been a huge shift in the public perception of the transsexual.

---

22 *P v S and Cornwall County Council*, Case C-13/94 [1996] IRLR 347, ECJ.

This is all rather ironic; the Court, the ECHR, which should have been able to provide protection to transsexuals through the notion of Human Rights has been unable to in the past, whereas the Court, the ECJ, which ostensibly deals solely with economic concerns has stepped into what appeared to be an irretrievable breach of human rights law.

I would argue that the reasons why the ECJ has been able to afford greater human rights protection than the ECHR stems from their juridical position. The ECHR, if it finds against a nation state, holds that the nation state has broken its obligations under the Convention. As such, it places a nation outside of the signatories to the Convention. To do so is a drastic step. It means that for a period of time, until that nation rectifies its domestic law, the treaty upholding the Convention is broken. The signatories are no longer unanimous in their condemnation of human rights violations. The ECHR uses the 'margin of appreciation' allowed to give warning shots across the bows of nation states, but is always wary of causing that break in the treaty. To do so means that they actually dismantle the body that maintains their existence. As such, they are very wary of making decisions against states, and prefer to merely indicate their unhappiness with any given situation. Of course, there are occasions when they do find against nation states, but that is when the breach of the Convention is more conventionally associated with human rights, as they are traditionally constructed, for example, in torture and asylum cases.

In contrast, the ECJ, when it finds against a nation state, does not place it outside of the treaty that brought the EEC (now EC) into being. Instead, the Court stands in a position to simply state that the nation state has misinterpreted its responsibilities under EU law. A decision is simply clear guidance on how the state must act to meet those responsibilities from now on. In other words, they provide a pathway for the nation state to re-integrate itself into the treaty.

Further, the decisions in the ECHR are about human rights and therefore the Court has the role of being a moraliser, an extremely difficult position in a multi-cultural collection of states, whereas in the ECJ, the Court never moralises, it simply promotes economic harmony through social justice. Consequently, the ECJ is much more readily placed to deal with difficult moral issues by sidestepping them. Issues of human rights can be played out in the ECJ through the issues of economic well being. This allows far greater social movement than can be obtained through the ECHR.

At a time when economic issues are so crucial to an individual's well being because of the gradual dismantling of many aspects of the welfare states of Europe, employment and a position in the workplace are increasingly becoming the access point to social status, economic well being, health care, education, etc. The ECJ has created for itself a crucial role in ensuring that employment access is available on an equal footing to all, and as such, has become a crucial player in ensuring that human rights, in their broader sense, are provided through the nation state.

CHAPTER 11

THE PRAXIS AND POLITICS OF POLICING: PROBLEMS FACING TRANS PEOPLE[1]

'FRAMING THE PROBLEM'

The praxis and politics of policing in relation to trans people raises two central issues: firstly, their employment rights as applicants and/or employees of the police service; and secondly, as members of the community being policed and in receipt of the services of the police. These are inevitably inextricably linked, as evidenced by the police approach to equal opportunities in policing. The focus of this chapter is the employment status of trans people in the police service in England and Wales (UK), which is currently in an anomalous position. There have been very few of these cases: *M v Chief Constable of West Midlands Police*[2] and *A v Chief Constable of West Yorkshire Police*,[3] both of which involved the refusal of employment to an mtf transsexual woman. Also, the case of *Ashton v Chief Constable of West Mercia Police*[4] in which an mtf transsexual woman claimed unfair dismissal following transfer to a clerical post in the police service after undergoing gender reassignment.

These cases pose some interesting issues for the debates around gender diversity in policing and the need to develop a theoretical framework that goes beyond binary oppositions generated by a lack of recognition of diversity. They also raise the question about the suitability of transsexual or transgender people to participate in policing as a police officer. One of the arguments used to exclude transsexual people from policing is the view that should they be employed, they would not be able to conduct lawful searches. Thus, transsexual people become categorised as 'other', a 'third sex', being neither male nor female for the purposes of conducting searches.

The refusal to employ transsexual people in the police service falls within the ambit of sex discrimination law, details of which are outlined in this chapter. These arguments justifying the exclusion of transgender people from policing are similar to those presented in the resistance of the police to the incorporation of women and other minority groups. The essence of discrimination against a transgender person is summarised by a statement made in the case of *M v Chief Constable of West Midlands Police*:

---

1   Co-authors for this chapter are Catherine Little, Principal Lecturer in Law, Manchester Metropolitan University, and Paula Stephens.

2   *M v Chief Constable of West Midlands Police*, Case No 08964/96 (1996) IT.

3   *A v Chief Constable of West Yorkshire Police*, Case No 1802020/98 (1999) IT.

4   *Ashton v Chief Constable of West Mercia Police*, Case No 2901131/98 (1999) IT.

As a legal male, although presenting as a female, searching a female, even by consent, would not be genuine, because the person being searched would not know the applicant was a transsexual. If the fact had to be spelt out each time, the force would lose credibility in the community. Within the force, there would be a loss of effectiveness – another officer would always be involved in a search, wasting time and resources.[5]

This statement goes against the grain of current rhetoric on equal opportunities and the management of diversity in policing in the UK.

THE POLICE APPROACH TO EQUAL OPPORTUNITIES AND DIVERSITY

Overall, the police approach to equal opportunities has arisen and developed as a response to external pressures rather than from a genuine commitment to reform from within. Pressure in the form of increasing and high profile sex and race discrimination cases, led Her Majesty's Inspectorate of Constabulary (HMIC) to issue a circular (Home Office, 1989) instructing all police force areas to introduce (where not already in existence) and implement an equal opportunities policy and internal grievance procedures. The circular stated:

> The effects of equal opportunities policies will be to secure for the organisation the best recruits from the widest available range of candidates; to ensure that the best use is made of the skills and abilities of all employees; and less directly, to reinforce the professionalism and image of the organisation itself. (Home Office, 1989, para 2.)

More recently, the approach to equal opportunities has been to develop and manage diversity to ensure that the police service represents the diverse communities that it polices. The approach now is to do more than simply take measures to further the advance of women, ethnic minorities or any other group (HMIC, 1995). Thus, the purpose of equal opportunities is about the creation of fairness, where every member of the police service, irrespective of difference, can 'flourish, develop and give their best' (HMIC, 1995, p 10).

Interest in policing and equal opportunities has heightened in the UK since the murder of the black teenager Stephen Lawrence and the subsequent inquiry by Sir William MacPherson into the police investigation of his death (MacPherson, 1999). This has primarily arisen as a result of the public debates about police institutional racism and organisational/occupational police culture. The impact of the MacPherson Report on developing the diversity approach to managing equal opportunities in policing has been considerable. HMIC for England and Wales has driven the policing agenda to ensure that all force areas are becoming more effective in dealing with cultural diversity

---

5   *M v Chief Constable of West Midlands Police*, Case No 08964/96 (1996) IT: 9 and 10.

within policing. Though scholars of policing have welcomed the MacPherson Report, one rather negative effect of its publication and the ensuing debate has been to stifle, if not silence, the debate around gender diversity in policing.

GENDER DIVERSITY AND POLICING

Research on gender discrimination in the police service has been dominated by studies on women's experiences, concluding that despite the existence of anti-discrimination law and policy, discrimination is still widespread (Jones, 1986; Heidensohn, 1992; Brown, 1998; Brown and Heidensohn, 2000). The volume of research on gay and lesbian officers has been rather more limited (Burke, 1993) and virtually none exists on the experiences of transgender officers.

It is hardly surprising that studies on gender relations and gender discrimination, or more specifically on women in policing, have developed in the way they have. Policing studies have been dominated by male discourse generated predominantly by male academics writing about policemen. Such discourse has not only failed to take account of women's experiences, but has also failed to consider men and masculinities as problematic. Consequentially, this has meant that feminist academics have been marginalised in policing studies and studies on women in policing have developed almost as a sub-category of mainstream policing studies (Heidensohn, 1992).

This is primarily because the concept of gender *difference* has been applied in many of the studies on policewomen, and the process of gender differentiation gives rise to the notion that such differences are natural. Nowhere is this illustrated more clearly than in studies on the performance and physical capability of policewomen, which question if policing is a suitable job for women (Bell, 1982; Balkin, 1988). Sex/gender difference is also the pivot of the debate about the inclusion of transgender people in the police service and their unsuitability to perform all policing tasks.

The concentration on gender differentiation results in the construction of dichotomous binary oppositions based primarily on assumed natural differences. For example, man/woman, male/female, masculine/feminine are categories based on a particular construction of sex and gender, one which fails to consider men and women as socially constructed 'gendered subjects'. The experiences of policewomen are often explained in the context of a 'masculine police culture' (Smith and Gray, 1985; Young, 1991), which fails to deconstruct the underlying gender constructions of man/woman, male/female, feminine/masculine, instead treating the definition of these concepts as 'taken-for-granted assumptions'. Furthermore, focus on these oppositional categories gives rise to the assumption that these categories are unified, that is, all men and all women are alike. Failure to focus on other factors such as gendered identities and subjectivities which take account of the fluidity of masculinities and femininities means that it is difficult to theoretically account for discrimination against gay, lesbian and trans officers in the police service. This is fundamentally because of the failure to recognise and consider the diversity of gender in the context of policing. Consideration of such factors illustrates the diversity of gender rather than the unitary categories of the binary divide.

Police cultural oppositions are based on gender dichotomies with aspects of police work being associated with either female or male characteristics. Binary police cultural oppositions based on female/male dichotomies can be identified thus:

- female/male;
- formal/informal;
- academy/street;
- inside/outside;
- management/street cop;
- administration/crime fighting;
- social service/rescue activity;
- paperwork/crime fighting;
- formal rules/informal rules;
- legal money/clean and dirty money (corruption);
- marital sex/illicit sex;
- domestic women/whore/dyke;
- emotional/instrumental;
- intellectual/physical;
- clean/dirty. (Hunt, 1990, p 11.)

Thus, policemen and policewomen are the antithesis of one another and must engage in the activities associated with their gender in order to maintain their masculinity or femininity.

Furthermore, this way of thinking about gender is part of the police organisational culture based on hegemonic masculinity. The effect of such a culture is to create the existence of rigid in-group/out-group distinctions (Fielding, in Newburn and Stanko, 1994). The consequences of this dichotomous relationship based primarily on gender and ethnic difference are the structural marginalisation and exclusion of those members of the out-group. In the context of gender divisions, members of the out-group include female, gay, lesbian and trans police officers, that is, those that do not comply with (white) male normative heterosexuality. Those in the out-group are constructed as 'other', that is, different from the cultural norm.

Discrimination, sexual and non-sexual harassment of officers in the out-group manifest exclusion and marginalisation.

DECONSTRUCTING THE BOUNDARIES: CHALLENGING GENDER DIFFERENCE AND DEFINITIONS OF 'OTHER'

The construction of gender as based on difference, either biological or socially constructed difference (role theory), poses a problem in attempting to locate gay, lesbian and trans officers in the police service into a theoretical framework. Their position is better understood from the viewpoint of gendered subjectivities and identities, which gives primacy to ways of thinking and valuing. Furthermore, the focus on 'identity in the context of masculinities/femininities emphasises how power works through constraining feelings, thoughts and actions' (Alvesson and Billing, 1997, p 97). The cultural values of policing and the acceptance of them by the individual officer (agency) within the structural constraints of policing allows for a better understanding of diversity. Police officers, both male and female, negotiate strategies for dealing with the cultural norms and values of policing. For women officers, this can entail choosing to 'become one of the boys'. Although police culture can be a controlling force, officers can and do challenge that culture. The very nature of undergoing gender reassignment is in itself challenging to police culture. The taking of a sex and/or race discrimination case is another way of challenging the cultural values inherent within policing.

The sexuality of officers has been commented upon in studies of women in policing (Hunt, 1990, p 11; Young, 1991; Levine, 1994) as a means of illustrating the social control of women in a male dominated organisation, and as an aspect of male/female interaction in the workplace (Martin, 1980, p 208). However, that social control extends to all those, that is, gay, lesbian and trans, officers who are identified as 'other' to male normative heterosexuality which is at the centre of police cultural norms based on hegemonic masculinity. Thus, a focus on gendered subjectivities and identities rather than gender-difference, which is based on comparing men and women in terms of biological and socially constructed difference, is more helpful because it assists in acknowledging the existence of gender diversity. The current emphasis on binary oppositions of gender suppresses/silences the voice(s) of gay, lesbian and trans police officers by constructing them as other.

EMPLOYING THE TRANS POLICE OFFICER

In 1999, after the decision of the ECJ in *P v S and Cornwall County Council*,[6] the UK government passed the Sex Discrimination (Gender Reassignment)

---

6   *P v S and Cornwall County Council*, Case C-13/94 [1996] IRLR 347, ECJ.

Regulations 1999 (see Chapter 6). The Regulations are intended to prevent discrimination against transsexual people, because of their gender reassignment, both in pay and treatment in employment and vocational training. However, in some circumstances, the Regulations make provisions (notably Section 7(2)(b)) whereby it may not be unlawful to discriminate on grounds of gender reassignment, in particular, where the job may involve conducting intimate searches pursuant to statutory powers (for example, the Police and Criminal Evidence Act 1984). The Regulations formalised discrimination in a way that directly contradicts the clear instruction of the ECJ in the case of *P v S*. The Regulations without a doubt intimate that transgender people are neither male nor female in those circumstances where they have to perform intimate physical searches.

The operational requirements of policing, including searching, pose some interesting issues for transsexual officers, particularly s 55 searches under the Police and Criminal Evidence Act 1984. The question of an officer's duties is one of operational requirements and those which are contained in the contractual employment arrangements between an officer and the police service. Where there are no standard practices, the details are matters for police managers to decide according to their resources and objectives, allowing for local practice and history of the particular service and the nature of the locality policed.

The duties of the police are very diverse, and it is clear that not all police constables perform, or are expected to perform, exactly the same duties or all possible duties. Police services are made up of different types of people in order to relate in different ways, and to different issues, in the community. Different officers have different strengths. The idea that they should be monolithic is not now considered to be desirable – note the concern about racism in the police and the need to attract recruits who can reflect different backgrounds and life experiences within, and to, the police, to ensure cultural diversity. It is also increasingly recognised within the police service itself and generally that the public interest requires the same approach to be adopted in relation to sexual orientation. Our police services are in general and increasingly required to be dynamic institutions adapting and responding to changing legislative, operational, social and cultural realities.

Police powers, however, are different from police duties, in that whereas a duty might be considered part of the contractual obligations of a police officer, a power enables an officer to fulfil those duties. There are three relevant police powers in relation to searching:

(1) The power to stop and search under s 1, Code A, para 3.5 of the Police and Criminal Evidence Act 1984 (PACE), which requires that any search involving more than the removal of outer clothing must be by an officer of the same sex and must not without consent be in the presence of an officer of the opposite sex.

(2) Searches of a detained person at a police station as part of the logging in process under s 54 of PACE must not involve an intimate search but must be conducted by a constable of the same sex.

(3) Under s 55 of PACE, persons of the opposite sex may not carry out intimate searches.

There is also a requirement in Code A para 3.1 that:

> ... every reasonable effort *must* be made to reduce to a minimum the embarrassment that a person being searched may experience.

Section 1 and Code A 3.5 PACE

These provisions govern the powers to stop and search by patrolling police officers and arise only where an officer has reasonable grounds for suspecting the person is in possession of certain identified prohibited articles. It is the Code and not the Act that specifies the precise manner in which the search is to be carried out. Section 67(10) and (11) provides that a breach of the code requirement does not, of itself, amount to a crime or civil offence. Such breach may be used, however, to show that any of the well established criminal or civil offences relating to the individual's rights over his person and property have been infringed, for example, assault or trespass.

Article 3.5 of the Code restricts searches in public to superficial examination of outer clothing. Any officer of either sex can carry out such a search on suspects. More thorough searches involving removal of the outer jacket, gloves, headgear or footwear should be conducted out of the public view, for example, in the police van or at the station. Again, any officer of either sex can carry out such a search on suspects. Such searches, non-sex specific searches, constitute the overwhelming majority of searches carried out by patrolling officers. It is only where the officer considers it necessary to remove more than an outer coat, jacket, gloves or footwear that there is a requirement that the officer be of the same sex and that the search may not be in the presence of anyone of the opposite sex without consent. This again should be conducted out of public view, the example being given of the police van or the police station.

Section 54 PACE

Section 54 searches are made as part of the 'logging in' when a person is detained at a police station. They must be made at the police station and a constable of the same sex must conduct the search.

Section 55 PACE

Section 55 searches are the only searches that could truly be described as intimate searches, that is, those involving the searching of intimate areas of the body. A person of the same sex must carry out these searches. However, a 'suitably qualified person other than a police officer' must carry out intimate searches unless an officer of the rank of superintendent or above authorises otherwise. A suitably qualified person is a registered doctor or nurse, and such a person must carry out all searches for drugs. It is only in the case of harmful articles (that is, dangerous weapons) that a constable may carry out the search, and then only if it is not practicable for a suitably qualified person to perform the search. Paragraph 3.1 of the Code states that:

> ... every reasonable effort must be made to reduce to a minimum the embarrassment that a person being searched may experience.

Section 1 PACE searches: a general overview

The available Home Office statistics, from 1996, show that during that year, there were 814,500 searches of persons or vehicles using police powers under s 1 of PACE (Home Office Research and Statistics Directorate, 1997). The statistics do not record the gender of those who were searched, nor of the officers who searched suspects. Neither are the statistics broken down into the categories of superficial searches, which may be performed by any officer, or more thorough searches, including the removal of outer clothing which are required under PACE to be performed by someone of the same sex as the suspect.

However, Art 3.5 of the code governing the powers to stop and search by patrolling police officers restricts searches in public to 'superficial examination of outer clothing', and an officer of either sex may carry out such a search. Any search involving the removal of 'outer jacket, gloves, head gear or footwear' should be conducted out of the 'public view', for example, in a police station or police van. However, an officer of either sex can also carry out such a search on a suspect. It is only where a police officer proposes a search that requires more than the removal of outer clothing that the code requires that the officer be of the same sex as the suspect. Again, the search must be conducted out of the view of the public and the code further requires that such a search be not done in the presence of anyone of the opposite sex without the consent of the suspect. With around 125,000 'front line' police officers, who are primarily police constables, we can say that on average, each officer would perform 6.5 searches per annum under s 1 of PACE. However, very few of these would be 'sex specific' searches and even where sex specific searches are called for, in fact, as these must take place out of the public view, they will take place in a police van or station where there are likely to be several officers available to perform the search.

As regards the gender of police officers, 14.6% of officers are women (Home Office, 1997). If we extrapolate from the prison population figures, it must sensibly be considered the case that the majority of suspects are male. In 1997 (White, 1998), there were 46,370 sentenced males in England and Wales as compared to 2,080 sentenced females. This means that only 4.3% of those in prison were female. If a similar proportion of those searched in 1996 were female, then of the 814,500 searches under s 1 of PACE, only around 35,000 of those searches would be of women. This means that there is a general disproportion of same gender officers to suspects, and we must assume that provisions already exist in the day-to-day management of a police service to ensure that appropriate officers are available if more thorough s 1 searches are required.

ONE POLICE SERVICE'S SITUATION

Section 1 PACE searches

According to the Home Office statistics (Home Office Research and Statistics Directorate, 1997) from 1996, there were 14,447 s 1 searches carried out in the West Yorkshire region.[7] The West Yorkshire police service had a total police workforce of 5,142 as at 31 March 1996 (West Yorkshire, 1998). Of these, 4,754 were of the rank of sergeant or constable, which are those officers most likely to be involved in s 1 searches. As such, in West Yorkshire, each front line officer averages three s 1 searches per annum.

708 officers of that rank were women, 14.8% of the service. If we estimate that of the 14,447 s 1 searches, only 621 were likely to be of women, then in fact each female officer is not likely to reach an average of one search per annum. Taken further, if the number of s 1 searches which require a same sex officer are a much smaller number than the total number of s 1 searches, then a police service such as the West Yorkshire service must already be making day-to-day operational adjustments to ensure that an officer of the same gender is available. There is already likely to be a requirement for proportionally (and numerically) more of the thorough type of search of male suspects, than there are proportionally male officers available.

It is therefore apparent that in many circumstances where a more thorough s 1 search is required, because a disproportionate number of suspects are male (as opposed to the proportion of police officers who are male), female officers are disqualified from undertaking these searches, and hence other arrangements must be made. Generally, as these searches have to be undertaken out of the public view, there are several police officers present either in a police van or at a police station, and these arrangements are quite easily made.

---

7   West Yorkshire is the police force in the case *of A v Chief Constable West Yorkshire Police.*

Section 54 PACE searches

Searches under s 54 take place as part of the 'logging in' of a suspect at a police station. Searches under s 54 must not involve an intimate search but must be conducted by a constable of the same sex. A study by Tom Bucke and David Brown (1997) showed that only 3% of detained suspects were strip-searched, the majority being searched in a non-intrusive manner. In only 3% of these cases, according to Bucke and Brown, was a nurse or doctor present. However, it would be the case that all of these searches would take place in a police station, under s 54. Given that searches under s 54 take place in the police station, there are likely to be several officers available who could carry out the search. Again, there would be a higher proportion of men detained and searched under s 54, as opposed to a smaller proportion of male officers available and vice versa for women and female police officers.

Section 55 PACE searches

Intimate searches are governed by s 55. These are searches involving a physical search of body orifices. They may only be carried out if there are reasonable grounds to believe a suspect may have concealed on him or her something which could be used to cause physical injury, or in the case of suspected couriers or dealers only, a Class A drug. In the case of harmful articles, a constable (authorised by an officer of the rank of superintendent or above) may carry out the search.

According to the Home Office, in 1996 only 132 s 55 intimate searches were carried out, throughout England and Wales, of which only four were carried out by a police officer alone (Home Office Research and Statistics Directorate, 1997, table 7). Another 30 were performed in the presence of a suitably qualified person. This means that 98 (74%) were carried out by a doctor or nurse rather than a police officer. The statistics for the West Yorkshire police service region in 1996 record only five such searches being carried out, and a police constable carried out only one of these. These figures are consistent with the Bucke and Brown study mentioned above (1997, p 9).

The day-to-day operational implications for a police service which employs a transsexual person as an officer, such as they relate to the requirements of PACE and its codes, are minimal. Police services already have to make operational allowances for the disproportionate ratio of male and female officers to suspects. It is highly likely that many female police officers will rarely, if ever, have the experience of being called upon to search suspects when the sex of the officer is relevant to the search that is taking place. Searches are a limited part of a constable's duties, and the requirements for strip or intimate searches are such that they can be easily accommodated to operational requirements.

DIVERSIFYING RECRUITMENT TO INCLUDE TRANS PEOPLE

In order to maintain law and order, the police must acquire the consent of the public (HMIC, 2000). In pursuit of this, the service requires the trust and confidence of the community in which it operates. Section 8 of the Police Act 1996 requires police authorities annually to set out what consultation has taken place between each force and its local community. Thus, the service has a legal requirement obligating it to interact with the diverse community it serves (Home Office, 2001).

Unless dialogue translates into the context of employment policy, so that trans people and others are able to police their communities as constables in the service, the social perspectives and understanding of trans people (and other diverse people) will never be fully realised (HMIC, 1995). Although, in a racial context, the views of Inspector Paul Wilson giving evidence to the Stephen Lawrence Inquiry are just as applicable to transgender people. He pointed to the fact that:

> ... predominantly, white officers only meet members of the black community in confrontational situations, (consequently) ... they tend to stereotype black people in general. This can lead to all sorts of negative views and assumptions about black people. (MacPherson, 1999.)

Thus, dialogue alone will not shift police attitudes to trans people. It is an employment issue, without which negative stereotyping and institutional transphobia will continue to thrive. As Her Majesty's Inspectorate points out:

> ... there is a direct and vital link between performance and the way an organisation obtains the best people and develops the knowledge, skills and attitudes of those newcomers and of existing staff. (HMIC, 1995.)

BARRIERS TO THE RECRUITMENT OF
TRANS PEOPLE TO THE POLICE SERVICE

In examining the barriers that exist to the recruitment of trans people, one of the contributors to this chapter was asked to advise the Metropolitan Police Service (MPS). The report was to comment on the limitations of the 'searching' exception, and advise on how multiple discrimination impacted on the MPS's ability to attract new recruits (Stephens, 2001). Hence, it was considered that any policy that discriminated against trans people was also a barrier to the recruitment of male, female, ethnic, gay and lesbian officers also (Stephens, 2001, para 1.2.2). In recounting one example, it was observed that, while applicants to the service were told that there were no set qualifications needed to become a police officer (MPS, 2000b, section 2), they were nevertheless asked to provide a list of all qualifications or examinations taken, or due to be taken (MPS, 2000a, section 2). Since many qualifications are gender specific and require dates in order to be verified, this requirement may not simply facilitate age or sex discrimination against trans people, but also disproportionately affect all minority people who, through decades of social and economic exclusion, may have been afforded the least opportunity of access to education and work-related training. The advice, in this respect, was that application forms should focus on achievements rather than qualifications. These would not only be less reliant on historical gender markers and chronological details but, additionally, would embrace a broader area of experience more relevant to members of those diverse groups that the service sought to represent (Stephens, 2001, para 2.3.2.3).

CRITERIA FOR ENTRY TO THE SERVICE

Generally, on examination of a range of recruitment literature, it was apparent that no common standard existed for appointment to the office of constable. Candidates were selected according to the range of criteria determined individually by forces, services or constabularies. Thus, it was possible (for example) for transsexual and transgender people to serve in the West Mercia Constabulary (West Mercia, 2001), whilst a ban existed on recruitment in West Yorkshire.[8] The prospect of appointment was therefore a lottery, devised not by matching personal skills, attributes and abilities to the requirements of the job, but by the differing criteria of a particular force in a postcode area. This has been further highlighted by recent newspaper reporting in the UK regarding the employment of a male to female transgender person by the North Yorkshire police. Sergeant Nicola Lamb appeared at a press conference with the Chief Constable of North Yorkshire who announced the existence, in his force, of two transgender police officers.[9] However, whilst the North Yorkshire force is 'celebrating gender diversity' in its force, its neighbouring force, West Yorkshire, is currently being challenged at the Court of Appeal at a second appeal in *A v Chief Constable West Yorkshire Police*.[10]

Similarly, the report to the MPS considered the application process extremely bureaucratic, inflexible and disadvantageous to a service that sought to represent the diverse community. Information sought by the application process was duplicated on numerous occasions, making forms and the medical questionnaires superfluous, time consuming and difficult to complete. It is believed that such a process served only to de-motivate those under-represented from applying (Stephens, 2001, para 2.1.4). This issue is one that was recognised by HMIC, who pointed out that:

---

8   *A v Chief Constable of West Yorkshire Police,* Case No 1802020/98 (1999) IT.

9   (2001) *The Guardian,* 21 July.

10 Case No 1802020/98 (1999) IT.

Officers who had recently joined the MPS, and were still in their probationary period, found recruitment to be a slow bureaucratic process. (HMIC, 2000, para 5.15.)

It was equally apparent that some aspects of the application forms and medical questionnaires were unlawful, serving as a barrier to the recruitment of diverse groups. The medical criteria applied specifically sought to expand the definition of 'disability', apparently facilitating indirect discrimination. The MPS thus tended to indirectly favour young, physically fit applicants possessing a minimum time frame of legal responsibility and life experience (Stephens, 2001, para 2.1.4). Arguably, the service therefore attempted to construct the society it sought to reflect rather than the society that actually exists. This was despite HMIC's belief that:

Positive and sensitive policing has a particular role in the quality of life of all communities. It is not, however, the sole determinant of quality of life. The police service serves society: it does not construct it. (HMIC, 2001, para 1.7.)

It is considered that the police service should assess (in terms of its 21st century 'intelligence-led and technology-based' *fair and responsive* policing role) whether it is ineffectual to exclude any group of people from serving, whether by ethnic background, disabled, gay, lesbian, trans, or those who self-identify with a combination of those labels. As HMIC pointed out in the preface of its publication *Developing Diversity in the Police Service*:

In today's diverse society, policing calls for a wider range of skills and abilities than ever before. All police forces need to use and develop their existing staff – police officers, civilian colleagues and special constables alike – and to attract and nurture talent from within the communities they serve. Striving for real equality of opportunity within the Service will make efficient use of our human resources and demonstrate our commitment to fair and responsive policing. (HMIC, 1995, preface.)

CHAPTER 12

PRISON PROVISION FOR TRANS PEOPLE

> After spending a short year in prison, most transsexuals will have forgotten what it means to actually be happy. (Brooks, 1998.)

Little if any research has been done with trans people who encounter the criminal justice system (CJS), whether as a victim, witness, offender or employee. In 1996, Petersen, Stephens, Dickey and Lewis (1996) published a survey of the policies of custodial facilities as they relate to transsexual prisoners in Europe, Australia, Canada and the US. The survey concluded that of the:

> ... 64 corrections departments that responded to the survey, only 20% reported any kind of formal policy in the housing or treatment of incarcerated transsexuals with another 20% reporting an informal policy. Perhaps in itself this should not be surprising since the incidence of transsexualism within the general population is relatively small. However, given the complexities of dealing with such inmates within a prison population, one would have to wonder at the lack of formal policy planning. (Petersen *et al*, 1996, p 229.)

In 2000, the Australian Institute of Criminology published Blight's review of the Australian state policies on transgender inmates. The review considered the matters of:

- choice of institution for the housing of transgender inmates;

- self-harm and/or sexual assault: possible methods of risk reduction;

- hormonal and surgical intervention: the basis for provision;

- need for statistics: the need to identify and record transgender inmates, and further research and policy development.

The review concludes that:

> Transgender inmates present a unique set of issues that, if not appropriately dealt with, could lead to a greatly increased incidence of assault and self-harm in that population. Failure to implement appropriate policies may also amount to a breach of anti-discrimination legislation and/or human rights obligations. (Blight, 2000, p 6.)

In order to address the lack of information in this area, the Home Office Research and Statistics Directorate commissioned a small pilot study in the UK. The study took place in the first quarter of 2001 and this chapter is based on the results.[1]

---

1   This chapter was co-written with the project's research assistant, Paula Stephens.

PREVALENCE OF TRANSSEXUAL AND TRANSGENDER PEOPLE IN CUSTODIAL SETTINGS

It is known that the social stigma associated with non-conventional gender behaviour or cross-gender identity still leads to social isolation for many trans people. The social stigma takes many forms, from experiencing personal violence in the home and in public arenas (Heredia, 2001)[2] to job or home loss, financial difficulties, loss of contact with families and communities, and having great difficulties in personal relationships. Further factors complicating the lives of trans people include the limited availability of gender reassignment services and the lack of personal privacy due to the failure to legally recognise a change of gender identity. As such, despite the enormous media interest in the exposure of a transsexual or transgender person's status, and in disclosing the minutiae of their lives, it is surprising that it is so rare to come across news reports of trans people being involved in the CJS. It is maintained that most transsexual and transgender people will do everything possible to avoid such contact (Whittle, 1995). My experience has been that, even when victims of serious crime, transsexual and transgender people will avoid making a report and, if that is unavoidable, will prefer not to have charges pressed. The combination of disclosure of status in court and social reaction often creates larger problems in themselves than the initial crime for the person involved. Similarly, it might be considered surprising that so few cases concerning to conviction or incarceration of transsexual or transgender people become public knowledge. However, despite the social exclusion that they suffer, most maintain that a criminal conviction would lead to the loss of so much, especially access to hormonal and surgical therapy, that there is little temptation to consider crime as a possible solution to any problem.

However, some transsexual and transgender people do find themselves charged and convicted of crimes. In March 2001, Home Office Minister, Paul Boateng, in reply to a parliamentary question on the prevalence of people within the prison system currently undergoing or requesting assessment for treatment for gender reassignment, replied:

> Information is not routinely collected centrally on the number of prisoners with gender dysphoria, or who are receiving treatment for that condition in prison. However, 16 cases of prisoners needing assessment, care or treatment for gender dysphoria have been drawn to the attention of Prison Service Headquarters in recent years.[3]

---

2   A recent report by Community United Against Violence, a San Francisco anti-violence advocacy group, reported that nationwide in the US, 2,475 people were victimised by anti-gay violence. Of these, one in six attacks were against transgender people (in Heredia, C, 'Hate crimes against gays on rise across US' (2001) *San Francisco Chronicle*, 13 April): www.sfgate.com:80/cgi-bin/article.cgi?file=/chronicle/archive/2001/04.

3   *Hansard*, Written No 140 (22/02/01) (155267), Tuesday 27 March 2001. The question asked by Dr Lynne Jones (MP for Birmingham, Selly Oak): 'To ask the Secretary of State for the Home Department, how many people who are currently serving a prison sentence (a) have undergone some part of the gender reassignment process, (b) are undergoing treatment for gender reassignment and (c) have requested an assessment for gender reassignment?'

Whether this is a true picture of the number of transsexual people currently incarcerated in the UK's prison system is difficult to evaluate. Overall, prevalence studies in the general population are very problematic, with little formal 'counting' of transsexual people being undertaken. Certainly, no attempt has been made at counting those people who are transgender, whether because they do not wish to have gender reassignment treatment, are unable to undergo such treatment or even those who are living in their new gender role but have not yet decided to undertake the route to gender reassignment.

The *Report of the Interdepartmental Working Group on Transsexual People* (Home Office, 2000b) states:

> Studies carried out in the Netherlands suggest that the prevalence of transsexualism is between 1:11,900 and 1:17,000 in men over 15 years of age. The number of female-to-male transsexual people is far smaller, possibly in the region of one to every five male-to-female transsexual people. These estimates are supported by a recent study carried out in primary care units in Scotland which estimated the relevance in men over 15 years at 1:12,400, with an approximate sex ratio of one to four in favour of male to female patients. These studies suggest that in this country there are between 1,300 and 2,000 male to female and between 250 and 400 female to male transsexual people. (Home Office, 2000b, p 3, para 3.)

On that basis, with a male prison population of 58,470 and a female population of 3,150 (Elkins, Olagundoye and Rogers, 2001), one would expect four or five mtf transsexual prisoners and only one ftm transsexual prisoner. In reality, despite the answer given by the Home Office minister when this study was being undertaken, these figures are clearly just the tip of a much more significant figure lurking underneath. During the course of this study, Press For Change, the lobby group for transsexual people, gave details of 14 prisoners currently serving sentences who had sought their advice.

Further, the support groups for transsexual and transgender people report a much higher overall incidence of transsexual and transgender people. For example, the national support organisation for ftm transsexual men has over 430 of its members claiming to be living in their new gender role, and undergoing or have completed gender reassignment treatment, out of a total current membership of just over 700.[4] It is highly unlikely that such a group would meet all of its target audience, and it is more likely the case that its membership consists of a minority, albeit sizeable, of the total number of ftm transsexual people in the UK.

Finally, during the research, probation officers and prison staff mentioned transsexual or transgender inmates they were currently working with, or who they had worked with in the past, on several occasions. Most said that staff

---

4   Figures obtained from the FTM Network, BM Network, London WC1N 3XX, March 2001.

and fellow prisoners knew the individuals concerned as transsexual or transgender. Some were receiving ongoing treatment for gender related issues. Some were 'living' in effect in their new gender role. Some were not and were seeking assessment or treatment, and some had been transitioned into their new gender role for some time and were simply receiving their continued hormone therapy, albeit that they were not able to live in role in their particular custodial setting. The conclusion is that although the number of transsexual and transgender people in custodial settings is small, it is certainly more than one might expect from current prevalence figures within the general population. And it may well be that there are others who do not feature in the official figures as they are not seen as needing special provision.

ISSUES IN THE IMPRISONMENT OF TRANSSEXUAL AND TRANSGENDER PEOPLE

Imprisonment for trans people presents a particular set of problems. If they have not yet undergone genital reconstructive surgery, they will almost certainly be incarcerated in a prison for people from their natal sex grouping. In that environment, it may well be impossible for them to continue or to commence living in their chosen gender role and, if they do, their transsexual or transgender status will always be known by both prison staff and other inmates. That makes them vulnerable to bullying, sexual assault and violence. Additionally, if prisoners have started hormone therapy, it may well be stopped in the short term whilst consideration is given to its continuance, and for some, this can cause particularly distressing problems, for example, the recurrence of baldness in mtf transsexual women, and menses in ftm transsexual men.

The continuance of hormone therapy is very much determined by medical professionals on whether the patient is continuing the 'real life test', during which they must live in their new gender role, and a prison environment often makes this virtually impossible. If hormone therapy is to be continued, research has shown that many institutions only permit the continuation of therapy at a 'level' setting. Even if, outside of prison, the hormonal therapy of an individual would normally be adjusted to a higher level after some period, within a custodial setting, it will only be allowed at those levels prescribed before arrival within prison. Further, the same research has shown that in the US, where such therapy actually increases feminisation or masculinisation, it will be withdrawn on the basis that the prisoner should be maintained at the same level of body configuration as on their arrival (Brown, 2001). Clinicians will rarely consider surgical reassignment procedures unless the 'real life test' has been undertaken for at least 12 months. Imprisonment will certainly delay any plans for such interventions and, if a long sentence has been received, it may well lead to the end of any such hope on the part of the prisoner.

There are other matters that must also be considered:

- appropriate and safe housing in prison;

- the need of the prisoner to feel secure and safe in their appropriate gender role, along with a way of expressing their identity;

- the re-introduction of the prisoner into society on their release, which can be particularly difficult for transsexual and transgender people who may well have little social support outside of prison.

For many trans people who come into the CJS, the probation services will provide their main contact with the outside world. They will be viewed as the prime source of support, and probation officers may well be placed in a position of having to quickly gain an expertise and understanding of a matter previously known only through their reading of the popular press. As such, they find themselves seeking help from outside organisations, but contact and information can be difficult to find.

Most support organisations for transsexual and transgender people are unfunded, providing support for their current members from stretched resources and, despite good intentions, are unable to meet the needs of the probation officers or this particularly vulnerable group of their membership. Some organisations feel that they are trying to provide mechanisms of support for those who are trying to 'blend in'. As such, they will consider those who have been convicted of crime as being either troublesome, in that they damage the reputation of other transsexual and transgender people, or likely to have become involved in social crimes such as prostitution, which again damage the reputation of their other members. As such, little work has been done as to the unmet needs of trans people in the CJS.

CRIMINOGENIC FACTORS AND THE ROLE OF THE PROBATION SERVICE

The probation services' primary duty is to protect the public from the harm of those it supervises (Furniss, in Chapman and Hough, 1998). This is achieved, among other things, by the setting of clear objectives based on theoretical or empirical evidence (Furniss, in Chapman and Hough, 1998). This should culminate in deterrence from re-offending or the elimination of the propensity to re-offend (Bingham, 1997).

As an offender, a trans person should be in exactly the same position as any other person who commits a crime (Home Office, 2000b, p 9). However, the issue of physical determinants that ultimately decide whether a transsexual person is placed in a male or female prison (Home Office, 2000b, p 14) may be precisely those that contributed to the criminogenic element that led to the offence being committed in the first place. As Lord Bingham of

Cornhill, Lord Chief Justice of England and Wales, put it in his speech to the Probation 2000 Conference:

> Most of us, I venture to think, have never had to resist the temptation to kill, or wound, or rob a bank, or commit rape, or traffic in drugs or forge £50 notes. This does not mean we are better people; it just means that we have been lucky enough to pass our lives in social milieus in which such temptations are not commonly encountered. (Bingham, 2000, p 2.)

Whilst there are no service guidelines on the treatment of trans people by the probation service, the treatment of such people is considered locally, taking account of 'local issues' (Home Office, 2000b, p 15). An outcome through which a trans offender ceases to re-offend and begins to make a positive contribution to the community (an outcome that the public rightly expects) therefore depends on probation officers having relevant and appropriate support and information so that factors of social exclusion cease to be a criminogenic element in the offender's behaviour (Furniss, in Chapman and Hough, 1998, p 6, figure 1.2). As Lord Irvine proposed in *Modernising Justice*:

> The more people are helped to become citizens with a stake in society, the less society has to fear from one of the worst effects, and causes, of social exclusion: crime. (Irvine, 1998, p 1.)

Though many offenders with which the probation service come into contact experience chaotic and disorganised lifestyles, research indicates that 'programmes which target needs related offending (criminogenic needs) are likely to be more effective' (Furniss, in Chapman and Hough, 1998, p 6).

Trans people are no different in this respect. However, the 'effective execution of the sentences of the courts so as to reduce re-offending and protect the public' (Home Office, 2000a, p 2) relies on an effective, individually designed, 'one-to-one' offender programme. This needs to take account of the limits of knowledge, skills and abilities available so that effective team work (which may include 'outside partnerships') are fully utilised and valued (Furniss, in Chapman and Hough, 1998, pp 8–9, figure 1.3).

PROBATION OFFICERS AND TRANS PEOPLE

Eleven probation service areas were surveyed, providing 172 responses from probation officers. Of these, 51.2% indicated that they had experienced working with a transsexual or transgender person, or someone they thought may be transsexual or transgender or had gender identity issues, as an offender or as a person awaiting trial. 30% of the officers had worked with a transsexual offender, and 12.4% had worked with a transsexual person who was awaiting trial. 10.6% worked with a transgender offender and 4.2% had worked with a transgender person awaiting trial. Although the officers who responded were more likely to be those for whom the questions provided a note of resonance (because of their work experience), the survey clearly indicated that transsexual and transgender people are not an uncommon feature of the working career of a probation service officer.

Ten officers were randomly selected from the respondents to take part in a semi-structured telephone interview. Whilst randomisation meant that a small proportion of those interviewed had never knowingly worked with a trans client, their perceptions were relevant to the aims and objectives of the study. This is especially so given the strong possibility from the figures above, that as probation workers, they will be required to support a trans person at some point during their career. 50% of those interviewed believed they did not have (or could not) access the appropriate information needed to respond to a trans client's questions, requests and perceived needs. Those who had worked with a trans offender said that they had sought information primarily by asking the trans client for details of information sources, as local libraries and gay and lesbian support services had not had anything relevant.

Most understood that incarceration would cause great problems for a trans person, and they could see the obvious problems of placing a trans person in a custodial setting. The fact that most of them had only met a trans person within the CJS environment was recognised as having 'skewed their views'. They perceived them as having multiple problems, such as alcoholism and drug addiction ,and mental health issues such as depression and anxiety; so as a group they were very problematic to the officers who worked with them. Probation officers saw the hostel system for offenders as having a part to play in picking up the pieces of 'difficult to place' people. Whereas prisons are bound by rules and regulations in terms of how they classify people, the probation service hostel system can be more flexible, sometimes providing sole occupancy accommodation and bathroom facilities and so affording more privacy and, possibly, safety.

Officers who had not met a trans person expressed some anxiety at the prospect of having a trans client, and some had experienced personal embarrassment with being faced with a 'man dressed up as woman'. All officers said they felt unskilled and unknowledgeable about trans issues and felt this would affect their confidence in communicating with the client. Those who had worked with a transsexual or transgender offender had, in fact, found the task difficult. The housing of trans people in prisons of their natal sex had caused many crises in their work and their clients had had multiple problems; one had even wanted to 'change back' because of the experience of prison.

All of them felt the need for better training and information on matters such as appropriate language. General diversity training was not specific enough to basic issues and needs, particularly those connected to custodial settings, being too theoretical and not sufficiently related to specific client group needs. They would have liked easily accessible information, say through a central manual or a named, knowledgeable and supportive person without their own agenda in the CJS, preferably a trans person who could be contacted via the phone. Several suggested an 'adopt your probation office' scheme by local trans support groups so as to raise profiles and awareness.

Overall, all of them recognised that incarceration would cause great problems leading (perhaps) to psychological difficulties, yet despite problems, trans people would inevitably be placed in custody. They felt that trans people would be better off in a hostel than prison as safety issues must be considered when housing trans people, but this would prove difficult in the case of serious offenders.

The telephone survey was followed up with a focus group of 14 probation officers possessing considerable 'actual' case experience, knowledge and expertise gained over many years' involvement in varying roles, environments and related occupations. The team was situated in a central area of England, providing services to a large town and a large rural area. In particular, the team was part of a service that had successfully managed the transition of a transsexual probation officer, and was known to be interested and proactively involved in developing awareness and improvements in its ability to support its diverse communities, clients and personnel.

This group explored five primary areas of concern:

(1) the nature of the probation officer's job;

(2) the knowledge probation officers had about trans people's social and healthcare issues;

(3) the methods and sources officers used to access information;

(4) issues concerning disclosure of trans status;

(5) work within custodial and resettlement settings.

The nature of the probation officer's job

The preparation of a pre-sentence report (PSR) was one of the primary powers available to effect a process of recommending a sentence. The PSR primarily concerned 'the effect that prison would have' on the client, but was also concerned with other issues such as assessing a client's suitability to complete a period of community service. Where there are issues of medical concern, the probation officer would typically seek access to medical information from the client's GP. This requires the client to sign a consent form granting permission of access.

Because of limits on the time available to complete a pre-sentence interview (PSI) (typically 1 to 1.5 hours), probation officers experience difficulty in conveying the relevance of a particular medical issue to the client, and its importance in assisting the court to decide what action they should take.

Officers recognised the difficulty in persuading clients to disclose medical details to a stranger. Whatever provisions the PSR recommended (in the event of a custodial sentence), these would comply with restricted guidelines. For example:

> In one case, it had been made clear to a transsexual remand prisoner that if she returned to the male prison in which she was held, she would not be placed on the health wing because she did not have an illness. However, it was also made clear to her that she could not be placed in a female prison. The issue about where she could safely be held was therefore a real and immediate concern.

On that occasion, the argument was advanced that the offender should reside in a hostel. However, this was difficult to arrange because hostel provision is largely classified as either male or female accommodation, with many using shared, communal facilities.

The knowledge probation officers have about trans people's social and healthcare issues

The view was expressed that the ability of clients to anticipate what problems might arise in a particular situation (for example, the prison environment) depended on whether they had previous experience of prison environment. For example, one person had conveyed clearly at the PSR stage that she did not want to go to prison because she was not only aware of the effect that the prison environment had on her (as a trans person), but also knew that her presence in that environment impacted on the other prisoners around her. She was only aware of those issues because she had been through the prison system before – the first time without a pre-sentence report having first being prepared.

However, the officers' knowledge was very basic, and often restricted to the facts that hormone therapy was taken, and that surgery would be required. None knew, for example, that a post-operative transsexual woman would need to dilate (often daily) to maintain her vagina. The ability, at present, of probation officers to gain knowledge of such issues depended largely on the client's ability to assess their own needs and convey those to their probation officer. Unfortunately, clients who are often socially excluded and sometimes possess poor communication skills might not know this to be a relevant issue at the PSR stage and/or be too embarrassed to mention it.

The ability of clients to anticipate potential issues and convey these to their probation officer varied considerably. While some clients said nothing until faced with a crisis in the prison environment, others were articulate and able to eloquently communicate any issues and concerns.

The group felt unhappy asking any client whether, at any time, they had undergone any major surgery or taken medication requiring special issues to be considered. Their consensus was that:

> ... a probation officer would never dream of saying to people 'well are you transsexual?' to every client who came in, just as (they) ... wouldn't say to people 'well have you had a colostomy?'

However, the officers did point out that the PSR interview does provide the opportunity, prior to closing the interview, to ask the client if there is anything else they needed to discuss which may assist the court in deciding how to deal with them.

The methods and sources officers use to access information

Information is provided by county court officers, whose responsibilities include providing clients with information 'by hand' that they will be undergoing a PSR before sentencing. Clients are also provided with an appointment letter, prepared by the probation service's administrative staff. It informs them about the purpose of the PSR interview.

However, there is no mechanism whereby information is given to clients who might expect to serve a custodial sentence which provides them with a realistic appraisal of the prison environment. For example, most male prisons have communal shaving areas (for daily use), whereas female prisons only allow a person to shave once a week.

As probation officers did not make the decision as to whether a person went to prison or not, they were concerned that it would be 'prejudicial' to appear in the interview to be making a judgment that someone would be likely to receive a custodial sentence. However, during the body of the interview, when the issue of custody is discussed, the client could be asked to convey their thoughts in terms of what might happen to them if they were sent to prison, whether they have any particular concerns, and advice could be provided by probation officers on how to deal with their first day inside.

The conclusion of the PSR specifically deals with issues around what unusually adverse effects a prison sentence might have on a particular client. Consequently, in order to ascertain that information, open-ended questions will be asked, effectively reminding the client what will happen unless they include in the report convincing reasons why they should not serve a custodial sentence. However, it is very much up to the client to provide appropriate information, even though they may lack confidence, communication skills, be stressed and unfamiliar with the process.

Officers said they would have to ascertain 'the issues' from the client before seeking sources of advice, etc, but the courts do expect probation officers to verify medical information with the client's GP, consultant, hospital, etc. Officers generally tried to 'add' to this information from various sources. These might include colleagues who had encountered a similar issue in the past, voluntary agencies and the Internet (but many felt they lacked confidence and skills in the use of this particular resource).

Issues concerning disclosure of trans status

Probation officers considered these to be difficult questions to answer, particularly if people are unclear about the role of the probation officer when preparing a pre-sentence report, which is not one of a friend, but one of providing an objective assessment to the court.

One probation officer believed that the issue of confidentiality within the court was a good reason to tell clients not to reveal anything they didn't wish to be known publicly, though due consideration had to be given to the fact that the court had asked them for their opinion and assessment. Consequently, anything they felt was crucial would need to be referred to in some way – although there are different ways of doing that. The court can be asked within the PSR to keep certain things confidential (that is, it wouldn't be mentioned in open court), but confidentiality can never be assured because the PSR is sent to the prison. There is a fine balance to be reached, with officers not wishing to facilitate discrimination by including issues that are unconnected with the offending behaviour yet which might ultimately affect the court's perceptions of the client, thus affecting the sentence imposed. Two things needed to be considered:

(1) whether an issue is relevant to the offending behaviour; and

(2) whether it is relevant to the effect of a particular sentence.

For example, in respect of transsexual and transgender people, where the offence is related in some way to prostitution, its relationship with that lifestyle is invariably initialised through a necessity to raise money for treatment. Ultimately, this feeds into the stereotyped perceptions of trans people as likely to be involved in prostitution. Nonetheless, it could be said that it is important that prisons have as much information as possible – including those matters which the offender might seek to keep confidential. How can a prison assist a person unless they are aware of all the issues? But prisons are not perfect and there are prisoners who would maim or even kill a person simply for being transsexual.

Where a custodial sentence is imposed, sealed envelopes are dispatched to the prison containing PSRs, psychiatric reports and post-sentence interview details (for example, whether the prisoner would be a suicide risk or not). A copy will also go to the Governor of the prison, the discipline staff and the probation department at that prison. Where a trans person has not disclosed their status prior to receiving a custodial sentence, there is an opportunity for disclosure before being sent from the court to a prison. The post-sentence report is completed in the cells of the court. It involves the completion of a form – basically concerned with ascertaining if there is a risk of self-harm – though other issues (such as health or family matters) are covered as well. Therefore, it is a possible point of 'fire-fighting' intervention. Unfortunately:

... because of time pressure on the court, a post-sentence report doesn't always take place. Whilst a prisoner could ask to see a probation officer following the sentence being delivered ... if the van's ready ... then they'll go.

As there are specific medical needs that are crucial to the maintenance of the transsexual individual's well being, they must be addressed, even if inherently embarrassing to talk about.

When a transsexual person arrives in the prison system, they may be unable to see a health officer for some time, therefore, some form of medical input from a practitioner as well as a separate psychiatric report would be beneficial in facilitating the proper medical care of the individual concerned. It is important that the trans community itself be aware that its members need to provide whatever intimate medical and personal information is relevant to their probation officer at the earliest opportunity, if they ever face incarceration. The earlier disclosure is made, the sooner time pressures on probation officers can be managed.

Achieving disclosure early on, though, may be easier said than done with a client group whose *raison d'être* was to keep their medical circumstances private. It was suggested that a tick list to be sent to clients prior to the PSR might help prompt disclosure. It could include a variety of 'case study' scenarios such as requiring stoma care, having diabetes or epilepsy, needing transsexual or transgender health care. This could prompt clients with all sorts of needs to consider what personal issues might be relevant and in their interests to disclose, along with the opportunity to consult with their GP, social worker, etc. It would also allow the probation service as a whole to demonstrate that transsexual or transgender issues are of real concern and ones which are more frequent than the client might think and for which resources and support available.

Work within custodial and resettlement settings

The probation officer's role is primarily concerned with protecting the public and preventing the offending behaviour. Consequently, just because a client has problems, unless those are related to the offence, it does not necessarily fall within the probation officer's remit to deal with these. Other agencies may also provide assistance and support that is much better suited than any that the probation service could provide. Trans people's issues (as with any other diverse community) are multi-factoral; for example, a socially excluded trans person living on the periphery of society may also be a recovering addict, suffer from depression and anxiety, use alcohol or drugs. Rehabilitation facilities are very limited, though, and finding rehabs that can facilitate the needs of transsexual or transgender people (that is, cross-dressing) may be almost impossible. In reality, the problems will fall on the probation service. Needs can only then be met by ensuring that the probation officer is well trained, and sufficiently confident to act as the liaison point for all parts of the CJS when a trans person becomes involved.

A NEEDS ASSESSMENT OF TRANSSEXUAL AND TRANSGENDER PEOPLE WITHIN THE CRIMINAL JUSTICE SYSTEM

The evaluation of the needs of trans people who find themselves involved with the CJS had never been undertaken before. This needs assessment was be based on:

- limited interviews of former prisoners;
- an informal discussion with a current prisoner;[5]
- letters received by Press For Change from serving prisoners, over the last four years;
- interviews with transsexual and transgender people who do not have experience of the CJS;
- the detailed knowledge of the researchers, who are themselves both transsexual people;
- informal discussions with professionals who work within prison environments including a solicitor, consultant psychiatrist, psychologist and several probation officers;
- previously published work in this area.

This needs assessment considered five stages of the process of involvement with the CJS:

- arrest and detention (including remand);
- court appearance;
- arrival at a custodial institution;
- serving a prison sentence;
- rehabilitation and release.

Each stage is considered in the light of the following stages in a transgender or transsexual person's process, with separate reference where necessary to the distinct needs of 'female to male' and 'male to female' people:

- prior to transition to the new gender role;

---

5   Access to current prisoners, though agreed in principle, was not made possible during the period of the study, due to bureaucratic processes within the prison health system.

- post-transition but prior to completion of all desired surgical procedures;

- completed procedures including, where appropriate, genital reconstructive surgery.

The needs assessment considered the following areas of life in pre-custodial and custodial institutions:

- housing;

- personal appearance and personal expression;

- the right to personal privacy in relation to:
  - personal status;
  - body morphology;
  - medical confidentiality;

- accessing or continuing medical therapy and surgical procedures;

- personal safety both from self-harm and assault (sexual or not).

The results of the needs assessment are contained in Tables 1 to 5 (below, pp 233–37). Broadly, the results may be summarised as follows:

- Needs are different at different stages within the CJS.

- There is a need for respect of the individual's chosen path, such as using appropriate gender pronouns and name at all times.

- There is a need to have respected the individual's ability to contribute to the decision making process, for example, about where to be housed within a facility, about how a search is to be conducted, about their own healthcare needs.

- Bodily integrity is crucial to the transgender and transsexual person. Consideration needs to be given to how personal privacy, whether for bathing, medical care, searching, or simply shaving or breast binding, can be given.

- A mechanism needs to be developed which would enable a medical assessment file to be created to follow the prisoner, from the point of sentencing to release.

- Prompt assessment of medical needs is required on entering a custodial institution, whether the prisoner is pre-transition, post-transition or post-operative, so enabling continuity of care.

- Commencement or continuation of medical processes that would be available if the person was not incarcerated should be available.

There are specific medical, personal and social needs relating to pre-operative and to post-operative transsexual people regarding their continuation on their chosen pathway. These need to be assessed on a personal basis, before receiving a sentence for a term of imprisonment, and need to be reassessed during the term of imprisonment. Medical needs are related not just to the process of obtaining gender reassignment, but also to the consequences of treatment for gender reassignment. There is a need to respect the confidentiality of medical care and circumstances, and not to make unnecessary disclosure about the trans person's status to other prisoners or staff, without an informed decision being made by the trans person and their express permission being given, if possible. Rehabilitation requires a successful re-integration into society. For many transsexual and transgender people, this is only possible if they are able to return to society successfully into their new gender role. Consideration needs to be given to enabling them to leave a prison of the appropriate gender role even when pre-operative, and to ensuring that their leaving records reflect that gender.

SUMMARY OF RESULTS AND RECOMMENDATIONS

Accepting that at any time, there will be a significant number of transsexual and transgender people involved with the CJS and that transsexual and transgender people who offend should be in no different situation than any other similar offender, it needs to be acknowledged that transsexual and transgender people are likely to have chaotic and disorganised lifestyles, which contribute to their criminogenic behaviour. This chaos and disorder often results from the social stigma surrounding the trans person's existence. Thus, for rehabilitative measures to have any chance of working, it is imperative that the social stigma and prejudice is not continued within the CJS and positive steps are taken to advance the social well being of the trans person.

Effective practice with transsexual and transgender people in the CJS needs to ensure the right to continue reasonable expression of the personal sense of gendered self and appropriate related personal appearance. This requires safe housing appropriate to gender role and an acknowledgment that solitary confinement is not a satisfactory placement for accommodation. There needs to be respect for personal privacy, particularly as regards medical matters, both in the past, ongoing and in the future. These needs require different consideration at the different points of contact with the CJS and are dependent upon the gender transition being undertaken, and the point of time within that transition. Crucially dependent upon both the point within the CJS and the point within transition is a need to have respected the individual's ability to contribute to the decision making process concerned with social factors during their incarceration, particularly as to issues of disclosure of their status to family members, employers, co-workers, court and prison staff and fellow prisoners.

Bodily integrity is crucial to the transgender and transsexual person, just as it should be for other inmates. Particular consideration needs to be given to how personal privacy, whether for bathing, medical care, searching, lavatory use, shaving or breast binding, can be given.

In order for continuation of care and appropriate social acceptance, a mechanism needs to be developed which would enable a medical and social well being assessment file to be created to follow the prisoner from the point of sentencing to release. This would require a prompt assessment of medical needs immediately on entering a custodial institution, whether the prisoner is pre-transition, post-transition or post-operative, so enabling continuity of care, as if the prisoner was not incarcerated.

Accepting that the probation service's primary duty is to protect the public from harm by the setting of clear objectives based on theoretical or empirical evidence and that this culminates in a deterrent from re-offending or the elimination of the propensity to re-offend through the supervisory and rehabilitative processes, and that the probation service is in the unique position of following offenders through from the pre-sentencing stage to the post-release stage of punishment, probation service officers should collate the information needed to determine the needs of individual transsexual and transgender people who are offenders and ensure the regular updating and safe passage of such information as it follows the prisoner from arrival in a custodial setting to their release and re-housing within the community.

In order to meet these needs successfully, probation service officers need to communicate the need for full disclosure of possible needs by transsexual and transgender people. This could be facilitated by sending, to all people facing a pre-sentence report, a clear leaflet explaining why they are having a PSR, what a PSR will inform the court of and what will be the consequences of failing to disclose relevant matters at this stage. This leaflet should include, amongst other conditions, specific mention of transsexual and transgender people and the sort of matters that might be relevant. Probation officers need easy to access information about transsexual and transgender people, not just about support groups but also about the day-to-day aspects of life which might be relevant to a custodial period. This information should include a 'tick list' relating to day-to-day health and social welfare issues for transsexual and transgender people, enabling the probation officer to cover the relevant matters.

NEEDS ASSESSMENT: Table 1: Arrest and detention (including remand)

	PRIOR TO TRANSITION TO THE NEW GENDER ROLE	POST-TRANSITION BUT PRIOR TO COMPLETION OF ALL DESIRED SURGICAL PROCEDURES	COMPLETED PROCEDURES INCLUDING, WHERE APPROPRIATE, GENITAL RECONSTRUCTIVE SURGERY
HOUSING		To be placed in police station facilities of appropriate gender	To be placed in police station or remand facilities of appropriate gender
PERSONAL APPEARANCE AND PERSONAL EXPRESSION	Not to have differently gendered underwear or other clothing items commented upon	To be referred to using appropriate gender pronouns. To be given facilities to adjust clothing, wigs, makeup if needed to maintain gendered appearance. To be allowed to shave (mtf) if needed, particularly before court appearance	To be referred to using appropriate gender pronouns. To be given facilities to adjust clothing, wigs, makeup if needed to maintain gendered appearance. To be allowed to shave (mtf) if needed, particularly before court appearance
THE RIGHT TO PERSONAL PRIVACY IN RELATION TO: PERSONAL STATUS, BODILY MORPHOLOGY, MEDICAL CONFIDENTIALITY	Not to have transgender status disclosed unnecessarily or made known to significant others who do not otherwise know	Not to have trans status disclosed unnecessarily, particularly to press or to employer or other prisoners. Not to be required to undress unless essential to investigation and arrest. To be consulted over sex of searching police officer, and provision to be made for appropriate privacy where search involves removal of clothing	Not to have transgender status disclosed unnecessarily, particularly to press, employers or to significant others who do not otherwise know, or to other prisoners. Not to be required to undress unless essential to investigation and arrest. To be searched by police officer of same gender role. To be given appropriate toilet access if standing urination is not possible (ftm)
ACCESSING OR CONTINUING MEDICAL THERAPY AND SURGICAL PROCEDURES	To be allowed to take hormone therapy as required by current healthcare programme	To be allowed personal medical and healthcare, provision, eg, take hormones as required by current healthcare programme	To be allowed personal medical and healthcare provision, eg, take hormones, or to dilate where post-operative care of neo-vagina is required (mtf) as required by current healthcare programme
PERSONAL SAFETY BOTH FROM SELF-HARM AND ASSAULT (SEXUAL OR NOT)	To be housed away from other prisoners in circumstances where full supervision cannot be provided, and there is any risk of assault	To be (exceptionally) housed away from other prisoners in circumstances if full supervision cannot be provided, and there is any risk of assault	To be (exceptionally) housed away from other prisoners in circumstances if full supervision cannot be provided, and there is any risk of assault

NEEDS ASSESSMENT: Table 2: Court appearance

	PRIOR TO TRANSITION TO THE NEW GENDER ROLE	POST-TRANSITION BUT PRIOR TO COMPLETION OF ALL DESIRED SURGICAL PROCEDURES	COMPLETED PROCEDURES INCLUDING, WHERE APPROPRIATE, GENITAL RECONSTRUCTIVE SURGERY
HOUSING			
PERSONAL APPEARANCE AND PERSONAL EXPRESSION		To be allowed to attend court in appropriately gendered dress without comment. To be referred to using appropriate gender pronouns	
THE RIGHT TO PERSONAL PRIVACY IN RELATION TO: PERSONAL STATUS, BODILY MORPHOLOGY, MEDICAL CONFIDENTIALITY	To not have trans status disclosed in open court, if not relevant to the matter being tried. If trans status is relevant, consideration to be given to restricted reporting order being made	To not have trans status disclosed in open court, if not relevant to the matter being tried. If trans status is relevant, consideration to be given to restricted reporting order being made	To not have trans status disclosed in open court, if not relevant to the matter being tried. If trans status is relevant, consideration to be given to restricted reporting order being made
ACCESSING OR CONTINUING MEDICAL THERAPY AND SURGICAL PROCEDURES	If an appearance for sentence, full preparation to be made for possible custodial sentence including preparation of personal file with details of ongoing medical programme, and other relevant matters	If an appearance for sentence, full preparation to be made for possible custodial sentence including preparation of personal file with details of ongoing medical programme, and other relevant matters	If an appearance for sentence, full preparation to be made for possible custodial sentence including preparation of personal file with details of ongoing medical programme, and other relevant matters
PERSONAL SAFETY BOTH FROM SELF-HARM AND ASSAULT (SEXUAL OR NOT)			

NEEDS ASSESSMENT: Table 3: Arrival at a custodial institution

	PRIOR TO TRANSITION TO THE NEW GENDER ROLE	POST-TRANSITION BUT PRIOR TO COMPLETION OF ALL DESIRED SURGICAL PROCEDURES	COMPLETED PROCEDURES INCLUDING, WHERE APPROPRIATE, GENITAL RECONSTRUCTIVE SURGERY
HOUSING		To be housed in facility of appropriate gender role	To be housed in facility of appropriate gender role
PERSONAL APPEARANCE AND PERSONAL EXPRESSION		To not have gender role commented on inappropriately. To be referred to at all times by appropriate gender pronouns, and by new name	
THE RIGHT TO PERSONAL PRIVACY IN RELATION TO: PERSONAL STATUS, BODILY MORPHOLOGY, MEDICAL CONFIDENTIALITY		To shower privately away from other prisoners. To shave if needed (mtf). To be able to retain and maintain current medication	To be able to retain and maintain current medication
ACCESSING OR CONTINUING MEDICAL THERAPY AND SURGICAL PROCEDURES		To have prompt access to medical services to maintain continuity of gender reassignment treatment	To have prompt access to medical services to assess continuing healthcare needs, including specific post-operative and hormonal needs, and contra-indications that arise, eg. osteoporosis (mtf and ftm), deep vein thrombosis risk (mtf) and liver damage (ftm)
PERSONAL SAFETY BOTH FROM SELF-HARM AND ASSAULT (SEXUAL OR NOT)		Accommodation should be made available affording personal bodily privacy and safety, but not in isolation. Note: Where a facility of the appropriate gender has not been made, for whatever reason, then it must be recognised that safety may well prove more problematic (mtf)	

NEEDS ASSESSMENT: **Table 4: Serving a custodial sentence**

	PRIOR TO TRANSITION TO THE NEW GENDER ROLE	POST-TRANSITION BUT PRIOR TO COMPLETION OF ALL DESIRED SURGICAL PROCEDURES	COMPLETED PROCEDURES INCLUDING, WHERE APPROPRIATE, GENITAL RECONSTRUCTIVE SURGERY
HOUSING		To be housed in facility of appropriate gender role, affording personal bodily privacy without complete isolation	
PERSONAL APPEARANCE AND PERSONAL EXPRESSION	To access electrolysis services if needed (mtf). To be allowed appropriate gender or unisex clothing where possible, eg, underwear in a male facility (mtf), masculine trousers in a female facility (ftm).	To have facilities for wig care if needed, including access to outside specialist facilities (mtf). To access electrolysis services if needed (mtf)	To access electrolysis services if needed (mtf). To have facilities for wig care if needed, including access to outside specialist facilities (mtf)
THE RIGHT TO PERSONAL PRIVACY IN RELATION TO: PERSONAL STATUS, BODILY MORPHOLOGY, MEDICAL CONFIDENTIALITY	To be allowed to register for educational courses in new name and gender	To not have trans status disclosed to other prisoners. To have privacy for bathing, showers, etc. To have recognised the limitations afforded by breast binding (ftm) and wig wearing (mtf) such as the difficulties of working in very warm environments, or in very physical jobs. To be allowed to register for educational courses in new name and gender	To not have trans status disclosed to other prisoners. To be afforded privacy for regular dilation of neo-vagina (mtf)
ACCESSING OR CONTINUING MEDICAL THERAPY AND SURGICAL PROCEDURES	To be allowed to continue medical assessment if commenced prior to incarceration, including continuation to 'Real Life Test' and surgical procedures if appropriate (particularly if a long term of imprisonment)	To be allowed to continue 'Real Life Test' and to commence surgical procedures if appropriate (particularly if a long term of imprisonment)	To be allowed regular checks of hormonal efficacy, and threat of deep vein thrombosis (mtf) and liver damage (ftm). To be allowed to consult appropriate gender specialists if post-operative problems occur
PERSONAL SAFETY BOTH FROM SELF-HARM AND ASSAULT (SEXUAL OR NOT)	To be afforded enhanced safety consideration in the event of the trans status being visible to other prisoners	To be housed in facility affording personal bodily privacy and safety away from other prisoners, without complete isolation (mtf)	

NEEDS ASSESSMENT: Table 5: Rehabilitation and release

	PRIOR TO TRANSITION TO THE NEW GENDER ROLE	POST-TRANSITION BUT PRIOR TO COMPLETION OF ALL DESIRED SURGICAL PROCEDURES	COMPLETED PROCEDURES INCLUDING, WHERE APPROPRIATE, GENITAL RECONSTRUCTIVE SURGERY
HOUSING		If placed in bail hostel or similar, to be placed in facility of appropriate gender role	If placed in bail hostel or similar, to be placed in facility of appropriate gender role
PERSONAL APPEARANCE AND PERSONAL EXPRESSION			
THE RIGHT TO PERSONAL PRIVACY IN RELATION TO: PERSONAL STATUS, BODILY MORPHOLOGY, MEDICAL CONFIDENTIALITY		To be released from a facility of the appropriate gender role, enabling a successful re-integration into society in that role. To have removed from prison release documentation any reference which might disclose former gender role or trans status	To be released from a facility of the appropriate gender role, enabling a successful re-integration into society in that role. To have removed from prison release documentation any reference which might disclose former gender role or trans status
ACCESSING OR CONTINUING MEDICAL THERAPY AND SURGICAL PROCEDURES	To have pre-release medical file prepared containing details of all ongoing medical treatment, for continuation of provision on release	To have pre-release medical file prepared containing details of all ongoing medical treatment, for continuation of provision on release	To have pre-release medical file prepared containing details of all ongoing medical treatment, for continuation of provision on release
PERSONAL SAFETY BOTH FROM SELF-HARM AND ASSAULT (SEXUAL OR NOT)			

CHAPTER 13

'GENDER IDENTITY': PROPOSED ADDITIONAL PROTOCOL BROADENING ART 14 OF THE EUROPEAN CONVENTION; THE NEED FOR EXPRESS INCLUSION[1]

This proposal was submitted to the European Council when Art 14 of the European Convention on Human Rights was being considered for amendment and updating in 2000. Article 14 is considered the catch-all mechanism of the Convention designed to ensure that all vulnerable groups of people should be protected from ill-treatment by the state, and states:

> The enjoyment of the rights and freedoms set forth in this Convention shall be secured without discrimination on any ground such as sex, race, colour, language, religion, political or other opinion, national or social origin, association with a national minority, property, birth or other status.

However, this has consistently been held not to cover matters of sexual orientation or transgender status.

The European Council did not accept the proposed amendment, but an adapted version of this submission was made to the Human Rights Commission in Northern Ireland. In the proposed Bill of Rights which the Belfast (Good Friday) agreement indicated as forming part of any lasting settlement, the Human Rights Commission have not suggested inclusion of 'gender identity' *per se*. But they do say in the proposed section on Equality and Discrimination that the term 'other status' would allow transgender individuals to be protected, at least acknowledging the need (Northern Ireland Human Rights Commission, 2001, p 27).

WHY 'GENDER IDENTITY' SHOULD BE INCLUDED AS AN EXPRESSLY PROHIBITED GROUND OF DISCRIMINATION IN THE NEW ART 14

ILGA-Europe respectfully submits that the new Art 14 should also include the ground 'gender identity' so as to make it clear that people who are transsexual or transgender are protected.

Transsexual and transgender people are one of the most vulnerable minorities in Europe. Their relatively small numbers make it extremely

---

1   Submission of ILGA-Europe, the European Region of the International Lesbian and Gay Association, to the Steering Committee on Human Rights, Council of Europe. Drafted for the Board of ILGA-Europe by Dr Stephen Whittle, School of Law, Manchester Metropolitan University, UK, with the assistance of Dr Robert Wintemute, School of Law, King's College, University of London.

difficult for them to obtain any protection against discrimination through new legislation. Like lesbians and gay men, they face violence, harassment and the denial of jobs or services because their gender identity or expression does not correspond with their recorded birth sex (Whittle, 1995). Further, much recorded homophobic discrimination and behaviour is in fact based upon perceptions of a person's apparent gender identity or expression, and hence implied sexual orientation rather than actual sexual orientation, which may well be unknown.

When a transsexual person undergoes gender reassignment, some member states of the Council of Europe refuse to acknowledge the change of their social gender and/or the change of their body morphology. In these states, transsexual people are forced to endure the almost daily humiliation of revealing their birth sex in many practical areas of life, so making them vulnerable to discrimination and prejudice regardless of the success of their gender role transition. The ECHR condemned this practice, where forced disclosure of birth sex is sufficiently frequent, by finding a violation of Art 8 in *B v France*.[2] In that case, the applicant could not legally change her male forename, and could not prevent the disclosure of her birth sex (male) in documents such as her national identity card and her passport, and in her social security number.[3]

Additionally, this failure to recognise their new gender role means that for many, they are effectively unable, in law, to found families and to take on the full social responsibilities embedded within the family. The European Commission of Human Rights was to condemn this practice by finding a violation of Arts 8 and 14 in *X, Y and Z v UK*.[4] Although the European Court was unable to agree with the Commission due to the facts of the particular case, they did, however, unanimously find that transsexual people were able to form *de facto* families and hence should be afforded protection under Art 8.

WHY THE APPLICATION OF 'SEX' OR 'SEXUAL ORIENTATION' IS NOT SUFFICIENT

One approach to the protection of transsexual and transgender people would be to treat discrimination against them as a form of discrimination based on 'sex'. The European Court of Justice adopted this approach in interpreting European Community sex discrimination law in *P v S and Cornwall County Council*.[5] The Court held that dismissal of a transsexual employee because she had announced her intention to undergo gender reassignment was:

---

2 *B v France* (1992) ECHR, Series A, No 57.
3 *Ibid*, paras 25–26, 59–63. The Court noted, at para 12, that the applicant was 'unable to find employment because of the hostile reactions she aroused'.
4 *X, Y and Z v UK* (1997) 24 EHRR 143, ECHR, www.echr.coe.int.
5 *P v S and Cornwall County Council*, Case C-13/94 [1996] IRLR 347, ECJ.

... discrimination ... based, essentially if not exclusively, on the sex of the person concerned ... To tolerate such discrimination would be tantamount ... to a failure to respect the dignity and freedom to which he or she is entitled, and which the Court has a duty to safeguard.[6]

The disadvantage of this approach is that it closely associates biological sex with gender role. Those states that do not legally recognise a change of social gender[7] maintain a situation whereby a transsexual person is still regarded as being of their recorded birth sex; therefore, any discrimination is based on recorded birth sex and resultant 'sex change' rather than new gender role.[8] Thus, any claim by the transsexual person provides a field day for the mass media as an individual's 'change of sex' becomes a crucial evidential element in any claim made. In this way, the judicial process becomes both a site for discriminatory treatment as individuals' (otherwise irrelevant) private medical histories are disclosed, and a source of further discrimination by others after such disclosure.

A transgender person who does not intend to, or is unable to, undergo gender reassignment is not regarded as having any possible claim based on grounds of sex. As they have not sought to 'change' their sex,[9] therefore, any discrimination is only construed in terms of their original recorded birth sex which, again, is revealed during the judicial process.

Another approach would be to treat discrimination against transsexual persons as a form of discrimination based on 'sexual orientation'. The Constitutional Court of South Africa adopted this approach in interpreting the non-discrimination provision (s 9(3)) of the 1996 Constitution of South Africa, in *National Coalition for Gay and Lesbian Equality v Minister of Justice*.[10] Justice Ackermann held that:

[T]he concept 'sexual orientation' as used in section 9(3) ... must be given a generous interpretation of which it is linguistically and textually fully capable of bearing. It applies equally to persons who are bisexual, or transsexual ...

The disadvantage of this approach is that transsexual and transgender people, like all other people, claim or express their sexual orientation in a variety of

6   *Ibid*, paras 21–22.

7   A change of social gender takes place when a transsexual or transgender person commences living full time in their new gender role.

8   Eg, discrimination against a transsexual woman would be considered as if it was discrimination against a man who had then undergone gender reassignment rather than against her as a woman. See the decision in *P v S and Cornwall County Council* (above), which effectively affords protection by virtue of P (a man) undergoing gender reassignment, rather than to P as a woman who happens to be a transsexual woman.

9   Eg, a discrimination case brought by a male transgender person concerning dress codes in the workplace would fail as the question would lie as to what other uniform rules related to men in the workplace. See the decision in *P v S and Cornwall County Council* (above) which only affords protection if a person 'intends to undergo, is undergoing or has undergone gender reassignment'.

10   *National Coalition for Gay and Lesbian Equality and Another v Minister of Justice and Others*, CCT11/98 (9 October 1998).

ways. Gender identity has little, if any, relation to sexual orientation other than that it can dictate how others perceive a person's sexual orientation. It would also not address issues such as arbitrary gender specific dress codes in the workplace or access to gender appropriate restroom facilities or recognition of any right of non-disclosure concerning gender reassignment. It would also fail to address situations involving discrimination on the grounds of sexual orientation, where such discrimination has not yet been made illegal.[11]

The ECHR has yet to adopt either of these approaches. Even if it were to adopt one of them, neither would provide symbolic recognition and condemnation of discrimination based on of the specific phenomenon of gender identity disorders and gender reassignment treatment, or simply just mistaken perceptions of gender identity. Only express inclusion of 'gender identity in Art 14 could do so.

THE GROWING NUMBER OF PRECEDENTS IN NATIONAL AND INTERNATIONAL LAW JUSTIFIES EXPRESS INCLUSION OF 'GENDER IDENTITY'

In spite of the extreme difficulties that transsexual people experience in attempting to invoke the legislative process, there was in the 1990s a growing number of precedents for express protection. The anti-discrimination legislation of a number of cities in the US includes 'gender identity' as a prohibited ground.[12] In the US state of Minnesota, anti-discrimination legislation defines 'sexual orientation' as including 'having ... a self-image or identity not traditionally associated with one's biological maleness or femaleness'[13] and in California, gender and gender expression are protected categories under the state's hate crimes legislation.[14]

Discrimination against transsexual persons is also expressly prohibited in South Australia[15] and in the Northern Territory of Australia,[16] where sexuality is defined to include 'transsexuality', and in the Australian Capital Territory, where 'transsexuality' is a separate, prohibited ground.[17] In New

---

11 See the American case of *Von Hoffburg v Alexander* 615 F 2d 633 (1980), in which a service woman who married a female to male transsexual, who was legally male, was honourably discharged as it was held that the relationship disclosed her alleged homosexual tendencies. This seems a very illogical state of affairs as although her husband was a legal male, he was held for the purposes of army regulations to be a biological female.

12 These cities include Minneapolis, San Francisco, Evanston (Illinois), Louisville (Kentucky) and Houston.

13 See Minn Stat Ann s 363.01(45).

14 Calif Stat AB 1999, signed on 28 September 1998.

15 Equal Opportunity Act 1984.

16 Anti-Discrimination Act (REPA007) 1996.

17 Discrimination Act No 81 of 1991.

South Wales,[18] discrimination is prohibited 'on transgender grounds' and the legislation refers to people as 'being transgender'.

The ECJ has also found that it is no longer appropriate to discriminate against a transsexual person. Advocate General Tesauro has stated:

> To my mind, the law cannot cut itself off from society as it actually is, and must not fail to adjust to it as quickly as possible. Otherwise it risks imposing outdated views and taking on a static role. In so far as the law seeks to regulate relations in society, it must on the contrary keep up with social change, and must therefore be capable of regulating new situations brought to light by social change and advances in science. From that point of view, there is no doubt that for present purposes the principle of the alleged immutability of civil status has been overtaken by events. This is so in so far as and from the time that the fact that one cannot change one's sex for bureaucratic and administrative purposes no longer corresponds to the true situation, if only on account of the scientific advances made in the field of gender reassignment.[19]

There is throughout Europe ever-wider recognition of transsexuality both by legislation and judicial decision, and sex change surgery is allowed in every member state of the European Community. Advocate General Tesauro, when calling upon the ECJ to afford protection to transsexual people, said:

> I am well aware that I am asking the Court to make a 'courageous' decision. I am asking it to do so, however, in the profound conviction that what is at stake is a universal fundamental value, indelibly etched in modern legal traditions and in the constitutions of the more advanced countries: the irrelevance of a person's sex with regard to the rules regulating relations in society. Whosoever believes in that value cannot accept the idea that a law should permit a person to be dismissed because she is a woman, or because he is a man, or because he or she changes from one of the two sexes (whichever it may be) to the other by means of an operation which – according to current medical knowledge – is the only remedy capable of bringing body and mind into harmony. Any other solution would sound like a moral condemnation – a condemnation, moreover, out of step with the times – of transsexuality, precisely when scientific advances and social change in this area are opening a perspective on the problem which certainly transcends the moral one.[20]

In 1989, the Parliamentary Assembly of the Council of Europe adopted Recommendation 1117 on discrimination against transsexuals and a

---

18 Anti-Discrimination Act No 48 of 1977, as amended by the Transgender (Anti-Discrimination and Other Acts Amendment) Act No 22 of 1996, Schedule 1.

19 *P v S and Cornwall County Council*, Case C-13/94 [1996] IRLR 347, ECJ, para 9.

20 *Ibid*, para 24.

Resolution on the condition of transsexuals, which in cases of transsexualism called on member states to introduce legislation whereby:

> ... all discrimination in the enjoyment of fundamental rights and freedoms is prohibited in accordance with Article 14 of the European Convention on Human Rights.[21]

Within the ECHR, there has been a gradual move towards recognising that transsexual people are suffering from violations of their human rights. The most recent decision of the Court ruled only by the narrowest of margins that there had not been a violation of Art 8 of the Convention.[22]

Albeit that there may not as yet be an international consensus that 'gender identity' should be treated like sex, race or religion, there is undoubtedly a growing awareness of and a recognisable trend towards acknowledging the extent of the discrimination that transsexual and transgender people face. When the existing list of grounds within Art 14 of the Convention are reviewed, those conducting the review must recognise the limitations that the ECHR has faced in attempting to provide protection through other Articles of the Convention. Because of the fundamental failure of many nation states to afford recognition of the 'change of sex' of transsexual and transgender people, gender identity in itself becomes an irrelevance within arguments based around recorded birth sex. As such, although the treatment individuals complain of is inevitably concerned with the contradictory appearance of civil documentation or legal status and the morphology of the person who has to daily represent themselves, the Court is unable to consider them as being treated any differently from any other person of the same recorded birth sex. It is only by adding to Art 14 that there will be no discrimination based on gender identity, that nation states will be obligated to initiate some steps towards addressing this contradiction and the other legal anomalies that transgender and transsexual people face.

However, including 'gender identity' will not mean that the Court will be obligated to find that every distinction based on 'gender identity' automatically violates the Convention. The Court has established that a difference in treatment on grounds expressly included in Art 14 may be permitted, provided that the difference in treatment has an objective and reasonable justification and is proportionate to a legitimate aim.[23] The Court will still be able to consider, in each case, the consensus amongst the Council of Europe member states regarding the particular issue and the resulting breadth of the margin of appreciation that should be afforded member states.

---

21 Recommendation 1117, 1989, Parliamentary Assembly of the Council of Europe.

22 *Sheffield and Horsham v UK* (1998) 27 EHRR 163, ECHR: www.echr.coe.int.

23 *Belgian Linguistic Case*, Case No 68/1 (1979–80) 1 EHRR 241.

THE LIST OF GROUNDS IN ART 14 DOES NOT INCLUDE SERIOUS KINDS OF DISCRIMINATION RECOGNISED IN EUROPE SINCE 1950 AND THEREFORE NEEDS TO BE REVISED

One argument that might be made against the inclusion of 'gender identity' is that the current list of 13 grounds contained within Art 14 is long enough, and is non-exhaustive. If the original list of grounds adopted in 1950 is opened up, there will be no end to the additions that could be proposed. It is better to leave the addition of new grounds to the ECHR.

However, in 1950, it would not have been possible to consider including the grounds proposed, as transsexualism had only just been recognised within medical circles, albeit as a form of pseudo-hermaphroditism.[24] The text of the Convention itself had been taken from the Universal Declaration on Human Rights written in 1948 before any recognition of this particular human condition. At that time, the emphasis was inevitably to be concerned with those particular matters that had led to the horrors of the war and the Holocaust. Although people with 'gender differences' had also been the target of the Nazi killing squads, it was not until the early 1980s that there was any recognition of that fact.[25] The Convention is a text of its time and yet it was intended that it be a text for a new Europe, not the old one. We are now in that new Europe and as such, the text needs updating for new social conditions and new social experiences.

To freeze the Convention at that historical moment in 1950 would fetter the Convention in a way that the ECHR has itself rejected.[26] The Court's approach to interpreting the Convention has been to ensure that it grows with changing conditions in Europe. It may well be asking the Council to take that 'courageous step' called for by Advocate General Tesauro of the ECJ. But, just as the ECJ did not shy away from providing the educational thrust called for, it is also an appropriate time to make improvements to Art 14 of the Convention to recognise both the social changes that have taken place and

---

24 The term 'transsexual' was not coined until 1950 when the Convention was being written. David Cauldwell, a populist medical writer, invented the term 'psychopathia transexualis' and the associated word transexual (*sic*). It was not used in a scientific paper until 1953, when the endocrinologist Harry Benjamin used the word 'transsexual' to describe a patient. Transsexualism was not separately categorised as a medical condition until its appearance in the *Revised Third Edition of the Diagnostic Statistical Manual of the American Psychiatric Association* in 1979.

25 The publication of *The Men with the Pink Triangle* (Heger, 1980) finally disclosed that homosexual people, and those perceived as homosexual (which would include transvestites and other people who were perceived as homosexual by their gender behaviour and who might have now considered themselves to be transgender or transsexual) were also victims of the Nazi killing machine.

26 The Court has said 'the Convention is a living instrument ... which must be interpreted in the light of present day conditions' (*Tyrer v UK* (1978) ECHR, Series A, No 26: para 31).

which are still needed in the future. Amending Art 14 will provide a way for the Council of Europe to better reflect the Europe of the new millennium rather than a Europe petrified for all time at the end of the Second World War.

CHAPTER 14

SURGICAL REQUIREMENTS FOR LEGAL RECOGNITION: WHY A VAGINECTOMY SHOULD NOT BE DEMANDED OF A TRANSSEXUAL MAN

This affidavit was prepared on 24 September 1997 for submission to the State Appeal Court on Ontario Canada. It was written in my capacity as a senior lecturer in law, a transsexual man myself and the co-co-ordinator of the Female to Male Transsexual Network in the UK. A transsexual man who had undergone irreversible hormone therapy and a bilateral mastectomy was refused permission to have his new gender role legally recognised until he underwent surgery to remove the vagina (vaginectomy) and close the vaginal entrance (vaginal occlusion). This almost certainly arose out of the fear that he might continue to use his vagina for sexual purposes.

Vaginectomy is a major surgical intrusion, often leading to massive blood loss and the attendant risks. Furthermore, the vaginal walls are intricately bound up with the clitoris, which is much larger than is commonly believed and which provides the posterior wall to the vagina. Vaginectomy can result in a loss of sexual sensation, and most transsexual men, even those who have full phalloplasty surgery to form a new 'penis', will choose not to undergo a vaginectomy, choosing rather simple occlusion of the vaginal entrance.

The application was successful, and the transsexual man was allowed to have his new gender recognised in law.

AFFIDAVIT

It is not appropriate or necessary to require a vaginectomy of those people who have undergone the transformation from female to male. There are several reasons for thinking this.

Current surgical provision as regards the provision of an acceptable phallus is very limited. Female to male transsexual men seek phalloplastic surgery which will produce a phallus that:

- looks realistic;

- through which urinary voiding is possible; and

- is sexually sensate.

Even 'state of the art' surgery can, at best, only ever afford two out of the three results that are desired by the ftm transsexual. However, currently, surgeons in this field promise at best a success rate of one in eight, with only two of these requirements being met as a general rule, for example, realistic looks and voiding, or sexual sensation and voiding.

Such surgery is extremely expensive – between $US 30,000 and $US 150,000. The surgical procedures vary in number, often requiring four to six hospital in-patient stays, and in some cases upward of 15 or 16 hospital stays. The surgical procedures have little guarantee of success, they will take a period of two to three years and the procedures are debilitating, often suffering catastrophic failure of the phalloplasty site. For many who commence upon this long road, the social cost is tremendous, with them losing their jobs and often their families and social support networks, and a few will suffer severe depressive illnesses as a result of undertaking this process.

As such, it is impossible to recommend this route to ftm transsexual men. The support networks, and all the many clinicians in the field, which includes many surgeons who perform this surgery, recommend that a period of peer group counselling be undertaken before any decision on phalloplasty is taken. The current recommendations are that with such counselling, most ftm transsexual men develop coping mechanisms to deal with their lack of a penis, and their partners, whether female or male, learn to respect the emotional limitations that ftm transsexual men face. As such, the ftm transsexual can live a full life as a man after hormone replacement therapy, a bilateral mastectomy, oophorectomy and hysterectomy.

Whether the ftm transsexual man then uses his full range of genital organs for sexual activity is a matter to be decided between him and his partner in the privacy of the bedroom. Some have penetrative sex, some do not (some, because of their shame and distaste with their body, will not have sexual relationships at all); however, most ftm transsexual men will discuss their sexual needs in terms of their genitals being male genitals but differently abled genitals, just as someone who is paraplegic might discuss their genitals. Furthermore, many ftm transsexual men speak of enjoyable vaginal sexual sensation at orgasm even without penetration occurring. Should ftm transsexual men be denied sexual satisfaction simply because they are differently abled men? We would not consider refusing a paraplegic who had no genital sensation the opportunity to use other parts of their body for sexual satisfaction.

Another reason for not demanding vaginectomy of the female to male before legal recognition is that the retention of the vaginal tissues is imperative if surgical procedures improve and phalloplasty becomes a more likely option. Vaginal tissues are often used in the procedure to line the urinary 'hook up' which will transfer urine to the site at the head of the new penis. If a vaginectomy is performed in advance of this procedure, then artificial means such as silicon tubing have to be used for such hook-ups. These are notorious for their failure rate, and one of the main problems currently incurred by ftm transsexual men who undergo phalloplasty is catastrophic failure of the site where such a tube is connected to the former urethral channel. As such, it is positively cruel and inhumane to demand that female to male transsexual men should undergo phalloplasty which will leave many of them incontinent, unable to work, in great pain, severely scarred and socially isolated.

If phalloplasty is not to be demanded, and it would be a human rights abuse to do so, then to demand a vaginectomy removes sexual satisfaction for the present and hope for the future for little reason. After a few months on hormone replacement therapy, the ftm transsexual man will be sterile for all procreative purposes, so the judicial and social fear of 'the man who has a baby' is extremely far-fetched.

To refuse legal recognition of what, after a short time, becomes a social reality for the ftm transsexual man, that is, their social position as male, not only can cause psychological harm, leaving the individual constantly doubting their social role and acceptance, but also leaves them open to abuse, prejudice and harassment in the workplace. This recognition should not be based in excessive demands which contravene basic human rights.

CHAPTER 15

TRANSSEXUAL PEOPLE IN THE MILITARY

Malone v RAF[1] concerned a weapons technician of the Royal Air Force. Having served for several years, the technician sought advice from the camp psychiatrist concerning several matters. The psychiatrist initially diagnosed 'incurable psychosis' and the technician was downgraded from the use of live arms. In 1993, after two years of therapy, the diagnosis was changed to one of 'gender identity disorder: transsexualism'. At that time, she was given notice of immediate termination of her employment on the grounds that 'she was unable to meet service obligations due to a permanently reduced employment standard'. This happened shortly before the decision of the European Court of Justice in *P v S and Cornwall County Council*, which had held that the Equal Treatment Directive of the EC provided protection to anyone 'intending to undergo, undergoing or who had undergone gender reassignment'. As the Equal Treatment Directive came into force in 1975, there was a good basis for those transsexual people who had suffered discrimination in the period 1975–96 to make a claim under the Sex Discrimination Act.[2]

Malone was settled out of court, not least because of the expert witness affidavits. Consequently, and some time before any protection was given to gay or lesbian people in the military, transsexual people had the opportunity to enlist or to transition within their branch of the services. This has not happened often, but a sergeant within the army has transitioned (Davies and Jones, 1999), and an RAF pilot has resumed flying duties since her gender reassignment (Barillas, 2000). The policy of the Ministry of Defence is quite clear. On one recruitment web page, they answer the question:

I am a transsexual; is it possible for me to join?

[with]

Yes. There is no bar to the employment of transsexuals in the Armed Forces. (Ministry of Defence, 2001.)

Achieving this whilst gay and lesbian people were still effectively barred[3] from the services was problematic, as can be seen from the affidavit below. The affidavit also illustrates the problem of explaining the complexities of trans lives within language and a framework that the courts will understand. Accordingly, the terms used are often antiquated as regards terms that the trans community would prefer to be used. This is indicative of the problem

---

1   *Malone v RAF* (1996) unreported, High Ct.
2   *Marshall v Dame Barbara Mills and the Crown Prosecution Service* (1998) IT.
3   This ban was only overturned after the decision of the ECHR in *Lustig-Prean and Beckett v UK; Smith and Grady v UK* (1999) 31 EHRR 23, ECHR, www.echr.coe.int.

often faced in bringing trans people's matters before the courts. Advocacy is the art of winning, and education is a secondary matter. No matter how much we, as trans people, and particularly in my case as a trans lawyer, might wish to change social attitudes, this cannot be done by words alone. It is only by successfully integrating people in a society that they can be accepted by that society. To do that, they must be able to participate, which means (using whatever methods available within reason) winning the cases which ensure that participation. This chapter is included as a specific example of the problems faced by practising lawyers and their advisors, and how these can be overcome. The fact that transsexual people can now serve in the armed services, in fire brigades, in police forces, as teachers and in many other roles means that participation, and ultimately integration, is taking place.

AFFIDAVIT: TRANSSEXUAL PEOPLE IN THE ARMED SERVICES

There are many transsexual people who have served or are serving, albeit not openly, within the armed forces. Research by Captain George Brown MD of the US Air Force has shown that in fact it is likely that:

> ... the prevalence of transsexualism in the armed forces may actually be much higher than in the civilian population (Brown, 1988). Brown's research was undertaken in the mid-1980s whilst an active duty military psychiatrist at an Air Force base situated in the mid-western United States in a community of over 300,000 military members, their families, and an associated civilian work force. He evaluated 11 biological males with severe gender dysphoria, well over the expected incidence of between 1:37,000 and 1:100,000 males.

There are many historical as well as contemporary examples that can be cited of transsexual people who have served their country in the forces, both in and out of combat. One of the more notable historical examples was Sir James (née Miranda) Barry who served in the British Army for more than 40 years and became colonial medical Inspector-General in South Africa, but who was discovered on death to have been born a biological female (Ray, 1958). More recent examples have included Jan (né James) Morris (Morris, 1974), Roberta (né Robert) Cowell (Cowell, 1954), Christine (né George) Jorgensen (Jorgensen, 1967), Robert (née Joyce) Allen (Allen, 1954) and Renee (né Richard) Richards (Richards, 1983). The question in fact to be addressed is not whether transsexual people serve in the armed forces, but whether upon discovery of their gender variant status, they should be discharged or alternatively reinstated.

TRANSSEXUALITY AND HOMOSEXUALITY

The question needs to be distinguished from that concerned with whether lesbian women and gay men should be discharged from the forces at the moment their sexuality becomes known to their commanding officers. Transsexuality has little relationship with sexuality and it is important to uncouple the concept of sexual orientation from the concepts of gender role and gender identity. Sexual orientation is defined by a person's responsiveness to sexual stimuli, the most salient dimension of which is probably the sex of one's sexual partner. Gender role is in fact:

> ... behaviours, attitudes, and personality traits that a society, in a given culture and historical period designates as masculine or feminine. (Zucker and Bradley, 1995.)

Gender role is that societal status which is assigned by others to a person and which is dependent upon the societal recognition of certain signifiers such as dress, whereas gender identity is the self's fundamental sense of being male or female.

In most people, their biological sex as determined at birth, and gender role and gender identity will be congruent. Transsexuals are those people in whom their personal sense of gender identity is at odds with the gender role assigned to them because of, initially, their body morphology. The use of the term 'transsexual' is an unfortunate one because it is often mistaken as a sexual problem, whereas it is better conceptualised as a gender identity disorder or a form of gender dysphoria.

As far as sexual orientation is concerned, in transsexuals, as in other persons, this can be directed towards individuals of the opposite or same natal sex grouping, or both (Reid, 1995). I have personally known many individual transsexual people who identify as gay, lesbian or bisexual after gender reassignment treatment, just as I have known many who identify as heterosexual in their confirmed gender identity and hence gender role. Of the membership of the FTM Network, for example, which is exclusively for ftm transsexuals, over one-third who declare sexual orientation identify themselves as gay men, with another 20% identifying themselves as bisexual.

Transsexualism is very different issue from transvestism or 'sexual orientation based cross-dressing'. A transvestite is a person who cross-dresses, in part, for the purposes of sexual arousal; a homosexual cross-dresser or drag queen will cross-dress, in part, to create a role for the self in a homosexual sub-culture and to make sexual contacts. A transsexual person cross-dresses for neither of these reasons, but in order to express their gender identity and gender role. It has little or no relationship to sexual behaviour except in indicating the gender role of the individual involved in a relationship, but that role could be exclusively heterosexual, homosexual or bisexual and would be in the expressed gender identity of the transsexual person.

It is nowadays possible to distinguish the true transsexual person from others who may manifest what appear to be similar behaviour patterns, or are diagnosed with other gender identity disorders, such as transvestites. If the correct differential diagnostic mechanisms are in place, then a person claiming transsexualism can be verified as such, and distinguished from a homosexual or heterosexual showing strong cross-dressing and cross-role behaviour. Such a homosexual would be referred to as a drag queen, a heterosexual as a transvestite.

Asserting your gender role can never constitute unacceptable behaviour, as gender role is an integral part of a person's sense of self and does not involve harassment or coercion of others, nor does it have any relationship to sexual behaviour. If a problem arises out of a transsexual person's sexual behaviour or sexual harassment to others, which might affect armed forces discipline or morale, there are mechanisms whereby disciplinary action can be taken. If a transsexual person transgresses the acceptable gender role mores, then they can be dealt with using the regulations that exist; that is, if there are sanctions against homosexual behaviour in the armed forces, and a transsexual person participates in lesbian or gay sexual activities in their new gender role, then the mechanisms that are in place can be used. But if the transsexual person does not transgress such regulations, then there should not be sanctions attached to their mere gender role transition and appropriate associated behaviour.

Other states do in fact provide mechanisms for such disciplinary action, such as those provided for the Australian Defence Force (Department of Defence, 1992), and these do not include as prejudicial behaviour, *per se*, either homosexual behaviour or transsexualism. As part of any good policy, any abusive or unacceptable sexual behaviour must call for discipline, but as transsexualism is not related to sexual behaviour, it cannot in itself be reason for disciplinary action.

Unlike the 'gay cases' in which the Defence Committee have examined and debated the policy relating to lesbians and gay men who serve in the military, no such argument or discovery has taken place in regard to transsexual people who serve. As such, the analysis regarding sexual orientation or associated behaviour has failed singularly to address the relevant issues as regards transsexuality which involves gender role transition and has little, if anything, to do with sexual activity.

COMPARATIVE EVIDENCE

According to surveys undertaken,[4] the situation for transsexual people in other countries is mixed, but increasingly, provision is being made to afford them legal confirmation of their reassigned gender status. Twenty one states that replied to a recent survey had some sort of provision for the transsexual's

---

4   These surveys were undertaken between 1991 and 1996, generally by questionnaires to embassies, ministries of justice and medical centres for gender reassignment provision.

change of status. Most were quite comprehensive in the provision they made, though Spain merely allowed for a change of name. Information regarding transsexual people in the armed forces is very scarce, as it is only now that the armed forces are being called upon to address these problems. Yet, it is apparent that other states do not treat transsexual persons as if they were lesbian or gay, if they have disciplinary regulations relating to homosexuality of armed forces members.

LEGISLATIVE APPROACHES

Some states, such as Sweden, Denmark, Germany, Turkey, Italy, South Africa, many Canadian states and Holland provide in their births and deaths legislation for the amendment of or reissuing of the birth certificate of the transsexual so that it reflects their new gender status. Such amendment or reissue will enable the holder to obtain changes to all their documentation that might distinguish their sex, and gives them full legal rights in their new status, such as the right to marriage or earlier retirement age where it is available. Accordingly, apparently, a transsexual person would be able to serve in the armed forces of these countries in their new gender role. Certainly, there appears to be no bar to transsexual people serving in the other uniformed public service groups such as the police, fire service and para-medical services, there have been no claims for unfair dismissal from any of these services or the armed forces and, as such, we can only assume that transsexual people do in fact serve their community in such organisations.

In Australia, there is currently a mixed situation as regards the protection of employment for transsexual people dependent upon whether the employer is a federal employer, as in the case of the armed forces or the post office, or a state employer, as in the case of the police or fire brigade.

South Australia provides for the legal recognition of a transsexual person's confirmed gender role through its 1988 Sexual Reassignment Act. This, alongside the 1991 Discrimination Act, means that a transsexual person is protected in employment, unless in a genuinely exempt occupation, and even then, discrimination would only be allowed in their legal status. Therefore, transsexual people can and do work in both the police service and the fire brigade.

The Parliament of New South Wales passed a bill to amend the 1977 Anti-Discrimination Act, inserting provisions outlawing discrimination or vilification on the grounds that a person is 'transgender' (the term actually used). The amending act (Transgender (Anti-Discrimination and Other Acts Amendment) Act 1996) provides for exceptions for religious organisations, superannuation, and sport. The Act also amends the 1995 Births, Deaths, and Marriages Registration Act to provide for alterations, on application, of the birth certificates of post-surgical reassignment transsexual people. The combined effect of this Act is to enable transsexual people to be protected if they work in the police service or the fire brigade.

Currently in Queensland, the Queensland Electoral and Administrative Review Commission has proposed changes to the Queensland 1992 Human Rights Bill which would allow recognition for all purposes of a transsexual person's reassigned gender and, if followed, would allow a similar situation to that which operates in New South Wales and South Australia to be in existence.

Thus, it is the case in Australia that as we see state laws being constantly amended, these, along with the regulations concerning unacceptable behaviour by members of the Australian Defence Force (Department of Defence, 1992), will soon mean that transsexual people will be able to serve openly in the armed services. Furthermore, the 1995 Sexuality Discrimination Bill proposes to make sexuality discrimination unlawful federally, and the Senate Legal and Constitutional References Committee held an inquiry on these issues which reported in March 1997.

In New Zealand, following the declaratory judgment in November 1994 of Judge Ellis in the High Court,[5] the Births, Deaths and Marriages Act 1995 was passed. Anti-discrimination legislation makes no mention of transsexuality, although it is an offence to discriminate on the grounds of sexual orientation.[6] Work involving National Security is excepted to some aspects of the personal self, such as ethical belief or disability,[7] but sexual orientation is not one of the specified as allowed exceptions.

In a conversation with Bruce Williams, the Secretary for Justice of the Legal Services Group for the Ministry of Justice on 10 June 1996, I asked whether transsexual people would be allowed to join the armed services or to continue in them post-reassignment treatment. Mr Williams said that many aspects of the Acts had yet to be tested, but the issue would be (in the case of armed service employment) whether it was a disability or a matter of sexual orientation. As it was likely to be regarded as a disability issue for the person involved, for example, an mtf transsexual could be regarded as a disabled woman, it might well be the case that it was not considered a proportionate response to dismiss a person because the effects of that particular disability would not necessarily hinder a person's ability to effectively perform their role in the armed services. However, he emphasised that the legislation is not comprehensive as regards all the potential issues.

---

5   *Attorney General v Family Court at Otahuhu* [1995] NZ Fam LR 57.

6   Human Rights Act 1993, No 82, Part II, s 21m.

7   *Ibid*, s 24.

As regards the US, many states provide a legislative or administrative approach to afford transsexual people legal recognition of their new gender role. But despite this, employment protection at a federal level has been notoriously difficult to achieve.[8] On the other hand, increasingly cities and states are developing ordinances and legislative approaches which afford protection at a local level.

The US military's policy to transsexual people is quite straightforward. The specific disqualifying regulation, common to all service branches, which bars appointment, induction and enlistment of transsexual people, reads:

Section IX GENITOURINARY SYSTEM

2.14 Genitalia

The causes for rejection for appointment, enlistment and induction are–

(a) Major abnormalities and defects of the genitalia such as a *change of sex*, a history thereof, or complications (adhesions, disfiguring scars, etc) residual to surgical correction of these conditions.[9]

There have been very few cases concerning transsexuals serving or applying to serve in the US forces. In the case of *Doe v Alexander*,[10] Doe, a post-surgical mtf transsexual, brought a suit for damages following rejection of her application for admission as an officer into the Army Reserves in 1976. The court held that they were particularly ill-equipped to develop judicial standards for commenting on the validity of judgments concerning medical fitness for the military.

In *Leyland v Orr et al*,[11] a 15 year veteran of the US Airforce/Airforce Reserve made the promotion list to Lieutenant Colonel immediately prior to gender reassignment surgery. Following a review board hearing, she was discharged from the service. She filed for relief in the Southern District Court of California, alleging that the discharge was invalid for a variety of constitutional reasons. The trial court found that the Airforce had acted in an arbitrary and capricious manner in their handling of the matter, but failed to rule on what should be done, preferring instead to refer back to the parties for resolution. Leyland appealed, and the Ninth Circuit Court of Appeals ruled that a discharge on the ground of physical unfitness after gender reassignment surgery did not violate regulations requiring individual assessment of a

---

8   In the US, to date, no court has found Title VII of the 1965 Civil Rights Act applicable to discrimination cases brought by transsexuals. The courts have repeatedly held that the word 'sex' in Title VII is to be given its plain meaning and is not to encompass transsexuals, the major thrust of the legislation being to provide equal opportunities for women. See the decision in *Kirkpatrick v Seligman & Latz Inc* MD Fl 636 F 2d 1047 (1979).

9   Air Force AR 40-501 Chapter 2, Section IX, paras 2–14, AFR 160-45; Army AR 40-501 Chapter 2, Section IX, paras 2–14; Navy BUMED manual Chapter 2, Section IX, paras 2–14. Emphasis added.

10 *Doe v Alexander* 510 F Supp 900 (1981).

11 *Leyland v Orr et al* 44 FEP 1636 (1987); 828 F 2d 584.

person's ability to perform for medical reasons *'given expert testimony that sex reassignment invariably impairs ability to perform'* (my italics).

It should be borne in mind that this case took place in 1987 and medical opinion has since altered in relation to gender reassignment treatment, and it is unlikely that medical testimony would now hold that such treatment invariably impairs ability to perform complex jobs, or hold leadership positions.

Interestingly, the regulations only cover genital surgery, and therefore the situation of the ftm transsexual who does not undergo genital surgery[12] is not covered. However, in the case of *Von Hoffburg v Alexander,*[13] a service woman who married an ftm transsexual, who was legally male, was honourably discharged as it was held that the relationship disclosed her alleged homosexual tendencies. This seems a very illogical state of affairs, as though her husband was a legal male, he was held for the purposes of army regulations to be a biological female, and again it must be considered that if this case were heard today, a very different result would be achieved.

As said before, many city ordinances and state regulations now protect the transsexual from discrimination in the workplace and, as such, many post-reassignment transsexual people openly serve in police forces, fire brigades and paramedic services in the US. One such example is Sergeant Stephen Thorne, an ftm transsexual who commenced work in the San Franciscan Police Force as a woman officer, but who was wholeheartedly supported by his senior officers and fellow police officers when he announced his intended gender role change. Another is Captain Melinda Whiteway of the New York Police Force, who successfully transitioned from male to female, with full support, after many years of service.

The reality in the US is that many pre-transition transsexual people serve in both the armed forces and the uniformed public services. Recently, there have been increasing moves to support transsexual people in the public service areas, both socially and through anti-discrimination legislation. As the issues relating to sexual orientation of armed forces members are increasingly aired, and reports like the Rand Report (1993) re-iterate that homosexual behaviour is not a threat to unit cohesion and performance, we are likely to see issues relating to transsexual people also being aired. Though, as said earlier, gender role has little to do with sexual orientation, the discussion of the one often leads to the discussion of the other. And as the Rand Report also finds, it will be seen that transsexual people join the armed forces, or other uniformed services, for exactly the same reasons as heterosexual and non-

---

12 Most female to males do not undergo genital surgery because of the limited and expensive nature of such surgery and its consistent failure to be effective, particularly here in the UK.

13 *Von Hoffburg v Alexander* 615 F 2d 633 (1980).

transsexual people, and though antipathetic feelings will still exist towards them, these will be moderated in time, and they will become valued members of any such units.

JUDICIAL AND ADMINISTRATIVE APPROACHES

Other states (generally those with a Napoleonic legal system) such as Belgium, Switzerland, Spain, Finland, Indonesia, France and Quebec do not provide a legislative solution. Instead, they provide a solution at law. This requires that the individual make an initial application to the court for a change of name and status. Many of these states make the procedure twofold: initially a change of forenames and then later, a change of sex designation. In some states, birth certificates may be amended, but if these are not publicly accessible, more often just identity cards and other civil status documents will be altered to recognise the individual's new gender role.

One such state is Greece. In Greece, there is no legislative regulation of a change of sex, but existing provisions allow a legal change of sex through judicial and administrative procedures which allow a person to obtain all the rights and responsibilities of the new sex. In a fax message received on 10 June 1996 from M Farmaki of the Hellenic Democracy Ministry of Justice General Management of Elaboration of Law, International Relations and Lawyers office, Mr Farmaki confirmed that this would mean that an ftm transsexual is permitted to join the all-male army, after completion of the judicial procedures.

East European and Soviet states have been undergoing great changes recently. Prior to 1990, many East European states such as Poland, all of the Soviet republics, Czechoslovakia and Yugoslavia provided legislative solutions to the status change required by transsexual people. Since the changes that have occurred, much legislation has disappeared and it will take some time to know what solutions will be developed in the new states. In Slovakia, for example, very recent legislation has allowed for the amendment of birth certificates upon receipt of medical evidence. In Poland, there are many hundreds of transsexual people who had their new gender status recognised before 1990. Currently, there is no legislation in this area, and the Polish Supreme Court has recently tightened their originally liberal attitude, though legal changes of status are still being provided under the jurisdiction of the Supreme Court if medical evidence of a change of sex is provided, but it is difficult to know the exact legal status of this change.

Some states provide no recognition of transsexual status at all. These include many of the African states, who do not recognise the phenomenon as existing in their society, but there is strong hearsay evidence of transsexuals who are able to recognise themselves as such in those societies making their way to South Africa for treatment. Black African transsexuals have for many years had equal access to treatment in South Africa.

Many Asian states do not provide any solution either, despite the fact that their societies do provide social solutions to the transsexuals in their midst, such as in India, Thailand and Japan. There are also occasional strange exceptions of states that seem to provide no solution, such as Luxembourg.

Other states such as the UK, Singapore and Portugal adopt a pragmatic and partially ameliorative approach to the problems that transsexuals face, and allow changes of certain documentation that may be used regularly in the public sphere, such as driving licences, passports and educational certificates. In this way, the 'sex' of the individual is not changed and hence they are unable to either marry in their new gender role, retire at an appropriate age, or have employment protection under domestic legislation. However, it has been reported in the *Asian Times* that discussion is currently taking place at a parliamentary level in Singapore to rectify this situation.

TRANSSEXUAL PEOPLE: MILITARY EXPERIENCES

I have never seen any evidence produced either by the Ministry of Defence or discussion in academic papers of other countries which allow transsexual people to serve openly. I have been informed by the leading gender reassignment surgeon Dr Joris J Hage of the Gender Identity Clinic at the Free University of Amsterdam that it would be illegal under Dutch law to discriminate against an individual who wished to serve in the Dutch armed forces because they were transsexual. In the event of conscription being in operation, the clinic would be willing to provide 'exemption pleas' for any transsexual person who did not wish to undertake military service, but this would not be because the clinical team necessarily deemed service inappropriate in all cases. In fact, they would also support the application of transsexual people who wished to participate in armed service. The clinic at the Free University is considered one the leading teams of clinicians in this field.

I personally know of many transsexual people who have served in the UK's armed forces, albeit without disclosure of their gender identity issues. To implement a blanket ban on transsexual people would be impossible, as many transsexual people are very successful at keeping their transsexuality a secret. Indeed, as the work of Brown (1988) has shown, many mtf transsexual people join the services in order to attempt to repress their transsexuality, in the hope that the services would make them a 'real man'.

For example, SM, who achieved the rank of Commander and who served as Admiral's Secretary and Supply Officer on HM Yacht *Britannia* before becoming Fleet Legal and Administrative Officer as part of the Staff of the Commander in Chief of the Fleet, joined the navy in 1965 in order to:

> ... make the best of things as I was: a man in what seemed to me to be a man's world.

Throughout the period of her service from 1965 to 1988, S knew of her transsexuality, and despite it, she obviously worked very successfully. From 1975 when upon reading Jan Morris's book *Conundrum* (1974), she realised she was not alone, she actively sought out support organisations. It was upon learning of the attitude that the navy would take to her gender identity that she worked towards retirement and the opportunity to undergo reassignment treatment.

Similarly, but in an almost reverse scenario, my work with ftm transsexual people has led me to know several who joined the forces in order to gain anonymity within an environment which would allow to take part in a more masculine career. However, they were to find themselves labelled as 'lesbian' if their gender identity issues became known. Mark Rees (1995) describes in his autobiography how his lack of femininity rather than any homosexual behaviour was to lead to problems when he was in the WRENS. He was labelled as being homosexual despite the fact that he had no sexual experiences with women, nor did he desire them whilst still living in a female gender role (Rees, 1995). JC, who served in the WRAC in the early 1980s, told me how he joined in order to get a 'man's job'. He became a heavy goods vehicle driver, but when he requested help from the unit doctor as regards his transsexual feelings, he was discharged – in this case, on medical grounds. In both of the above cases, the individuals continued to serve successfully during their period of assessment, and were able to perform their jobs consistently and effectively.

I personally applied to join the WRAC in 1974 in the hope that I would get a suitable career. It was only when informed that I had done so well in the entrance exam that I would be assigned to being trained as a TELEX operator in the Intelligence Unit rather than my chosen jobs of driver or dog handler that I realised that it would be a grave mistake. I was aware of my transsexuality and I realised that if discovered, it would be mistaken for lesbianism (which it was not). I did not show up for the bus to take me to Guildford.

The armed forces have shown a somewhat consistent response to transsexual people in their midst. In the cases of both Mark Rees and JC, they were medically discharged, and in JC's case, the army medical personnel arranged his assessment with a psychiatrist, his hormone therapy and his surgery in an army hospital, after his dismissal from the service. This then further delineates the question in hand. If the dismissal of the transsexual person is to be on medical grounds, then the issues are as to whether the transsexual person, whether pre-reassignment or post-reassignment, can perform the necessary duties to fulfil their role within the branch of the armed forces they are enlisted in.

As has been seen, transsexual people have often served in the forces and fulfilled their duties, albeit without disclosure of their transsexual status. There are the arguments that transsexual people would be either unfit to perform these once they commence or when they have completed gender reassignment treatment, or that they require such specialised medical services that it would not be possible to provide them, particularly in a zone of combat. Further, that their presence in a highly disciplined force, which provides little in terms of personal privacy, would be demoralising to other personnel, cause embarrassment or be a threat to discipline.

These arguments are facetious, in that it can be seen that transsexual people perform many highly technical or onerous duties in other professions. I know of several transsexual people, for example, the post-reassignment ftm transsexual man JL, who has been involved in the offshore drilling industry, which often involves a lack of privacy in terms of accommodation, and which makes particularly onerous demands in terms of strength, stamina and teamwork.

During reassignment treatment, the assessment process undertaken is such that it would make few demands in terms of sick leave. Once differential diagnostic procedures have been completed, most clinics require two or three one-hour visits before hormone therapy is authorised. At that time, the patient begins the real life test, whereby for maybe a year they are somewhat androgynous in appearance, but in many cases, after a suitable and clear explanation, their fellow employees have been happy with the situation and the decisions made, and will support their fellow worker through this period. There is a likelihood of up to 12 weeks away from work during which the surgical procedures will be completed, but after reassignment treatment has been completed, the medical intervention needed is minimal – the occasional check on hormonally influenced aspects of morphology, such as liver function. But apart from the regular taking of hormone preparations, in most cases, the transsexual person would require no more medical involvement than any other person who might suffer the normal medical issues in life. Most transsexual people will never address their transsexual medical needs any more than a migraine sufferer might address theirs.

In some cases, the process of transition can take longer than this, but this is invariably because of the associated problems of ending formalised family relationships that have been constructed in the old gender role, as well as the legal and social stigma still associated with 'sex change' treatment. However, if such legal and social stigmas were removed, for those transsexual people who have not been married in their previous gender role, the process of transition can be very easy and can be reduced considerably, as has been seen to be the case in Holland and other countries that make legal provision and provide social protection.

As to the presence of a transsexual person being a problem in a highly disciplined force that might need to go into combat, there are two issues. Firstly, very few armed forces personnel would be called upon to go into combat zones, and the job of the individual within the service must be looked at on an individual basis. Secondly, as seen, many pre-reassignment transsexuals have served in combat zones. The Transgendered Veterans Association in the US has many members who served in Vietnam. To my knowledge, several post-reassignment transsexuals were called up from the reserves to serve in the US forces in the Gulf Conflict. I have been told that WK, an American mtf transsexual woman, served in the US Navy at the time of the conflict, flying into combat zones at that time as a female officer with the rank of Commander, responsible for the targeting systems of onboard missile systems.

The case of Sister Mary Elizabeth of the Order of Elizabeth of Hungary, aka Joanna Clarke, brings into further question the issues of discipline problems. Sister Mary Elizabeth served for 17 years as a male in the US Navy and Naval reserve, becoming an Anti-submarine Warfare Electronics technician. At that time, she did not disclose that she was going to seek reassignment treatment. After discharge in the early 1970s she underwent a 'sex-change'. In 1975, she took a job as a woman with the Army Reserves as a supply technician, and was promoted to Staff Training Assistant 30 days later. She had been completely open about her gender reassignment, disclosing it to the recruiter Colonel A Walford of the 49th Medical Battalion before completing her enlistment papers. On all forms, she always gave her prior name and medical history.

In June 1977, she was recommended for promotion to Warrant Officer with full disclosure of her status. One month later, she was charged with immoral sexual activities and fraudulent enlistment. Her enlistment was voided, but not before a full evaluation at the US Naval Hospital in Long Beach, whereby her final report found her to be:

> ... disqualified only on the basis of the present wording of AR 40-501, qualified both physically and mentally to perform the duties of her rank and position. Recommend full retention.[14]

The *Los Angeles Times* broke the story on 14 September 1977 under the title 'Transsexual wars with army'. An investigation was ordered and though all allegations of misconduct were cleared, the Army retained its position that transsexual people were not sociologically or psychologically suited for military service. Her final discharge, after an appeal,[15] which was settled out of court by the army, was honourable with credit for time served. Throughout the period of her army career, her fellow soldiers knew of her status and there were apparently no problems.

---

14   Reported in letter to myself, 5 June 1996.
15   *Clarke v United States* No 443-80C (1980), US Court of Claims.

TRANSSEXUALS AND EMPLOYMENT

My research into employment practices concerning transsexuals showed that many transsexual people fulfil professional duties without issue, with over 50% of the survey respondents being in professional posts such as doctors, teachers, engineers, accountants, business executives, etc. Furthermore, 97% of the 146 respondents said that they were much happier after gender reassignment, despite over 44% having suffered financially as a result of taking this path and 35% suffering job loss as a result of their decision (Whittle, 1995, App C).

Though transsexual people have in the past had little or no protection within jobs, in fact, the tide of public opinion is turning and increasingly employers are putting in place personnel practices which ensure that transsexuals need not lose their jobs when they choose the moment of their transition. Many large employers now provide mechanisms whereby the worker is retained. Examples of these include British Telecom, most National Health Service Trusts, British Gas, etc.

Furthermore, the Department of Employment has stated in a letter to Sir George Young MP that:

> Although there is no specific legislation to cover discrimination against transsexuals, we are keen to eliminate all forms of discrimination.[16]

Thus, we see a commitment at a government level to respond to the current lack of employment protection afforded to transsexual people.

SECURITY IMPLICATIONS

Many transsexual people have retained or obtained security ratings that allow them to perform sensitive duties. I know of one who works in a senior and sensitive position for British Aerospace, and SB, a post-operative transsexual woman, now works for the Italian national aerospace company 'Alenia', which is part of the Euro-Fighter Consortium, responsible for the aircrew/ground crew training programmes and is responsible for the management and maintenance of Alenia's flight simulator. She is now 36 years old, started to live as a woman when aged 32, the company and her colleagues from many European countries know her history and she has a security rating up to 'Nato Secret'.

In order for security not to be an issue, it is important that transsexual people are not made to be 'illegal'. It is only if they are of a dubious legal status that they are likely to try and keep their past a secret. If employers were

---

16 Letter to Sir George Young MP, from the Employment Service, 22 March 1994.

not able to dismiss somebody because of their transsexual status, then there would be less of a need to keep it a secret, hence the issue of vulnerability would cease to exist.

PARTICULAR ISSUES IN RELATION TO MILITARY LIFE

Having seen the affidavit of the Air Chief Marshal Sir John Willis in the case of *R v Secretary of State for Defence ex p Smith et al*, I feel it is important to address the specific heads that arise from that affidavit. Though the affidavit concerns homosexual people within the military, the heads might well be seen as being relevant to the issues here. The heads are: morale and unit effectiveness, the services are *in loco parentis*, communal living and security implications.

Morale and unit effectiveness

Accepting that a high state of discipline, morale and unit effectiveness is essential to create and maintain an operationally efficient and effective fighting force, the question then arises as to how transsexual people might affect this. As has been seen, transsexual people have always served and often reached high rank. These people were not open about their transsexuality and therefore it must be presumed that the unit continued to be effective. But there is the evidence of those who have continued to serve during assessment of the syndrome and there has been no report of a breakdown of unit effectiveness. Furthermore, in the non-military uniformed services, transsexual people have been able to openly serve and to participate as full and valued members of the service.

Though individuals may not like the fact that someone is transsexual, it is on a similar basis that they do not like people of a different race, skin colour, or sex. In the Rand Report (RAND, 1993), which discussed the possibility of ending discrimination against homosexuals in the US military, it was emphasised that in police and fire departments where homosexuals were allowed to serve:

- Anti-homosexual sentiment does not disappear. However, heterosexuals generally behave towards homosexuals more moderately than would have been predicted based on their stated attitude.

- Policies of non-discrimination against homosexuals in these departments had no discernable effect on the ability of their departments to recruit or retain personnel.

- Implementation is most successful where the message is unambiguous, consistently delivered and uniformly enforced. Leadership is critical in this regard.

- Training that emphasised expected behaviour, not attitudes, was judged most effective.

Accordingly, what is important is that others are disciplined not to act upon feelings that they may have to discriminate against other individuals, and that they are told that within a disciplined force, they are expected to rise above their personal prejudices.

A force where people are expected to put their lives at risk, often for things that may be of no personal concern, must encompass a high discipline level. That discipline level is such that individuals are expected to respond to orders, and to perform appropriately. This aspect of military life is what can be called upon to ensure that what is expected of all ranks is an allegiance to the principles of service life, and in fact, in fields of combat, it is essential that prejudice against 'innocent' civilian populations is controlled amongst soldiers. Therefore, it must be quite easy for the leadership of the armed forces to ensure that non-discriminatory behaviour is practised, and that unit discipline is controlled and maintained through education and expectation.

It is only logical that if the armed forces now recognise and prohibit discrimination on the grounds of race or sex, which were seen as immense problems in the past, the next step must be on the grounds of an individual's transsexuality – another feature of a person that is literally only 'skin deep' and which does not impair their ability to function and do their job.

The services are *in loco parentis*

It has been argued that the services are *in loco parentis* for some 35% of new recruits who enter the services aged under 18. As such, the services have a responsibility for the morale and welfare of these young people. It is argued that the confidence of both them and their parents would be damaged if it was thought that their interests were at risk. Transsexual people would answer that they are of no risk to children or young people. The main aim in undergoing gender reassignment is in fact to blend in, to just be the woman or man you really are according to your gender identity. Transsexual people are just like other adults – a full range through all the walks and interests of life.

Transsexual people now participate in all walks of life; they are as involved in nursing and teaching as any other profession. I myself am a university teacher. I know many teachers in secondary and further education and some in primary education, all with their employers' knowledge, some with the knowledge of the parents of the children they teach – though as years go by, many transsexuals find that it becomes an 'open secret' and of very little importance to anyone. I also know one transsexual, Sharon, who worked for some years for Lambeth Social Services as head of a residential unit for children with behavioural difficulties, with the full knowledge of her employers. When she was 'outed' by the tabloid press in a most scurrilous article (Burden and Williams, 1986), which implied that she was being investigated for abusing a child in care (whereas in fact it was another member of staff), Lambeth Social Services stood solidly behind her and refused to bow to the media pressure. She also received total support from the parents of the children concerned.

It must be re-iterated that transsexuality has nothing to do with sexual orientation or behaviour, that transsexuals want to become part of their communities as the people they really are, and they want to fully participate in the society in which they live. There are now estimated to be between 5,000 and 15,000 post-surgical reassignment transsexuals in the UK, and many more living the one to two year 'real life test' in their new gender role that is required of them before they are placed on the list for surgical reassignment. Consequently, many people, and the children of many people, now know a transsexual person as either a family member, as a work colleague or as a neighbour. This does not appear to cause problems except to those people, like the military chiefs, who in their positions of authority take it upon themselves to protect the rest of society from things they often do not need protection from. This used to be the situation in employment for many transsexual people, whereby employers would try to protect the fellow employees of the transsexual by dismissing the transsexual person. In fact, fellow employees have often been horrified at the outcome, and have insisted on the reinstatement of the transsexual person, as happened in GEC plc in 1983.

So, if acting *in loco parentis*, services chiefs must remember that a parent allows a child gradual independence and does not attempt to protect a child from the realities of the world into which they will grow. In an armed force, this is even more important. The young people involved may end up in all sorts of cultural and social environments and must be prepared totally for the full range of people they might meet and with whom they must negotiate. If this training is poorly done, then the lives of those young people may well be put at risk. Secondly, those same chiefs must remember that they are also *in loco parentis* to the transsexual service person, and it is not appropriate to throw somebody out of their home and their job for merely having a now easily treated syndrome for which there is treatment available which will enable the individual to function more efficiently than before, to be much happier in themselves, to form long standing relationships and to perform their job effectively and probably better than they were doing before.

Communal living

It is argued that the special conditions of service life which require individuals to live in close proximity to one another would mean that it would be inappropriate to retain homosexual people in the armed forces, as young people might be unhappy to share close quarters with them. This, as is in fact the case with homosexual people, would not be an issue with transsexual people. They are no more of a sexual threat to others than other adults are. Furthermore, following the initial period of the 'real life' test, wherein some do have an androgynous appearance, after hormone therapy and surgery, transsexual people look no different from other members of their gender group. There is no need for others to know of their transsexuality apart from those who need to know for social (ie, someone forming a long standing relationship with the transsexual person), administrative or medical reasons. They will not be viewed as a sexual threat, and the issues of the priority of privacy between men and women need not become an issue.

Security implications

The transsexual person is only vulnerable to pressure or improper influence because of the legal limbo they are in which insists that they are female for some purposes and male for others. Increasingly, as transsexuality is being seen to be due to physiological factors rather than as a psychological disorder, transsexual people are able to be open to their family, friends and colleagues where appropriate. The biggest reason for transsexual people keeping their past a secret must be the fact that they could lose their jobs at any time merely for being transsexual. Accordingly, details had to be withheld from employers or potential employers. Conversely, if one of the main results of the legal stigma that exists were removed by providing protection to the transsexual person in the workplace, then employers could be told the basic fact, just as a partially deaf person might disclose that they were hard of hearing and needed to wear a hearing aid. Families will of course know of the transsexual person's status; it is impossible to hide it in the way a homosexual person might hide their sexual orientation. However, the transsexual person, as has been seen above, can be discreet, but also able to have a high security rating as long as employment discrimination is removed.

CONCLUSION

It must be asserted that exclusion of transsexual people from the services is contrary to Art 8 of the European Convention on Human Rights, which holds that everyone has a right to respect for his private and family life, and that there should be no interference except as is in the state's interests, such as national security. Even in the case of a conviction for murder, as happened with Private Lee Clegg, the armed services did not automatically link that to exclusion from service. Though homosexual orientation may still be a reason for exclusion, transsexuality is not the same, nor can it, nor should it, be equated under the same heads.

Increasingly, civilian personnel are performing many of the duties previously undertaken by members of the armed forces. To refuse to retain transsexual people within the forces is likely to mean that personnel could find themselves facing a 'double value' system, whereby some workers are protected and others are not. Transsexual people are, both before and after treatment, likely to wish to prove that they are 'as good as the rest'; furthermore, research has shown that treatment in 87% to 97% (Green and Fleming, 1990) of cases is successful. Their retention, rather than threatening morale and discipline, is likely to produce a hard working and loyal group of people who contribute a great deal to the good morale of any unit. Furthermore, the very disciplinary structure that the military services employ would enable any problems that might ensue because of the prejudices of other personnel to be easily repudiated within the structures that already exist.

CHAPTER 16

A TEMPORARY ASYLUM APPEAL FOR A TRANSSEXUAL PRISONER

This affidavit concerns a (ftm) transsexual man who was serving a prison sentence inside a women's prison. He had originally entered the UK as a 15 year old teenager, having made his way across Europe after being brutalised and thrown out of his family home in Turkey for being a 'lesbian'. He was able to present himself as a young man within the Turkish community in London where he successfully worked for several years. When he got older, he obtained a bilateral mastectomy from a private surgeon. The surgeon never suggested that he receive hormone therapy or required any psychiatric assessment. Consequently, he paid over his savings for what resulted in a very out-of-date surgical procedure that left him with unacceptable scarring on his chest. Not knowing any other (ftm) transsexual men, he accepted this as a normal result. When the surgeon offered to 'make him a penis' if he could produce £25,000, he got involved in illegal activity to raise the money.

His subsequent arrest and conviction led to a 12 year sentence with immediate deportation on his release. During his time in prison, he contacted a support group, and a lawyer who had expertise both in immigration and transsexual issues was obtained for him. Despite having to serve his time in a female prison, which resulted in most of that time being served in solitary in a hospital wing, he received support from some members of the prison staff and ultimately he was provided with hormone treatment, and he obtained a degree level education. He was also referred for phalloplasty surgery which, if he had received it whilst in prison, would have resulted in his transfer to a male prison. He was keen to obtain this as it would mean that he could leave prison from a men's unit and so be met by his friends on his release. Just before the date for this surgery and after seven years in prison, he came before the parole board who were keen to afford early release because of his exemplary behaviour, but there was a fear that this would result in his immediate deportation to Turkey. An immigration application was lodged and as his parole date approached, he received a final appeal hearing. The affidavit was intended to afford the immigration appeal board with information about the life of transsexual men and to explain why a return to Turkey would be disastrous. Fortunately, just as the parole came through, he heard that his appeal had been successful and he received temporary leave to stay.

AFFIDAVIT

I am writing this in my capacity as the co-ordinator of the FTM Network, a support group for female to male transsexual men, which has over 750 members throughout the UK. I am a female to male transsexual man myself. My personal experience and also the knowledge and experience I have gained through my involvement in campaigning and advising on issues relating to transsexual people gives me considerable insight into the difficulties faced by transsexual people as they 'transition' and the treatment of transsexual people by the wider community.

My personal experience as a transsexual is that at the age of four or five, I realised that I was very unhappy being a girl and wished that I was a boy. At the age of 9 or 10, I realised that something was 'very wrong'. I now know that these ages of awareness are common to many transsexual people. However, I was not diagnosed at that stage. My parents held very conventional views on gender roles and I was 'forced' into being more feminine. I succeeded in adapting small parts of my life, for example, at school I would wear a shirt and tie (although this was optional for girls) and I would immediately change into trousers on returning home. My peer group saw me as being rather strange and called me 'queer'.

At the age of 17, I went to my GP who referred me to a psychiatrist. At this stage, the medical authorities were completely non-accepting. In the UK in 1975, only 12 or so female to male people before me had received treatment for their transsexuality. I was considered rather a rarity. My transition process commenced in January 1974 with almost two years of psychiatric assessment at the Withington Hospital. I began living in a male role from May 1974 and testosterone hormone treatment was started in August 1975. In July 1978, I underwent a bilateral mastectomy and a hysterectomy. I was not offered any ongoing counselling or psychiatric support during this transition. I met my partner in 1978. From 1975 to 1990, I attempted to keep my transsexual identity a secret. I lived as a man with my partner. On the occasions I was discovered to be a transsexual, I was subjected to blatant discrimination and prejudice. I have been sacked from my job, subjected to blackmail and my partner was refused access to fertility treatment. It was, indeed, when we were expecting our first child (by donor insemination) that I decided that I should 'stand up and be counted', otherwise our child might never be able to do so. We now have four children and, as stated above, I have become an active spokesperson and campaigner on transsexual issues.

I commenced treatment for phalloplasty in the summer of 2001. The first stage involves the lifting of skin from the torso wall, and the connection of blood vessels and nerves. The second stage is scheduled for February 2002. This will involve further lifting of skin and the formation of the phallus. The third stage involves the reconnection of the urethra. The fourth stage involves minor cosmetic adjustments and surgery to form the scrotal sack, and the fifth and final stage involves the insertion of prosthetics into the scrotum and the phallus to enable an erection for sexual intercourse. The whole process is expected to take from 18 months to two years to complete. Each surgical procedure requires two to four weeks off heavy work.

The period of transition is a very difficult period for transsexual people. Transsexual people frequently see it as the solution to many of their problems in everyday life because it allows recognition as a man (or a woman in the case of mtf transsexual people). However, at the time of transition, many transsexual people experience the loss of family, friends and other relationships. There is other stigmatisation including the possible loss of job, homophobic aggression on the street, discrimination in shops, bars, restaurants and in accessing housing and other services.

For ftm transsexual people, there is also a problem with dealing with a mixed body form. It is necessary to bind breasts and there is masculine hair growth on the face and body and a deepening of the voice. These problems are emotionally draining and particularly wearing on relationships with others. The taking of testosterone puts the individual through puberty (again – but this time adolescent male puberty). For a year or more, there is often a lack of ability to control emotional stability (resulting in lots of shouting and tears). There is a markedly increased libido and male sex drive, but no 'outlet' for this as the transsexual's body is still 'mixed'. Further, the appetite for food is greatly increased and the individual becomes either very fat or extremely hungry.

The consequences of the effects of testosterone treatment, the experience of social stigmatisation and the 'peculiar' body form places the individual very much adrift and without a social place in the world. This may result in profound depression.

The Harry Benjamin International Gender Dysphoria Association (HBIGDA) promotes good standards of care for the treatment of transsexual people. These have been adopted by all gender clinics in Great Britain. All (reputable) doctors, surgeons and psychiatrists who treat transsexual people are members of the HBIGDA. The application of these standards has been shown, through clinical research, to reduce the suicidal tendencies of transsexual people going through transition and, also, to better facilitate adjustment into the gender role. Indeed, all follow-up studies of transsexual people undertaking transition, according to these standards of treatment care, show a 96–98% success rate in terms of a positive sense of social well being.

I am informed that a copy of these standards of care will be before the Immigration Appellate Authority. It is considered good practice that an individual has undergone a minimum of one year of psychiatric care before commencing irreversible hormonal or surgical treatment, and that psychotherapeutic support continues for at least one more year after the commencement of hormone treatment. The minimum suggested by the gender clinic at the Charing Cross Hospital is one hour of psychotherapeutic support every three months, throughout the assessment and treatment period, in cases where the individual is considered 'well adjusted'.

I have known AB since 1994 when he first contacted the FTM Network for support and advice and we have corresponded regularly since then. I first met him whilst undertaking research into transsexual prisoners for my report to the Home Office (see Chapter 12). I have, more recently, met with him again, at the request of Winstanley-Burgess, Solicitors. I am aware of his personal history and his past and present treatment as a transsexual. It is evident that he fell into the hands of scurrilous charlatans. He underwent a mastectomy prior to receiving any hormone treatment or psychotherapeutic counselling, in clear contravention of the guidelines in place at that time. The mastectomy AB received was in the form of an outdated surgical procedure last performed on transsexual men in the late 1960s by respectable surgeons. The results are very poor and AB is never likely to feel confident in exposing his chest in public.

As I have outlined, the experience of transition from female to male is a difficult one in any circumstances. I can only assert that this experience has been more difficult for AB in a female prison environment. I am aware that he commenced hormone treatment immediately prior to trial in 1996, when he had been on remand at HM Prison Holloway for almost seven months. This was following a serious suicide attempt. He is continuing to receive hormone treatment but no ongoing therapeutic intervention. The therapeutic services offered have, to date, been inappropriate, that is, the focus has been on whether AB is transsexual or not rather than therapeutic support through transition from female to male.

Inevitably, AB is experiencing all the difficulties of transition (as previously outlined) in the emotional and physical isolation of prison. In addition, detention in a female prison means that he faces greater problems in 'evolving' as a man in the wider community. He has no male friends or role models. This inevitably compounds his sense of isolation. AB has not received any meaningful counselling or psychiatric support throughout his treatment nor pending phalloplasty surgery. As stated above, failure to apply the HBIGDA guidelines[1] places the transsexual at greater risk of suicidal tendencies and their social and personal adjustment into their gender role is less likely to succeed.

In general, the prison authorities have recognised that there is a problem in this area. There has been a noticeable shift in attitudes over the past two to three years. Prior to this, there was little or no acceptance of the issue. This change (in respect of the prison service) appears to have been a consequence of the prison service medical services now being the responsibility of the NHS.

---

1   HBIGDA, *Standards of Care for Gender Identity Disorders,* Sixth Version, 2001, www.hbigda.org/socv6.html#09.

There remains a significant problem of the appropriate accommodation of transsexual people in prisons. It is important that the prison facilitates the social acceptance of transsexual people within the prison environment. At present, the prison service requires the transsexual person to have undergone genital reassignment surgery before the individual can be placed within the gender-appropriate prison. This causes problems in adjustment to the male role as mentioned above; for transsexual men, it also prevents transsexual people maintaining contacts with friends outside of prison, as to do so would automatically 'out' the transsexual status of the prisoner and make it impossible to re-enter their former social grouping on release.

The placing of AB in a women's prison will have had profound repercussions on his process of transition to the male role. His position is that he is currently never recognised as a man either by other prisoners or by staff. Instead, he is regarded as a 'freak', someone to be laughed at, possibly mentally ill and certainly a 'weird' woman. This means that he gets no emotional satisfaction in having his true self recognised. Ironically, it is for recognition of the true self that transsexual people undergo such major health interventions. AB will instead view himself as a failure and he will doubt his ability to be a man. It is crucial to the adjustment of the transsexual person to achieve successes, even small successes such as being referred to as 'son' or 'sir' in a shop. These affirm that the route being taken is the right route and that the future place in society as a man is likely to be accepted and successful.

Furthermore, genital surgery is complex and 'risky' surgery, particularly for ftm transsexuals, and the results are still problematic, with complications in results still a normal part of the procedures. It is important therefore that the transsexual man is able to make an informed decision to undergo this surgery without external pressures. Unfortunately for those in prison, the requirement of genital surgery before being placed in a prison of the appropriate gender places makes these surgical procedures highly desirable and this will affect the decision making process.

Bearing in mind though that there is a risk of sexual assault in some men's prisons, it is probably the case that the pre-genital surgery transsexual man would be placed at some risk in that environment. However, AB has spent much of his time in Holloway in solitary, due to the prejudice he has suffered from appearing as a man in a women's prison. This has doubly stigmatised him. I am certain that his mental health would have fared better if he had been placed in solitary, for his physical safety, in a men's prison. There he would, at least, have been able to maintain contact with his social circle and he would have felt that he was recognised and treated as a man by other prisoners and by staff – a vital aspect of reducing the psychological distress of the gender disorder.

As such, almost any transsexual man would fare better and be more likely to achieve rehabilitation by being accepted as a man in a men's prison, with the attendant risks, rather than to appear constantly as a failed woman inside a women's prison.

It is in this context that I fear for AB's ability to cope psychologically with expulsion to Turkey. His experiences in prison make him ill-equipped to adjust to life in Turkey where the lack of adequate treatment for the gender disorder will be compounded by the many problems he faces on return and where proper medical treatment and support is unlikely to be available to him. It is precisely in this type of circumstances that the relatively high risk of suicide associated with gender identity disorder manifests.

I am extremely concerned at the prospect of AB's deportation to Turkey at the end of his prison sentence. Since 1973, Turkey has had a formal mechanism whereby legal recognition can be given of a change of sex. However, in practice, this has meant little. Police persecution of transsexual people is notorious. For example, in 1997, a transsexual woman, Demet Demir, was given a human rights award by the International Gay and Lesbian Human Rights Commission. This was for her continued work with transsexual people in Istanbul, despite years of police persecution. Within hours of her return home from the awards ceremony, she was arrested and tortured during her interrogation. Her arrest resulted in no charges against her.

AB's transsexual status will be known from his arrival in Turkey. I believe he will be immediately picked up by the police and face violence, and it is highly likely that because he has not undergone genital reconstructive surgery, he will be particularly vulnerable to sexual abuse, which is a common experience of vulnerable transsexual people, even in western states. In my work with transsexual people from Arab states, central Africa and South America, I have been told by several of such experiences. Even if that does not happen, because of the social stigma surrounding transsexuality in Turkish society, he will almost certainly be ostracised and isolated, and he may well even face physical danger. His family in Turkey have made it very clear that they will not tolerate his situation at all, and have said that as far as they are concerned, he has been expelled from the family.

There will be no one he can turn to for help, as there is no support structure for transsexual people in Turkey. It is highly unlikely he would find an employer who would tolerate his gender change, and he will be at risk of becoming dependent upon illegal activities to survive, or alternatively live a life of severe deprivation. These factors would mean his ability to lead a successful social life will be severely curtailed, and he is likely to become depressed and anxious, leading him to develop very serious mental health problems.

AB has used his time in prison, despite the hardships, usefully. He has almost completed his Open University degree in Psychology. AB has worked hard to put the past behind him, and to gain the prospect of becoming a constructive citizen. With an opportunity to complete appropriate training and, if allowed, to continue his social development and his gender reassignment undisturbed, he is very unlikely to return to crime. In fact, my research has shown that transsexual people greatly appreciate the opportunity to live their life recognised as a member of the gender group they are. As such, they are very aware of the loss that a criminal conviction could cause them, and almost all of them lead exemplary law abiding lives, rarely having any contact with the police, courts, or the Criminal Justice System. I believe that AB, if given the opportunity to complete his education and his gender reassignment, is likely to become a hard working and successful member of British society, if allowed to, on his release.

BIBLIOGRAPHY

ABC News Investigative Unit, *'Bell Curve' and the Eugenics Foundation*, 22 November 1994, *Tonight Programme*

Ackroyd, P, *Dressing Up*, 1979, Norwich: Thames and Hudson

Addis, WE and Arnolds, T (revised by Hallett, PE), *A Catholic Dictionary*, 1951, London: Virtue & Co

Agence France Press, *Chinese Minister Defends New Eugenics Law*, 1 June 1995, Paris: AFP release

Allen, R, *But For The Grace: The True Story of a Dual Existence*, 1954, London: WH Allen

Alvesson, M and Billing, YD, *Understanding Gender and Organisations*, 1997, London: Sage

American Psychiatric Association, *Diagnostic and Statistics Manual of Mental Disorders Third Edition*, revised (DSM IIIR), 1980, New York: American Psychiatric Association

American Psychiatric Association, *Diagnostic and Statistics Manual of Mental Disorders Fourth Edition*, (DSM 4), 1994, New York: American Psychiatric Association

Anderson, RJ and Sharrock WW, *Applied Sociological Perspectives*, 1984, London: Allen and Unwin

Bainham, A, 'Family law in a pluralistic society' (1995) 22 Journal of Law and Society 234

Balkin, J, 'Why policemen don't like policewomen' (1988) 16(1) Journal of Police Science and Administration 29–38

Barillas, C, *Transsexual RAF Pilot to Fly Again*, 16 August 2000, The Data Lounge, www.datalounge.com/datalounge/news/record.html?record=9429

Baudrillard, J, 'The virtual illusion: or the automatic writing of the world' (1995) 12(4) Theory, Culture and Society, pp 96–107

Baynes, S, *Breeching The Barriers*, 1991, New Zealand: The Minorities Trust

Bell, D and Valentine, G, *Mapping Desire*, 1995, London: Routledge

Bell, DJ, 'Policewomen: myths and reality' (1982) 10(1) Journal of Police Science and Administration 112–20

Beemyn, B and Eliason, M, *Queer Studies: A Lesbian, Gay, Bisexual and Transgender Anthology*, 1996, New York: New York UP

Benjamin, H, 'Newer aspects of the transsexual phenomenon' (1969) 5(2) Journal of Sex Research, pp 135–44

Best, S and Kellner, D, *PostModern Theory: Critical Interrogations*, 1991, London: Macmillan

Bingham, LJ, *Speech to the National Probation Convention*, 1997, www.open.gov.uk/lcd/speeches/1997lcj-spe.htm

Bingham, LJ, *Speech to the Probation 2000 Conference: QEII Conference Centre*, London, 27 January 2000, www.open.gov.uk.lcd/judicial/speeches/27-1-00.htm

Blight, J, 'Transgender inmates', 2000, in Graycar, A, (ed), *Trends and Issues in Crime and Criminal Justice, No 168*, Canberra: Australian Institute of Criminology

Bockting, WO and Coleman, E (eds), *Gender Dysphoria: Interdisciplinary Approaches in Clinical Management*, 1992, New York: Haworth Press

Bornstein, K, *Gender Outlaw: On Men, Women and the Rest Of Us*, 1994, London: Routledge

Bray, A, *Homosexuality in Renaissance England*, 1982, London: Gay Men's Press

Brooks, JM, *Transsexuals in Prison, Twenty; The Official Newsletter of The Twenty (XX) Club Inc*, Nov–Dec 1998, www.twentyclub.org/novdec98.html

Brown, GR, 'Transsexuals in the military: flight into hypermasculinity' (1988) 17 Archives of Sexual Behaviour, pp 527–37

Brown, GR, *Further Research Findings: Transgender Prisoners*, unpublished paper presented at the International Foundation for Gender Education Conference, 23–25 March 2001, Chicago

Brown, J, 'Aspects of discriminatory treatment of women police officers serving in forces in England and Wales' (1998) 38(2) British Journal of Criminology 265–83

Brown, J and Heidensohn, F, *Gender and Policing: Comparative Perspectives*, 2000, London: Macmillan

Brundage, JA, *Law, Sex and Christian Society in Medieval Europe*, 1987, Chicago: Chicago Press

Bucke, T and Brown, D, *In Police Custody: Police Powers and Suspects Rights under the Revised PACE Codes of Practice*, 1997, Home Office Research and Statistics Directorate, Home Office Research Study No 174, London: Home Office

Bullough, B, Bullough, VL and Elias, J (eds), *Gender Blending*, 1997, New York: Prometheus

Bullough, VL, 'Transvestites in the Middle Ages' (1974) 79(6) American Journal of Sociology, pp 1381–94

Bullough, VL and Bullough, B, *Crossdressing, Sex and Gender*, 1993, Philadelphia: University of Pennsylvania

Burden, P and Williams, D, 'Sex change shock at council home' (1986) *Daily Mail*, 2 September

Burman, E and Parker, I, *Discourse Analytic Research*, 1993, London: Routledge

Burke, M, *Coming Out of the Blue*, 1993, London: Cassells

Butler, J, *Bodies That Matter: On the Discursive Limits of 'Sex'*, 1993, London: Routledge

Colapinto, J, 'The true story of John Joan' (1987) *Rolling Stone*, 11 December, pp 54–97

Card, C, *Adventures In Lesbian Philosophy*, 1994, Bloomington and Indianapolis: Indiana UP

Cauldwell, D, 'Psychopathia Transexualis' (1949) 16 Sexology, pp 274–80

Cauldwell, D, *Questions and Answers on the Sex Lives and Sexual Problems of Trans-Sexuals*, 1950, New York: Haldeman-Julias

Change, FTM Network, G & SA, The Gender Trust, GIRES, Liberty, Press For Change, *Meeting the Needs of Transsexual People: A Presentation to the Interdepartmental Working Group on Transsexual Issues* (2000a), 19 January 2000, www.pfc.org.uk/workgrp/jan2000.htm

Change, FTM Network, G & SA, The Gender Trust, GIRES, Liberty, Press For Change, *The Problems of Gender Re-Registration: A Consultation Paper to the Interdepartmental Working Group on Transsexual People's Issues* (2000b), 16 February 2000, www.pfc.org.uk/workgrp/feb2000.htm

Chapman, T and Hough, M (eds), *Evidence Based Practice: A Guide to Effective Practice*, 1998, London: HMIP Home Office, www.homeoffice.gov.uk/hmiprob/ebp.htm

Choisy, Abbé de, (Scott, RHF (trans)), *The Transvestite Memoirs*, 1994, London: Peter Owen

Cohen, S, *Visions of Social Control*, 1985, Cambridge: Polity

Cohen-Kettenis, PT and van Goozen, SHM, 'Sex reassignment of adolescent transsexuals: a follow-up study' (1997) 36(2) American Academy Child Adolescent Psychiatry, pp 263–71

Cohen-Kettenis, PT and van Goozen, SHM, *Pubertal Delay as an Aid in Diagnosis and Treatment of a Transsexual Adolescent*, 1998, unpublished paper

Cole-Wilson, YI, *Corbett v Corbett: Is It Still Good Law?*, unpublished paper presented at the Third International Congress on Sex and Gender, Oxford, 1998

Connell, RW, *Gender and Power*, 1987, Cambridge: Polity

Cossey, C, *My Story*, 1991, London: Faber & Faber

Cowell, R, *Roberta Cowell's Story By Herself*, 1954, London: W Heinemann

Council of Europe, *Proceedings of the XXIII Colloquy on European Law: Transsexualism, Medicine and Law*, 1995, Strasbourg: Council of Europe

Cox, C, *The Enigma of the Age*, 1966, London: Longmands, Green and Co

Cromwell, J, 'Default assumptions or the Billy Tipton phenomenon' (1994) FTM Newsletter, Issue 28, July, pp 4–5

Davenport-Hines, R, *Sex, Death And Punishment*, 1990, London: W Collins and Son

Davies, H and Jones, G, 'Sex change soldiers can stay in the army' (1999) Electronic Telegraph, 2 August, www.pfc.org.uk/news/1999/army-dt.htm

Dekker, RM and van de Pol, LC, *The Tradition of Female Transvestism in Early Modern Europe*, 1989, Hampshire: Macmillan

Department for Education and Employment, *Consultation Paper: Legislation Regarding Discrimination on Grounds of Transsexualism in Employment*, January 1998, London: DfEE

Department for Education and Employment, *Sex Discrimination (Gender Reassignment): A Guide to the Sex Discrimination (Gender Reassignment) Regulations*, 1999, London: Stationery Office

Department of Defence, *Unacceptable Sexual Behaviour by Members of the Australian Defence Force*, 22 June 1992, Australia: Department of Defence

Devor, H, *Gender Blending*, 1989, Bloomington: Indiana UP

Di Cegli, D, *Conference Proceedings: Gender Identity and Development in Childhood and Adolescence*, 1992, London: Child and Adolescent Section, Department of Mental Health Sciences, St George's Hospital

Doerfal, J, *Transsexuality and the European Convention on Human Rights*, 1998, unpublished essay

Doerfal, J, Marshall, S, Playdon, Z-J, Whinnom, A and Whittle, S, *Transsexual People in the Workplace: A Code of Practice*, 1998, London: Press For Change

Doerner, K, *Madmen and the Bourgeoisie*, 1981, Oxford: Blackwell

Dollimore, J, *Sexual Dissidence*, 1991, Oxford: Clarendon

Dorenkamp, M and Henke, R, *Negotiating Lesbian and Gay Subjects*, 1994, London: Routledge

Douglas, G, Hebenton, B and Thomas, T, 'The right to found a family' (1992) 142 NLJ 488

Douzinas, C, Warrington, R and McVeigh, S, *Postmodern Justice: The Law of Text in the Texts of the Law*, 1991, London: Routledge

Duberman, M, *About Time, Exploring the Gay Past*, 1991, New York: Penguin

Duberman, MB, Vicinus, M and Chauncey Jr, G, *Hidden from History*, 1989, London: Penguin

Dylan More, S, 'The pregnant man – an oxymoron?' (1998) 17(3) Journal of Gender Studies, pp 319–27

Ekins, R and King, D, *Blending Genders: Social Aspects of Cross-dressing and Sex-changing*, 1996, London: Routledge

Electronic Telegraph, 'Transsexual fights RAF dismissal rule' (1996) *Electronic Telegraph*, 21 May, www.pfc.org.uk/news/1996/raf-sack.htm

Elkins, M, Olagundoye, J and Rogers, K, *Prison Population Brief, England and Wales, December 2000*, 2001, London: Home Office Research Development Statistics Unit

Ellis, H, *Studies in the Psychology of Sex Vol 7*, 1928, Philadelphia: FA Davis and Co

Ellis, H, *Studies in the Psychology of Sex Vol 1*, 1948a, London: Random House

Ellis, H, *Studies in the Psychology of Sex Vol 7, Pt 4 – Sexual Inversion*, 1948b, London: Heinemann

Elnadi, AB, 'Noelle Lenoir', September 1994, Unesco Courier, Iss 0304-3118, pp 5–9

Epstein, J and Straub K, *Body Guards: The Cultural Politics of Gender Ambiguity*, 1991, London: Routledge

Feldman, D, *Civil Liberties and Human Rights in England and Wales*, 1993, Oxford: OUP

Foster, S, 'Transsexuals, sexual identity and the European Convention' (1998) *Law Teacher*, p 32

Foucault, M, *Madness and Civilisation*, 1971, London: Tavistock

Foucault, M, *I, Pierre Riviere, Having Slaughtered my Mother, my Sister and my Brother*, 1975, New York: Random House

Foucault, M, *The History of Sexuality*, Vol 1, 1978, London: Penguin

Foucault M, *The Order of Things*, 1994, London: Routledge

Garbor, M, *Vested Interests: Cross Dressing and Cultural Anxiety*, 1992, London: Routledge

Garton, S, 'Sound minds and healthy bodies: re-considering eugenics in Australia 1914–1940' (1994) 26 Australian Historical Studies, Pt 103, pp 163–81

Gender Trust, *The Gender Trust Handbook*, 1990, Belper: The Gender Trust

Gender Trust, *Submission to the DfEE*, February 1998, Press For Change, www.pfc.org.uk/employ/gentrst1.htm

GFI, *Internet Access Control, Ensuring Productive Internet Use at Work*, 2000, www.gfi.com/languard/wpinternetaccesscontrol.htm

Goffman, E, *Stigma: Notes on the Management of Spoiled Identity*, 1990, London: Penguin

Goodich, M, *The Unmentionable Vice*, 1979, Santa Barbara: ABC-Clio

Goodrich, P, *Languages of Law*, 1990, London: Weidenfeld and Nicolson

Gooren, LJG, *Biological Aspects of Transsexualism and their Relevance to its Legal Aspects*, unpublished paper presented at the XXIIIrd Colloquy on European Law of the Council of Europe, Amsterdam, 1993

Graham, M, 'Jazz star's 55-year secret from sons ... he was a she' (1989) *Today*, 2 February

Green, J, *Investigation into Discrimination Against Transgendered People*, September 1994, San Francisco: Human Rights Commission, City and County of San Francisco

Green, J and Wilchins RA, 'New men on the horizon', January 1996, San Francisco: FTM Newsletter, Issue 33

Green, R, *Sexual Identity Conflict in Children and Adults*, 1974a, London: Duckworth

Green R, 'Sexual identity of 37 children raised by homosexual or transsexual parents' (1974b) 135(6) American Journal of Psychiatry, pp 692–97

Green, R and Fleming, DT, 'Transsexual surgery follow-up: status in the 1990s' (1990) 1 Annual Review of Sex Research, pp 163–74

Green, R and Money, J, *Transsexualism and Sex Reassignment*, 1969, Baltimore: Johns Hopkins UP

Grossberg, L, Nelson, C and Treichler, P, *Cultural Studies*, 1992, New York: Routledge

Halberstam, J, 'Skinflick: posthuman gender in Jonathan Demme's *The Silence of the Lambs' Camera Obscura*, Issue 27, 9 September 1992, pp 35–52

Hall, S, *Minimal Selves*, ICA Documents, 1987, Series 6, p 14

Hall, S, 'Cultural studies and its theoretical legacies', in Grossberg, L et al (eds), *Cultural Studies*, 1992, New York: Routledge

Hargreaves, R, *Women at Arms*, 1930, London: Hutchinson

HBIGDA, *Standards of Care for Gender Identity Disorders, Sixth Version*, 2001, HBIGDA, www.hbigda.org/socv6.html#09

Heger, H, *The Men with the Pink Triangle*, 1980, Boston: Allyson

Heidensohn, F, *Women in Control? The Role of Women in Law Enforcement*, 1992, Oxford: Clarendon

Hennessey, S, 'A man's a man for all that', *Rouge*, Winter 1990–91

Herdt, G (ed), *Third Sex, Third Gender: Beyond Sexual Dimorphism in Culture and History*, 1994, New York: Zone

Heredia, C, *Hate Crimes Against Gays on Rise Across US*, 13 April 2001, www.sfgate.com:80/cgi-bin/article.cgi?file=/chronicle/archive/2001/04

Her Majesty's Inspectorate of Constabulary (HMIC), *Developing Diversity in the Police Service: Equal Opportunities Thematic Inspection Report*, 1995, London: Home Office

Her Majesty's Inspectorate of Constabulary, *Police Integrity*, 1999, London: Home Office

Her Majesty's Inspectorate of Constabulary, *Policing London 'Winning Consent'*, 2000, London: Home Office

Her Majesty's Inspectorate of Constabulary, *Winning the Race – Embracing Diversity*, 2001, London: Home Office Communication Directorate

Hernstein, RJ and Murray, C, *The Bell Curve: Intelligence and Class Structure in American Life*, 1994, London: Free Press

Hirschfeld, M, *Sexual Anomalies*, 1948, London: Emerson

Home Office, *Equal Opportunities in the Police Service, Circular No 87*, 1989, London: Home Office

Home Office, *Police: Serving the Community*, 1997, London: Home Office

Home Office, *Stephen Lawrence Inquiry: Home Secretary's Action Plan*, 1998, London: Home Office

Home Office, *Her Majesty's Inspectorate of Probation Statement of Purpose*, 2000a, London: Home Office, www.homeoffice.gov.uk/hmiprob/plan.htm

Home Office, *The Interdepartmental Working Group Report on Transsexual People*, 2000b, London: Home Office

Home Office, *Winning the Race – Embracing Diversity*, 2001, London: Home Office Communication Directorate

Home Office Research and Statistics Directorate, *Home Office Statistical Bulletin, Issue 27/97*, 4 December 1997, London: Home Office

hooks, bell, *Outlaw Culture, Resisting Representations*, 1994, New York: Routledge

Hoyer, N, *Man Into Woman*, 1937, Essex: Anchor

Hunt, J, 'The logic of sexism among police' (1990) Vol 1(2) Women and Criminal Justice

ICTLEP, *Proceedings from The Second International Conference on Transgender Law and Employment Policy*, 1993, Houston: ICTLEP

ICTLEP, *International Bill of Gender Rights*, 1995, Houston: ICTLEP

Irigary, L (Porter, C and Burke, C (trans)), *The Sex Which is Not One*, 1977, New York: Cornell UP

Irish Times, 'Of race and right' (1994) *Irish Times Education and Living*, 6 December, p 6

Irvine, LJ, *Modernising Justice*, 1998, www.open.gov.uk/lcd/consult/jmfword.htm

Jacobs, S and Cromwell, J, *Visions and Revisions of Reality: Reflections on Sex, Sexuality, Gender and Gender Variance*, 1992, unpublished, University of Washington

Jeffreys, S, 'FTM Transsexualism and grief' (2002) 64 Lesbian Network, pp 16–17

Jones, A, *All She Wanted*, 1996, New York: Simon and Schuster

Jones, J, 'FTM crossdresser murdered', February 1994, FTM Newsletter, Issue 26, p 3

Jones, S, *Policewomen and Equality: Formal Policy v Informal Practice*, 1986, London: Macmillan

Jorgensen, C, *A Personal Autobiography*, 1967, New York: Eriksson

Kempton, W and Kahn, E, 'Sexuality and people with intellectual disabilities: a historical perspective' (1991) 9(2) Sexuality and Disability, Special Issue: Sexuality and Developmental Disability, pp 93–111

King, D, *The Transvestite and the Transsexual*, 1993, Aldershot: Avebury

Kipnis, K and Diamond, M, 'Pediatric ethics and the surgical assignment of sex' (1998) 9 Journal of Clinical Ethics, pp 398–410

Krafft-Ebing, R, *Psycopathia Sexualis*, 1893, London: FA Davis and Co

Langley Simmons, D, *Dawn: A Charleston Legend*, 1995, Charleston: Wyrick & Co

Lauw, I, *Recognition of Same-Sex Marriage: Time for Change?*, 1994, www.murdoch.edu.au/elaw/issues/v1n3/lauw2.txt

Lee, R and Morgan, D, *Birthrights, Law and Ethics at the Beginning of Life*, 1991, London: Routledge

Leshko, I, *Determine, Define, Modify Gender*, 1996, http://planetq.com/pages/lfeinberglnt.html

Levine, P, 'Walking the streets in a way no decent woman should: women police in World War One' (1994) Journal of Modern History, March, p 66

Liberty, *Integrating Transsexual and Transgendered People: A Comparative Study of European, Commonwealth and International Law*, 1997, London: National Council for Civil Liberties

Little, H, 'Non-consensual sterilisation of the intellectually disabled in the Australian context: potential for human rights abuse and the need for reform' (1992) Australian Year Book of International Law, pp 203–26

Lupton, D, 'The embodied computer/user', in *Cyberspace, Cyberbodies*, Cyberpunk, Body and Society No 3–4, November 1995, London: Sage

MacPherson, W, *Report on the Inquiry into the Stephen Lawrence Murder*, 1999, London: Home Office

Maier, S, 'Preventative eugenics', *World Press Review*, May 1995, p 26

Martin, SE, *Breaking and Entering: Policewomen on Patrol*, 1980, Berkeley: University of California

McIntosh, M, 'Queer theory and the war of the sexes', in Bristow, J and Wilson, AR (eds), *Activating Theory*, 1993, London: Lawrence and Wishart

McKnorrie, K, 'Reproductive technology, transsexualism and homosexuality: new problems for international private law' (1994) 43 International and Comparative Law Quarterly, pp 757–75

McMullen, M and Whittle, S, *Transvestism, Transsexualism and the Law*, 1994, London: The Gender Trust, The Beaumont Trust

Messerschmidt, JW, *Masculinities and Crime, Critiques and Reconceptualisation of Theory*, 1993, Maryland: Rowman & Littlefield

Metropolitan Police Service, *Application for Appointment as Police Constable*, 2000a, London: Metropolitan Police Service

Metropolitan Police Service, *Application Pack – Application Form Guidance Notes*, 2000b, London: Metropolitan Police Service

Millot, C, *Horsexe: Essays on Transsexuality*, 1990, New York: Autonomedia Inc

Ministry of Defence, *The Armed Forces – Questions and Answers*, 2001, www.mod.uk/index.php3?page=601

Modleski, T, *The Woman Who Knew Too Much*, 1988, New York: Methuen

Money, J, 'Ablatio penis: normal male infant sex-reassigned as girl' (1975) 4 Archives of Sexual Behaviour, pp 65–71

Money, J, *Gay, Straight and In-Between*, 1988, New York: OUP

More, K and Whittle, S (eds), *Reclaiming Genders: Transsexual Grammars at the Fin de Siècle*, 1999, London: Cassell

Morris, J, *Conundrum*, 1974, London: Coronet

Murray, C, *The Emerging British Underclass*, 1990, London: IEA Health and Welfare Unit

Newburn, T and Stanko, EA (eds), *Just Boys Doing Business? Men, Masculinities and Crime*, 1994, London: Routledge

Northern Ireland Human Rights Commission, *Making a Bill of Rights for Northern Ireland*, 2001, Belfast: NIHRC

Norton, R, *Mother Clap's Molly House, The Gay Subculture in England 1700–1830*, 1992, London: GMP

Norton, R, 'The Vere Street coterie', updated 21 December 1999, Queer Culture, www.infopt.demon.co.uk/vere.htm

Norton, R, 'The gay subculture in early eighteenth-century London', updated 21 April 2000, *Homosexuality in Eighteenth-Century England: A Sourcebook*, www.infopt.demon.co.uk/molly2.htm

O'Donovan, K, *Sexual Divisions In The Law*, 1985, London: Weidenfeld and Nicholson

O'Donovan, K, *Family Law Matters*, 1993, London: Pluto

Office of National Statistics, *Civil Registration: Vital Change*, 2002a, London: ONS, www.statistics.gov.uk/registration/whitepaper/downloads/wpeng.pdf

Office of National Statistics, *Labour Statistics*, 2002b, London: ONS

Ofori, T, 'Where only the gowns are black' (1996) *The Guardian, Education,* 7 May, p 3

O'Hartigan, MD, 'She's baaa-aaack: *The Transsexual Empire*' (1994) 6 TransSisters, The Journal of Transsexual Feminism, Autumn, pp 24–25

P, *Dinner in Cornwall*, 1997, Press For Change, www.pfc.org.uk/legal/cdinner.htm

Pace, P, *Family Law*, 1992, London, Pitman

Parker, I, *Discourse Dynamics*, 1992, London: Routledge

Pateman, C, *The Disorder of Women: Democracy, Feminism and Political Theory*, 1989, Cambridge: Polity

Payne, J, *The Criminal Law Amendment Act and Sexual Assault on Minors*, 1998, www.geocities.com/Athens/Aegean/7023/Consent.html

Petersen, M, Stephens, J, Dickey, R and Lewis, W, 'Transsexuals within the prison system: an international survey of correctional services policies' (1996) 14 Behavioural Sciences and the Law, pp 219–29

Plummer, K (ed), *The Making Of The Modern Homosexual*, 1981, London: Hutchinson & Co

Press For Change, *PFC Newsletter*, No 4, November 1996, London: Press For Change

Press For Change, *Metropolitan Police Guidelines for Officers Working with the Transsexual and Transvestite*, 1997, London: Press For Change

Press For Change, *PFC Newsletter No 10*, May 1998, London: Press For Change

Radical Deviance, *A Journal of Transgender Politics Vol 2 Issue 3*, 1996, London and Middlesbrough: Gender and Sexuality Alliance

Rafter, N, 'Claims-making and socio-cultural context in the first US eugenics campaign' (1992) 39(1) Social Problems, pp 17–34

RAND, National Defense Research Institute, *Sexual Orientation and US Military Personnel Policy: Options and Assessment, (RAND) MR-323-OSD*, 1993, www.rand.org/publications/MR/MR323

Ray, I, *The Strange Story of Dr James Barry*, 1958, London: Longmans, Green and Co

Raymond, J, *The Transsexual Empire*, 1979, London: The Women's Press

Raymond, J, *The Transsexual Empire*, 1994, New York: Teacher's College Press

Rees, M, *Dear Sir or Madam*, 1995, London: Cassell

Rebello, S, *Alfred Hitchcock and the Making Of Psycho*, 1990, New York: Dembner

Reid, R, 'Psychiatric and psychological aspects of transsexualism', in *Transsexualism, Medicine and Law*, XXXIII Colloquy on European Law, 1995, Strasbourg: Council of Europe

Richards, R, *The Renee Richards Story: Second Serve*, 1983, New York: Stein and Day

Riley, DM, 'Women, children, animals and the like: protecting an unwilling electronic population', in *Proceedings of the Fifth Conference on Computers, Freedom and Privacy*, 1995, California: Burlingame

Robins, K, 'Cyberspace and the world we live in', in *Cyberspace, Cyberbodies, Cyberpunk*, Body and Society No 3–4, November 1995, London: Sage

Rogers, L, 'Children of 14 get sex change treatment on NHS' (1997) *The Times*, 12 October

Rushkoff, D, *Cyberia: Life in the Trenches of Hyperspace*, 1994, London: Harper-Collins

San Francisco, *San Francisco Gender Information Leaflet*, 1992, San Francisco

Segal, L, *Straight Sex: The Politics of Pleasure*, 1994, London: Virago

Sheilds, R (ed), *Cultures of Internet, Virtual Spaces, Real Histories, Living Bodies*, 1996, London: Sage

Skidmore, P, 'Dressed to impress: employer regulation of gay and lesbian appearance' (1999) 8(4) Social and Legal Studies, pp 509–29

Smith, DJ, 'Institutionalization, involuntary sterilization, and mental retardation: profiles from the history of the practice' (1993) 31(4) Mental Retardation, pp 208–14

Smith, DJ, 'Reflections on mental retardation and eugenics, old and new: Mensa and the human genome project' (1994) 32(3) Mental Retardation, pp 234–38

Smith, D and Gray, J, *Police and People of London: the PSI Report*, 1985, Aldershot: Gower

Stephens, P, *Report to the Metropolitan Police Service Gender Project – Assessing the Impact of the MPS Application Form on Gender Diversity in the Service*, 2001, unpublished

Stoller, RJ, *The Transsexual Experiment*, 1975, London: Hogarth

Stryker, S, 'My words to Victor Frankenstein above the village of Chamonix: performing transgender rage' (1994) 1(4) A Journal of Lesbian and Gay Studies, pp 237–54

Sullivan, L, *Information For The Female To Male Cross Dresser and Transsexual*, 3rd edn, 1990, Washington: Ingersoll

Szaz, T, *The Myth Of Mental Illness*, 1970, New York: Doubleday

Tally, T, *The Silence of the Lambs: Screenplay*, 1989, www.godamongdirectors.com/scripts/lambs.shtml

Trumbach, R, 'London's sodomites: homosexual behaviour and western culture in the 18th century' (1977) Journal of Social History, Fall, pp 1–33

Walworth, J, 'Michigan Womyn's Music Festival 1994: transsexual protesters allowed to enter', 1994, *Cross-Talk*, Issue 61

Weatherill, S and Beaumont, P, *EC Law*, 1995, London: Penguin

Weeks, J, *Sex, Politics and Society: The Regulation of Sexuality since 1800*, 1981, London: Longman

Weeks, J, *Sexuality*, 1989, London: Routledge

Weeks, J, *Coming Out: Homosexual Politics from the Nineteenth Century to the Present*, 1990, London: Quartet

West Yorkshire, *Police Strength and Workforce Distribution*, 11 May 1998, www.wypolice.gov.uk/randc3.htm

West Mercia Constabulary, *Managing Diversity Policy Statement*, 2001, www.westmercia.police.uk/local.htm

Wheelwright, J, *Amazons and Military Maids*, 1989, London: Pandora

Whinnom, A, *Introductory letter of PFC's Response to the DfEE's Consultation Paper*, 1998, Press For Change, www.pfc.org.uk/employ/pfcresp.htm

White, P, *The Prison Population in 1997: A Statistical Review, Home Office Research and Statistics Directorate Research Findings No 76*, 1998, London: Home Office

Whittle, S, *Transsexuals and the Law*, PhD thesis, 1995, Manchester Metropolitan University

Whittle, S, *Jumping the Hurdles of Gender: Transsexuals Finally Make Legal Headway*, 1996, Press For Change, www.pfc.org.uk/legal/ecjnews.htm

Whittle, S, 'An association for as noble a purpose as any' (1996) NLJ, 15 March, pp 366–67

Whittle, S and Wong, S, *The FTM Networks' Response to the DfEE's Consultation Paper*, February 1998, Press For Change, www.pfc.org.uk/employ/ftmresp.htm

Wiley, J, 'No BODY is "doing it": cybersexuality as a postmodern narrative' (1995) 1(1) Body and Society 145–62

Williams, WL, *The Spirit and the Flesh, Sexual Diversity in American Indian Culture*, 1988, Boston: Beacon

Wills, MR, *Legal Conditions of Sex Reassignment by Medical Intervention – Situation in Comparative Law*, 1993, unpublished paper presented at the XXIIIrd Colloquy on European Law of the Council of Europe, Amsterdam

Wintemute, R and Andenaes, M, *Legal Recognition of Same-Sex Partnerships*, 2001, Oxford: Hart

Wood Middlebrook, D, *Suits Me: The Double Life of Billy Tipton*, 1998, New York: Houghton Mifflin Co

Woods, PA, *Ed Gein – Psycho*, 1992, London: Nemesis

Young, M, *An Inside Job*, 1991, Oxford: Clarendon

Zhou, J, Hoffman, M, Gooren, L and Swaab, D, 'A sex difference in the human brain and its relation to transsexuality' (1995) 378 Nature, 2 November, pp 68–70

Zucker, KJ and Bradley, SJ, *Gender Identity Disorder and Psychosexual Problems in Children and Adolescents*, 1995, New York: Guildford

Zuger, B, *Early Effeminate Behaviour in Boys: Outcome and Significance for Homosexuality* (1984) 172 Journal of Nervous and Mental Diseases 90–97

INDEX